Prudential Supervision

What Works and What Doesn't

A National Bureau
of Economic Research
Conference Report

Prudential Supervision
What Works and What Doesn't

Edited by **Frederic S. Mishkin**

The University of Chicago Press

Chicago and London

FREDERIC S. MISHKIN is the Alfred Lerner Professor of Banking and Financial Institutions at the Graduate School of Business, Columbia University, and a research associate of the National Bureau of Economic Research. He is a former director of research and executive vice president at the Federal Reserve Bank of New York.

The University of Chicago Press, Chicago 60637
The University of Chicago Press, Ltd., London
© 2001 by the National Bureau of Economic Research
All rights reserved. Published 2001
Printed in the United States of America
10 09 08 07 06 05 04 03 02 01   1 2 3 4 5

ISBN: 0-226-53188-0 (cloth)

Library of Congress Cataloging-in-Publication Data

Prudential supervision : what works and what doesn't / edited by
    Frederic S. Mishkin.
        p.   cm.—(A National Bureau of Economic Research
    conference report)
        Papers presented at a conference held at Cheeca Lodge,
    Islamorada, FL, Jan. 13–15, 2000.
        Includes bibliographical references and index.
        ISBN 0-226-53188-0 (alk. paper)
        1. Bank management—Congresses.   2. Risk management—
    Congresses.   3. Banks and banking—Government policy—
    Congresses   I. Mishkin, Frederic S.   II. Series.
    HG1615 .P78   2001
    332.1′.068—dc21   00-066783

Contents

Acknowledgments

This volume contains papers and comments presented at a conference held at Cheeca Lodge, Islamorada, Florida, 13–15 January 2000. I am grateful to the Ford Foundation, the Andrew W. Mellon Foundation, and the Center for International Political Economy for financial support. I thank Martin Feldstein, president of the NBER, and Greg Mankiw, program director for monetary economics at the NBER, for their advice over the course of this project. I also thank Marc Saidenberg of the Federal Reserve Bank of New York's Research and Markets Analysis Group for preparing the summaries of the general discussions, Kirsten Foss Davis and Brett Maranjian of the NBER Conference Department for efficient support of the conference, and Helena Fitz-Patrick of the NBER Publications Department for excellent assistance with the publication process.

1

Prudential Supervision
Why Is It Important and
What Are the Issues?

Frederic S. Mishkin

1.1 Introduction

Prudential supervision, broadly construed, involves government regulation and monitoring of the banking system to ensure its safety and soundness. This conference volume contains papers that examine prudential supervision: What works and what doesn't. To understand the importance of this topic, it is worth taking a step back and examining more basic questions: Why is prudential supervision so important, and why does it take the form it does? This chapter introduces this volume by doing exactly this.

To understand why getting prudential supervision right is so crucial to the efficient functioning of the financial system, first we need to know how asymmetric information plays a key role in the way the financial system operates. This chapter first outlines what problems asymmetric information creates for the financial system and shows that the presence of asymmetric information explains why banks are so important. The chapter then goes on to explain why prudential supervision of these institutions is needed, and what forms it takes.

The chapter ends by outlining the key issues in the design of prudential supervision and uses them to organize a general discussion of the papers

Frederic S. Mishkin is the Alfred Lerner Professor of Banking and Financial Institutions at the Graduate School of Business, Columbia University, and a research associate of the National Bureau of Economic Research. He is a former director of research and executive vice president at the Federal Reserve Bank of New York.

The author would like to thank Allen Berger, Mark Carey, Mark Flannery, Patricia Jackson, Randall Kroszner, and other conference participants for their helpful comments. Any views expressed in this paper are those of the author only and not those of Columbia University or the National Bureau of Economic Research.

in this volume, providing a brief overview of their contents. The linkages between these papers are explored in order to highlight some general conclusions.

1.2   The Role of Asymmetric Information in the Financial System

The financial system is critical to the health of the economy because it performs the essential function in an economy of channeling funds from savings to those individuals or firms that have productive investment opportunities. If the financial system does not perform this role well, then the economy cannot operate efficiently, and economic growth will be severely hampered. A crucial impediment to the efficient functioning of the financial system is asymmetric information, a situation in which one party to a financial contract has much less accurate information than the other party. For example, borrowers who take out loans usually have much better information about the potential returns and risks associated with the investment projects they plan to undertake than do lenders. Asymmetric information leads to two basic problems in the financial system: adverse selection and moral hazard.

Adverse selection is an asymmetric information problem that occurs before the transaction because lower-quality borrowers with higher credit risk are the ones who are most willing to take out a loan or pay the highest interest rate. Thus, the parties who are most likely to produce an undesirable (adverse) outcome are most likely to be selected. For example, those who are poor credit risks are likely to be the most eager to take out a loan and pay a high interest rate because they know that they are unlikely to pay it back. Because adverse selection makes it more likely that loans might be made to bad credit risks, lenders may decide not to make any loans even though there are good credit risks in the marketplace. This outcome is a feature of the classic "lemons problem" analysis first described by Akerlof (1970). Clearly, minimizing the adverse selection problem requires that lenders screen out good from bad credit risks.

Moral hazard occurs after the transaction takes place because the lender is subjected to the hazard that the borrower has incentives to engage in activities that are undesirable from the lender's point of view—that is, activities that make it less likely that the loan will be paid back. Moral hazard occurs because a borrower has incentives to shift into projects with high risk in which the borrower does well if the project succeeds but the lender bears most of the loss if the project fails. Also, the borrower has incentives to misallocate funds for his or her own personal use, to shirk and just not work very hard, or to undertake investment in unprofitable projects that increase his or her power or stature. The conflict of interest between the borrower and lender stemming from moral hazard implies that many lenders will decide that they would rather not make loans, so that lending and investment will be at suboptimal levels. (Asymmetric information is clearly not the only source of the moral hazard problem. Moral hazard can also occur because high enforcement costs might make it too costly for the lender to prevent moral hazard even when the lender is fully informed about the borrower's activities.) To minimize the moral hazard problem, lenders must impose restrictions (restrictive covenants) and other contract terms on borrowers so that borrowers do not engage in behaviors that make it less likely that they can pay back the loan; then lenders must monitor the borrowers' activities and enforce the restrictive covenants if the borrower violates them.

Another concept that is very important in understanding the impediments to a well-functioning financial system is the so-called free-rider problem. The free-rider problem occurs because people who do not spend resources on collecting information can still take advantage of (get a free ride off) the information that other people have collected. The free-rider problem is particularly important in securities markets. If some investors acquire information that tells them which securities are undervalued and then buy these securities, other investors who have not paid for this information may be able to buy right along with the well-informed investors. If enough free-riding investors can do this, the increased demand for the undervalued securities will cause their low price to be bid up to reflect the securities' full net present values given this information. As a result of all these free riders, investors who have acquired information will no longer be able to earn the entire increase in the value of the security arising from this additional information. The weakened ability of private firms to profit from producing information will mean that less information is produced in securities markets, so that the adverse selection problem, in which overvalued securities are those most often offered for sale, is more likely to be an impediment to a well-functioning securities market.

More important, the free-rider problem makes it less likely that securities markets will act to reduce incentives to commit moral hazard. As we have seen, monitoring and enforcement of restrictive covenants and other contract terms are necessary to reduce moral hazard incentives for borrowers to take on risk at the lenders expense. However, because monitoring and enforcement are costly, the free-rider problem discourages this kind of activity in securities markets. Once some investors know that other securities holders are monitoring and enforcing the restrictive covenants, they can free-ride on the other securities holders' monitoring and enforcement. When these other securities holders realize that they can do the same thing, they also may stop their monitoring and enforcement activities, with the result that not enough resources are devoted to monitoring and enforcement. The outcome is that moral hazard can be a serious hindrance to the issuance of marketable securities.

One important feature of financial systems explained by the asymmetric information framework is the prominent role played by banking institutions and other financial intermediaries that make private loans. These institutions play such an important role because they are well suited to reduce adverse selection and moral hazard problems in financial markets. They are not as subject to the free-rider problem and profit from the information they produce because they make private loans that are not traded. Because the loans of these institutions are private, other investors cannot buy them. As a result, investors are less able to free-ride off financial intermediaries and bid up the prices of the loans that would prevent the intermediary from profiting from its information production activities. Similarly, it is hard to free-ride off these monitoring activities of financial intermediaries when they make private loans. Financial institutions making private loans thus receive the benefits of monitoring and so are better equipped to prevent moral hazard on the part of borrowers.

Banks have particular advantages over other financial intermediaries in solving asymmetric information problems. For example, banks' advantages in information collection activities are enhanced by their ability to engage in long-term customer relationships and to issue loans using lines of credit arrangements (Petersen and Rajan 1994; Berger and Udell 1995). In addition, their ability to scrutinize their borrowers' checking account balances may provide banks with an additional advantage in monitoring the borrowers' behavior (Nakamura 1993). Banks also have advantages in reducing moral hazard because, as demonstrated by Diamond (1984), they can engage in lower cost monitoring than can individuals, and because, as pointed out by Stiglitz and Weiss (1983), they have advantages in preventing risk taking by borrowers because they can use the threat of cutting off future lending to improve a borrower's behavior. Banks also have advantages in contracting, that is, specifying interest rates, collateral requirements, and other contractual terms that help sort borrowers into risk pools that reduce adverse selection and moral hazard incentives for borrowers to engage in risky activities. Banks' natural advantages in collecting information and reducing moral hazard explain why banks have such an important role in financial markets throughout the world.[1] In addition, banks have the advantage of the synergy from providing liquidity provision at the same institution offering line of credit lending and deposits (see Kashyap, Rajan, and Stein 1999).

The asymmetric information framework explains why banks play an even more important role in the financial systems of emerging market and transition countries because of the greater difficulty of acquiring informa-

---

1. As pointed out in Edwards and Mishkin (1995), the traditional financial intermediation role of banking has been in decline in both the United States and other industrialized countries because of improved information technology that makes issuing securities easier. Nonetheless, banks continue to be important in the financial system.

tion on private firms in these countries.[2] When the quality of information about firms is worse, asymmetric information problems will be more severe, and it will be harder for firms to issue securities. Thus, the smaller role of securities markets in emerging market and transition countries leaves a greater role for financial intermediaries such as banks.

1.3   Why is Prudential Supervision Needed?

The previous section shows how asymmetric information leads to adverse selection and moral hazard problems that both have an important impact on the financial system and explain the importance of banks. The same asymmetric information analysis is especially useful in understanding why prudential supervision of the banking system is necessary and why governments choose the types of supervision they do.

1.3.1   The Rationale for a Government Safety Net

As shown in the previous section, banks are particularly well suited to solving adverse selection and moral hazard problems because they make private loans that help avoid the free-rider problem. However, this solution to the free-rider problem creates another asymmetric information problem because depositors lack information about the quality of these private loans. This asymmetric information problem leads to two reasons why the banking system might not function well.

First, in the absence of government intervention, a bank failure means that depositors would have to wait to get their deposit funds until the bank is liquidated and its assets turned into cash, and at that time they would be paid only a fraction of the value of their deposits. Unable to learn if bank managers were taking on too much risk or were outright crooks, depositors would be reluctant to put money in the bank, thus making banking institutions less viable. Second, depositors' lack of information about the quality of bank assets can lead to bank panics, which can have serious harmful consequences for the economy.

To see this, consider the following situation. After an adverse shock hits the economy, 5 percent of the banks have such large losses on loans that they become insolvent (i.e., they have a negative net worth and therefore are bankrupt). Because of asymmetric information, depositors are unable to tell whether their bank is a good bank or one of the 5 percent that are insolvent. Depositors at bad and good banks recognize that they may not get back 100 cents on the dollar for their deposits and will want to withdraw them. Indeed, because banks operate on a sequential service constraint (i.e., a first-come, first-served basis), depositors have a very strong

---

2. Rojas-Suarez and Weisbrod (1996) document that banks play a more important role in the financial systems in emerging market countries than in industrialized countries.

incentive to show up at the bank first because if they are last in line, the bank may run out of funds and they will get nothing. Uncertainty about the health of the banking system in general can lead to runs on banks both good and bad, and the failure of one bank can hasten the failure of others (a contagion effect). If nothing is done to restore the public's confidence, a bank panic can ensue. Because banks solve asymmetric information problems and thus facilitate productive investment in the economy, a bank panic in which many banks go out of business reduces the amount of financial intermediation undertaken by banks and so leads to a decline in investment and aggregate economic activity. Indeed, the most severe economic contractions in U.S. history have always been associated with bank panics (see Friedman and Schwartz 1963; Bernanke 1983; and Mishkin 1991).

A government safety net for depositors can short-circuit runs on banks and bank panics; and by providing protection for the depositor, it can overcome reluctance to put funds in the banking system. One form of the safety net is explicit deposit insurance, a guarantee such as that provided by the Federal Deposit Insurance Corporation (FDIC) in the United States, in which depositors are paid off in full on the first $100,000 they have deposited in the bank, no matter what happens to the bank. With fully insured deposits, depositors do not need to run to the bank to make withdrawals—even if they are worried about the bank's health—because their deposits will be worth 100 cents on the dollar, no matter what.

Deposit insurance is not the only way in which governments provide a safety net for depositors. Governments have often stood ready to provide support to domestic banks when they face runs, even in the absence of explicit deposit insurance. This support is sometimes provided by the central bank, which operates as a lender of last resort, either by lending directly to troubled institutions or by injecting liquidity into the financial system through open market operations (which may be less effective). In other cases, funds are provided directly by the government to troubled institutions, or these institutions are taken over by the government, which then guarantees that depositors will receive their money in full.

1.3.2 Moral Hazard and the Government Safety Net

Although a government safety net can be very successful at protecting depositors and preventing bank panics, it is a mixed blessing. The most serious drawback of the government safety net stems from moral hazard, the incentives of one party of a transaction to engage in activities detrimental to the other party. Moral hazard is a prominent concern in government arrangements to provide a safety net. Because depositors know that with a safety net they will not suffer losses if a bank fails, they do not impose market discipline on banks by withdrawing deposits when they suspect that the bank is taking on too much risk. Consequently, banks with a government safety net have an incentive to take on greater risks than they otherwise would. The problem here is not just that a government safety net exists, but that it results in a payoff function for bank owners that encourages excessive risk taking. If the insurance provided by the safety net could be priced properly so that the payoff for the bank would no longer encourage excessive risk taking—obviously a tall order—then the moral hazard problem would disappear.

1.3.3   Adverse Selection and the Government Safety Net

A further problem with a government safety net arises because of adverse selection: The people who are most likely to engage in activities that may cause bank failure are those who most want to take advantage of the insurance. Because depositors who are protected by a government safety net have little reason to impose discipline on the bank, risk-loving entrepreneurs might find the banking industry a particularly attractive one to enter; they know that they will be able to engage in highly risky activities.

1.3.4   Too Big To Fail

Because the failure of a very large bank makes it more likely that a major financial disruption will occur, governments are naturally reluctant to allow a big bank to fail and cause losses to its depositors and perhaps to other stakeholders. Indeed, when large banks have failed (as happened in the United States with the failure in May 1984 of Continental Illinois, one of the ten largest banks in the United States at the time), governments have often not only guaranteed insured deposits but also prevented losses for uninsured deposits or even bondholders. (Note that the term *too big to fail* is somewhat misleading because when a bank is closed or merged into another bank, at least in the United States but not always elsewhere, the managers are usually fired, and the stockholders in the bank lose their investment.)

One problem with the too-big-to-fail policy is that it increases the moral hazard incentives for big banks. If a government is willing to close a bank and prevent losses only for insured depositors, uninsured depositors or other creditors would suffer losses if the bank failed. Thus they would have an incentive to monitor the bank by examining the bank's activities closely and pulling their money out if the bank were taking on too much risk. To prevent such a loss of credit, the bank would be more likely to engage in less risky activities. However, once uninsured creditors know that a bank is too big to fail, they have no incentive to monitor the bank and pull out their funds when it takes on too much risk; no matter what the bank does, uninsured creditors will not suffer any losses. The result of the too-big-to-fail policy is that big banks might take on even greater risks, thereby making bank failures more likely. Boyd and Gertler (1993) find evidence consistent with this view: Large banks in the United States took on riskier loans than did smaller banks, and this led to higher loan losses for the large banks.

1.3.5 Rationale for Prudential Supervision

Because all governments provide some form of a safety net for the banking system, whether it is explicit or implicit, they need to take steps to limit the moral hazard and adverse selection that the safety net creates. Otherwise, banks will have such a strong incentive to take on excessive risks that the safety net may do more harm than good and promote banking crises rather than prevent them. Prudential supervision, in which the government establishes regulations to reduce risk taking and then supervisors monitor banks to see that they are complying with these regulations and not taking on excessive risk, is thus needed to ensure the safety and soundness of the banking system. Preventing excessive risk taking with prudential supervision is even more critical in emerging market countries, as recent events have indicated. Inadequate prudential supervision has led to severe problems in these countries' banking sectors, which have been an important factor triggering the currency and financial crises in these countries in recent years, and which have created so much economic hardship (see Mishkin 1996, 1999; and Corsetti, Pesenti, and Roubini 1998).

1.4 Forms of Prudential Supervision

Prudential supervision takes on nine basic forms: (a) restrictions on asset holdings and activities; (b) separation of the banking and other financial service industries such as securities, insurance, or real estate; (c) restrictions on competition; (d) capital requirements; (e) risk-based deposit insurance premiums; (f) disclosure requirements; (g) bank chartering; (h) bank examination; and (i) a supervisory versus a regulatory approach.

1.4.1 Restrictions on Asset Holdings and Activities

Even in the absence of a government safety net, banks still have the incentive to take on too much risk. Risky assets may provide the bank with higher earnings if they pay off; but if they do not pay off and the bank fails, depositors are left holding the bag. If depositors are able to monitor the bank easily by acquiring information on its risk-taking activities, they would immediately withdraw their deposits if the bank was taking on too much risk. To prevent such a loss of deposits, the bank would be more likely to reduce its risk-taking activities. Unfortunately, acquiring information on a bank's activities to learn how much risk the bank is taking can be a difficult task. Hence, depositors may be incapable of imposing discipline that might prevent banks from engaging in risky activities. A rationale for government regulation to reduce risk taking on the part of banks therefore exists even without the presence of a government safety net, such as deposit insurance.[3] The need for restrictions on risky activities is even greater when there is a government safety net that increases the incentives for risky behavior.

Governments therefore impose banking regulations that restrict banks from holding risky assets—common stock, for example, in the United States—and these restrictions are a direct means of making banks avoid too much risk.[4] Bank regulations also promote diversification, which reduces risk by limiting the amount of loans in particular categories or to individual borrowers. Regulations also restrict banks from engaging in commercial activities that are considered to be outside the core banking business and that might subject the bank to too much risk.

1.4.2 Separation of Banking and Other Financial Service Industries

One particular type of activity that may involve more risk than traditional banking activities is underwriting securities. Concerns that moral hazard incentives created by the government safety net might encourage excessive risk in this business have led some governments to prevent the combination of banking and securities activities. For example, the Glass-Steagall Act of 1933 forced a separation of the banking and securities industries in the United States until its repeal with the passage in 1999 of the Gramm-Leach-Bliley Financial Services Modernization Act.

Another concern with banks engaging in other financial activities such as securities underwriting, insurance, or real estate is that these may lead to extension of the government safety net in these industries also, even if they are not inherently riskier than traditional banking. As we have seen, expansion of the safety net could increase the incentives for risk taking in nonbanking industries, which could make the financial system more fragile. In addition, extending the safety net to units of banking institutions that engage in securities, insurance, and real estate activities might give banking institutions an unfair competitive advantage in these industries relative to companies not affiliated with banks. Thus, governments often restrict banks from entering these other businesses in order to prevent extension of the safety net.

1.4.3 Restrictions on Competition

Increased competition can also increase moral hazard incentives for banks to take on more risk. Declining profitability and hence a lower franchise value as a result of increased competition could tip the incentives of

---

3. However, even if most depositors are unable to monitor banks activities sufficiently well to discipline them, banks structured with more equity or subordinate claims would not rely on depositors for discipline, and junior claimants might then be able to provide more of the required discipline.

4. Preventing banks from holding individually risky assets does not necessarily reduce the variance of their portfolios, and this is why regulators also focus on the overall riskiness of the bank's balance sheet and activities.

bankers toward assuming greater risk in an effort to maintain former profit levels (see Marcus 1984 and Keeley 1990). Thus, governments in many countries have instituted regulations to protect banks from competition. These regulations have taken four forms. First are regulations separating banking and nonbanking business, like those in the Glass-Steagall legislation just mentioned, which prevent nonbank institutions from competing with banks by engaging in banking business. Second are restrictions on entry of foreign banks (or, in the United States, restrictions on entry of out-of-state banks that occurred before implementation of the Riegle-Neal Interstate Banking and Branching Efficiency Act of 1994). Third are restrictions on branching. Fourth are ceilings on rates charged on loans or ceilings on rates charged on deposits, as with the Regulation Q restrictions on deposit rates in the United States that were abolished in the mid-1980s.

Although restricting competition may prop up the health of banks, restrictions on competition have obvious serious disadvantages: They can lead to higher charges to consumers and can decrease the efficiency of banking institutions, which do not have to compete as hard (Berger and Hannan 1998). Thus, although the existence of asymmetric information provides a rationale for anticompetitive regulations, it does not mean that they will be beneficial. Indeed, in recent years the impulse of governments in industrialized countries to restrict competition has been waning.

1.4.4   Capital Requirements

Requiring that banks have sufficient capital is another way to change the banks' incentives to take on less risk. When a bank is forced to hold a large amount of equity capital, the bank has more to lose if it fails and is thus more likely to pursue less risky activities.

Bank capital requirements typically take three forms. The first type is based on the so-called leverage ratio: the amount of capital divided by the bank's total assets. For example, to be classified as well capitalized in the United States, a bank's leverage ratio must exceed 5 percent; a lower leverage ratio—especially one below 3 percent—triggers prompt corrective action with increased restrictions on the bank.

In the wake of banking problems in the 1980s, regulators in the United States and the rest of the world have become increasingly worried about banks' holdings of risky assets and about the increase in banks' off-balance-sheet activities, particularly activities that involve trading financial instruments and generating income from fees, which do not appear on bank balance sheets but nevertheless expose banks to risk. This led to the establishment of a second type of capital requirements in 1988 that attempted to make adjustments for risk, referred to as the Basel Accord on bank capital requirements because they were agreed to by banking officials from industrialized nations who met under the auspices of the Bank for International Settlements in Basel, Switzerland. Under this risk-based capital requirement, minimum capital standards are linked to off-balance-sheet activities such as loan commitments, letters of credit, interest-rate swaps, and trading positions in futures and options.

The Basel Accord required that banks hold capital of at least 8 percent of their risk-weighted assets. Assets and off-balance-sheet activities were allocated into four categories, each with a different weight to reflect the degree of credit risk. The first category carried a zero weight and included items that have little default risk, such as reserves and government securities in the Organization for Economic Cooperation and Development (OECD) countries. The second category had a 20 percent weight and included claims on banks in OECD countries. The third category had a weight of 50 percent and included municipal bonds and residential mortgages. The fourth category had the maximum weight of 100 percent and included credits to consumers and corporations. Off-balance-sheet activities are treated in a similar manner by assigning a credit-equivalent percentage that converts them to on-balance-sheet items to which the appropriate risk weight applies.

A third type of capital requirement was introduced in 1996 to cover risk in trading activities at the largest banks. For example, since January 1998 the Federal Reserve has required these banks to use their own internal models to calculate how much they could lose over a ten-day period and then set aside additional capital equal to three times that amount. Banks can meet this new capital requirement with more standard forms of capital or by issuing a new form of capital, called Tier 3, which consists of short-term securities that holders cannot cash in at maturity if the bank is under-capitalized.

1.4.5   Risk-Based Deposit Insurance Premiums

As mentioned earlier, the government safety net creates a moral hazard problem because it leads to a payoff function for bank owners that encourages excessive risk taking. The moral hazard problem could therefore be eliminated if premiums for the insurance provided by the government were priced appropriately to reflect the amount of risk taken by a bank. The Federal Deposit Insurance Corporation Improvement Act (FDICIA) of 1991 pursued this approach to reducing the moral hazard problem by mandating the implementation of risk-based deposit insurance premiums. As a result, deposit insurance premiums in the United States are based on bank's classifications into one of three capital adequacy groups and one of three supervisory groups. The higher capital adequacy is and the better the bank's supervisory rating is, the lower its insurance premium is.

Although risk-based deposit insurance premiums are desirable in theory, they have not worked very well in practice. The basic problem is that it is hard to determine accurately the amount of risk a bank is actually taking. For example, at the beginning of 1999, 95 percent of the Bank Insurance Fund institutions in the United States (with 98 percent of commercial bank deposits) and 92 percent Savings Association Insurance

Fund institutions (with 96 percent of savings and loan deposits) ended up being put in the least risky insurance category, paying a zero insurance premium. Clearly, the risk-based deposit insurance scheme in the United States does not discriminate adequately among banks and has not provided the appropriate incentives to reduce risk taking.

1.4.6 Disclosure Requirements

The free-rider problem described earlier indicates that individual depositors and other bank creditors will not have enough incentive to produce private information about the quality of a bank's assets. To ensure that there is better information for depositors and the marketplace, regulators can require that banks adhere to certain standard accounting principles and disclose a wide range of information that helps the market assess the quality of a bank's portfolio and the amount of the bank's exposure to risk. More public information about the risks incurred by banks and the quality of their portfolio can enhance market discipline by enabling stockholders, creditors, and depositors to evaluate and monitor banks and thus act as a deterrent to excessive risk taking. Disclosure requirements can also be the primary focus of a bank regulatory system, as with the approach implemented in New Zealand in 1996 in which every bank must supply a comprehensive quarterly financial statement to the public and prominently post its rating from private credit agencies at all bank branches. An unusual feature of the New Zealand system is that it requires bank directors to validate financial statements, and they are subject to unlimited liability if the bank goes into bankruptcy and if these financial statements are found to be misleading.

1.4.7 Bank Chartering

Overseeing who operates banks is an important method for reducing the adverse selection problem created by the government safety net. Because banks can be used by dishonest people or overly ambitious entrepreneurs to engage in highly speculative activities, such undesirable people (from the safety and soundness perspective) would be eager to run a bank. Chartering banks is one method for preventing this adverse selection problem; through chartering, proposals for new banks are screened to prevent undesirable people from controlling them. The typical chartering process requires the people planning to organize the bank to submit an application that shows how they plan to operate the bank. In evaluating the application, the chartering authority looks at whether the bank is likely to be sound by examining the quality of the banks' intended management, the likely earnings of the bank, and the amount of the bank's initial capital.[5]

---

5. Chartering can also be used to restrict entry and competition. For example, to get a charter from the Office of the Comptroller of the Currency in the United States in the past,

1.4.8   Bank Examination

To limit moral hazard incentives for excessive risk taking, it is not enough to have regulations that encourage less risk taking, but banks must be monitored to see if they are complying with these regulations. If not, enforcement actions must be taken. Banks are required to file periodic (usually quarterly) reports (called *call reports* in the United States) that contain such information as the bank's assets and liabilities, income and dividends, ownership, and foreign exchange operations. Bank examiners also evaluate the quality of a bank's loans and classify them into problem categories if they are unlikely to be repaid in order to assess the bank's balance-sheet position and the amount of its capital. This information, along with regular on-site bank examinations, allows regulators to monitor whether the bank is complying with capital requirements (including sufficient provisioning for loan losses), restrictions on asset holdings, disclosure requirements, and so on, and is crucial to limiting the moral hazard created by the government safety net.[6]

In the United States, with variants in other countries, examiners give banks a so-called CAMELS rating (the acronym is based on the six areas assessed: capital adequacy, asset quality, management, earnings, liquidity, and sensitivity to market risk). With this information about a bank's activities, regulators can enforce regulations by taking such formal actions as cease and desist orders to alter the bank's behavior or even by closing a bank if its supervisory rating is sufficiently low. Actions taken to reduce moral hazard by restricting banks from taking on too much risk also help reduce the adverse selection problem, because with less opportunity for risk taking, risk-loving entrepreneurs will be less likely to be attracted to the banking industry.

1.4.9   Supervisory versus Regulatory Approaches

Traditionally, prudential supervision has focused primarily on assessment of the quality of the bank's balance sheet and loans at a point in time, then determining whether the bank complies with capital requirements and restrictions on asset holdings. Because this kind of prudential supervision is based on regulatory rules, it is often referred to as the *regulatory approach.* Although the traditional regulatory approach is important for reducing excessive risk taking by banks, it is no longer felt to be adequate in today's world, in which financial innovation has produced new markets and instruments that make it easy for banks and their employees

---

a bank had to demonstrate a need for a new bank. However, the use of chartering to restrict competition is no longer a feature of the chartering process in the United States.

6. For a description of the bank examination process in the United States, see the paper by Berger, Kyle, and Scalise in this volume.

to make huge bets easily and quickly. In this new financial environment, a bank that is quite healthy at a particular point in time can be driven into insolvency extremely rapidly from trading losses, as forcefully demonstrated by the failure of Barings in 1995. Thus an examination that focuses only on the quality of the bank assets or whether a bank is following the rules at a point in time may not be effective in indicating whether a bank will in fact be taking on excessive risk in the near future.

This change in the financial environment for banking institutions has resulted in a major shift in thinking about the bank supervision process throughout the world to what is called the *supervisory approach*. In the supervisory approach bank examiners focus less on compliance with specific regulatory rules and the risks of the financial instruments currently in the bank's portfolio and more on the soundness of the bank's management practices with regard to controlling risk. This shift in thinking was reflected in a new focus on risk management in the Federal Reserve System's 1993 guidelines to examiners on trading and derivatives activities. The focus was expanded and formalized in the Trading Activities Manual issued early in 1994, which provided bank examiners with tools to evaluate risk management systems. In late 1995, the Federal Reserve and the Office of the Comptroller of the Currency (OCC) announced that they would be assessing risk management processes at the banks they supervise. Now bank examiners give a separate sensitivity to risk rating from 1 to 5 that feeds into the overall management rating as part of the CAMELS system. Four elements of sound risk management are assessed to determine the sensitivity to risk rating: (a) the quality of oversight provided by the board of directors and senior management, (b) the adequacy of policies and limits for all activities that present significant risks, (c) the quality of the risk measurement and monitoring systems, and (d) the adequacy of internal controls to prevent fraud or unauthorized activities on the part of employees.

This shift toward focusing on management processes is also reflected in recent guidelines adopted by the U.S. bank regulatory authorities to deal with interest-rate risk. At one point, U.S. regulators were contemplating requiring banks to use a standard model to calculate the amount of capital a bank would need to have to allow for the interest rate risk it bears. Because coming up with a one-size-fits-all model that would work for all banks has proved difficult, the regulatory agencies have instead decided to adopt guidelines for the management of interest rate risk, and bank examiners will continue to consider interest rate risk in deciding on the bank's capital requirements. These guidelines require the bank's board of directors to establish interest rate risk limits, appoint officials of the bank to manage this risk, and monitor the bank's risk exposure. The guidelines also require that senior management of a bank develop formal risk management policies and procedures to ensure that the board of directors' risk limits are not violated and to implement internal controls to monitor interest-rate risk and compliance with the board's directives.

The Basel Committee on Banking Supervision has also moved more toward the supervisory approach in deciding on capital requirements. One part of its June 1999 proposal allows banks to use their own credit risk models for setting capital requirements, whereas the internal management procedures that banks use to decide how much capital to hold would be subject to supervisory review, after which in some circumstances banks might be required to hold capital beyond the regulatory minimum. The movement away from rules-based prudential supervision (the regulatory approach) toward a more forward-looking supervisory approach will probably increase over time. However, bank regulations will still play a prominent role in prudential supervision, not only because they are a first defense against excessive risk taking, but also because their existence provides supervisors with a stick they can wield to get banks to implement proper risk management procedures.

1.5   What Are the Issues?

The framework used here to understand why prudential supervision is needed and the forms that it takes can also be used to examine key issues affecting whether prudential supervision will work well in preserving the safety and soundness of the banking system, the topic of this conference. There are eight basic issues that we look at here, and the papers in this conference volume have something to say about all of them.

1.5.1   How Restrictive Should a Regulatory Environment Be?

We have seen that prudential supervision often takes the form of restricting bank activities, either by not allowing them to hold certain assets or by restricting them from engaging in certain businesses. Although restricting banks from certain activities may limit the opportunities for banks to take on risk, this does not mean that doing so will always be beneficial or will promote the safety and soundness of the financial system.

For example, those who are opposed to restrictions separating the banking and other financial industries believe that allowing banks to enter these industries would increase competition. Bank entry into securities underwriting can lower the spreads between the price guaranteed to the issuer of the security and the price paid for the security by the public, possibly increasing the efficiency of securities markets (see Beatty, Thompson, and Vetsuypens 1998 and Gande, Puri, and Saunders 1999). Bank entry into insurance could create more efficient networks to deliver insurance to consumers, thereby lowering costs. Furthermore, the combination of banking and nonbanking businesses under one roof could lead to more diversified financial institutions, which may thus be less likely to fail. Therefore, allowing banks to enter other financial industries could actually increase the safety of the financial system, rather than make it more fragile.

Proponents of the separation of banking from other industries such as investment banking and real estate, which can be quite risky, believe that allowing commercial banks to engage in this business might produce more bank failures and a less stable financial system. They are concerned also about potential conflicts of interest if banks engage in underwriting securities. Congressional hearings in the United States prior to the enactment of the Glass-Steagall Act in 1933 turned up abuses in which banks that were underwriting new issues of securities sold them to trust funds they managed when they could not sell them to anyone else, and these trust funds often suffered substantial losses when the securities were sold later. Cases also surfaced in which the bank would buy securities that it was underwriting when the securities could not be sold elsewhere. Proponents of the separation of banking from other financial industries worry also that the extension of the safety net to these other industries will remove market discipline and encourage risk taking in these industries, which could reduce their safety and soundness.

Proponents of abolishing the separation of banking from the securities industries point out that the extent of underwriting abuses that occurred before the passage of Glass-Steagall was probably exaggerated (Benston 1990), and regulatory authorities now have much greater power to find and punish people who would abuse commercial banking's securities activities. Empirical research suggests that conflicts of interest that would lead to underwriting abuses are not a serious problem (see Ang and Richardson 1994; Kroszner and Rajan 1994, 1997; Puri 1994, 1996; Gande et al., 1997; and Gande, Puri, and Saunders, 1999). Furthermore, the erection of fire walls to separate various bank operations can help prevent conflicts of interest. Fire walls could also be useful in limiting the expansion of the safety net to other businesses, including securities and insurance underwriting.

A key issue for the design of prudential supervision is thus, what regulatory environment works best, and how restrictive it should be? The paper by James Barth, Gerard Caprio Jr., and Ross Levine in this volume examines this issue by exploiting a unique data set they created at the World Bank that documents the nature of the regulatory environment and restrictions in a panel of over sixty countries. Through statistical analysis, they evaluate the links among different regulatory/ownership practices, financial sector performance, and banking-system stability. They ask three basic questions and get the following answers.

First, do countries with regulations that impose tighter restrictions on the ability of commercial banks to engage in securities, insurance, and real estate activities have less efficient but more stable financial systems? Barth, Caprio, and Levine uncovered no reliable statistical relationships between regulatory restrictions on banks engaging in securities, insurance, and real estate activities and the level of financial development or industrial competition. However, they do find that restrictions on banks engaging in securities activities tend to be associated with higher interest rate margins, suggesting that these restrictions hamper efficiency. Furthermore, countries with greater regulatory restrictions on securities activities of commercial banks have a significantly and substantially higher probability of suffering a financial crisis. The evidence in this paper thus suggests that regulatory restrictions separating banking and other financial industries, especially the securities industry, are harmful. Allowing banks to enter the securities industry not only promotes efficiency but can actually promote a more stable financial system. Evidence of the type in this paper can never be conclusive, as Mark Gertler points out in the comment, but the paper shifts the burden of proof to those who advocate separation of banking and the securities industries to demonstrate harmful effects of allowing banks into this industry.

The second question Barth, Caprio, and Levine ask is whether countries that restrict the mixing of banking and commerce have less efficient but more stable financial systems. They do not find that restrictions on mixing banking and commerce hurt efficiency or financial development, but they do find that these restrictions are associated with greater financial instability. Thus, one of the major reasons for restricting the mixing of banking and commerce—to reduce financial fragility—is not supported by the evidence in this paper. This evidence, along with the evidence on the first question, weakens the case for more restrictive regulatory environments in the banking system.

The third question asks whether having state-owned banks play a large role in the financial system leads to more poorly functioning financial systems. They find that the answer is yes because greater state ownership of banks in a country tends to be associated with more poorly developed banks, nonbanks, and securities markets. This result accords well with the intuition of economists who believe that the private sector has much better incentives to create financial institutions that will make the financial system operate efficiently. This evidence also accords well with many economists' recommendations that the government should not be in the financial business but should instead leave it to the private sector.

1.5.2   Limiting Too Big To Fail

As we have seen, the too-big-to-fail problem provides a particular challenge for prudential supervision. Governments are reluctant to let the failure of particularly large banking institutions cause losses for depositors and often other stakeholders, because the failure is then more likely to have a systemic effect on the financial system, thereby precipitating a financial crisis. On the other hand, this reluctance increases moral hazard incentives for large banking institutions to take on excessive risk, which makes the financial system more fragile. Thus a key issue for prudential supervision is how to limit the moral hazard incentives for large banking institutions.

The speech given at the conference by Lawrence Meyer, a governor of the Federal Reserve System, addresses the issue of how the Federal Reserve System is approaching the supervision of what he calls *large complex banking organizations.* This issue has grown in importance recently, with the growth of financial consolidation and the passage of the Gramm-Leach-Bliley Act of 1999, both of which encourage the development of larger and more complex financial organizations. Meyer's speech indicates that the Federal Reserve has groups that are engaged in intensive study of how best to supervise these large organizations and that the Federal Reserve's thinking is taking two directions. First, there is a growing emphasis on a supervisory approach in which examiners focus on the adequacy of banks' risk management and internal models to determine the amount of capital needed to cope with market and credit risk. Second, there is increased emphasis on the use of market discipline to create the right incentives for these large, complex banking organizations.

In order to enhance market discipline, Meyer cites two steps that can be taken. First are requirements to increase public disclosure of information about residual risk in securitizations; the distribution of credits by internal risk classifications; and concentrations of credits by industry, geography, and borrower. This disclosure should make it easier for the market to judge whether these large banks are managing risk properly and to pull out funds if they have concerns about the way the bank is managing risk. Second, an increase in issuance by large banking organizations of subordinated debt (junior debt that is paid off only after more senior claims have been paid). This subordinated debt will subject them to increased market discipline because subordinated debt holders have strong incentives to monitor these organizations.

1.5.3   Market Discipline

The importance of market discipline and how it might work to promote safety and soundness of the financial system are themes present not only in Meyer's speech but also in the papers by Robert Bliss and Mark Flannery and Charles Calomiris and Andrew Powell.

The term *market discipline* has often been used quite loosely in the literature, and Bliss and Flannery make the important point that the concept of market discipline needs to be refined if we are to understand its effectiveness. Bliss and Flannery distinguish between two aspects of market discipline: (a) *monitoring,* in which investors are able to understand changes in a firm's condition accurately and incorporate these assessments promptly into the firm's security prices; and (b) *influence,* in which a security price decline causes firm managers to respond by counteracting adverse shocks. There is substantial evidence that markets are able to monitor and reflect a firm's financial condition in securities prices (see the survey in Flannery 1998). On the other hand, there is very little evidence in the literature on whether there is market influence in nonextreme situations.[7] Without market influence in which market prices cause managers to alter their behavior in normal times, market monitoring will not necessarily limit managers of financial institutions from taking on excessive risk. Thus without market influence, market discipline will not work.

Bliss and Flannery study market influence by examining what happens to the condition of bank holding companies after changes in stock and bond prices in order to see if there is evidence that these price changes affect managerial actions. They do not find convincing evidence of market influence, but as is indicated in the paper and in the comment by Raghuram Rajan, because securities prices may primarily reflect predictions of future financial conditions, managerial actions that counteract adverse shocks may be extremely difficult to find in the data, even if this is exactly what the managers are doing. Instead of indicating that market influence is weak, the Bliss and Flannery paper demonstrates how difficult it is to use market prices to obtain evidence on the existence of market influence. However, their paper suggests that without strong evidence for the ability of markets to influence managerial actions, prudential supervisors should retain responsibility for influencing managerial actions to restrict risk taking.

In recent years, Argentina has undertaken a sweeping reform of its system of prudential supervision, particularly in the aftermath of the tequila crisis in 1994, by using greater reliance on market discipline to promote a safe and sound banking system. The paper by Calomiris and Powell outlines what changes Argentina has made in its supervisory system and assesses how well these changes have worked to create credible market discipline of the banking system. The Argentine experience is worth studying not only for the lessons it provides to emerging market countries, but also for the lessons it may provide for industrialized countries like the United States, which, as Meyer's speech indicates, are considering increasing the use of market discipline in their supervisory systems.

In the aftermath of the tequila crisis, Argentina adopted the Bonds, Auditing, Supervision, Information, and Credit Rating (BASIC) system of banking oversight, administered by the central bank. The main concept behind this system is that market discipline and regulatory discipline are each imperfect by themselves, but there is a strong complementarity between the two. The Argentines recognized, as Meyer does in his speech,

---

7. An example of extreme situations would be one of near insolvency or very poor firm performance that might trigger a takeover.

that information is a prerequisite to market or regulatory discipline. Thus a key feature of the BASIC system is increased disclosure of information (the *I* in BASIC), including development of a credit bureau in which information about all loans in the financial system more than $50 in value are made publicly available. Information disclosure is useful only if the information is accurate. Thus another key feature of the BASIC system is the supervisory authority's standards and supervision of the auditing process (the *A* in BASIC). To increase information, the BASIC system also has a credit rating requirement (the *C* in BASIC), in which banks are required to obtain credit ratings and disclose them to the public. To increase market discipline, the BASIC system requires banks to issue subordinated debt for 2 percent of their deposits each year (the *B*, for bonds, in BASIC). If banks are forced to attract investors by going to the market and issuing subordinated debt, this process reveals information about the bank to both debt holders and supervisors. In addition, subordinated debt holders have incentives to monitor banks and pull out their funds if the bank is taking on too much risk. In addition to the elements just mentioned, which focus on information and market discipline, the BASIC system has an important role for supervision (the *S* in BASIC). The supervisory authority adopted a version of the CAMELS system used in the United States and used CAMELS ratings to set capital requirements.

Calomiris and Powell find that although the BASIC system has worked reasonably well, some elements are problematic. The subordinated debt requirement, which was to be in place by January 1998, has not worked as well as some of its advocates had hoped. The Asian crisis in mid-1997 and the Russian crisis in the fall of 1998 made debt issues very difficult for the banks. Thus the central bank put back the compliance date for subordinated debt requirements several times and weakened the requirement by increasing the range of liabilities that banks could issue to satisfy the requirement. In addition, the central bank has been unwilling to disclose which banks have been unable to comply with the subdebt requirement. However, the subdebt requirement has been beneficial in that it is the weak banks that have had trouble issuing subdebt and that there have been penalties for noncompliance, giving banks incentives to decrease the riskiness of their activities. The credit ratings requirement has also run into some difficulties because obtaining the ratings appeared to be expensive and because the ratings were not of uniform quality. The central bank has tried to fix these problems by asking banks to have only one rating to reduce the cost, and the central bank has restricted the number of authorized agencies to only internationally active ones.

On the whole, Calomiris and Powell give a fairly favorable assessment of the BASIC system. Not only has the Argentine banking system grown rapidly and withstood shocks from the Asian and Russian crises, but the BASIC system also seems to have injected credible market discipline into the banking system. The authors find that there are market reactions to bank default risk as measured by deposit interest rates and deposit growth, and that deposit interest rates means revert quickly, especially after BASIC was implemented. These findings, though subject to some criticisms as indicated in the comment by Douglas Diamond, suggest that the market can measure bank risk and punish banks that are riskier, and that banks try to reduce risk after they are exposed to risk-increasing shocks. Calomiris and Powell thus provide a more encouraging view of the effectiveness of market discipline than do Bliss and Flannery. However, their assessment of Argentina's BASIC system does indicate that bank examination and supervision still play an important role in promoting safety and soundness of the banking system and that market discipline is not enough.

1.5.4 Limiting the Principal-Agent Problem in Supervision

An important impediment to successful prudential supervision of the financial system is the principal-agent problem, in which the agent (a regulator or supervisor) does not have the same incentives as the principal (the taxpayer it works for) and so acts in its own interest rather than in the interest of the principal. To act in the taxpayer's interest, regulators and supervisors have several tasks, as we have seen. For example, they need to set restrictions on holding assets that are too risky, to impose sufficiently high capital requirements, and to close down insolvent institutions. However, because of the principal-agent problem, regulators have incentives to do the opposite and engage in regulatory forbearance. One important incentive for regulators that explains this phenomenon is their desire to escape blame for poor performance by their agency. By loosening capital requirements and pursuing regulatory forbearance, regulators can hide the problem of an insolvent bank and hope that the situation will improve, a behavior that Kane (1989) characterizes as "bureaucratic gambling." Another important incentive for regulators is that they may want to protect their careers by acceding to pressures from the people who strongly influence their careers—the politicians.

Limiting the principal-agent problem by making bank supervisors accountable if they engage in regulatory forbearance is important to improve incentives for them to do their job properly. For example, as pointed out in Mishkin (1997), an important but very often overlooked part of FDICIA that has helped make this legislation effective is that the supervisory agencies must produce a mandatory report if the bank failure imposes costs on the FDIC. The resulting report is made available to any member of congress and to the general public upon request, and the General Accounting Office must do an annual review of these reports. Opening the actions of bank supervisors to public scrutiny makes regulatory forbearance less attractive to them, thereby reducing the principal-agent problem. In addition, subjecting the actions of bank supervisors to public scrutiny reduces the politicians' incentives to lean on supervisors to relax their supervision of banks.

Although limiting the principal-agent problem in bank supervision was not the main focus of any paper in the conference, the Calomiris and Powell paper and the paper by Allen Berger, Margaret Kyle, and Joseph Scalise do have some useful things to say about this issue. Calomiris and Powell point out that an additional benefit of the subordinated debt requirement in Argentina is that it helps monitor bank supervisors: Failure to comply sends a signal that can discourage regulatory forbearance. When a weak bank fails to comply with the subordinated debt requirement, the supervisors cannot easily claim that they were unaware of the bank's problems because the market has provided a clear signal of its lack of confidence in the bank. The presence of the subordinated debt requirement thus avoids plausible deniability by supervisors, which makes it more likely that they will close down a weak bank or take actions to encourage it to return to health.

One question examined in the Berger, Kyle, and Scalise paper is whether supervisors got tougher during the 1989–92 period and then got easier in the following 1993–98 period. Although Berger, Kyle, and Scalise found some limited evidence that supervisors were tougher in the 1989–92 period, they found even stronger evidence that bank supervisors eased up on banks during the 1993–98 period. This finding of easing in the 1993–98 period is particularly interesting because it was during this period that there was tremendous political pressure on supervisors to relax standards: Politicians claimed that supervisory actions during the 1989–92 period were to blame for creating the "credit crunch" that put a significant damper on the economy. In 1993, supervisors formally recognized a problem of credit availability and began a joint program directed at dealing with this problem, taking actions designed to alleviate the apparent reluctance of institutions to lend. The results of this paper thus suggest that despite the supposed independence of bank supervisors in the United States and provisions in FDICIA to reduce the principal-agent incentives for supervisors to relax standards, bank supervisors in the United States might still be responsive to political pressure—although an alternative view is that they were just trying to respond appropriately to a problem in the economy. The paper's results thus suggest that the principal-agent problem may not have been completely solved in the United States despite efforts to do so.

1.5.5   Refining Capital Requirements

The Basel Accord on capital requirements was developed to make capital requirements responsive to the amount of credit risk borne by the bank. Over time, limitations of the Basel Accord have become apparent because the broad-brush, regulatory measure of bank risk as stipulated by the credit risk weights can differ substantially from the actual risk the bank faces. For example, a loan to a AAA-rated corporation receives the same 100 percent risk weight (i.e., 8 percent capital requirement) as a highly risky loan to a CCC-rated corporation. As a result, banks may engage in what is called *regulatory (capital) arbitrage* in which they end up substituting riskier assets in their portfolio for safer assets that have the same risk weight. Thus risk-based capital requirements like the Basel requirements may end up encouraging risk taking by banks rather than limiting it. In his speech Meyer notes this problem and worries that the incentive to arbitrage economic and regulatory capital will increase, giving regulatory capital less and less meaning.

A key issue for effective prudential supervision is whether capital requirements can be refined so that requirements ensure that banks have adequate capital to deal with the amount of credit risk in the bank's activities. The Basel Committee on Banking Supervision (1999) has outlined two potential approaches to credit risk capital requirements for consideration: (a) a revised, standardized approach similar in style to the current requirements that leaves in place many of the distortions that lead to capital arbitrage, and (b) an internal ratings approach in which required capital would be computed using formulas based on internal credit risk ratings done by the bank. Over the longer term, a move to an internal models approach, similar to that used for market risk, may be possible. Under this approach banks' internal models would be used to calculate the risk requirement. The internal ratings and internal models approaches would attempt to get regulatory capital requirements to match economic capital more closely. The internal models approach takes a supervisory approach to capital regulation because the bank would make decisions about the models used, and then the supervisory authorities would monitor these models to see if they are reasonably accurate and follow best practice. The internal ratings approach has more elements of a regulatory approach because the parameters and architecture of the system would be set by regulators, although supervisors would still monitor the bank's procedures for determining the internal ratings.

For the two new approaches to risk-based capital requirements to get regulatory capital close to economic capital, so that regulatory arbitrage would be minimized, technical knowledge about what portfolio characteristics and factors are important in exposing the bank to credit risk is crucial. Mark Carey's paper conducts Monte Carlo simulation exercises to see which asset or portfolio characteristics and types of behavior substantially expose the bank to risk and whether a linear structure, in which different credit risks are added up independently, accurately reflects total credit risk for the bank. The basic findings of this work, and also the results from similar work done at the Bank of England, reported in the comment by Patricia Jackson, are that credit risk is substantially influenced by the following factors: borrower default ratings, estimates of likely loss given a default, and measures of portfolio size and granularity (the extent to which loans to a few borrowers make up a large fraction of the portfolio). In addition, the linear structure that is inherent in the internal ratings approach seems to produce reasonable estimates of overall credit risk for the bank. This research is useful both to banking institutions that need to develop their own internal models to assess credit risk and to supervisors who may have to evaluate these internal models or regulators who might be designing an internal ratings approach to credit risk–based capital requirements.

1.5.6   How Are Regulations Produced?

Economic analysis is useful for designing regulation to achieve certain objectives, and many of the papers in this conference are attempts to provide exactly this analysis. However, even when economists reach a consensus about what form regulation should take, we often see that the real world produces something quite different. For example, almost all American banking economists have agreed for over two decades that abolishing restrictions on branching across state lines would not only improve the efficiency of the banking sector, but would also increase diversification and make the banking system more stable. Despite this consensus, it was only in 1994, with the passage of the Riegle-Neal Interstate Banking and Branching Efficiency Act, that these restrictions were finally abolished. Why does it take so long for welfare-enhancing reforms to get implemented, and what finally leads to passage of these reforms?

The paper by Randall Kroszner and Phillip Strahan looks at this question by using a political economy approach to analyze why regulations evolve as they do and what forces lead to passage of legislation that changes regulations. They analyze voting patterns in congress on three amendments to the FDICIA of 1991 and find that private interests are a key determinant of votes on banking regulations, although partisanship and ideology also play an important role. Although the ability of their private-interest model to explain individual votes is impressive, Jeremy Stein points out in his comment that their model of interest group competition and battle among private interests may not be quite as good at explaining regulatory outcomes as the regression results indicate. The problem is that median votes and not individual votes determine whether legislation is passed, so that accurate prediction of individual votes may not always translate into accurate prediction of whether legislation is actually passed.

Nonetheless, Kroszner and Strahan's results do provide important clues as to why particular legislation passes at some times but not at other times.

For example, technological and economic shocks reduced the market share of small banks, the traditional beneficiaries of branching restrictions, which weakened their ability to block interstate branching reform. Their results thus suggest how to think about getting desirable regulatory reforms passed. If legislation is designed to dissipate the efforts of different private interests against each other using a divide-and-conquer strategy, these private interests are less likely to support narrow special interest legislation. This research thus suggests how economists can increase the political sophistication of their recommendations (i.e., how to skin the cat) to address the interests of different constituencies to make passage of welfare-improving legislation more likely.

1.5.7   Where Should Bank Supervision Be Done?

Countries have made different choices about which government agencies are responsible for prudential supervision. Some countries like Argentina have bank supervision housed entirely inside the central bank. Others completely separate the monetary policy function and bank supervision function and give no supervisory role to the central bank. In the United States, the Federal Reserve does have a supervisory function, but shares it with other supervisory agencies at both the state and federal levels.

In their paper, Joe Peek, Eric Rosengren, and Geoffrey Tootell focus on an economic consideration for where supervision should be done that has been largely neglected in discussions about the design of the bank supervisory structure. Peek, Rosengren, and Tootell show that there is a synergy between the supervisory and monetary policy functions because information provided by bank examinations helps increase the accuracy of macroeconomic forecasts. Forecast accuracy of macroeconomic variables is essential to the monetary policy function because successful monetary policy is necessarily forward-looking. Without accurate macroeconomic forecasts, monetary policy makers cannot know which values are the right ones to set for their policy instruments in order to achieve their goals. Peek, Rosengren, and Tootell examine recent proposals in the United States for redesign of the bank supervisory system to see which of them gives the Federal Reserve the most useful information to improve macroeconomic forecasts relevant for monetary policy. They find that supervisory information from banks regulated by the Federal Reserve does improve macroeconomic forecasts of inflation and unemployment rates, but the greatest improvement comes from supervisory information on state-chartered banks that are typically supervised by the FDIC or the OCC. Thus the authors' results might indicate that there is a potential cost to monetary policy if the central bank is excluded from participation in bank supervision, or even if the central bank is limited to supervising only the largest institutions.

In his comment, Ben Bernanke raises the issue—which the Peek, Rosengren, and Tootell paper is well aware of—that the most important consideration for where banking supervision should be done is not the improvement of monetary policy, but rather whether supervision promotes financial stability. He argues that bank supervision needs to be in the central bank in order to facilitate the central bank's role as lender of last resort. The Peek, Rosengren, and Tootell paper sparked a lively discussion by the participants in the conference about whether bank supervision should be inside the central bank, and there were many different views expressed on this issue.

An interesting issue raised by the Peek, Rosengren, and Tootell paper is whether there are other ways for information to be shared by supervisory agencies, so that even if it is not engaged in supervision the central bank still gets the supervisory information that helps it improve the accuracy of its macroeconomic forecasts. Peek, Rosengren, and Tootell suggest that hands-on experience is necessary for the central bank to get the supervisory information it needs, a view echoed by Alan Greenspan in a quote cited in the paper. However, different institutional designs of the relationship of the central bank with outside supervisory agencies may enable the central bank to get the information it needs, and this could be an interesting topic for future research.

1.5.8   Banking Supervision and the Aggregate Economy

Although the primary purpose of banking supervision is to promote financial stability, supervision can also have ancillary effects on the aggregate economy by affecting bank lending. There is a large literature suggesting that the capital crunch that occurred in the late 1980s and early 1990s—due to loan losses that ate away bank capital and increased capital requirements—led to a credit crunch in which bank lending was restricted, with a negative effect on aggregate demand that slowed down the economy (e.g., Bernanke and Lown 1991; Federal Reserve Bank of New York 1993; Berger and Udell 1994; Berger, Kashyap, and Scalise 1995; Hancock, Laing, and Wilcox 1995; Peek and Rosengren 1995). The paper by Berger, Kyle, and Scalise provides further evidence of the potential impact of prudential supervision on the aggregate economy by looking at whether supervisors changed their toughness during the 1989–92 credit crunch period and in the 1993–98 period following, and whether these changes in toughness had an impact on aggregate bank lending.

As mentioned earlier, Berger, Kyle, and Scalise do find some limited evidence that bank examiners became tougher in the 1989–92 period, but they found even stronger evidence that bank examiners eased up on banks during the 1993–98 period. They then find that these changes in supervisory toughness did affect bank lending behavior in the expected direction, with increased toughness leading to a contraction in lending and easing to expansion in lending. However, all of these measured results were rather small, suggesting that changes in supervisory toughness do not explain much of the dramatic changes in aggregate bank lending over the last decade or so. This evidence suggests that changes in supervisory toughness can have effects on the aggregate economy that might be important information for monetary policy makers who may want to adjust policy instruments because of these effects. However, as pointed out in the comment by Stephen Cecchetti, the measured effects that Berger, Kyle, and Scalise find may in part reflect changes in the general economic environment, rather than changes in supervisory toughness per se. It should also be noted that because Berger, Kyle, and Scalise do not look at all the channels through which changes in bank balance sheets affect the aggregate economy, their results do not rule out potential large cyclical effects from capital requirements on the aggregate economy.

1.6   Conclusions

This chapter has tried to show that getting prudential supervision right is extremely important to the health of the economy. The papers following in this volume have many interesting things to say about some of the key issues in prudential supervision. They will hopefully provide results that can help guide policy makers in enhancing the effectiveness of prudential supervision in the future.

References

Akerlof, George. 1970. The market for lemons: Quality uncertainty and the market mechanism. *Quarterly Journal of Economics* 84:488–500.
Ang, James S., and Terry Richardson. 1994. The underwriting experience of commercial bank affiliates prior to the Glass-Steagall Act: A re-examination of evidence for passage of the act. *Journal of Banking and Finance* 18 (2): 351–95.
Basel Committee on Banking Supervision. 1999. *A new capital adequacy framework.* Basel, Switzerland: Bank for International Settlements.
Beatty, Randolph P., Rex W. Thompson, and Michael Vetsuypens. 1998. Issuance costs and regulatory change in the investment banking industry. Southern Methodist University. Mimeograph.
Benston, George. 1990. *The separation of commercial and investment banking: The Glass-Steagall Act revisited and reconsidered.* Oxford: Oxford University Press.
Berger, Allen N., and Timothy H. Hannan. 1998. The efficiency cost of market power in the banking industry: A test of the quiet life and related hypotheses. *Review of Economics and Statistics* 80 (3): 454–65.
Berger, Allen N., Anil K. Kashyap, and Joseph M. Scalise. 1995. The transformation of the U.S. banking industry: What a long strange trip it's been. *Brookings Papers on Economic Activity,* issue no. 2:55–201.

Berger, Allen N., and Gregory F. Udell. 1994. Did risk-based capital requirements allocate bank credit and cause a "credit crunch" in the United States? *Journal of Money, Credit and Banking* 26:585–628.

———. 1995. Relationship lending and lines of credit in small firm finance. *Journal of Business* 68 (July): 351–82.

Bernanke, Ben S. 1983. Non-monetary effects of the financial crisis in the propagation of the Great Depression. *American Economic Review* 73:257–76.

Bernanke, Ben S., and Cara Lown. 1991. The credit crunch. *Brookings Papers on Economic Activity,* issue no. 2: 205–39.

Boyd, John, and Mark Gertler. 1993. U.S. commercial banking: Trends, cycles and policy. In *NBER Macroeconomics Annual 1993,* ed. Olivier Blanchard and Stanley Fischer, 318–68. Cambridge, Mass.: MIT Press.

Corsetti, Giancarlo, Paolo Pesenti, and Nouriel Roubini. 1998. What caused the Asian currency and financial crisis? Part I and II. NBER Working Papers no. 6833 and 6844. Cambridge, Mass.: National Bureau of Economic Research.

Diamond, Douglas W. 1984. Financial intermediation and delegated monitoring. *Review of Economic Studies* 51 (3): 393–414.

Edwards, Franklin, and Frederic S. Mishkin. 1995. The decline of traditional banking: Implications for financial stability and regulatory policy. *Federal Reserve Bank of New York Economic Policy Review* 1 (3): 27–45.

Federal Reserve Bank of New York. 1993. The role of the credit slowdown in the recent recession. *Federal Reserve Bank of New York Quarterly Review* 18 (1).

Flannery, Mark J. 1998. Using market information in prudential bank supervision: A review of the U.S. empirical evidence. *Journal of Money, Credit and Banking* 30 (3): 273–305.

Friedman, Milton, and Anna J. Schwartz. 1963. *A monetary history of the United States, 1867–1960.* Princeton: Princeton University Press.

Gande, Amar, Manju Puri, and Anthony Saunders. 1999. Bank entry, competition and the market for corporate securities underwriting. *Journal of Financial Economics* 54 (2): 165–95.

Gande, Amar, Manju Puri, Anthony Saunders, and Ingo Walter. 1997. Bank underwriting of debt securities: Modern evidence. *Review of Economic Studies* 10 (4): 1175–202.

Hancock, Diana, Andrew J. Laing, and James A. Wilcox. 1995. Bank capital shocks: Dynamic effects on securities, loans and capital. *Journal of Banking and Finance* 19 (3–4): 661–77.

Kane, Edward J. 1989. *The S&L insurance mess: How did it happen?* Washington, D.C.: Urban Institute Press.

Kashyap, Anil, Raghuram Rajan, and Jeremy Stein. 1999. Banks as liquidity providers: An explanation for the coexistence of lending and deposit-taking. NBER Working Paper no. 6962. Cambridge, Mass.: National Bureau of Economic Research.

Keeley, Michael C. 1990. Deposit insurance, risk and market power in banking. *American Economic Review* 80 (5): 1183–200.

Kroszner, Randall S., and Raghuram G. Rajan. 1994. Is the Glass-Steagall Act justified? A study of the U.S. experience with universal banking before 1933. *American Economic Review* 84 (4): 810–32.

———. 1997. Organizational structure and credibility: Evidence from commercial bank securities activities before the Glass-Steagall Act. *Journal of Monetary Economics* 39:475–516.

Marcus, Alan J. 1984. Deregulation and bank financial policy. *Journal of Banking and Finance* 8 (4): 557–65.

duced by researchers. The paper in several respects substantially extends the preliminary investigation reported in Barth, Caprio, and Levine (1999). We do this by enlarging our earlier sample of forty-five countries to more than sixty countries, updating existing data, materially improving the quality of the data, adding new information on the banking environment in different countries, and testing additional hypotheses. We provide documentation showing the substantial cross-country variation in regulatory restrictions on various activities of banks, in legal restrictions on the mixing of banking and commerce, and in the structure of bank ownership. Although we examine the socioeconomic determinants of regulatory choices by governments, the focus is on examining which types of regulatory practices and ownership structures are associated with well-functioning, stable banking systems.

Motivated by a long and divisive policy debate (especially in the United States)[3] over the extent to which the activities of banks should be limited, this paper examines the following questions:

1. Do countries with regulations that impose tighter restrictions on the ability of commercial banks to engage in securities, insurance, and real estate activities have (a) less efficient but (b) more stable financial systems?

2. Do countries that restrict the mixing of banking and commerce—both in terms of banks owning nonfinancial firms and nonfinancial firms owning banks—have (a) less efficient but (b) more stable banking systems?

3. Do countries in which state-owned banks play a large role have more poorly functioning financial systems?

Those who favor restricting commercial banks to traditional deposit taking and loan making argue that inherent conflicts of interest arise when banks engage in such activities as securities underwriting, insurance underwriting, real estate investment, and owning nonfinancial firms. Expanding the array of permissible activities, moreover, may provide greater opportunities for moral hazard to distort the investment decisions of banks, especially when they operate within a deposit insurance system (Boyd, Chang, and Smith 1998). Furthermore, in an unrestricted environment, the outcome may be a few large, functionally diverse, and dominant banks that could (a) complicate monitoring by bank supervisors and market participants[4] and (b) lead to a more concentrated and less competitive

3. For reviews of the literature regarding this issue, see Kwan and Laderman (1999) and Santos (1998a,b,c). Also, see Barth, Brumbaugh, and Yago (1997); Kane (1996); Kroszner and Rajan (1994); and White (1986) for discussions of some of these issues. On 12 November 1999 laws in the United States restricting banks from engaging in securities and insurance activities were repealed (see Barth, Brumbaugh, and Wilcox 2000).

4. Camdessus (1997) describes this as: "the development of new types of financial instruments, and the organization of banks into financial conglomerates, whose scope is often hard to grasp and whose operations may be impossible for outside observers—even [sic!] banking supervisors—to monitor" (537).

nonfinancial sector. Relatively few regulatory restrictions on commercial banking activities and relatively few legal impediments to the mixing of banking and commerce may therefore produce less efficient and more fragile financial systems.

Those who favor substantial freedom with respect to the activities of commercial banks argue that universal banking creates more diversified and thereby more stable banks. Fewer regulatory restrictions may also increase the franchise value of banks and thereby augment incentives for bankers to behave more prudently, with positive implications for bank stability. Furthermore, the opportunity to engage in a wide range of activities enables banks to adapt and hence provide more efficiently the changing financial services being demanded by the nonfinancial sector. Thus, fewer regulatory restrictions on the activities of commercial banks and the mixing of banking and commerce may produce more efficient and more stable financial systems.[5] The lack of appropriate cross-country data, however, has impeded the ability to examine the relationship between commercial bank regulations and both the functioning and the stability of the financial system.

This paper attempts to rectify this situation and in so doing provides the following answers to the questions posed above. First, we do not find a reliable statistical relationship between regulatory restrictions on the ability of commercial banks to engage in securities, insurance, and real estate activities and (a) the level of banking sector development, (b) securities market and nonbank financial intermediary development, or (c) the degree of industrial competition. Indeed, based on the cross-country evidence, it would be quite difficult for someone to argue confidently that restricting commercial banking activities impedes—or facilitates—financial development, securities market development, or industrial competition. We do, however, find that regulatory restrictions on the ability of banks to engage in securities activities tend to be associated with higher interest rate margins for banks.[6] Thus, even though there may be some negative implications for bank efficiency due to restricting commercial bank activities, the main message is that there is little relationship between regulatory restrictions on banking powers and overall financial development and industrial competition.

Second, in terms of stability, we find a strong and robust link to the regulatory environment. Countries with greater regulatory restrictions on the securities activities of commercial banks have a substantially higher probability of suffering a major banking crisis. More specifically, countries with a regulatory environment that inhibits the ability of banks to engage

---

5. Mishkin (1999, 686), furthermore, states that the "benefits of increased diversification open up opportunities for reform of the banking system because it makes broad-based deposit insurance less necessary and weakens the political forces supporting it."

6. This may reflect the fact that in such a situation banks are limited to the extent that they can cover costs with fee income.

Table 2.1 Country Data on Bank Regulations and State Ownership of Bank Assets

	Securities	Insurance	Real Estate	Banks Owning Nonfinancial Firms	Restrict	Nonfinancial Firms Owning Banks	State-Owned Bank Assets
Argentina	3	2	2	3	2.50	1	0.305
Australia	1	2	3	2	2.00	2	0.000
Austria	1	2	1	1	1.25	1	0.044
Barbados	3	4	3	4	3.50	2	0.195
Belgium	2	2	3	3	2.50	1	0.000
Bolivia	2	2	4	4	3.00	1	0.000
Botswana	2	4	4	4	3.50	2	0.000
Brazil	2	2	3	3	2.50	1	0.510
Canada	2	2	2	3	2.25	3	0.000
Chile	3	2	3	3	2.75	3	0.238
Colombia	2	2	2	4	2.50	3	0.19
Cyprus	2	2	4	3	2.75	3	0.034
Denmark	1	2	2	2	1.75	1	0.000
Ecuador	2	4	4		3.33		
Egypt, Arab Rep.	2	2	3	3	2.50		0.666
El Salvador	2	2	4	4	3.00	2	0.069
Fiji	2	3	4	2	2.75	3	0.085
Finland	1	3	2	1	1.75	1	0.411
France	2	2	2	2	2.00	2	0.145
The Gambia	2	4	2	4	3.00	2	0.000
Germany	1	3	2	1	1.75	1	0.429
Ghana	2	1	4	2	2.25	2	0.388
Greece	2	3	3	1	2.25	1	0.628

(continued)

Table 2.1 (continued)

	Securities	Insurance	Real Estate	Banks Owning Nonfinancial Firms	Restrict	Nonfinancial Firms Owning Banks	State-Owned Bank Assets
Guatemala	4	4	4	3	3.75	2	0.051
Guyana	1	3	3	3	1.75	3	0.233
Hong Kong	1	2	2	3	2.00	3	0.000
Iceland	2	2	4	3	2.75	1	0.644
India	2	4	4	2	3.00	2	0.800
Indonesia	2	4	4	4	3.50	1	0.415
Ireland	1	4	1	1	1.75	1	0.000
Israel	1	1	1	1	1.00	1	
Italy	1	2	3	3	2.25	3	0.250
Japan	3	4	3	3	3.25	3	0.000
Jordan	2	4	3	2	2.75	1	0.000
Republic of Korea	2	2	2	3	2.25	3	0.000
Lesotho	2	4	3	3	3.00	2	0.720
Luxembourg	1	3	1	1	1.50	3	0.000
Madagascar	2	4	3	3	3.00	2	0.220
Malaysia	2	2	3	2	2.25	2	0.096
Malta	1	3	3	3	2.50	4	0.475
Mexico	3	4	3	3	3.25	2	0.415
Netherlands	1	2	2	1	1.50	1	0.000
New Zealand	1	1	1	2	1.25	2	0.000
Nigeria	1	2	2	2	1.75		0.130

tables 2.4–2.10. First, it would be very difficult for someone to argue confidently that restricting the activities of commercial banks adversely affects financial development, securities market development, or industrial competition. At the same time, it would be very difficult for someone to argue confidently that easing restrictions on commercial banking activities facilitates greater financial development, securities market development, or industrial competition. Specifically, although countries with more restrictive regulations tend to have less well developed banking sectors and securities markets as well as lower levels of industrial competition, the correlations are frequently not statistically significant; nor do they retain their values when controlling for other factors in a regression context. Indeed, Securities, Insurance, and Real Estate do not enter any of the regressions significantly when one includes Private Credit, Bank Concentration, Industrial Competition, Total Value Traded, or Nonbank Credits. As discussed earlier, these conclusions are robust to a wide assortment of measures of banking sector development, industrial competition, and securities market development.

Second, it would be very difficult to argue that restricting the mixing of banking and commerce—either by restricting bank ownership of nonfinancial firms or by restricting nonfinancial firm ownership of banks—impedes or facilitates overall financial development or industrial competition. Banks Owning Nonfinancial Firms and Nonfinancial Firms Owning Banks do not enter *any* of the regressions significantly. These findings hold when using alternative measures of banking sector development, industrial competition, and securities market development.

Third, there is some evidence that restricting commercial banks from securities and real estate activities tends to raise net interest margins. Thus, restricting commercial banks from securities and real estate activities may have some negative implications for bank efficiency. Taken as a whole, however, the analysis of the data indicates little link between the restrictiveness of commercial bank regulations and the mixing of banking and commerce, on the one hand, and financial development (taken broadly) and industrial competition, on the other.

Fourth, in terms of state ownership, the empirical evidence suggests a negative relationship between the degree of state ownership of banks and financial development.[8] Countries with greater state ownership of banks tend to have less-developed banks and nonbanks. It should also be noted in this context that underdeveloped financial systems tend to exert a negative influence on long-run growth (see Levine, Loayza, and Beck 2000 and Levine 2001). Although considerably more research needs to be done

---

8. In this regard, Cetorelli and Gambera (2001, 23), in a study assessing the relevance of the market structure for the "finance-growth relationship," state that "it would be interesting to investigate whether it matters if banks are privately or state-owned."

Table 2.4   Relationship Between Bank Regulatory Restrictiveness and Alternative Measures of Financial Development

	Net Interest Margin	Private Credit	Bank Concentration	Industrial Competition	Total Value Traded	Nonbank Credits
			A. Correlations			
Restrict	0.365	−0.299	−0.182	−0.324	−0.249	−0.068
	(0.005)	(0.020)	(0.174)	(0.032)	(0.070)	(0.671)
			B. Regressions			
Restrict	0.007	−0.016	−0.101	−0.163	−0.022	0.067
	(0.020)	(0.832)	(0.046)	(0.422)	(0.480)	(0.188)
No. of countries	57	60	57	44	54	41
R^2	0.28	0.47	0.12	0.29	0.18	0.46

Notes: Regressions include a constant, the logarithm of real per capita GDP, and the variable Good Government, which combines measures of expropriation risk, the law and order tradition of the country, and the level of corruption. Numbers in parentheses are p-values. Restrict = the average of regulatory restrictions on the ability of banks to engage in (a) securities activities, (b) insurance activities, (c) real estate activities, and (d) the ownership of non-financial firms.

Table 2.5   Relationship Between Restriction of Securities Activities of Banks and Alternative Measures of Financial Development

	Net Interest Margin	Private Credit	Bank Concentration	Industrial Competition	Total Value Traded	Nonbank Credits
			A. Correlations			
Securities	0.369	−0.121	−0.199	−0.273	−0.152	0.155
	(0.005)	(0.359)	(0.137)	(0.073)	(0.274)	(0.332)
			B. Regressions			
Securities	0.007	0.010	−0.065	−0.131	−0.007	0.056
	(0.016)	(0.860)	(0.197)	(0.316)	(0.809)	(0.121)
No. of countries	57	60	57	44	54	41
R^2	0.30	0.47	0.09	0.29	0.17	0.47

Notes: Regressions include a constant, the logarithm of real per capita GDP, and the variable Good Government, which combines measures of expropriation risk, the law and order tradition of the country, and the level of corruption. Securities = the ability of banks to engage in the business of securities underwriting, brokering, dealing, and all aspects of the mutual fund business. Larger values imply greater restrictions on bank activities. 4 = prohibited; 3 = banks (and subsidiaries) restricted in activities; 2 = permitted in subsidiaries; 1 = permitted directly in the bank. Numbers in parentheses are *p*-values.

Table 2.6   **Relationship Between Restriction of Insurance Activities of Banks and Alternative Measures of Financial Development**

	Net Interest Margin	Private Credit	Bank Concentration	Industrial Competition	Total Value Traded	Nonbank Credits
	A. Correlations					
Insurance	-0.035	-0.194	-0.086	-0.110	-0.200	-0.031
	(0.797)	(0.138)	(0.527)	(0.477)	(0.147)	(0.845)
	B. Regressions					
Insurance	-0.003	-0.011	-0.038	-0.010	-0.023	0.026
	(0.321)	(0.843)	(0.272)	(0.926)	(0.405)	(0.382)
No. of countries	57	60	57	44	54	41
R^2	0.25	0.47	0.06	0.27	0.18	0.43

Notes: Regressions include a constant, the logarithm of real per capita GDP, and the variable Good Government, which combines measures of expropriation risk, the law and order tradition of the country, and the level of corruption. Insurance = the ability of banks to engage in the business of insurance underwriting and selling insurance products/services as principal and as agent. Larger values imply greater restrictions on bank activities. 4 = prohibited; 3 = banks (and subsidiaries) restricted in activities; 2 = permitted in subsidiaries; 1 = permitted directly in the bank. Numbers in parentheses are *p*-values.

Table 2.7   **Relationship Between Restriction of Real Estate Activities of Banks and Alternative Measures of Financial Development**

	Net Interest Margin	Private Credit	Bank Concentration	Industrial Competition	Total Value Traded	Nonbank Credits
			A. Correlations			
Real Estate	0.395	−0.346	−0.068	−0.236	−0.360	−0.218
	(0.002)	(0.007)	(0.617)	(0.123)	(0.008)	(0.171)
			B. Regressions			
Real Estate	0.006	−0.035	−0.045	−0.074	−0.042	0.022
	(0.021)	(0.445)	(0.181)	(0.631)	(0.105)	(0.480)
No. of countries	57	60	57	44	54	41
R^2	0.29	0.47	0.07	0.28	0.22	0.42

Notes: Regressions include a constant, the logarithm of real per capita GDP, and the variable Good Government, which combines measures of expropriation risk, the law and order tradition of the country, and the level of corruption. Real Estate = the ability of banks to engage in real estate investment, development, and management. Larger values imply greater restrictions on bank activities. 4 = prohibited; 3 = banks (and subsidiaries) restricted in activities; 2 = permitted in subsidiaries; 1 = permitted directly in the bank. Numbers in parentheses are *p*-values.

Table 2.8   Relationship Between Restriction of Banks Owning Nonfinancial Firms and Alternative Measures of Financial Development

	Net Interest Margin	Private Credit	Bank Concentration	Industrial Competition	Total Value Traded	Nonbank Credits
			A. Correlations			
Banks Owning Nonfinancial Firms	0.339	−0.209	−0.081	−0.316	0.001	−0.101
	(0.011)	(0.111)	(0.552)	(0.037)	(0.993)	(0.534)
			B. Regressions			
Banks Owning Nonfinancial Firms	0.004	0.021	−0.033	−0.102	0.027	0.049
	(0.066)	(0.629)	(0.266)	(0.411)	(0.270)	(0.131)
No. of countries	56	59	56	44	53	40
R^2	0.26	0.47	0.06	0.29	0.19	0.46

Notes: Regressions include a constant, the logarithm of real per capita GDP, and the variable Good Government, which combines measures of expropriation risk, the law and order tradition of the country, and the level of corruption. Banks Owning Nonfinancial Firms = the ability of banks to own and control nonfinancial firms. Larger values imply greater restrictions on bank activities. 4 = prohibited; 3 = less than 100% ownership; 2 = unrestricted, but ownership is limited based on bank's equity capital; 1 = 100% ownership permitted. Numbers in parentheses are *p*-values.

Table 2.9   Relationship Between Restriction of Nonfinancial Firms Owning Banks and Alternative Measures of Financial Development

	Net Interest Margin	Private Credit	Bank Concentration	Industrial Competition	Total Value Traded	Nonbank Credits
			A. Correlations			
Nonfinancial Firms Owning Banks	−0.056	0.065	−0.130	−0.193	0.029	0.132
	(0.690)	(0.996)	(0.354)	(0.216)	(0.842)	(0.429)
			B. Regressions			
Nonfinancial Firms Owning Banks	−0.003	0.072	−0.032	−0.123	0.011	0.043
	(0.364)	(0.165)	(0.412)	(0.272)	(0.701)	(0.139)
No. of countries	53	56	53	43	50	38
R^2	0.27	0.48	0.06	0.35	0.15	0.44

Notes: Regressions include a constant, the logarithm of real per capita GDP, and the variable Good Government, which combines measures of expropriation risk, the law and order tradition of the country, and the level of corruption. Nonfinancial Firms Owning Banks = the ability of nonfinancial firms to own banks. Larger values imply greater restrictions on bank activities. 1 = limits placed on ownership; 0 = no limits placed on ownership. Numbers in parentheses are *p*-values.

Table 2.10   Relationship Between State Ownership of Bank Assets and Alternative Measures of Financial Development

	Net Interest Margin	Private Credit	Bank Concentration	Industrial Competition	Total Value Traded	Nonbank Credits
A. Correlations						
State-Owned Bank Assets	0.216	−0.345	0.095	−0.247	−0.273	−0.380
	(0.117)	(0.009)	(0.496)	(0.115)	(0.052)	(0.017)
B. Regressions						
State-Owned Bank Assets	0.011	−0.275	0.007	−0.414	−0.129	−0.242
	(0.522)	(0.088)	(0.962)	(0.562)	(0.065)	(0.012)
No. of countries	54	57	54	42	51	39
R^2	0.24	0.48	0.05	0.28	0.18	0.49

Notes: Regressions include a constant, the logarithm of real per capita GDP, and the variable Good Government, which combines measures of expropriation risk, the law and order tradition of the country, and the level of corruption. State Ownership of Bank Assets = percentage of bank assets accounted for by state-owned banks. Numbers in parentheses are *p*-values.

before a causal interpretation can be given to these findings, it may justify some concern among policy makers in countries where state banks play a major role in credit allocation. In this sample alone it appears that about half the world's people live in countries with banking systems that are a majority state-owned (Brazil, China, Egypt, India, Pakistan, and recently Indonesia), which underscores the importance of this concern.

In sum, the lack of a close and reliable link between the regulatory environment and overall financial development and industrial competition is robust to various alterations in the conditioning information set and to redefinitions of the regulatory indicators. In the analysis, however, the regulatory variables take values ranging from 1 through 4. This particular scaling may create an interpretation problem because the difference between a 2 and a 3 may not be the same as the difference between a 3 and a 4, or a 1 and a 2. We therefore examine the sensitivity of the empirical results to this scale in three ways. First, we created a new regulatory indicator that assumed values of 1 through 3, rather than 1 through 4. This new variable equals 1 if the original indicator equals 1; the new variable equals 2 if the original indicator equals 2 or 3; and the new variable equals 3 if the original indicator equals 4. Second, we created an additional regulatory indicator for each category (Securities, Insurance, Real Estate, Banks Owning Nonfinancial Firms, and Nonfinancial Firms Owning Banks) with values of either 1 or 0. The additional regulatory indicator takes the value 1 if the original indicator was 1 or 2, and 0 otherwise. Finally, we also used separate dummy variables for each value between 1 and 4. In this case, we created four dummy variables: Securities1, Securities2, Securities3, and Securities4. Securities1 equals 1 if Securities equals 1, and 0 otherwise; Securities2 equals 1 if Securities equals 2, and 0 otherwise; and so on. We created these new variables for all the regulatory indicators. Using these alternative indicators, however, did not change this section's conclusions. The results are robust to changes in the other regressors too. Also, it is important to note that these conclusions are robust to the inclusion of regional dummy variables. Thus, the results are not simply reflecting regional differences in regulatory policies. Furthermore, we conducted the analysis using the individual components of Good Government instead of the conglomerate index. This modification also did not alter the results. Lastly, we confirmed our empirical results using indexes of bureaucratic efficiency, government red tape, and the degree to which governments repudiate contracts.

2.3 Regulatory Restrictions, Ownership, and Banking Crises

This section evaluates the relationship between banking crises and (a) regulatory restrictions on the activities of commercial banks, (b) regulatory restrictions on the mixing of banking and commerce, and (c) state ownership of banks. Allowing banks to engage in a wide range of activities may increase bank fragility by expanding the set of external risks affecting banks and by allowing banks themselves to choose among a broader assortment of risky ventures. On the other hand, allowing banks more freedom may lower bank fragility through greater diversification of the sources of profits for banks. This paper assesses which of these two opposing forces tends to dominate. In terms of state ownership of banks, we believe the links will be more opaque. State-owned banks that encounter difficulties may receive subsidies through various channels, so that the banks are never identified as being in a crisis. Nonetheless, we conduct the analysis with the information available. After describing our definition of whether a country experienced a banking crisis or not, we present probit regressions incorporating the regulatory/ownership variables and a wide array of factors to control for other potential influences on bank fragility. We find that regulatory restrictiveness is positively linked with financial fragility. We then present evidence suggesting that this result is *not* due to reverse causation.

2.3.1   Definition of a Crisis

To investigate the relationship between the regulatory/ownership environment and financial fragility, we use two measures of whether a county's banking system suffered a crisis during the last fifteen years.

Systemic is based upon Caprio and Klingebiel's (1999) determination of whether a country experienced a systemic banking crisis. The variable takes the value 1 if there was a systemic crisis, and 0 otherwise. The authors define a systemic crisis as meaning that all or most of the banking system's capital was eroded during the period of the crisis. The assessments are made for countries from the late 1970s into early 1999.

Major equals Systemic except for two adjustments. First, the Caprio and Klingebiel (1999) indicator of systemic banking crises is expanded to include countries that experienced major, though perhaps not systemic, banking crises over the 1985–97 period. This results in the addition of Canada (fifteen members of Canadian Deposit Insurance Company failed), Denmark (cumulative losses of 9 percent of loans), Hong Kong (nine out of eighteen banks failed over the period), India (nonperforming loans estimated as 16 percent of total loans), Italy (fifty-eight banks accounting for 11 percent of total loans were forcibly merged), and the United States (estimated savings and loans clean-up costs of 3.2 percent of GDP). Second, we exclude two countries (Israel and Spain) from the Caprio/Klingebiel list of systemic banking crises because their crises occurred in the late 1970s and therefore are outside our sample period. We report the results using Major but reach similar conclusions using Systemic. The values of Major and Systemic are listed in table 2A.3.

2.3.2   Empirical Results

The empirical results indicate that countries that restrict commercial banks from engaging in securities activities and countries that restrict commercial banks from owning nonfinancial firms have a higher probability of suffering a major banking crisis. Table 2.11 summarizes these findings. Besides simple correlations, we present probit regressions that control for other characteristics of the national environment. Specifically, we control for the level of economic development (Development) and the quality of the government (Good Government) in the probit regressions. As shown, countries with greater regulatory restrictions on commercial bank securities activities and the ability of banks to own and control nonfinancial firms have a higher probability of experiencing major banking sector distress.

The positive and significant relationship between financial fragility and regulatory restrictions on the securities activities of banks and restrictions on commercial bank ownership of nonfinancial firms is robust to a number of alterations in the econometric specification. First, we obtain the same results using a logit estimation procedure. Second, we obtain similar results when controlling for the degree of private property rights protection, the degree to which regulations restrict the opening and operation of businesses, a measure of bureaucratic efficiency, the rate of economic growth, inflation, the existence of a deposit insurance scheme, and the size of the financial intermediary sector (*Private credit*). Thus, we control for the standard variables used in the large and growing empirical literature that tries to explain banking crises. The coefficients on Securities and Banks Owning Nonfinancial Firms remain significantly positive in the crisis regressions (when also including Development and Good Government). Third, as noted earlier, we obtain similar results when using Systemic instead of Major as the indicator of whether a country experienced a banking crisis or not. Fourth, we obtain similar results when using the alternative measures of Securities and Bank Ownership of Nonfinancial Firms as just discussed. Specifically, we also use the regulatory measures based on (a) values from 1 through 3, (b) values of 0 or 1, and (c) values of individual dummy variables for each of the values 1 through 4. These alternative specifications do not alter the findings. Fifth, these conclusions are robust to the inclusion of regional dummy variables; the results are not driven by regional factors. Sixth, because the degree of securities market development may influence financial fragility, we also included measures of the degree of securities market development. Specifically, we used measures of (a) equity market liquidity, (b) the issuance of equity (in the primary market) as a share of GDP, and (c) the issuance of long-term bonds (in the primary market) as a share of GDP. This modification did not alter

Table 2.11   **Relationship Between Bank Crises and Bank Regulations and Policies**

	Good Government	Restrict	Securities	Insurance	Real Estate	Banks Owning Nonfinancial Firms	State-Owned Bank Assets	Nonfinancial Firms Owning Banks	Financial Structure
				A. Correlations					
Bank Crisis	−0.301	0.393	0.377	−0.006	0.298	0.418	0.217	0.188	−0.157
	(0.019)	(0.002)	(0.003)	(0.964)	(0.020)	(0.001)	(0.102)	(0.161)	(0.267)
				B. Simple Probit Regressions					
Bank Crisis	−0.056	0.689	0.584	−0.154	0.300	0.527	0.873	0.237	−0.265
	(0.372)	(0.020)	(0.015)	(0.436)	(0.123)	(0.010)	(0.296)	(0.233)	(0.643)
No. of countries	61	61	61	61	61	60	58	57	52
Probability (LR stat)	0.052	0.009	0.006	0.089	0.039	0.005	0.105	0.124	0.014

Notes: Simple probit regressions include a constant, the logarithm of real per capita GDP, and the variable Good Government, which combines measures of expropriation risk, the law and order tradition of the country, and the level of corruption. The Good Government regression includes Development only. Probability (LR statistic) is the *p*-value for the test that the coefficients on the (nonconstant) regressors equal zero. Numbers in parentheses are *p*-values.

the results, and these securities market indicators enter the crisis regressions insignificantly. Similarly, we also tried controlling for the net interest income of banks (*Net interest margin*), the degree of banking sector concentration (*Bank concentration*), and a measure of the degree to which the financial system is primarily bank-based or market-based (*Structure*).[9] These additional variables did not enter the crises regressions significantly. Moreover, including these measures did not alter this section's major conclusion: There is a positive, significant, and robust relationship between bank fragility and regulatory restrictions on securities market activities and bank ownership of nonfinancial firms.[10]

2.3.3 Endogeneity

Endogeneity is an issue that merits further consideration. Countries that experience banking crises might have responded to them by adopting regulatory restrictions on the activities of banks. If this situation actually happened, it would be inappropriate to interpret the results in table 2.11 as suggesting that regulatory restrictions increase the probability that a crisis will occur. To control for potential simultaneity bias, we have used a two-step instrumental variable estimator. Using instrumental variables did not alter the main results: Countries in which banking systems face greater regulatory restrictions on securities activities and on owning nonfinancial firms have a higher probability of suffering a major crisis (see Barth, Caprio, and Levine 1999). However, because the instrumental variables are not very good predictors of regulatory restrictions, we decided to examine the issue of endogeneity using a more laborious—albeit less statistically rigorous—procedure.

Table 2.12 presents the results of this effort. As the table indicates, for those countries in our sample experiencing a crisis, information is provided regarding the dates of the banking crises, the scope of the problems, and the estimated costs of resolution. In addition, information is provided about whether or not there was any change in regulations with respect to securities, insurance, and real estate activities as well as to the mixing of banking and commerce during or shortly after a banking crisis occurred. For some countries and for some time periods, the required regulatory information has not yet been obtained. For the majority of our countries, however, such information was available from publications of the Institute of International Bankers, materials from the OCC and the World Bank Survey.

Banking crises generally did not induce governments to enact more

---

9. For a detailed discussion and analysis of bank-based versus market-based financial systems, see Allen and Gale (2000) and Levine (2000).

10. The source of the additional variables used in this analysis is Beck, Demirgüç-Kunt, and Levine (2001).

Table 2.12   Banking Crises: Dates, Costs and Bank Regulatory Responses

| | Year of Crisis | Scope of Problem | Estimate of Total Losses/Costs | Change in Regulations for Allowable Activities: Yes or No | | | | Bank Ownership of Nonfinancial Firms | Nonfinancial Firm Ownership of Banks | Coding of Banking Crises | |
				Securities	Insurance	Real Estate				Systemic	Major
Argentina	1980–82[a]	More than 70 institutions were liquidated or subject to central bank intervention accounting for 16 percent of assets of commercial banks and 35 percent of total assets of finance companies.	55.3 percent of GDP.	n.a.	n.a.	n.a.	n.a.	n.a.	1	1
	1989–90[a]	Nonperforming assets constituted 27 percent of the aggregate portfolio and 37 percent of the portfolios of state-owned banks. Failed banks held 40 percent of financial system assets.		Yes, since 1991, allowed to act as underwriter in issuing private debt.	No	No	No	No		
	1995[a]	Suspension of eight banks and collapse of three banks. Overall through the end of 1997, 63 out of 205 banking institutions were either closed or merged.	Direct and indirect cost to public estimated at 1.6 percent of GDP.	No	No	No	No	No		

Country	Dates	Scope of crisis									
Bolivia	1986–87[a]	Five banks were liquidated. Total NPLs of banking system reached 29.8 percent in 1987; in mid-1988 reported arrears stood at 92 percent of commercial banks' net worth.		n.a.	n.a.	n.a.	n.a.	n.a.	n.a.	1	1
	1994[a]	Two banks with 11 percent of banking system assets were closed in November 1994. In 1995, four out of 15 domestic banks, which accounted for 30 percent of banking system assets experienced liquidity problems and suffered from high levels of NPLs.		No	No	No	No	No			
Brazil	1990[a]	(deposit to bond conversion)		No	No	No	No	No		1	
	1994–ongoing[a]	By end 1997, the Central Bank had intervened in, or put under the Temporary Special Administration Regime (RAET) system, 43 financial institutions. Also by end 1997 nonperforming loans of the entire banking	In 1996, negative net worth of selected state and federal funds banks estimated at 5–10 percent of GDP. Costs of individual bank recapitalization, by end 1997:	No	No	No	No	No	No	1	1

(continued)

Table 2.12 (continued)

| | Year of Crisis | Scope of Problem | Estimate of Total Losses/Costs | Change in Regulations for Allowable Activities: Yes or No | | | | | Coding of Banking Crises | |
				Securities	Insurance	Real Estate	Bank Ownership of Nonfinancial Firms	Nonfinancial Firm Ownership of Banks	Systemic	Major
		system had reached 15 percent.	Banco Economico, USD 2.9 billion; Bameridus, USD 3 billion; Banco do Brazil, USD 8 billion.							
Canada	1983–85[b]	Fifteen members of the Canadian Deposit Insurance Corporation, including two banks, failed.		No, but changed from prohibited to permitted in 1987.	No, but changed from prohibited to permitted in 1992.	No	No	No	0	1
Chile	1981–83[a]	Authorities intervened in four banks and four nonbank financial institutions (with 33 percent of outstanding loans) in 1981. In 1983, seven banks and one financiera accounting for 45 percent of total assets. By the end of 1983, 19 percent of loans were nonperforming.	1982–85: government spent 41.2 percent of GDP.	No, but changed from restricted to permitted in 1997/98.	No, but starting in 1997 banks were allowed to intermediate (sell) insurance through subsidiaries.	No, but starting in 1993 banks were allowed to invest in real estate through subsidiaries that specialized in (housing and office space) leasing.	No	No, but changed from unrestricted to permitted in 1993.		

Country	Period										
Colombia	1982–87[a]	Central Bank intervened in six banks accounting for 25 percent of banking system assets.	Costs of restructuring estimated to be around 5 percent of GDP.	No	No, but changed from permitted to prohibited in 1998.	No	No	No, but changed from permitted to prohibited in 1994.	No	1	1
Denmark	1987–92[b]	Cumulative loan losses over the period 1990–92 were 9 percent of loans; 40 of the 60 problem banks were merged.	No	No	No	No	No	No	No	0	1
Ecuador	early 1980s[a]	Implementation of exchange program (domestic for foreign debt) to bail out banking system	n.a.	n.a.	n.a.	n.a.	n.a.	n.a.	n.a.	1	1
	1996–ongoing[a]	Authorities intervened in several smaller financial institutions in late 1995 to early 1996 and in the fifth largest commercial bank in 1996. Seven financial institutions, which accounted for 25–30 percent of commercial banking assets, were closed in 1998/99. In March 1999, authorities declared a one week bank holiday.	n.a.	n.a.	n.a.	n.a.	n.a.	n.a.	n.a.		
Egypt, Arab Rep.	early 1980s[a]	Government closed several large investment companies. Four	Nine state-owned commercial banks recorded	n.a.	n.a.	n.a.	n.a.	n.a.	n.a.	1	1

(continued)

Table 2.12 (continued)

	Year of Crisis	Scope of Problem	Estimate of Total Losses/Costs	Change in Regulations for Allowable Activities: Yes or No					Coding of Banking Crises	
				Securities	Insurance	Real Estate	Bank Ownership of Nonfinancial Firms	Nonfinancial Firm Ownership of Banks	Systemic	Major
		public sector banks were given capital assistance.	NPL ratios of 37 percent on average in 1989.							
	1991–95[b]	Four public sector banks were given capital assistance.		n.a.	n.a.	n.a.	n.a.	n.a.		
El Salvador	1989[a]	Nine state-owned commercial banks recorded NPL ratios of 37 percent on average in 1989.		n.a.	n.a.	n.a.	n.a.	n.a.	1	1
Finland	1991–94[a]	Savings banking sector badly affected; Government took control of three banks that together accounted for 31 percent of total system deposits.	Recap. costs amounted to 11 percent of GDP.	No	No	No	No	No	1	1
Ghana	1982–89[a]	Seven audited banks (out of 11) insolvent; rural banking sector affected.	Restructuring costs estimated at 6 percent of GNP.	n.a.	n.a.	n.a.	n.a.	n.a.	1	
	1997–ongoing[b]	NPL levels increased sharply during 1997 from 15.5 percent of loans outstanding to 26.5 percent. Two state-owned commercial banks	One large investment bank fails. Nonperforming assets of the 27 public sector banks estimated	No	No	No	No	No		

(continued)

Country	Period	Description						
		accounting for 33.9 percent of market share in bad shape. Three banks, accounting for 3.6 percent of market share in terms of deposits failed. Seven banks or Deposit Taking Institutions were either liquidated or taken over.						
		at 19.5 percent of total loans and advances as of end of March 1995. Nonperforming assets to total assets reached 10.8 percent in 1993–94. At end 1998, NPLs estimated at 16 percent of total.						
Hong Kong	1982–83[b]	Nine Deposit Taking Companies failed.	n.a.	n.a.	n.a.	n.a.	n.a.	1
	1983–86[b]	Seven banks or Deposit Taking Institutions were either liquidated or taken over.	n.a.	n.a.	n.a.	n.a.	n.a.	1
	1998[b]	One large investment bank fails.	No	No	No	No	No	0
India	1993–ongoing[b]	Nonperforming assets of the 27 public sector banks estimated at 19.5 percent of total loans and advances as of end of March 1995. Nonperforming assets to total assets reached 10.8 percent in 1993–94. At end 1998, NPLs estimated at 16 percent of total loans.	No	No	No	No	No	1

Table 2.12 (continued)

	Year of Crisis	Scope of Problem	Estimate of Total Losses/Costs	Change in Regulations for Allowable Activities: Yes or No					Coding of Banking Crises	
				Securities	Insurance	Real Estate	Bank Ownership of Nonfinancial Firms	Nonfinancial Firm Ownership of Banks	Systemic	Major
Indonesia	1994[b]	Classified assets equal to over 14 percent of banking system assets with over 70 percent in the state banks.	Recapitalization cost for five state banks expected to amount to 1.8 percent of GDP.	Yes, a regulation prohibiting banks from underwriting securities was issued in Aug. 1995. The decree however allowed banks to act as arranger, issuer, dealer, investor or buying agent.	No	No	No	No	1	1
	1997–ongoing[a]	As of March 1999, Bank of Indonesia had closed down 61 banks and nationalized 54 banks, of a total of 240. NPLs estimates for the total banking system range from 65–75 percent of total loans.	Fiscal costs estimated to range from 50–55 percent of GDP.	No	No	No	No	No		
Italy	1990–95[b]	During 1990–94, 58 banks (accounting		No	No	No	No, but changed from	No	0	1

Country	Date											

for 11 percent of total lending) were merged with other institutions.

prohibited to restricted in 1995.

| Japan | 1990s | Banks suffering from sharp decline in stock market and real estate prices; official estimate of NPLs: 40 trillion yen (US$ 469 billion) in 1995 (10 percent of GDP); unofficial estimates put NPLs at 1 trillion or 25 percent of GDP; for some of bad loans, banks have already made provisions. At the end of 1998, total banking system NPLs estimated at yen 87.5 trillion (US$ 725 billion), about 17.9 percent of GDP. In March 1999, Hakkaido Takushodu bank closed, Long Term Credit Bank nationalised; Yatsuda Trust merged with Fuji Bank, and Mitsui Trust merged with Chuo Trust. | In 1996, rescue costs estimated at over USD 100 bn. In 1998, government of Japan announced the Obuchi Plan which provides 60 trillion yen (US$ 500 billion), about 12.3 percent of GDP, in public funds for loan losses, recapitalization of banks and depositor protection. | No | No | No | No | No | 1 | 1 |
| Republic of Korea (continued) | 1997– ongoing[a] | By March 1999, two out of 26 commercial | Fiscal costs of crisis estimated | No | No, but changed from | No | No | No | 1 | 1 |

Table 2.12 (continued)

Country	Year of Crisis	Scope of Problem	Estimate of Total Losses/Costs	Change in Regulations for Allowable Activities: Yes or No					Coding of Banking Crises	
				Securities	Insurance	Real Estate	Bank Ownership of Nonfinancial Firms	Nonfinancial Firm Ownership of Banks	Systemic	Major
		banks accounting for 11.8 percent of total banking system assets nationalized; 5 banks, accounting for 7.8 percent of total banking system assets closed. Seven banks accounting for 38 percent of banking system assets, placed under special supervision. Overall, banking system NPL expected to peak at 30–40 percent.	to reach 34 percent in 1999.		prohibited to permitted in 1995.				1	1
Madagascar	1988[a]	25 percent of banking sector loans deemed irrecoverable.		No	No	No	n.a.	n.a.	1	1
Malaysia	1985–88[b]	Insolvent institutions account for 3.4 percent of financial system deposits; marginally capitalized and perhaps insolvent institutions account for another 4.4	Reported losses equivalent to 4.7 percent of GNP.	n.a.	n.a.	n.a.	n.a.	n.a.	1	1

	Date	Net loss / Description						
	1997–ongoing[a]	percent of financial systems deposits. Finance company sector is being restructured and number of finance companies is to be reduced from 39 to 16 through mergers. Two finance companies were taken over by Central Bank including MBf Finance, the largest independent finance company. Two banks, deemed insolvent, acounting for 14.2 percent of financial system assets, to be merged with other banks. Overall, at end 1998, NPLs estimated between 25–35 percent of total banking system assets.						
		Net loss estimated at USD 14.9 bn, or 20.5 percent of GDP by 1999.	No, but changed from restricted to permitted in 1991.	No	No, but changed from restricted to permitted in 1991.	No	No, but changed from restricted to permitted in 1991.	No
Mexico	1981/82 (perhaps until reprivatized 1990/91)[a]	Government took over troubled banking system.	n.a.	n.a.	n.a.	n.a.	n.a.	1
	1995–ongoing[a]	Distressed banks accounted for	No	No	No	No	No	1
		Out of 34 commercial banks as of 1994, nine banks						1

(*continued*)

Table 2.12   (continued)

| | | | Change in Regulations for Allowable Activities: Yes or No | | | | | Coding of Banking Crises | |
	Year of Crisis	Scope of Problem	Estimate of Total Losses/Costs	Securities	Insurance	Real Estate	Bank Ownership of Nonfinancial Firms	Nonfinancial Firm Ownership of Banks	Systemic	Major
		were intervened in and 11 more banks participated in the loan/purchase recapitalization program. These nine intervened banks accounted for 18.9 percent of total financial system assets and were deemed insolvent; 1993: insolvent banks account for 20 percent of total assets and 22 percent of banking system deposits; 1995: almost half of the banks reported to be in financial distress.	3.9 percent of banking system assets.							
Nigeria	1990s[a]	1993: insolvent banks account for 20 percent of total assets and 22 percent of banking system deposits; 1995: almost half of the banks reported to be in financial distress.		No	No	No	No	No	1	1

Country	Dates									
Norway	1997[b]	Distressed banks accounted for 3.9 percent of banking system assets.	No	No	No	No	No	No	1	1
	1987–93[a]	Central Bank provided special loans to six banks, suffering from post-oil recession of 1985–86 and from problem real estate loans; state took control of three largest banks (equivalent to 85 percent of banking system assets, whose loan losses had wiped out capital), partly through a Government Bank Investment Fund (Nkr 5 billion) and the state-backed Bank Insurance Fund had to increase capital to Nkr 11 billion.	Recapitalization costs amounted to 8 percent of GDP.	No	No	No	No	No	1	1
Peru	1983–90[a]	Two large banks failed. The rest of the system suffered from high levels of nonperforming loans and financial disintermediation following the nationalization of the banking system in 1987.	No	No	No	No	No	No	1	1

(continued)

Table 2.12 (continued)

			Change in Regulations for Allowable Activities: Yes or No					Coding of Banking Crises	
	Year of Crisis	Scope of Problem	Estimate of Total Losses/Costs	Securities	Insurance	Real Estate	Bank Ownership of Nonfinancial Firms	Nonfinancial Firm Ownership of Banks	Systemic	Major
The Philippines	1981–87[a]	Two public banks accounting for 50 percent of banking system assets, six private banks accounting for 12 percent of banking system assets, 32 thrifts accounting for 53.2 percent of thrift banking assets and 128 rural banks.	At its peak, central bank assistance to financial institutions amounted to 19.1 bn pesos (3 percent of GDP).	n.a.	n.a.	n.a.	n.a.	n.a.	1	1
	1998– ongoing[a]	Since January 1998, one commercial bank, seven out of 88 thrifts and 40 out of 750 rural banks have been placed under receivership. Banking system NPLs reached 10.8 percent by August of 1998 and 12.4 percent by November 1998. Expected to reach 20 percent in 1999.	Net loss estimated at USD 4.0 bn, or 6.7 percent of GDP by 1999.	No	No	No	No	No		
Sri Lanka	1989–93[a]	State-owned banks comprising 70 percent of banking	Restructuring cost amounted to 25 bn rupees	n.a.	n.a.	n.a.	n.a.	n.a.	1	1

Sweden	1991[a]	system estimated to have nonperforming loan ratio of about 35 percent. Nordbanken and Gota Bank insolvent, accounting for 21.6 percent of total banking sytem assets. Sparbanken Foresta intervened, accounting for 24 percent of total banking system assets. Overall, five of six largest banks, accounting for over 70 percent of banking system assets experienced difficulties.	(5 percent of GDP). Cost of recapitalization amounted to 4 percent of GDP.	No	No	No	No	Yes, changed from prohibited to restricted in August 1991.	No	1	1
Tanzania	Late 1980s; 1990s[e]	1987: the main financial institutions had arrears amounting to half of their portfolio; 1995: The National Bank of Commerce which accounted for 95 percent of banking system assets, insolvent since 1990–92, possibly longer.	1987: implied losses amount to nearly 10 percent of GNP.	n.a.	n.a.	n.a.	n.a.	n.a.	n.a.	1	1
Thailand	1983–87[a]	Authorities intervened in 50 finance and security firms and 5 commercial banks or	Government cost for 50 finance companies estimated at 0.5	n.a.	n.a.	n.a.	n.a.	n.a.	n.a.	1	1

(continued)

Table 2.12 (continued)

Year of Crisis	Scope of Problem	Estimate of Total Losses/Costs	Change in Regulations for Allowable Activities: Yes or No			Bank Ownership of Nonfinancial Firms	Nonfinancial Firm Ownership of Banks	Coding of Banking Crises	
			Securities	Insurance	Real Estate			Systemic	Major
	about 25 percent of total financial system assets; 3 commercial banks judged insolvent (14.1 percent of commercial banking assets).	percent of GNP; government cost for subsidized loans amounted to about 0.2 percent of GDP annually.							
1997– ongoing[a]	Up to March 1999, Bank of Thailand intervened in 70 finance companies (out of 91) which together accounted for 12.8 percent of financial system assets of 72 percent of finance company assets. It also intervened in six banks that together had a market share of 12.3 percent. At end 1998, banking sytsem NPLs had	Net losses estimated at USD 59.7 bn, or 42.3 percent of GDP in 1999.	No	No	No	No	No		

Country	Year									
Turkey	1994[b]	reached 46 percent of total loans. Three banks failed in April 1994.	Up to June 1994, authorities spent 1.1 percent of GDP.	No	No	No	No	Yes, changed from unrestricted to permitted. As of 1993, banks may only acquire shares, including bonus shares, of a nonfinancial firm up to a maximum of 15 percent of their own fund, and the total sum of investment in these companies may not exceed 60 percent of the banks' total funds.	1	1
United States	1984–9[f]	More than 1,400 savings & loans and 1,300 banks failed.	Cost of savings & loan clean up amounted to an	No	No	No	No	No	0	1

(continued)

Table 2.12 (continued)

| Year of Crisis | Scope of Problem | Estimate of Total Losses/Costs | Change in Regulations for Allowable Activities: Yes or No | | | | | Coding of Banking Crises | |
			Securities	Insurance	Real Estate	Bank Ownership of Nonfinancial Firms	Nonfinancial Firm Ownership of Banks	Systemic	Major
		estimated USD 180 billion equivalent to 3.2 percent of GDP.							
Uruguay	1981–84[a]	Affected institutions accounted for 30 percent of financial system assets; insolvent banks accounted for 20 percent of financial system deposits.	Costs of recapitalizing banks estimated at USD 350 million (7 percent of GNP); Central Bank's quasi-fiscal losses associated with subsidized credit operations and purchase of loan portfolios amounted to 24.2 percent of GDP during 1982–85.	n.a.	n.a.	n.a.	n.a.	n.a.	1	1

Venezuela	Late 1970s[b] and 1980s	Notable bank failures: Banco Nacionale de Descuento (1978); BANDAGRO (1981); Banco de los Trabajadores de Venezuela (1982); Banco de Comercio (1985); BHCU (1985); BHCO (1985); Banco Lara (1986).	n.a.	n.a.	n.a.	n.a.	n.a.	1	1
	1994– ongoing[a]	Insolvent banks accounted for 30 percent of financial system deposits. Authorities intervened in 13 out of 47 banks which held 50 percent of deposits in 1994, and in five additional banks in 1995.	No	No	No	No	No		
Zimbabwe	1995– ongoing[a]	Two out of five commercial banks recorded high NPL ratio.	No	No	No	No	No	1	1

Sources: Authors, based on Caprio and Klingebiel (1999); *Global Survey,* Institute of International Bankers, various years; and the Office of the Comptroller of the Currency.

Note: n.a. = not available.

[a]Systemic banking crises.

[b]Nonsystemic banking crises.

restrictive regulations. Indeed, the overall indication is that there was not much change in these regulations: Of the 250 possible entries in the table, 141 showed no subsequent change at all (neither during nor immediately after the crisis), 14 showed a change in the direction of fewer restrictions (only 2 of which could be linked to a crisis), and only 3 showed greater restrictions after the crisis; in 92 cases we have no data. Thus, even in the relatively few cases in which there was a change during or after a crisis, it was in the direction of broader powers for banks, meaning that we were using fewer restrictions than actually existed. This biases the results against the conclusion that greater restrictions increase the likelihood of a crisis.

Governments generally do respond to banking crises, but the response has typically been in the direction of limiting the bank safety net or raising its cost, as in the cases of the early crises from the 1980s in Argentina and Chile, rather than attempting to restrict banks' powers. Interestingly, both countries in fact have moved in the other direction, providing added powers to banks, which is consistent with the general trend toward broader powers. More generally, any concern about the endogeneity in the crisis regressions would appear to be unwarranted.[11] Reestimating the probit regressions in table 2.11 with the data from table 2.12, moreover, does not produce any significant changes.

Thus, although the analysis does not fully resolve the endogeneity issue, the results clearly suggest that greater regulatory restrictions on the ability of commercial banks to engage in securities activities and the ability of commercial banks to own and control nonfinancial firms tend to increase the probability that a country will experience a major banking crisis.[12]

2.4   Summary and Conclusions

The purposes of this paper have been twofold. The first is to present comprehensive and detailed information on the regulatory environment and ownership structure of commercial banks in a large number of countries around the world. There is substantial variation among the more than sixty countries in our sample about what banks are allowed to do with

11. The inability to make limits on powers stick may be one reason for this trend. Bandiera and colleagues (1999) characterized financial reforms as a vector of variables pertaining to changes over long periods of time in interest rate regulation, reserve requirements, directed credit, bank ownership (moves toward privatization), liberalization of securities markets, prudential regulation, and international financial liberalization. They did not include changes in banks' powers insofar as there were so few changes. Note also that in the particular case of the United States, banks were allowed to underwrite corporate debt in 1989 and corporate equity in 1990 through subsidiaries, but subject to a revenue restriction. In 1999 there were more than forty banking organizations that had established such subsidiaries.

12. In this respect, Kwan and Laderman (1999, 24), in a review of literature pertaining to the United States, state that "On the effects of securities activities on banking organizations' safety and soundness, the bulk of empirical evidence indicated some potential for risk reduction in expanding banks' securities powers."

respect to securities, insurance, and real estate activities. A bank in one country, in other words, is not necessarily the same as a bank in another country. As a result of all the banking crises in different countries in recent years, there have been numerous calls for banking reforms. Yet, they typically fail to address the issue of exactly which regulatory environment is most appropriate for simultaneously promoting bank performance and stability. The information presented here helps one address this issue by initially recognizing the substantial cross-country variation that exists in bank regulation. This variation occurs, moreover, in countries that differ in terms of geographical location and level of economic development, among other ways. At the same time, it is found that state ownership of banks varies from a high of 80 percent to a low of 0 percent in our sample of countries.

The second purpose is to assess whether or not it matters what a bank is permitted to do with respect to securities, insurance, and real estate activities. As summarized in table 2.13, whether restrictions are placed on securities activities matters most. The tighter the restrictions placed on this activity, on average, the more inefficient banks are and the greater the likelihood of a banking crisis is. The likelihood of a banking crisis is also greater, on average, the tighter are the restrictions placed on bank ownership of nonfinancial firms. Perhaps surprisingly, not one of these restrictions produces any beneficial effects with respect to financial development, nonbank sector and stock market development, or industrial competition. Nor is it found that any of them lessen the likelihood of a banking crisis or enhance bank efficiency. At the same time, the greater the share of bank assets controlled by state-owned banks, on average, the less financial development as well as the development of the nonbank sector and the stock market will be.

It is important to emphasize that this paper is the product of an ongoing research project. Thus, as more information is collected and analyzed, the findings and conclusions reported here may be modified. This means that the paper actually represents a progress report on a timely and important public policy issue. Much more work remains. We are in the process of collecting and analyzing information on supervision. Optimal regulatory restrictions may depend importantly on the type of supervisory regime. Indeed, the choice of regulatory restrictions may be importantly influenced by the efficiency of supervision. We plan to explore these relationships in future research. The bottom line, however, is that this paper presents new cross-country data and analyses of what a bank is and whether or not it matters. For now it does indeed matter what a bank is permitted to do. The imposition of tight restrictions on some activities of banks appears not to be beneficial and, worse yet, downright harmful in some important ways.

Table 2.13   Summary of Empirical Results

	Bank Inefficiency	Financial Development	Concentration & Bank per capita	Industrial Competition	Nonbank & Stock Market	Bank Crisis
Securities restrictions	SPR					SPR
Insurance restrictions						
Real estate restrictions	SPR	SNC			SNC	SPC
Bank owning nonfinancial firms restrictions			SNC			
Nonfinancial firms owning banks restrictions	SPC					SPR
State-owned bank assets	SPC	SNC			SNR	

Notes: SPC indicates a significant positive correlation; SPR indicates significant positive relationship, controlling for GDP per capita and government quality; SNC indicates a significant negative correlation; SNR indicates a significant negative relationship, controlling for GDP per capita and government quality.

Appendix A

Bank Regulations and the Socioeconomic Environment

This appendix presents correlations between the commercial bank regulatory indicators and the degree of state ownership of banks and a variety of political, cultural, legal, and economic characteristics. These socioeconomic factors may influence bank regulations and state ownership of banks. For instance, it has been found that income diversity and ethnic diversity influence many policy decisions (see Engerman and Sokoloff 1997 and Easterly and Levine 1997). Consequently, we examine the associations between ethnic and income diversity and the commercial bank regulatory decisions of governments. Furthermore, La Porta and colleagues (1998) emphasize that common law countries tend to provide greater protection to outside investors in firms (creditors and minority shareholders). This may influence public demand for regulation. Thus, we examine the relationship between the legal environment and both regulatory regime and state ownership of banks. Also, regulatory policies reflect the outcome of political decisions. Thus, it is worth examining whether countries with good public institutions tend to select particular financial sector policies. Lastly, we include the level of economic development. Not only is it worth examining whether relatively successful countries tend to have particular regulatory/ownership patterns, but economic development may also be highly correlated with a variety of institutional and other national traits that are both associated with financial sector policies and for which we do not have direct measures. The goal here is to present some summary statistics regarding the relationship between the bank regulatory environment and the socioeconomic environment more generally. More specifically, the six indicators that we study are as follows:

1. *Development:* Real per capita GDP in 1980 (source: Penn World Tables).
2. *Good Government:* Average value of three variables: (a) risk of expropriation by the government, (b) the degree of corruption, and (c) the law-and-order tradition of the country. Each variable is based on a scale from 0 to 10, where higher values signify better government (La Porta, Lopez-de-Silanes, and Shleifer 1999).
3. *Income diversity:* Average of Gini coefficients for each country over the period 1980–95 (Deininger and Squire 1996).
4. *Ethnic diversity:* Average value of five indexes of ethnolinguistic fractionalization, with higher values denoting greater diversity. The scale extends from 0 to 1 (Easterly and Levine 1997).
5. *Common law country:* Dummy variable with a value of 1 if the coun-

try has an English, common law heritage, and 0 otherwise (La Porta, Lopez-de-Silanes, and Shleifer 1999).

6. *Legal rights of investors:* An index of the legal rights of creditors and minority shareholders (computed from La Porta, Lopez-de-Silanes, and Shleifer 1998).[13]

Table 2A.1 presents simple correlations (and *p*-values for the correlations) between the regulatory/ownership indicators and the six indicators of the national environment. A few findings worth mentioning are as follows. First, legal heritage and the legal rights of investors are not strongly associated with commercial banking regulations or state ownership of banks. Second, although ethnic diversity is not highly correlated with the regulatory/ownership environment, income diversity is strongly linked. Countries with greater income diversity tend to have more restrictions on their commercial banks with respect to (a) engaging in securities market activities and (b) owning nonfinancial firms. Third, governments in richer countries (and good governments—those with low corruption, a strong law-and-order tradition, and low risk of expropriation) tend to (a) impose fewer regulatory restrictions on their banks and (b) own a small percentage of the banking industry. The level of economic development and the quality of the government are very highly correlated (0.82).

13. We calculate this from La Porta and colleagues (1998). Specifically, for shareholder rights, we add 1 if (1) the country allows the shareholders to mail their proxy to the firm; (2) shareholders are not required to deposit their shares prior to the General Shareholders' Meeting; (3) cumulative voting or proportional representation of minorities in the board of directors is allowed; (4) an oppressed minorities mechanism is in place; (5) the minimum percentage of share capital that entitles a shareholder to call for an Extraordinary Shareholders' Meeting is less than or equal to 10 percent (the sample median); or (6) shareholders have preemptive rights that can only be waived by a shareholder's vote. Then, we add 1 for creditor rights if (7) the country imposes restrictions, such as creditors' consent, to file for reorganization; (8) secured creditors are able to gain possession of their security once the reorganization petition has been approved (no automatic stay); (9) secured creditors are ranked first in the distribution of the proceeds that result from the disposition of assets of a bankrupt firm; and (10) the debtor does not retain the administration of its property pending the resolution of the reorganization. Thus, the legal rights of investors index can potentially assume values between 0 and 10.

Table 2A.1   Correlations for Bank Regulations and Environment in which Banks Operate

	Restrict	Securities	Insurance	Real Estate	Banks Owning Nonfinancial Firms	Nonfinancial Firms Owning Banks	State-Owned Bank Assets
Development	-0.440	-0.110	-0.378	-0.450	-0.342	-0.050	-0.346
	(0.000)	(0.379)	(0.002)	(0.000)	(0.005)	(0.700)	(0.005)
Good Government	-0.374	-0.224	-0.176	-0.374	-0.380	-0.161	-0.286
	(0.003)	(0.083)	(0.174)	(0.004)	(0.003)	(0.230)	(0.030)
Income diversity	0.347	0.396	0.106	0.158	0.371	0.195	0.080
	(0.010)	(0.003)	(0.447)	(0.255)	(0.006)	(0.171)	(0.571)
Ethnic diversity	0.092	-0.006	0.067	0.134	0.048	0.139	0.042
	(0.464)	(0.959)	(0.592)	(0.285)	(0.707)	(0.283)	(0.744)
Common law country	-0.060	-0.086	0.093	-0.042	-0.078	0.233	-0.042
	(0.634)	(0.493)	(0.458)	(0.735)	(0.535)	(0.068)	(0.744)
Legal rights of investors	-0.069	-0.061	0.092	-0.035	-0.193	0.141	-0.027
	(0.653)	(0.690)	(0.547)	(0.818)	(0.208)	(0.380)	(0.866)

Note: Numbers in parentheses are *p*-values.

Table 2A.2   Data on Financial Development and the Political/Economic Environment

	Development	Good Government	Net Interest Margin	Private Credit	Bank Concentration	Industrial Competition	Total Value Traded	Nonbank Credits
Argentina	6,506	12.7	0.082	0.15	0.57	3.05	0.017	0.01
Australia	12,520	20.4	0.019	0.81	0.67	3.04	0.144	0.34
Austria	10,509	20.8	0.019	0.87	0.72	4.03	0.040	0.04
Barbados	6,379	0.0	0.033	0.40	1.00		0.003	0.08
Belgium	11,109	20.9	0.023	0.37	0.62	3.93	0.034	
Bolivia	1,989	8.0	0.035	0.20	0.46		0.000	0.02
Botswana	1,940	16.5	0.052	0.11	0.95		0.005	
Brazil	4,303	15.2	0.120	0.25	0.68	3.31	0.064	0.09
Canada	14,133	21.7	0.018	0.77	0.58	3.90	0.153	0.28
Chile	3,892	14.9	0.045	0.50	0.49	3.62	0.038	0.06
Colombia	2,946	11.2	0.064	0.27	0.46	2.17	0.007	0.13
Cyprus	5,295	15.7	0.067	0.77	0.88		0.015	0.21
Denmark	11,342	21.7	0.049	0.42	0.75	4.76	0.064	0.04
Ecuador	3,238	13.7	0.072	0.19	0.41		0.017	0.04
Egypt, Arab Rep.	1,645	11.1	0.012	0.28	0.65	4.19	0.004	0.04
El Salvador	2,014	8.3	0.039	0.24	0.86			0.00
Fiji	3,609	0.0		0.30	0.86			0.02
Finland	10,851	21.7	0.016	0.67	0.86	2.77	0.044	
France	11,756	20.5	0.035	0.91	0.41	3.72	0.084	0.09
The Gambia	1,017	15.0		0.16				
Germany	11,920	20.8	0.025	0.92	0.44	4.53	0.187	0.07
Ghana	976	10.3	0.071	0.03	0.94		0.004	
Greece	5,901	15.2	0.035	0.40	0.77	3.18	0.016	0.18
Guatemala	2,574	8.2	0.054	0.15	0.43		0.000	0.01
Guyana	1,927	7.9	0.044	0.30	1.00			0.08
Hong Kong	8,719	18.3	0.020	1.36	0.80	3.88	0.506	
Iceland	11,566	21.6		0.39		2.00	0.005	
India	882	13.0	0.030	0.27	0.42	2.87	0.048	0.03
Indonesia	1,281	10.8	0.041	0.26	0.43	3.29	0.018	

Ireland	6,823	19.5	0.016	0.63	0.79	4.07	0.144	0.36
Jordan	3,384	12.0	0.022	0.62	0.90	2.63	0.091	0.07
Republic of Korea	3,093	14.7	0.023	0.81	0.33	2.45	0.266	0.35
Lesotho	994	0.0		0.16	1.00			0.02
Luxembourg	11,893	22.0	0.007	0.24	0.38	3.00	0.016	
Madagascar	984	11.7	0.060	0.16	0.96			
Malaysia	3,799	16.5	0.025	0.80	0.54	3.88	0.427	0.21
Malta	4,483	14.0	0.023	0.60	0.97			0.11
Mexico	6,054	13.4	0.053	0.18	0.59	2.76	0.063	0.03
Netherlands	11,284	22.0	0.015	1.28	0.73	4.77	0.191	0.54
New Zealand	10,362	21.7	0.025	0.54	0.77	3.40	0.080	0.13
Nigeria	1,438	8.8	0.047	0.15	0.83		0.000	0.02
Norway	12,141	21.9	0.031	0.89	0.85	3.47	0.061	0.40
Pakistan	1,110	9.2	0.029	0.23	0.78		0.019	
Peru	2,875	9.9	0.072	0.10	0.72	2.94	0.014	0.03
The Philippines	1,879	8.6	0.042	0.29	0.47	2.67	0.053	0.07
Portugal	4,982	18.5	0.035	0.63	0.45	4.27	0.021	
Rwanda	757	0.0	0.044	0.08	1.00			0.01
Seychelles	2,906	0.0		0.10				
Singapore	7,053	19.4	0.021	0.95	0.73	4.16	0.446	0.16
South Africa	3,496	14.9	0.039	0.79	0.78	2.28	0.076	0.28
Spain	7,390	18.6	0.038	0.72	0.46	4.06	0.062	0.06
Sri Lanka	1,635	10.2	0.051	0.19	0.83		0.013	
Suriname	3,737	8.6		0.37				
Sweden	12,456	21.4	0.027	1.09	0.89	2.86	0.137	0.64
Switzerland	14,301	22.0	0.016	1.78	0.74	4.00	0.975	0.34
Tanzania	480	13.2						
Thailand	2,178	14.3	0.030	0.68	0.54	2.62	0.203	0.17
Turkey	2,874	13.2	0.094	0.14	0.45	3.14	0.062	0.01
United Kingdom	10,167	20.3	0.020	0.74	0.58	4.46	0.355	
United States	15,295	21.2	0.039	1.31	0.18	4.22	0.344	0.66
Uruguay	5,091	12.6	0.056	0.31	0.86		0.001	
Venezuela	7,401	13.5	0.078	0.39	0.52	2.28	0.014	0.18
Zimbabwe	1,206	11.1	0.044	0.22	0.82	2.40	0.010	0.09

Table 2A.3   Banking Crises Around the Globe

	Systemic	Major		Systemic	Major
Argentina	1	1	Jordan	0	0
Australia	0	0	Republic of Korea	1	1
Austria	0	0	Lesotho	0	0
Barbados	0	0	Luxembourg	0	0
Belgium	0	0	Madagascar	1	1
Bolivia	1	1	Malaysia	1	1
Botswana	0	0	Malta	0	0
Brazil	1	1	Mexico	1	1
Canada	0	1	Netherlands	0	0
Chile	1	1	New Zealand	0	0
Colombia	1	1	Nigeria	1	1
Cyprus	0	0	Norway	1	1
Denmark	0	1	Pakistan	0	0
Ecuador	1	1	Peru	1	1
Egypt, Arab Rep.	1	1	The Philippines	1	1
El Salvador	1	1	Portugal	0	0
Fiji	0	0	Rwanda	0	0
Finland	1	1	Seychelles	0	0
France	0	0	Singapore	0	0
The Gambia	0	0	South Africa	0	0
Germany	0	0	Spain	0	0
Ghana	1	1	Sri Lanka	1	1
Greece	0	0	Suriname	0	0
Guatemala	0	0	Sweden	1	1
Guyana	0	0	Switzerland	0	0
Hong Kong	0	1	Tanzania	1	1
Iceland	0	0	Thailand	1	1
India	0	1	Turkey	1	1
Indonesia	1	1	United Kingdom	0	0
Ireland	0	0	United States	0	1
Israel	0	0	Uruguay	1	1
Italy	0	1	Venezuela	1	1
Japan	1	1	Zimbabwe	1	1

References

Allen, F., and Douglas Gale. 2000. *Comparing financial systems.* Cambridge, Mass.: MIT Press.

Bandiera, O., G. Caprio, P. Honohan, and F. Schiantarelli. 2000. Does financial reform raise or reduce savings? *Review of Economics and Statistics* 82 (2): 239–63.

Barth, J. R., R. D. Brumbaugh Jr., and J. A. Wilcox. 2000. The repeal of Glass-Steagall and the advent of broad banking. *Journal of Economic Perspectives* 14 (2): 191–204.

Barth, J. R., R. D. Brumbaugh Jr., and G. Yago. 1997. Breaching the walls between banking and commerce. *Banking Strategies* 10 (July/August): 47–52.

Barth, J. R., G. Caprio Jr., and R. Levine. 1999. *Financial regulation and performance: Cross-Country Evidence.* World Bank Policy Research Working Paper no. 2037. Santa Monica, Calif.: Milken Institute.

Barth, J. R., D. E. Nolle, and T. N. Rice. 2000. Commercial banking structure, regulation, and performance: An international comparison. In *Modernizing Financial Systems,* ed. D. B. Papadimmitriou, 119–251. New York: St. Martin's Press.

Beck, T., A. Demirgüç-Kunt, and R. Levine. 2001. A new database on financial development and structure. *World Bank Economic Review,* forthcoming.

Beck, T., R. Levine, and N. Loayza. 2000. Finance and the sources of growth. *Journal of Financial Economics* 58 (1): 261–300.

Boyd, J. H., C. Chang, and B. D. Smith. 1998. Moral hazard under commercial and universal banking. *Journal of Money, Credit, and Banking* 30 (3, pt. 2): 426–68.

Camdessus, M. 1997. The challenges of a sound banking system. In *Banking soundness and monetary policy,* ed. C. Charles Enoch and J. H. Green, 535–39. Washington, D.C.: International Monetary Fund.

Caprio, G., Jr., and P. Honohan. 1999. Restoring banking stability: Beyond supervised capital requirements. *Journal of Economic Perspectives* 13 (4): 43–64.

Caprio, G., Jr., and D. Klingebiel. 1999. Episodes of systemic and borderline financial crises. Washington, D.C.: World Bank. Mimeograph.

Cetorelli, N., and M. Gambera. 2001. Banking market structure, financial dependence and growth: International evidence from industry data. *Journal of Finance,* forthcoming.

Deininger, K., and L. Squire. 1996. A new data set on measuring income inequality. *World Bank Economic Review* 10 (3): 565–92.

Demirgüç-Kunt, A., and V. Maksimovic. 1998. Law, finance, and firm growth. *Journal of Finance* 53:2107–137.

Dutz, M., and A. Hayri. 1999. Does more intense competition lead to higher growth? Washington, D.C.: World Bank. Mimeograph.

Easterly, W., and R. Levine. 1997. Africa's growth tragedy: Policies and ethnic divisions. *Quarterly Journal of Economics* 112:1203–50.

Engerman, S., and K. Sokoloff. 1997. Factor endowments, institutions, and differential paths of growth among new world economies. In *How Latin America fell behind,* ed. S. Haber, 260–304. Stanford, Calif.: Stanford University Press.

Gertler, M. 1988. Financial structure and aggregate economic activity: An overview. *Journal of Money, Credit, and Banking* 20:559–88.

Jayaratne, J., and P. E. Strahan. 1996. The finance-growth nexus: Evidence from bank branch deregulation. *Quarterly Journal of Economics* 111:639–70.

Kane, E. J. 1996. The increasing futility of restricting bank participation in insurance activities. In *Universal banking: Financial system Design Reconsidered,* ed. I. Walter and A. Saunders, 338–417. Chicago: Irwin.

King, R. G., and R. Levine. 1993a. Finance and growth: Schumpeter might be right. *Quarterly Journal of Economics* 108:717–38.

———. 1993b. Finance, entrepreneurship, and growth: Theory and evidence. *Journal of Monetary Economics* 32:513–42.

Kroszner, R. S., and R. G. Rajan. 1994. Is the Glass-Steagall Act justified? A study of the US experience with universal banking before 1933. *American Economic Review* 84:810–32.

Kwan, S. H., and E. S. Laderman. 1999. On the portfolio effects of financial convergence: A review of the literature. *Federal Reserve Bank of San Francisco Economic Review* 2:18–31.

Lamoreaux, N. 1994. *Insider lending: Banks, personal connections, and economic development in industrial New England.* New York: Cambridge University Press.

La Porta, R., F. Lopez-de-Silanes, and A. Shleifer. 2000. Government ownership of commercial banks. Cambridge, Mass.: Harvard University. Mimeograph.
La Porta, R., F. Lopez-de-Silanes, A. Shleifer, and R. W. Vishny. 1998. Law and finance. *Journal of Political Economy* 106:1113–155.
———. 1999. The quality of government. *Journal of Law, Economics, and Organization* 15:222–79.
Levine, R. 1997. Financial development and economic growth: Views and agenda. *Journal of Economic Literature* 35:688–726.
———. 2000. Bank-based or market-based financial systems: Which is better? Finance Department, University of Minnesota, Carlson School of Management. Mimeograph.
———. 2001. Napoleon, Bourses, and growth: With a focus on Latin America. In *Market augmenting government,* ed. O. Azfar and C. Cadwell. Ann Arbor: University of Michigan Press, forthcoming.
Levine, R., N. Loayza, and T. Beck. 2000. Financial intermediation and growth: Causality and causes. *Journal of Monetary Economics* 46 (August): 31–77.
Levine, R., and S. Zervos. 1998. Stock markets, banks, and economic growth. *American Economic Review* 88:537–58.
Mishkin, F. S. 1999. Financial consolidation: Dangers and opportunities. *Journal of Banking and Finance* 23:675–91.
Penn World Tables. Available at http://pwt.econ.upenn.edu.
Rajan, R. G., and L. Zingales. 1998. Financial dependence and growth. *American Economic Review* 88:559–86.
Santos, J. A. C. 1998a. Banking and commerce: How does the United States compare to other countries? *Federal Reserve Bank of Cleveland Economic Review* 34 (4): 14–26.
———. 1998b. Commercial banks in the securities business: A review. *Journal of Financial Services Research* 14 (1): 35–60.
———. 1998c. Mixing banking with commerce: A review. *Bank for International Settlements.* Mimeograph.
White, E. 1986. Before the Glass-Steagall Act: An analysis of the investment banking activities of commercial banks. *Explorations in Economic History* 23:33–55.
Wurgler, J. 2000. Financial markets and the allocation of capital. *Journal of Financial Economics* 58 (1): 187–214.

Comment   Mark Gertler

Overview

There are two parts to the paper: The first develops a data set that provides cross-country measures of the stringency of legal restrictions on the mix of banking and commerce and on bank ownership structure. The second part explores the extent to which these measures help explain (a) vari-

Mark Gertler is the Henry and Lucey Moses Professor of Economics and Director of the C. V. Starr Center for Applied Economics at New York University, and a research associate of the National Bureau of Economic Research.

ous measures of financial development and real development and (b) financial crises. The most striking finding is that more restrictive ownership structures tend to raise the likelihood of a financial crisis.

Overall, I find the paper a very useful addition to the literature. The development of the data set is a particularly important contribution. The empirical results are thought provoking. I do think, however, that there are some serious identification problems that make the findings hard to interpret. But I also believe that there may be ways to address this issue, as I discuss here.

The data are of three types:

1. Qualitative indicators of restrictions on the mix of banking and commerce and on bank ownership structure. Specifically, each indicator is a grade of 1 to 4 for a variety of regulatory categories.

2. Quantitative measures of the degree of financial sophistication and real development.

3. An indicator (unity or zero) of whether or not a country experienced a banking crisis, based on the Caprio and Klingebiel (1999) rating.

The overall empirical strategy of the paper is to consider the explanatory power of variables in category 1 for variables in categories 2 and 3. The first part of the paper considers regressions of variables in 2 on variables in 1; the second considers regressions of variables in 3 on variables in 1. Following I discuss each part in turn. Because the results on financial crises are the most striking and controversial, I spend most of the time on the second part and only briefly touch on the first.

Part I: Does Regulatory Structure Affect Financial or Real Development, or Both?

The authors' answer is generally no. There appears to be little correlation between measures of regulatory tightness and financial development. In some ways this result is disappointing because it offers no clear guidance for regulatory reform—"try it; it can't hurt" is not exactly a compelling argument for regulatory reform.

However, the lack of statistical significance could in part reflect the nature of the data in conjunction with the way the econometric model is specified. As just discussed, the independent variables that measure legal restrictions are qualitative indicators. It is accordingly difficult to measure intensity (e.g., is going from category 2 to 3 the same in percent terms as going from 3 to 4?). On the other hand, the authors impose a linear relation in the estimation between the quantitative dependent variables and the qualitative independent variables. To the extent that the restriction of linearity is not correct (as is likely to be the case in general), low statistical significance could result.

Another factor is that with the current data, the authors are unable to control for the adequacy of supervision and regulation. Having legal restrictions on the books is of little meaning if these restrictions cannot be enforced. In this regard, it would obviously be desirable to extend the data set to include a measure of the quality of regulatory enforcement.

One positive finding is that a more restrictive regulatory structure implies a higher net interest margin. This result is consistent with the argument that relaxing ownership restrictions could produce efficiency gains. Rather than reflect true efficiency gains, however, a high net interest margin could simply reflect legal deposit rate ceilings, which force down the cost of liabilities. It could be the case that countries that heavily regulate ownership structure are also more likely to restrict deposit rates. If the latter scenario is true, then the evidence does not necessarily support relaxing ownership structure. I believe, however, that there is sufficient data on deposit rate restrictions to get to the bottom of the issue.

Part II: Does Regulatory Structure Affect the Likelihood of Financial Crisis?

The authors' answer is yes, very much so. Probit regressions yield statistically and quantitatively significant effects of regulatory structure on the likelihood of a crisis for post-1980 data. The authors make a convincing case, furthermore, that the results are not due to reverse causation. That is, by and large regulations were not imposed in the wake of a crisis.

The authors' preferred explanation for the link between ownership restrictions and financial crises is that limits on the diversification of activities raised risk exposure. Although I do not necessarily disagree, note that this argument runs directly counter to the argument used to justify imposing the restrictions in the first place. The original justification for the now-defunct Glass-Steagall Act was that it would reduce risk taking by banks. Obviously, there are some theoretical issues to sort out here.

Overall, the results are impressive, but they raise a huge puzzle. In particular, variables are found to predict financial crises that bear no obvious relation to the factors emphasized in conventional descriptions of recent financial turmoil. Indeed, the entire discussion and formal analysis is orthogonal to the standard literature. The conventional theories indeed make almost no mention of ownership structure. They instead (e.g. Borio, Kennedy, and Prowse 1994) stress the following factors:

1. Financial liberalization, which leads to increased competition.

2. Increased risk taking by financial institutions due to the first factor along with failure by the regulatory authority to adjust the safety net to account for the change in competition and also along with weak supervision and enforcement of existing regulations.

3. Macro shocks; for example, asset price contractions (real estate, exchange rate, stock market, etc.) and associated recessions that have an

unduly harmful effect due to the increased risk taking by financial institutions.

Hutchinson and McDill (1999) provide formal support for the conventional theory, using a very similar methodology and, indeed, the exact same dependent variable (the Caprio and Klingebiel [1999] measure of financial crisis). In particular, they find that three factors contribute significantly to the likelihood of a crisis: (a) financial liberation; (b) explicit deposit insurance protection; and (c) macroeconomic distress, as measured by either real GDP growth or the change in real stock prices. This kind of empirical relation is exactly what the convention story suggests.

How do we reconcile the authors' findings with those of Hutchinson and McDill? The authors implicitly assume that the regulatory variables they include in their regressions are orthogonal to everything else that might affect the likelihood of a financial crisis, including the Hutchinson and McDill variables. (The orthogonality assumption is required to justify the coefficients on the regulatory variables as capturing the true effect of these variables on the likelihood of a crisis.)

There is, however, a clear geographic pattern to financial crises. In figure 2C.1, the darkly shaded countries experienced a financial crisis; the lightly shaded ones did not; and the countries not shaded do not appear in the sample. The crises are concentrated in four regions: Latin America, North America, East Asia, and Scandinavia. Europe, for the most part, and Oceania (Australia and New Zealand) escaped formal banking crises.

Furthermore, in regions dominated by crises, it is unlikely that the countries that escaped financial turmoil did so because they had fewer restrictions on ownership. Table 2C.1 lists the countries by region, along with the authors' measure of the stringency of ownership restrictions. It is clear, for example, that the countries in Latin America, East Asia, and Scandinavia that did not have crises also did not have restrictions significantly weaker than the norm for the region.

It is true, though, that the regions that largely escaped crises (Europe and Oceania) did have less restrictive systems. In other words, there is a correlation between geography and the nature of the financial system, which reconciles the authors' findings with the clear regional pattern in figure 2C.1. On the other hand, there is an identification problem because geography might be correlated with other relevant factors. For example, Europe and Oceania may simply have suffered less severe aggregate shocks than the other regions.

Evidence from Higgens and Osler (1997), however, suggests that the simple asymmetric shock hypothesis may not be correct. In particular, Europe and Australia did experience asset price contractions similar in magnitude. Thus, there is some reason to believe that the banking systems in these countries were more resilient than those in the regions experiencing

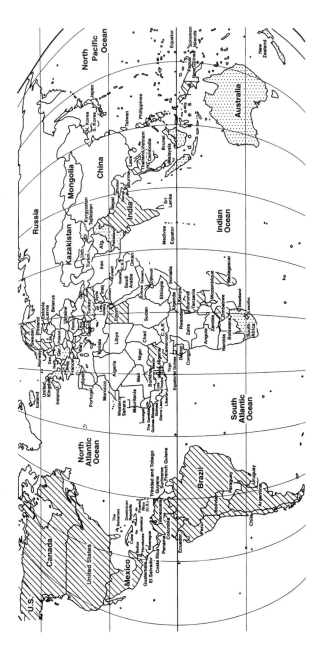

Fig. 2C.1   The regional pattern of financial crises

Table 2C.1   **Regional Crises and Ownership Restrictions**

South America	Central America	North America	Scandinavia	Europe	Australia
Argentina	Ecuador	Canada	Denmark (1.75)	Italy (2.25)	Australia[a] (2.00)
Bolivia	El Salvador	United States	Finland (1.75)	Turkey	New Zealand[a] (1.25)
Brazil	Mexico		Norway (2.00)	Belgium[a] (2.50)	Fiji[a] (2.75)
Chile	Barbados[a] (3.50)		Sweden	Cyprus[a] (2.75)	
Colombia	Guatemala (3.75)		Iceland[a] (2.75)	France[a] (2.00)	
Peru (2.00)				Germany[a] (1.25)	
Uruguay				Greece[a] (2.25)	
Venezuela				Ireland[a] (1.25)	
Guyana[a] (1.75)				Luxembourg[a] (1.50)	
Suriname[a] (1.50)				Malta[a] (2.50)	
				Netherlands[a] (1.50)	
				Portugal[a] (2.00)	
				Switzerland[a] (1.50)	
				United Kingdom[a] (1.25)	

Africa	Middle East	Asia	East Asia	Australia
Egypt	Israel[a] (1.00)	India	Hong Kong (2.00)	
Ghana (2.25)	Jordan[a] (2.75)	Sri Lanka	Indonesia	
Madagascar		Pakistan[a] (2.50)	Japan	
Tanzania (1.75)			Republic of Korea (2.25)	
Zimbabwe			Malaysia (2.25)	
The Gambia[a] (3.00)			The Philippines (2.00)	
Rwanda[a] (3.25)			Thailand (2.25)	
Seychelles[a] (2.00)			Singapore[a] (2.25)	
South Africa[a] (1.50)				

Note: Numbers in parentheses correspond to Restrict variable in table 2.1.

[a] No financial crisis.

crises. On the other hand, this alone does not prove the authors' theory, which stresses that alternative lines of business helped smooth banks' cash flow. For example, it might have been the case that banks in these regions were simply less exposed to real estate risk. Fortunately, the data exist to sort out these competing hypotheses.

In addition to sorting out these competing stories, it would be worthwhile to integrate the formal panel data analysis with other studies on financial crises (e.g., Hutchinson and McDill 1999). For example, it might be worthwhile to interact the authors' regulatory variables with other factors that appear to cause crises (e.g., liberalization and macroshocks). At a minimum, there should be regional dummies, as figure 2C.1 makes clear.

References

Borio, C. E. V., N. Kennedy, and S. D. Prowse. 1994. Exploring aggregate asset price fluctuations across countries: Measurement, determinants, and monetary policy implications. BIS Economics Papers no. 40. Bank for International Settlements, April.

Caprio, G., Jr., and D. Klingebiel. 1999. Episodes of systemic and borderline financial crises. Washington, D.C.: World Bank. Mimeograph.

Higgens, M., and C. Osler. 1997. Asset market hangover and economic growth: The OECD during 1984–93. *Oxford Review of Economic Policy* 13 (3): 110–134.

Hutchinson, M., and K. McDill. 1999. Are all banking crises alike? The Japanese experience in international comparison. NBER Working Paper no. 7253. Cambridge, Mass.: National Bureau of Economic Research.

Discussion Summary

Charles Calomiris began the general discussion by raising an empirical question about business-bank linkages. He noted that the regulatory environment is not fully captured by laws that prevent ownership of banks by firms and vice versa. He argued that in some of the crisis countries, insider lending is high because of concentration in the industrial sector that has a claim on bank lending resources. He wondered if another variable might not be appropriate—an interaction between industrial concentration and insider lending. He concluded by noting that ownership variables used in the paper do not fully capture the regulatory environment.

Raghuram Rajan began by asking about the role of changes in regulation and ownership to complement the cross-sectional evidence presented in the regressions. He asked whether the authors had examples of changes in regulation and ownership where the regulation is getting tighter. *Mark Flannery* asked about the role of foreign banks. He noted that in Singapore, for example, significant banking assets are held in foreign bank branches instead of domestic institutions. He suggested that the authors look at restraints on real estate holdings as well. He also wondered about the endogeneity of the regulatory structure.

Andrew Powell raised the issue of entrance by foreign banks. He wondered if the entrance of foreign banks could be correlated with the restrictions. *Martin Feldstein* also questioned the role of foreign banks—in particular the scope and size of their activities.

Eric Rosengren raised the question of whether one regulatory structure should fit all. He noted that restrictions might be optimal in a volatile economic environment, and that in such an environment banks might not be able to act effectively as intermediaries. He observed that in a stable environment, a different and less-restrictive environment might be better. He noted that the regulatory environment might, in fact, be endogenous to the macroeconomic environment.

Following up on comments made by the discussant *Mark Gertler,* Stephen Cecchetti emphasized the role of deposit insurance. He noted that the authors could try to exploit any information that is available on both the amount and changes of deposit insurance coverage.

Gerard Caprio began by responding to Rosengren and agreeing that one size does not fit all. He noted that if the world is changing or international agencies are pushing in that direction, this could be a mistake. In response to Rajan, Caprio observed that most countries have moved in the other direction, going from restrictive rules to looser rules. Fewer data are available for those countries, however.

James Barth also replied, noting that evidence on foreign ownership needs to distinguish wholesale from retail operations. Foreign ownership may also be correlated with government ownership. He also noted that, in part, the wealth variable captures family involvement. He also noted that along the same lines it would be helpful to look at government-directed lending.

Finally, *Ross Levine* noted that additional research on deposit insurance is currently underway (in particular, at a large World Bank research project). He observed that the inclusion of the deposit insurance variable available does not seem to affect the paper's findings. He also observed that, as expected, there is an increase in the probability of a crisis with more and explicit deposit insurance. Finally, he noted that data for foreign bank ownership and the regulation of foreign participation have also been included and that these variables do not seem to affect the ownership or securities results presented.

3

Supervising Large Complex Banking Organizations
Adapting to Change

Laurence H. Meyer

Conference themes, rhetoric, and commentary have emphasized the nature of dramatic change in the banking industry for so long that it has become one of the clichés that dominate our professional lives. The reality of change in banking—significant and dramatic change—has become, well, humdrum. It has, in fact, become so well understood and so real that Congress has finally enacted financial modernization legislation. This is not a cheap shot. The Gramm-Leach-Bliley Financial Services Modernization Act was a massive and complicated effort to make the legal structure consistent with the new reality while accommodating the myriad of new and old interests affected by the economic and legislative changes. Arguably, the legislation, to a considerable degree, validated law changes that had already occurred—or were soon to occur—in the marketplace with the aid of both loopholes and regulatory actions. Nevertheless, it is worth emphasizing that structural and other efficiency gains brought about by statutory revision are important in and of themselves.

The supervisory response to change—the real theme, I hope, of this conference—is quite another matter. That is to say, the official response of the banking agencies to the changes in banking is, I think, incomplete. To be sure, we have made some real progress with risk-focused examinations that recognize the reality that effective risk management systems are critical to the safe operation of a modern bank. Similarly, using models to determine capital for market risk on traded securities and derivative positions is another genuine step forward.

Despite these advances, however, our capital rules have been undermined by the state of the art. The one-size-fits-all risk weight for credit

Laurence H. Meyer is a member of the Board of Governors of the Federal Reserve System.

risk on commercial loans has induced creative ways to arbitrage whenever regulatory capital exceeds economic capital. At the same time, banks have taken advantage of being undercharged for capital for loans with above-average risk. The result has been that banks have placed a greater emphasis on unproductive capital arbitrage schemes and bank capital ratios that are significantly less relevant and informative than intended. Indeed, as banks become more adept at internal risk classifications, their incentives to arbitrage economic and regulatory capital can only increase, and regulatory capital will carry less and less meaning.

In addition, the growing scale and complexity of our largest banking organizations—and, I might add, not only ours but also those of many other nations—raise as never before the potential for systemic risk from a significant disruption in (let alone failure of) one of these institutions. We seem, in this regard, to face the unattractive options of exposing our economies to additional risk in order to obtain financial efficiencies and market choices or of imposing more regulation with both its attendant moral hazard and inefficiencies.

Bank supervisors have been trying to respond to this new reality—to adapt to change, as it were. The response is taking longer than we wish. But it is important to get our response as right as we can because so much is at stake.

At the Federal Reserve System, we are working through three major channels: through the evolution of the Fed's supervisory practices in cooperation with the other banking agencies; through the Basel Committee on Banking Supervision, where we meet with officials from other G10 countries; and through work in a Fed-based group called the F-6, which I chair. Much of the effort in each case is directed at what we call the large complex banking organizations (LCBOs). By talking of F-6s and LCBOs, I'm about to share with you some of the secrets of the temple. You, too, will soon be able to talk the talk of the central banker by spicing your conversation with the same catchwords.

Before I discuss the evolution in supervisory practice in the Federal Reserve and other agencies, let me briefly note the highlights of our work with the Basel supervisors' committee, for this work sets the stage for some of the issues I want to discuss with you. For those of you interested in the economics of bank supervision, the research of Dave Jones and John Mingo on capital arbitrage, Mark Carey and Bill Treacy on internal risk classifications, and Mark Flannery and Charlie Calomiris on market discipline contributed importantly to the work on improving the international accord in Basel.

As you know, the evolving consensus of the Basel supervisors is to base a new accord on the so-called three pillars of capital, supervision, and market discipline. More specifically, the capital pillar—at least for larger banks, as I will discuss momentarily—is to be designed so as to link *regu-*

latory capital more tightly to the same *economic* capital that banks use for their own internal management. Large banks already have been directed by the Fed to create internal risk classification systems for such purposes, and cutting-edge banks have made substantial progress. We fully anticipate that within the next decade or sooner, these systems will evolve into full internal risk models that could be used to measure market and credit risks throughout large banks.

Bankers do not want their institutions to fail and—with the exception of periods when failure may be close at hand—never plan to take excessive risk with inadequate capital. They will, no doubt, strive on their own to establish strong and meaningful internal risk classification systems and internal risk models. But the second pillar (supervision) is to be used in a trust-but-verify mode. That is, a major role of supervision will be to independently test and compare systems and models to best practices. This is already occurring at the Fed and the Office of the Comptroller of the Currency (OCC).

Although supervisory reviews of risk management systems will become even more important in the years ahead, they are not enough by themselves. As large banking institutions become increasingly complex—and fund themselves more from noninsured sources—market discipline and its prerequisite, public disclosure, must play a greater role. Indeed, increased transparency and market discipline can also help substantially to address concerns about increased systemic risk associated with ever-larger institutions and to avoid the potentially greater moral hazard associated with more intrusive supervision and regulation.

The edifice that these pillars are to support is not designed to cover all banks in the United States. For most, the existing system works just fine with only minor modifications and probably will continue to do so for the foreseeable future. Rather, the edifice covers the LCBOs that engage in capital arbitrage and often operate at the edge of the envelope in risk-return tradeoffs and in the creation of new instruments and strategies. Thus, the U.S. banking agencies have been strong supporters of bifurcation in the Basel deliberations—central bankese for having separate policy applications for large banks and other banks.

Indeed, the OCC has had a large bank program for some time, and the Fed has established a separate supervisory arrangement for LCBOs. The Fed has designated about thirty entities—accounting for about 60 percent of total U.S. bank assets—as LCBOs. The number and distribution of these organizations will no doubt change over time; one-third, by the way, are now foreign owned—a fact that vividly highlights the globalization of banking. Each LCBO has a designated team of Federal Reserve supervisors whose job is to understand thoroughly the organization's business strategy, management structure, key policies, and risk control systems. Each team is led by a senior examiner who is designated a central point of contact (CPC). The CPC and his or her team of examiners draw on specialists in risk management, payments, credit- and market-risk modeling, information technology, and other technical areas.

I've already mentioned the increasing emphasis of the OCC and the Fed on the largest banking organizations as well as our emphasis on examining and evaluating risk management systems. In addition, in summer 1999 the Fed established a supervisory policy requiring LCBOs to evaluate their capital relative to their internal risk evaluations. Jointly with other agencies, we have also established policies on the use of synthetic credit instruments in securitizations and will soon announce a policy on asset sales with recourse. All of these efforts are designed to limit the disproportionate reduction in regulatory capital requirements that might otherwise occur.

The Fed is also dealing with implications arising from changing market structures through senior-level ad hoc groups. During the past year, for example, the Fed formed the F-6 group to study the systemic implications of changing banking markets. The group was originally composed of three Federal Reserve governors and three Reserve Bank presidents and chaired by me. Along the way, we added a fourth president but didn't change the name. The F-numbered ad hoc groups, with the number depending on size, have existed from time to time for the last ten years or so and began when a governor decided to make a bit of sport of the various G-designated groups that meet internationally. Now you know all of our secrets!

During 1999, the current F-6 commissioned and reviewed several studies that have played a significant role in shaping our evolving supervisory policy. These studies addressed issues involving systemic risk, the potential regulatory role of subordinated debentures, the value of public disclosure, staff resource needs for supervising LCBOs, and other supervisory issues. I would like to discuss some of these topics in greater detail.

3.1   Public Disclosure

Greater public disclosure at LCBOs is an idea whose time has come. As my colleagues and I struggled with the complexities of capital reform in Basel, the systemic concerns of increasing scale and concentration, the rising weight of the C in LCBO, the burden and moral hazard of additional supervision and regulation, and the accelerated speed with which markets respond to shock, we concluded that harnessing markets to work in our behalf was a necessity, not a choice. And, as I have already noted, markets cannot operate well without transparency. Put another way, the prerequisite for market discipline is more rapid dissemination of information by the regulators and, more importantly, the direct provision to market participants of critical and timely information about risk exposures by the LCBOs themselves.

We are painfully aware of a potentially difficult downside to public disclosure: the herdlike withdrawal of funding in the event of bad news or surprise. As one of my colleagues notes, the good news is that market discipline will work, and the bad news is that market discipline will work. That risk is there but it needs to be balanced by the ex ante change in bank behavior that expanded public disclosure will induce. We should also consider that more disclosure will induce changes in funding costs when individual banks take on more risk. Such responses should increase bank safety and soundness and reduce risks and surprises.

Market discipline is not, of course, the only instrument for disciplining banks' risk-taking; it may not even be the strongest pillar among the three. But I have great expectations that it will become an effective supplement to the supervisory process. I also hope that it will, at least to some extent, substitute for additional future regulation, if not permit a reduction in regulation. However, if public disclosure does not induce meaningful market discipline, there could be significant additional regulation—and more intrusive supervision—as organizations increase in scale and complexity.

A public version of the staff F-6 paper on public disclosure will be published by the Board in a month or so. It documents the significant amount of public disclosure that already occurs at LCBOs, makes a case that current disclosure is not sufficient, and suggests examples of kinds of disclosures that might be helpful for the problem at hand. They relate to the residual risks held in securitizations, the distribution of credits by internal risk classification, and concentrations of credits by industry, geography, and borrower. As an aside, we understand that the work that the Fed has published to date on internal systems for credit risk classification and on analyses of economic capital has been actively sought out by rating agencies, investors, and analysts who have repeatedly expressed strong support for more meaningful disclosure about bank risk profiles.

Let me underline that we are still developing the LCBO public disclosure initiative, and we hope to engage senior bank executives in helping us design the program. We are fairly far along in designing what we have in mind, but it is very much a work in progress. Let me share with you our conceptual framework.

At least initially, we are limiting application of the program to the LCBOs. For the domestic LCBOs, only a little more than half of the organizations' worldwide consolidated assets are funded from deposits, and not all of their deposits are insured; 42 percent of assets are funded by nondeposit debt, and 7 percent by equity. Market discipline thus has a potential for significant impact. I noted that one-third of the LCBOs are foreign-chartered banks. Any U.S. disclosure policy would apply to only the U.S. operations of foreign-chartered banks, but to the consolidated worldwide operations of U.S.-chartered organizations.

Even though there are only about thirty LCBOs, a one-size-fits-all disclosure requirement simply would not work. The strategies, business mixes, and risk control methods and policies among banks are simply too diverse and rapidly changing. Rather than imposing a predetermined set of statistics and reporting schedules for all LCBOs, we may require some reverse engineering tailored for each bank. Each LCBO might be asked to disclose information on the frequency and at the level of detail that would be necessary for uninsured creditors and other stakeholders to evaluate that LCBO's unique risk profile.

Lest you conclude that this is some voluntary effort that LCBOs could meet in principle, but not in fact, let me make three observations. First, I hope that the Fed and the banking community can jointly develop a best-practices standard for public disclosure. Second, a best-practices standard will, it seems clear, place considerable market pressure on all LCBOs (as well as other large banks) to disclose similar kinds of information. Third, examiners will be reviewing an LCBO's disclosures to confirm that the organization's policy is consistent with best practices and to confirm that the bank's actual disclosures are consistent with its own policy.

Public disclosure is not going to be easy for bankers because it may well bring new pressures that they may not like in the short run. It is not going to be easy on creditors and other stakeholders because they will have some tough analyses to do, although it will greatly help them to do a more effective job. It is not going to be easy on examiners because they will have to make some tough judgments. But the alternatives—more supervision and regulation—are not easy either.

3.2 Subordinated Debentures

Beyond the broad public disclosure effort, Charlie Calomiris has helped focus attention on the potential for subordinated debentures as a way of increasing the degree of market discipline in banking. Charlie has a quite specific proposal in mind, but I would like to address a more generic model that is applicable to LCBOs. That broader model—built around the issuance of investment-grade unsecured long-term debt—is now almost required by the Gramm-Leach-Bliley Act and is one of the hoops through which large banks must jump if they want to operate securities subsidiaries of the bank. In December 1999, the Board published a staff study, under the direction of Myron Kwast and drawn from a paper for the F-6, that analyzes the potential for using subordinated debt as an instrument of market discipline. And the Gramm-Leach-Bliley Act requires the Treasury and the Fed to conduct a joint study evaluating the use of mandatory subordinated debentures for large banks and financial holding companies.

Let me just highlight some of the reasons policymakers might be interested in requiring LCBOs to make subordinated debentures a part of (or a supplement to) Tier 2 capital requirements. Of course, the general principle from which all else flows is that these instruments would provide a market signal of the perceived riskiness of the issuer—directly at the time of issue and indirectly in its secondary market price. These instruments are particularly relevant because the holders have interests similar to those of the Federal Deposit Insurance Corporation. Subordinated debt holders have an interest in discouraging excessive risk taking because their claims are both long-term and junior to all depositors and any senior debt holders, and they share in upside potential in very limited ways. If the train crashes, the subordinated debt holders sit not in the caboose but in the cab of the engine. They are thus quite sensitive to the speed of the train and the quality of the tracks.

Another factor supporting the regulatory use of subordinated debentures is that the market is already well established: Thirty-six of the fifty largest bank holding companies have such instruments outstanding and held by third parties today; eight of the fifty largest *banks* do as well. The market is well defined and homogenous. Rates on outstanding instruments adjust promptly to events, and the market appears to monitor the spreads across issuers closely. Issuers disclose considerable information at the time of issuance, and such disclosure refreshes secondary market prices.

There are several things we do not yet know. We do not know if the market behavior of these instruments provides information to supervisors that they do not already appreciate, if such information is provided earlier than from other sources, or if it is simply confirming. We do not yet have a good understanding of how much additional market discipline would be provided by mandatory subordinated debt relative to equity, voluntary subordinated debt, and other uninsured liabilities. The F-6 has asked the staff to study these and related matters, and that effort is under way. In addition, we have asked the staff to help us resolve some thorny analytical and practical questions. Would a *mandatory* policy provide greater advantages than current *market* practices? If there were a mandatory policy, should it apply to banks or to holding companies? Which banks or holding companies? Should it be a part of Tier 2 requirements or a supplement? What should be the required minimum? How frequently should issuance be required? What sort of issuance flexibility should be permitted, especially at times of market or individual bank stress?

Although the Fed is not committed to a specific policy as yet, my own view is that subordinated debt will be shown to be quite useful as a supplement to supervision, especially in conjunction with a broader program of additional public disclosure and greater reliance on market discipline. Perhaps we should not expect too much from these instruments, taken alone, but I think they could be a useful part of a broader program.

Let me end this discussion of subordinated debt and public disclosure by noting and underlining an obvious point. None of this will be worth the effort—indeed, will not work—unless the market believes that the authorities will refuse to rescue uninsured creditors of failed or reorganized institutions. And that expectation cannot be sustained unless the government and its agencies demonstrate it by their actual behavior.

3.3 Other Issues

With my eye on the clock, let me briefly mention a couple of other items that the F-6 has reviewed in recent months.

Decentralization is fundamental to the culture of the Federal Reserve System, and I have been impressed by how beneficial it is for obtaining intelligence about banking, financial markets, and the macro- and micro-economy. The presidents, their boards of directors, and the staffs of the Reserve Banks are invaluable for providing the Fed with an understanding of what is going on and helping ensure that the policies developed in Washington are meaningful and relevant.

Nonetheless, the lack of congruity between the geographical distribution of banks and Federal Reserve Districts creates the potential for a maldistribution of resources: Not every District can afford to maintain the expert specialists that are required to examine the LCBOs for which they are responsible, and other Districts may be allocating their experts on District assignments with a lower national priority. Therefore, to ensure reasonable resource allocations consistent with Fed priorities, and as a result of our F-6 discussions, we are in the process of recruiting a staff coordinator to facilitate the allocation of scarce staff experts at all the Reserve Banks to the highest Fed priority in LCBO exams.

Another important issue involves the cooperation and coordination among the many financial services supervisors with complementary and sometimes overlapping responsibilities within banking organizations. The wider scope of financial activities for banking organizations authorized by the Gramm-Leach-Bliley Act has made this an increasingly important concern. There are potential tensions in the interaction between the Federal Reserve as umbrella supervisor, on the one hand, and the specialized functional regulators of nonbank activities—the Security and Exchange Commission and the state insurance commissioners—on the other. Moreover, the increased complexity of banking organizations requires improved cooperation and coordination between the Federal Reserve as umbrella supervisor and the primary bank supervisors, particularly the OCC, given that most LCBOs have lead banks with national charters.

One final issue. As a matter of prudent contingency planning, the F-6 reviewed the implications of changes in markets and financial structure for central bank management of LCBO failures. The review made clear that the speed of financial market reactions to shocks has increased greatly. This faster response reflects globalization, information technology, banks' increased emphasis on short-term nondeposit funding and securitization by banking organizations, the greater participation in dealing and hedging markets by LCBOs, and the increased scale of operations of the largest organizations. At the same time, statutory and policy reforms have limited the options available for addressing difficulties at individual institutions, although I hasten to add that the tools available for macropolicy and short-term assistance to individual institutions remain unchanged.

My colleagues and I carried away from this review a greater appreciation of the need for contingency planning by bank management for significant disruptions—including the sale of units and business lines and more active participation by outside directors. In addition, the review emphasized the need for supervisors to be ready and willing to intervene aggressively and rapidly when significant difficulties occur. As a result, we are in the process of reviewing and implementing a series of technical recommendations to facilitate the resolution of a problem or failing bank by regulatory agencies.

Although such actions are needed, the analysis and discussion of these issues have greatly reinforced my view that we must rely more on market discipline in an effort to create ex ante conditions that minimize excessive risk taking and provide supervisors with rapid signals when there are difficulties.

3.4   Conclusion

As I consider how to end my remarks today, I am reminded of the story about the time Chico Marx was playing a zippy little melody on the piano in Groucho's presence. It went on and on, repeating the same silly little tune with what seemed to be neverending regularity. Chico observed, "That's funny, I can't think of how to end this." To which Groucho responded, "That's funny, that's *all* I can think about."

4

Market Discipline in the Governance of U.S. Bank Holding Companies
Monitoring versus Influencing

Robert R. Bliss and Mark J. Flannery

4.1 Introduction

That markets discipline firms and their managers is an article of faith among financial economists, with surprisingly little direct empirical support. The market discipline paradigm requires (a) that the necessary information is publicly available and that the private benefits to monitoring outweigh the costs, (b) that rational investors continually gather and process information about traded firms whose securities they hold and about the markets in which they operate, (c) that investors' assessments of firm condition and future prospects are impounded into the firm's equity and debt prices, and (d) that managers operate in the security holders' interests. The prices of a firm's traded securities are the most obvious public signal by which stakeholder/monitors make their evaluations known to management.

The idea that market prices provide informative signals that affect how managers run their companies occupies pride of place in most introductory microeconomic classes. Likewise, finance textbooks assert that investors lead firms toward appropriate decisions by changing security prices

Robert R. Bliss is an economic advisor at the Federal Reserve Bank of Chicago. Mark J. Flannery is the BankAmerica Eminent Scholar at the University of Florida.

The authors thank Lisa Ashley, Allen Berger, Mark Carey, Doug Evanoff, Jon Garfinkel, Alton Gilbert, Rick Mishkin, Raghuram Rajan, two anonymous referees, and conference participants, as well as the Indiana University Finance Symposium, the Federal Reserve Bank of Chicago, and the Atlanta Finance Workshop for information and helpful discussions. John Banko, Genny Pham-Kantor, Kasturi Rangan, Mike Rorke, and Reem Tanous provided excellent research assistance. Remaining errors are our own. The analysis and conclusions expressed here represent the authors' personal opinions, which do not necessarily coincide with those of the Federal Reserve Bank of Chicago.

in response to apparent trends and managerial policies. Only in the more advanced classes do students learn that product market externalities or deviations from the perfect capital market assumptions can undermine financial market discipline. Indeed, much of modern corporate finance concerns the ways in which markets may *fail* to discipline firms or firm managers appropriately.

Financial regulators are concerned that the increasing complexity of large banking organizations makes them difficult to monitor and control using traditional supervisory tools. Financial regulators have been increasingly drawn to the idea that private investors can affect the actions of financial firms. This interest in harnessing market disciplinary forces to assist regulatory goals reflects the growing evidence that investors can assess a financial firm's true condition quite well. The Basel Committee on Banking Supervision's (1999) consultative paper on capital adequacy asserts that "[m]arket discipline imposes strong incentives on banks to conduct their business in a safe, sound and efficient manner" and designates market discipline as one of the three pillars on which future financial regulation should be based.[1] A Federal Reserve task force has recently investigated whether requiring large banking firms to issue subordinated debt on a regular basis would enhance supervision. The 1999 Gramm-Leach-Bliley Act, which overhauled banking regulation in the United States, required that the fifty largest nationally insured banks, if nationally chartered, have at least one issue of debt outstanding rated A or better.

The concept of market discipline incorporates two distinct components: the ability of investors to evaluate a firm's true condition, and the responsiveness of firm managers to the investor feedback impounded in security prices. Although the banking literature often fails to distinguish clearly between these components, their implications for regulatory reform differ substantially. For the sake of clarity, we define two distinct aspects of market discipline in this paper: market monitoring and market influence.[2]

- *Monitoring* refers to the hypothesis that investors accurately understand changes in a firm's condition and incorporate those assessments promptly into the firm's security prices. Monitoring generates the market signals to which managers hypothetically respond.

1. The other two pillars are minimum capital standards and supervisory review of capital adequacy.

2. Just as the term market discipline is frequently used without sufficient refinement, so too do academics tend to use the term monitoring in various senses. Diamond's (1984) pathbreaking paper on delegated monitoring requires that the lender make advance arrangements to assess what actually happens to a borrower's cash flows. Other writers envision monitoring as an ongoing process by which a lender deters manager/owners from transferring wealth from the debt holders to themselves, usually through monitoring and enforcement of ex ante negotiated covenants that restrict managerial discretion. Williamson (1986) models monitoring as an ex post activity: given default, a bank pays to audit and uncover fraud.

- *Influence* is the process by which a security price change engenders firm (manager) responses to counteract adverse changes in firm condition.

The market discipline paradigm is inherently asymmetric. Negative market signals indicate that investors may want management to make changes, whereas positive signals generally do not suggest that change is desired. Regulatory discipline also focuses primarily on avoiding or reversing *adverse* changes in firm condition.

Extensive evidence supports the hypothesis that markets can effectively identify a firm's true financial condition, at least on a contemporaneous basis.[3] However, accurate market signals are not sufficient to ensure that investors can collectively influence the actions of firm management. The finance literature provides numerous reasons to be circumspect about the ability of market participants to influence managers: asymmetric information, costly monitoring, principal-agent problems, and conflicts of interest among stakeholders.[4] The optimal contracting literature is premised on the idea that investor/owners are disadvantaged vis-à-vis managers in ensuring that the firm is run in the investors' interests. Furthermore, different types of claimants may evaluate managerial actions differently. Bondholders are less interested in upside potential than in seeing that default is avoided. Stockholders, on the other hand, may prefer a riskier investment strategy as long as the expected return compensates them for the additional risk. Thus, the idea of market discipline raises the question of *which* market.[5]

We have comparatively little evidence about the ability of equity or (especially) debt owners to influence routine managerial actions. Stockholders and bondholders can surely influence managers in extremis. For example, Penn Central's management was forced to take action when money market participants refused to roll over its commercial paper. The firm was forced to file for Chapter 11, substantially affecting all concerned. Stockholders can also vote out management, and poor firm performance increases the likelihood of managerial turnover. Sufficiently disgruntled stockholders can also create an environment that facilitates a hostile takeover. However, policy proposals for using market discipline to enhance

---

3. See the recent survey by Flannery (1998) and earlier papers by Gilbert (1990) and Berger (1991).

4. Another impediment to market discipline is sometimes a legal environment that makes stockholder activism and hostile takeovers difficult. The recent failures of a number of hostile takeover attempts in France and Germany, with the active participation of governments on the side of target management, are examples.

5. Markets—other than the securities markets considered in this paper and in recent regulatory proposals—also influence managers. These include the market for corporate control (takeovers), the managerial labor market (turnover), and the direct influence exerted by large stockholders. See Shleifer and Vishny (1997) for a review of the relevant theory and evidence.

banking supervision usually envisage something more commonplace, constructive, and benign than precipitating bankruptcy or replacing management through takeovers.

This paper seeks to complement the existing literature on market monitoring by looking for direct evidence of stockholder and bondholder influence in the U.S. banking sector. Because financial regulators are actively considering the formal use of market discipline in their supervisory processes, an empirical investigation of market influence on bank holding companies (BHCs) is quite timely. Even beyond the obvious policy implications, however, BHCs provide a fruitful area for examining investor influence more generally. First, banking firms have relatively high leverage, which makes shareholders unusually sensitive to changes in asset value or risk. Second, BHC deposits have absolute priority over other financial liabilities, which should increase the urgency with which subordinated bondholders feel the results of adverse changes in asset value or risk. Third, the Federal Reserve collects extensive financial data about BHCs, and the industry is relatively homogeneous. It is thus feasible to examine detailed BHC asset, liability, and cash flow changes from one calendar quarter to the next.[6]

We begin by showing that stock and bond prices frequently move in opposite directions, which presumably gives them opposing preferences about managerial action. We then investigate whether managerial actions appear to be associated with prior returns on BHC stocks and bonds. We experiment with multiple measures of market signals, a large number of managerial "action" variables, and various lags between signal and potential action. What evidence we find of market influence is weak and, at best, mixed. Certainly, we find no prima facie support for the hypothesis that managers consistently respond to quarter-to-quarter changes in bond or stock prices.

The paper is organized as follows: Section 4.2 discusses agency problems pertaining to complex U.S. BHCs that generate the need for disciplinary forces. Section 4.3 discusses the construction of the study's data set. Section 4.4 presents evidence on the extent to which bondholders and shareholders have common—as opposed to conflicting—goals in disciplining firm managers. Section 4.5 describes and motivates our tests for market influence, and the results of those tests are presented in Section 4.6. The last section discusses the regulatory implications of our findings.

---

6. Prowse (1997) concludes that government supervisors are more likely than investors to impose extreme discipline (such as managerial turnover or forced mergers) for banking firms. To the extent that institutional arrangements have reduced investors' incentives to monitor and influence, our study will be biased toward finding no effective market influence.

4.2   Agency Problems and the Rationale for Stakeholder Influence

The governance problem in a levered firm generally involves three groups: shareholders, bondholders, and (unless the managers also own the firm) managers. Correspondingly, there are three possible types of agency conflict in the typical corporation:

1. Stockholders must induce managers to maximize firm value by working hard and making appropriate risk-return tradeoffs.
2. Bondholders have an analogous attitude toward managerial effort, but different preferences about risk bearing.
3. Stockholders may use their control rights to impose unanticipated risks on the firm's bondholders.

Numerous theoretical analyses have evaluated the first and third of these conflicts, but we have relatively little empirical information about the importance of either. Jensen and Meckling (1976) first observed that shareholders need to align managers' interests with their own. This can occur through performance-related managerial compensation (e.g., Morck, Shleifer, and Vishny 1988; Kaplan 1994a, b; Hadlock and Lummer 1997).[7] Managers' employment prospects are also related to prior firm performance (Mikkelson and Partch 1997; Martin and McConnell 1991; Denis and Denis 1995; Canella, Fraser, and Lee 1995; Brickley, Linck, and Coles 1999). Finally, firm value responds significantly to board composition (Cotter, Shivdasani, and Zenner 1997; Hirshleifer and Thakor 1998; and, for banking in particular, Brickley and James 1987) and the presence of block shareholders (DeYoung, Spong, and Sullivan 2001 for banking, and Ang, Cole, and Lin 2000 more generally).

It is difficult to demonstrate the efficacy of these control mechanisms. Although they appear to work well in most situations, sufficiently large private gains from perquisite consumption or self-dealing could still lead managers to ignore the compensation consequences of their actions.[8] Furthermore, much of the existing literature deals with "large" events such as takeovers or managerial terminations, as opposed to more mundane events that can cumulatively affect firm performance.

The existing studies concern the ability of shareholders to affect managerial actions. We have located no previous research into the ability of bondholders to influence managers. Both bondholders and stockholders may wish to monitor managerial slacking and perquisite consumption. An increase in a firm's asset value raises both share and (weakly) debt

---

7. Hubbard and Palia (1995) specifically evaluate management compensation in banking.
8. See, for example, Jensen and Murphy (1990), or Core, Holthausen, and Larcker (1999).

prices.[9] Ceteris paribus, bondholders and stockholders share an interest in the firm's continued profitability. But ceteris rarely is paribus. Bondholder and stockholder interests strongly diverge regarding the risk that may accompany higher firm profits. Greater asset risk or financial leverage, for example, may raise the value of stockholders' option-like claim on the firm's residual cash flows. Stockholders benefit from risk as long as it is associated with a sufficiently high rate of expected return, but an unanticipated increase in risk generally reduces the value of fixed-income claims. Bond covenants are designed to limit a firm's ability to shift risk by giving bondholders some control rights under some circumstances. Stockholders accept such covenants because they can increase overall firm value (Smith and Warner 1979; Myers 1977).

The incentives of managers, beyond consuming perquisites, are ambiguous. If managers' incentives are well aligned with those of shareholders (e.g., through performance-based compensation), their actions may tend to harm bondholders. If managers receive insufficient pay for performance, managerial claims on the firm resemble bonds more closely than equity, and managers may reduce equity values by acting too conservatively.

Section 4.4 provides some evidence about the relative frequency with which bond and stock investors are affected in opposite directions when new market information arrives.

4.3 Sample Selection and Data Sources

We assembled our BHC sample by forming the intersection of three data sets: the Y-9 Reports (Consolidated Financial Statements for Bank Holding Companies, available on the Federal Reserve Bank of Chicago website, http://www.chicagofed.org), the Center for Research in Security Prices (CRSP) Stock Returns and Master Files, and the Warga/Lehman Brothers Corporate Bond Database (Warga 1995). Our sample period began in 1986, prior to which the Y-9 Reports lacked sufficient detail, and continued through December 1997. We did not require that a firm exist for the entire period but used whatever data were available for each BHC. A total of 107 BHCs were simultaneously listed in all three data sources for at least part of the 1986–88 period.

The Y-9 Reports provide information on BHC balance sheets and income statements. Although specific Y-9 variable definitions changed over time, we could combine data series to construct variables with reasonably consistent definitions throughout the sample period.

Stock returns, dividends, prices, and shares outstanding were obtained

9. The impact of a debt overhang on shareholders' investment incentives is one exception to this statement. Again, this is an extreme circumstance.

from the CRSP monthly stock files. We computed quarterly returns and two measures of excess returns. The simple excess return is the difference between the stock return and the contemporaneous stock market index returns (the CRSP value-weighted index of all stocks listed on the NYSE, Amex, and Nasdaq). We also estimated the market model parameters for each firm, using a sixty-month moving window. The resulting parameters were used to compute the following month's market model excess return. The process was repeated for each month, rolling forward the estimation window and forecast period. Our results are robust to the definition of excess returns used. The excess returns provide the smallest number of usable observations because their computation requires a continuous five-year stock price history. We therefore present results only for raw returns and simple excess returns when analyzing the interaction between stocks and bonds in section 4.4, and only simple excess returns when analyzing evidence of market influence in section 4.6.

BHC bond information, taken from the Warga/Lehman Brothers Corporate Bond Database, includes price, monthly credit rating, yield, price, accrued interest, and face value outstanding applicable to the end of each calendar month. We computed quarterly holding period returns and quarter-to-quarter yield changes. The 107 BHCs had a total of 761 bonds outstanding for at least some part of the sample period. The literature provides little guidance for constructing benchmarks to measure excess bond performance. We constructed multiple indexes to ensure robustness of our reported results. Within indexes, bonds were assigned to buckets containing bonds of similar terms to maturity and ratings (using Moody and Standard & Poor's [S&P] ratings to produce two sets of indexes). Ratings were grouped into eleven categories that corresponded to Moody and S&P ratings, suppressing the + or − qualifiers attached to the basic rating definitions. Three term-to-maturity categories were used: zero to five years, five to ten years, and more than ten years. Two alternative bond populations were used to form indexes. "All Firms" indexes were constructed using all domestic industrial, utility, transportation, and financial industry bonds in the Warga database. The "All Financials" indexes were constructed using only bonds of corporations classified as financial institutions. Both the "All Firms" and "All Financials" indexes included the BHC bonds used in this study. For each rating/term classification bucket, index yields, yield changes, and returns were constructed using both equal and value weighting as measured by face value of amounts outstanding at the end of the previous quarter. The result was eight indexes—each containing thirty-three yield, yield-change, and return series—against which to measure excess bond performance.

Each BHC has a single common stock issue outstanding (we restricted our analysis to common stock—those with Committee on Uniform Security Identification Procedures [CUSIP] numbers ending in 10) but may have multiple bonds outstanding at any given time. For BHCs with multiple bonds outstanding in a given quarter, we constructed BHC-wide bond measures by aggregating the raw and excess bond performance measures across outstanding bonds within each BHC each quarter.[10] Aggregation was done using both arithmetic and principal-weighted averages of each performance measure. For each BHC-quarter we thus have two sets of raw yields, yield changes, and returns, and 16 sets of yield, yield changes, and return spreads over various indices.

There is no obviously appropriate manner for aggregating and comparing yields of bonds of differing maturities. We have evaluated a variety of index construction methods, and our results are robust across methods. Therefore, we present results only for raw bond returns and excess returns measured against the principal-weighted "All Firms" bonds index. BHCs with multiple bonds are assigned returns for a principal-weighted average of their individual bond returns and excess returns. Hereafter, in referring to bonds we will mean these measures aggregated within BHCs.

The final data set includes stock and bond returns and contemporaneous accounting information for 2,490 firm-quarters over the period June 1986 to March 1998.

4.4 Correlations between Bond and Stock Returns

As we pointed out in section 4.2, the potential divergence of stock- and bondholders' preferences affects the search for evidence of market influence. Previous studies presenting evidence on the comovements of stock and bond returns include Kwan (1996) for all industrial firms and Ellis and Flannery (1992) for bank equity and CD rates. In both studies, the evidence suggests that changes in the value of a BHC's security reflect, for the most part, the expected asset payoffs, and not the assets' return volatility. Accordingly, a firm's stock and bond returns tend to be positively correlated because both groups tend to evaluate new developments similarly. In this situation, the influence of bondholders may be difficult to separate from that of shareholders. Requiring banks to issue subordinated debentures might then be a questionable policy, because bondholders' assessments and influence would simply replicate those of shareholders. We therefore begin by evaluating whether bond and shareholder preferences are sufficiently different to permit us to identify separate bondholder and stockholder influences on bank managers.

Table 4.1 reports the Pearson correlations and rank order correlations for stock and bond returns and excess returns. Given the leptokurtic distri-

---

10. Treating each outstanding bond for a given BHC separately, matching each bond with repeated stock and BHC variables, would have given undue weight to BHCs with large numbers of bonds outstanding.

Table 4.1   **Stock and Bond Return Correlations**

	Stock Returns		Bond Returns	
	Raw	Excess	Raw	Excess
A. Pearson Correlations				
Stock returns				
Raw	1.00			
Excess	0.652	1.00		
Bond returns				
Raw	0.310	0.212	1.00	
Excess	0.238	0.179	0.815	1.00
B. Rank Correlations				
Stock returns				
Raw	1.00			
Excess	0.848	1.00		
Bond returns				
Raw	0.271	0.189	1.00	
Excess	0.157	0.129	0.449	1.00

Notes: Raw stock returns are quarterly, inclusive of dividends. Raw bond returns are quarterly, inclusive of accrued interest. Excess stock returns are the difference between the stock return and the CRSP value-weighted combined NYSE, Amex, and Nasdaq market index. Excess bond returns are the bond return relative to the rating/term-matched bucket in the value weighted all bonds S&P-based index.

bution of returns, the rank correlations provide a robust confirmation of the Pearson correlation measures. Table 4.1 indicates a strong positive correlation between raw and excess returns within each type of security. The excess stock and bond returns are much less strongly correlated with each other than are the raw returns. Nonetheless, both the Pearson and the rank-order correlations are all significantly positive (at the 5 percent level). Other stock and bond excess return measures yield results similar to those shown in table 4.1.

Table 4.2 provides information about an alternative way to summarize the interaction of BHC stock and bond values: according to the sign of their contemporaneous quarterly movements. Headings A and B classify each (raw or excess) return as either positive or negative. Whether we measure returns as raw or excess, chi-square tests reject (with p-values of 0.001) the hypothesis that stock and bond return classifications were independent.[11] Raw stock and bond returns have the same sign in a majority of the BHC-quarters we analyze. (Raw returns are like-signed 65.1 percent of the time, whereas excess stock and bond returns move together 55.0

---

11. If x is the percentage of stock-up (S^u) moves and y is the percentage of bond-up (B^u) moves, then if stock and bond movements were independent we would expect to see xy $S^u B^u$ moves, $x(1 - y)$ $S^u B^d$ moves, and so on.

Table 4.2　　　　Coincidence of Quarterly Stock and Bond Returns' Signs

| | Bond Returns | | Stock Signal Marginal Distribution |
	Down	Up	
A. Raw Returns			
Stock returns			
Down	290	662	952
	10.6%	24.2%	34.8%
Up	293	1489	1782
	10.7%	54.5%	65.2%
Bond signal marginal distribution	583	2151	2734
	21.3%	78.6%	100%
B. Excess Returns			
Stock returns			
Down	764	534	1,289
	27.9%	19.5%	47.5%
Up	694	742	1,436
	25.4%	27.1%	52.5%
Bond signal marginal distribution	1,458	1,276	2,490
	55.3%	46.7%	100%

| | Bond Returns | | | Stock Signal Marginal Distribution |
	Down	Flat	Up	
C. Raw Returns Tertiary Breakdown				
Stock returns				
Down	411	283	217	911
	15.0%	10.3%	7.9%	33.3%
Flat	333	286	293	912
	12.2%	10.5%	10.7%	33.3%
Up	167	343	401	911
	6.1%	12.5%	14.7%	33.3%
Bond signal marginal distribution	911	912	911	2734
	33.3%	33.3%	33.3%	100%
D. Excess Returns Tertiary Breakdown				
Stock returns				
Down	391	251	269	911
	14.3%	9.2%	9.8%	33.3%
Flat	276	344	292	912
	10.1%	12.6%	10.7%	33.3%
Up	244	317	350	911
	8.9%	11.6%	12.8%	33.3%
Bond signal marginal distribution	911	912	911	2,734
	33.3%	33.3%	33.3%	100%

percent of the time.) This positive correlation between stock and bond returns is consistent with the hypothesis that most security returns reflect changes in the firm's overall value, and not simply a redistribution of value between equity and debt.

We would expect market influence to be most readily apparent in the upper-left cells of headings A and B, where all investors lose money. By contrast, the impact on firm claimants derived from (advertent or inadvertent) changes in the firm's leverage or asset volatility is evidenced by stock and bond returns moving in opposite directions (upper-right and lower-left cells). In these instances, stockholder and bondholder preferences conflict, and we may be able to identify which group, if either, influences firm managers more strongly.

Headings C and D of table 4.2 elaborate this analysis with a three-part taxonomy for security returns. Each stock and bond return was assigned to one of three equally sized groups: Up, Flat, or Down. Chi-square statistics reject the hypothesis that the stock and bond returns are independent in either C or D. We expect to see the strongest evidence of market influence when the signals are large and negative—in Down-Down cells. Conversely, strong but contradictory signals (Up-Down and Down-Up) should provide the best opportunity to compare the efficacy of equity versus bond preferences. Stockholder-only influence will be reflected in particularly strong responses to cells along the top row, while bondholder-only influence should manifest itself in the left-most column. Contradictory stock and bond signals are common, with strong contradictory signals (Up-Down or Down-Up) occurring about 14 percent of the time for raw returns and 19 percent of the time for excess returns.

Figures 4.1 and 4.2 present year-by-year information about the proportion of firm-quarters falling into each of the four binary categories.[12] If the direction of market signals from stocks and bonds were perfectly correlated, the inner two bars ($S^u B^d$ and $S^d B^u$) would both be zero. This clearly is not the case: a chi-square test rejects the hypothesis that bond and stock values move independently of one another in six of the twelve sample years for the raw returns in figure 4.1 (at the 5 percent level of significance). Although the excess returns are more symmetrically distributed, chi-square tests reject the independence of stock and bond returns in eight of twelve sample years. Finally, these two figures indicate that the distribution of stock and bond return signs varies substantially across years. Accordingly, we will include a dummy variable identifying each calendar year in our regression models below.

To summarize, a typical BHC's stock and bond returns are moderately positively correlated overall. However, the data include enough contrasting

---

12. 1998 data were omitted from the figures because the Warga/Lehman Brothers database ends in March of that year.

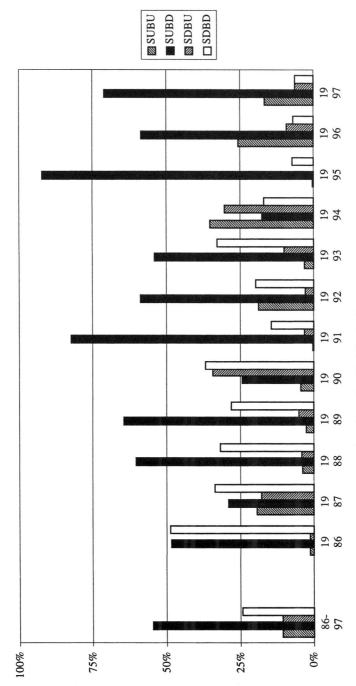

Fig. 4.1 Raw stock and bond returns, proportions in each cell of the 2×2

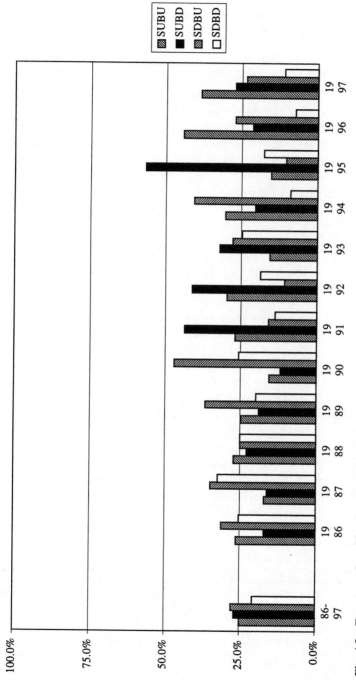

Fig. 4.2 Excess stock and bond returns, proportions in each cell of the 2×2

price signals to provide hope that we can identify separate stock market and bond market influences (if there are any), and to determine if one source of discipline dominates or reinforces the other.

4.5   Methodology for Detecting Stock and Bond Market Influences

We begin with a working definition of market influence: Market influence obtains when the return on the firm's securities induces managerial actions, which in turn increases security value.[13] In order to detect market influence we look for an effect of stock and bond returns on managerial actions. We first illustrate our methodology with a simplified version of the regressions we actually run. An extensive discussion of this simplified model in section 4.5.1 indicates which inferences can (or cannot) be drawn about market influence. Section 4.5.2 describes how we implement the model estimation.

4.5.1   Identifying Influence

Consider a firm whose value is affected by a single exogenous variable (X) and one endogenous variable (A) controlled by the manager. The firm has a single security, a stock, whose price reflects the firm's expected future value. At time $t - 1$ stockholders observe the exogenous shock, form an expectation of the action the manager will take in response, and adjust the stock price. The net effect of all these changes is the stock's quarterly return R_{t-1}. The manager's *expected* action during quarter t depends on the past stock return R_{t-1} and/or X_{t-1}: $E_{t-1}(A_t) = f_A(R_{t-1}, X_{t-1})$. We linearize this relationship and estimate $E_{t-1}(A_t) = a_0 + a_1 R_{t-1} + a_2 X_{t-1}$, which provides an expected managerial action conditional on information available at $t - 1$.[14] The manager's action is observed at the end of quarter t, and it is composed of an expected and an unexpected component: $A_t = E_{t-1}(A_t) + \varepsilon_t$. If the stockholders are rational, the unexpected component (ε_t) of the action A_t will be mean zero and uncorrelated with the information available at time $t - 1$.[15] We can therefore combine these last two equations to get

13. Our methodology for seeking what we call influence is tied to observed managerial actions. Allen Berger has pointed out that influence can also result in managers deciding *not* to take certain actions—for example, not undertaking certain risky types of investments because the bondholders would be harmed and this would subsequently drive up the firm's cost of capital. Such absence of action cannot be measured, so we cannot conclude whether this anticipatory influence exists. However, if influence is apparent in the observed managerial actions, it may provide some support for the belief that unobserved anticipatory influence also obtains.

14. The structure of our model assumes that the manager's response to shocks in one period cannot be completed in the same period. In our empirical implementation this means that managers cannot offset, in the same quarter, exogenous shocks that we observe as changes in the firm balance sheet over the same quarter.

15. Another implication of rational expectations is that returns will be serially uncorrelated, even if market influence (discipline) obtains.

(1) $$A_t = a_0 + a_1 R_{t-1} + a_2 X_{t-1} + \tilde{\varepsilon}_t,$$

which can be estimated with OLS. Investor influence appears in the form of a *nonzero* a_1.

Unfortunately, investor rationality may cause a bias in the estimated coefficient a_1. Investors' expectations about managerial actions will be impounded in R_{t-1}:

(1a) $$R_{t-1} = g[X_{t-1}, E_{t-1}(A_t)] + \tilde{\delta}_{t-1}.$$

Here, $\tilde{\delta}_{t-1}$ is a random residual. Linearizing equation (1a) and substituting it into equation (1) gives

(1b) $$A_t = a_0 + a_1[g_0 + g_1 X_{t-1} + g_2 E_{t-1}(A_t) + \tilde{\delta}_{t-1}] + a_2 X_{t-1} + \tilde{\varepsilon}_t.$$

The bracketed term in equation (1b)—the lagged stock return—contains the (unbiased) expected value of A_t, hence biasing the estimated a_1 coefficient upward (away from zero). We try to minimize the impact of this endogeneity by proxying for security returns with dummy variables in one of our implemented regressions models, as is shown in equation (3b).

The linear specification in equation (1) assumes that managers respond equally to positive and negative equity returns. This seems unlikely—why change a winning strategy? We therefore partition R_{t-1} into two variables, R_{t-1}^+ and R_{t-1}^-, defined as:

$$R_{t-1}^+ = \begin{cases} |R_{t-1}| & \text{if } R_{t-1} > 0 \\ 0 & \text{otherwise} \end{cases}$$

$$R_{t-1}^- = \begin{cases} |R_{t-1}| & \text{if } R_{t-1} \leq 0 \\ 0 & \text{otherwise} \end{cases}$$

and change equation (1) to

(1c) $$A_t = a_0 + a_1^+ R_{t-1}^+ + a_1^- R_{t-1}^- + a_2 X_{t-1} + \varepsilon_t.$$

If managers make fewer changes in response to positive stock returns than to negative returns, a_1^- should be more prominent than a_1^+. Moreover, an action taken in the wake of a negative stock return is readily interpreted as a corrective response, whereas a managerial action following a positive stock return is more difficult to interpret. The specification in equation (1c) should thus provide more power than the specification in equation (1).

At time t, the firm's value responds to the *surprise* component of A_t, plus any new exogenous shock X_t.[16] Stockholders then update their estimate of firm value, giving a (linearized) realized return over period t of

16. We assume that neither the manager nor the stockholder can predict future exogenous shocks.

$$(2) \quad R_t = b_0 + b_1[A_t - E_{t-1}(A_t)] + b_2 X_t + \tilde{\eta}_t = b_0 + b_1\hat{\varepsilon}_t + b_2 X_t + \tilde{\eta}_t,$$

where $\hat{\varepsilon}_t$ is the estimated residual from equation (1c). The sign of b_1 indicates what action shareholders desire. Suppose the action being evaluated is a cut in dividends. Under most circumstances, a dividend cut is interpreted as bad news for the firm. At the start of period t, investors know there is some probability that their dividend will be cut. If the cut actually happens, $\hat{\varepsilon}_t > 0$ and R_t falls. If the dividend cut does not happen, $\hat{\varepsilon}_t < 0$ and R_t rises. Equation (2) thus has $b_1 < 0$ if an action is *not* thought to enhance firm value. By contrast, if stockholders thought that the action under consideration was a good idea—e.g., an increase in consumer loans—a surprise realization of this policy would *increase* R_t and we should find $b_1 > 0$ in equation (2).

Market influence requires that both $\hat{a}_1$ and $\hat{b}_1$ differ significantly from zero: Lagged returns help predict managerial actions, and security values increase when those actions are actually taken. If $\hat{a}_1 = 0$, managers seem *not* to respond reliably to recent security returns. This finding would not support the hypothesis of investor influence.[17] An estimated $\hat{\alpha}_1 \neq 0$ implies that managers respond to past returns in choosing how to act, but we must still determine if the action enhances share value.

Turning now to the response regression in equation (2), our most common finding (shown later) is that $\hat{b}_1 = 0$, indicating that the action surprise does not affect investor beliefs about firm value. A possible alternative explanation for this result is that we have chosen inappropriate measures of managerial action. (Investors do not care about changes in our measured actions, or management cannot closely control the "action" variables.) However, we selected a large number of disparate action variables in hopes that at least a few would be relevant. Still a third possibility is that we have appropriate action variables, but equation (1c) poorly estimates their surprise component. (The relatively high R^2 statistics in table 4.6 suggest that this is not a serious problem for at least some of the action variables.)

Advocates of market discipline generally think of *beneficial* influence, but agency problems in the firm's governance may cause managers to behave perversely. We use a combination of the b_1 and a_1 coefficients to distinguish good from bad managerial responses. Consider first the case of $b_1 > 0$, for which a positive action surprise at time t is associated with a positive contemporaneous stock return. Beneficial influence thus requires that managers be more likely to take this action when preceding stock

17. Regression misspecification or errors in variables can also cause $\hat{a}$ to equal 0. One such problem is particularly relevant to examining market influence. Suppose investors expect that managers will always take the most appropriate action in response to an external shock, but that action varies across shocks. This is an omitted (unobservable) variables problem that mistakenly biases us against finding evidence of investor influence.

Table 4.3   **Interpretation of Influence as "Beneficial" or "Perverse"**

Influence Regression $A_t = a_0 + a_1^+ R_{t-1}^+ + a_1^- R_{t-1}^- + a_2 X_{t-1} + \varepsilon_t$

where $R_{t-1}^+ = \begin{cases} |R_{t-1}| & \text{if } R_{t-1} > 0 \\ 0 & \text{otherwise} \end{cases}$

$R_{t-1}^- = \begin{cases} |R_{t-1}| & \text{if } R_{t-1} \leq 0 \\ 0 & \text{otherwise} \end{cases}$

	$a_1^- > 0$	$a_1^- < 0$
$b_1 > 0$	beneficial	perverse
$b_1 < 0$	perverse	beneficial

returns were negative.[18] That is, we want $a_1^- > 0$; large negative returns make it more likely that managers will do the appropriate thing. Conversely, if $b_1 < 0$, shareholders want *less* of this action to follow a stock price decline. Beneficial influence would therefore have $a_1^- < 0$ for this sort of managerial action. These requirements are summarized in table 4.3.

Equations (1c) and (2) lay out the basic framework for detecting market influence. Applying this methodology to actual data requires a considerable increase in complexity, although the core ideas remain unchanged.

4.5.2   Implementation

Estimating the regression model in equations (1c) and (2) requires explicit selection of security returns, action variables under close managerial control, and a set of balance sheet variables not (completely) under managerial control that proxy for the exogenous shocks to BHC value. We have also included a set of control variables to proxy for changes in the economic environment.

It is usual to think that security returns have a systematic component that reflects exogenous shocks to the economy and an idiosyncratic component that reflects firm-specific factors including managerial actions. Because an individual firm's managers cannot be held accountable for the systematic component of returns, we measure each BHC's stock and bond returns as the *excess* return, over appropriate market return indexes.[19] We

18. Interpreting managerial responses to positive security returns is difficult to justify as an indication of investor control. Accordingly, we concentrate our subsequent discussion on the a_1^- coefficients from equation (1c), rather than the a_1^+ estimates.

19. We investigated whether our results depend on the particular return variables used. They do not. We therefore used the simple stock excess return—the return relative to the value-weighted stock market index—and the within-BHC value-weighted bond excess return measured relative to the value-weighted index using S&P credit classifications.

denote these excess returns R_t^{stk} and R_t^{bnd} respectively. Firm excess returns reflect (actual and anticipated) managerial actions, plus idiosyncratic exogenous shocks.[20] Because our interest lies with managerial influence, we will need to control for the latter.

The Influence Equation

The corporate governance literature has focused primarily on stockholder-manager interactions, but the regulatory benefits of market discipline focus on bank debt. Bondholders and regulators confront similar risk-return tradeoffs: They do not share in the upside return to risky projects but are exposed to loss if the projects fail. In order to evaluate whether investors can reliably influence managers, we must control for both stockholders' and bondholders' preferences. Moreover, we must *interact* these preferences in order to account for potentially offsetting pressures coming from the two groups. Finally, we conjecture that positive market signals may elicit less reaction from managers than do negative signals (why change a winning strategy?). Although an across-the-board *rise* in equity and bond values appears to require no managerial changes, an across-the-board *decline* might elicit the most intense pressure for change.

Our illustrative specification of the influence equation (1c) indicates that past returns may affect managers, but theory provides no indication of the appropriate lag between signal and action. How long should it take a market signal to influence managers? We wished to let the data describe the delays associated with market influence, while preserving a reasonable number of degrees of freedom for our estimates. Accordingly, we include three lags of the market signals in our regressions, and three lags of the exogenous shock variables. We also investigated single-lag models, in which the explanatory variables were lagged one, two, or three, quarters, and these produced qualitatively similar results (not reported). The specifications we employ permit shareholders and bondholders to have differential influence and for the influence to differ for between "up" and "down" return signals.

In our first implementation of equation (1c) we classify excess stock and bond returns as either positive or negative, and interact the resulting four dummy variables with the absolute value of each security's return. For each possible action variables, we estimate:

---

20. Our use of bond returns as one measure of BHC value necessarily assumes that subordinated debenture holders felt exposed to default risks. Although there is some question whether this was true for most of the 1980s, by the end of that decade BHC debenture rates clearly reflected cross-sectional variations in default probabilities (Flannery and Sorescu 1996; DeYoung et al. 2001).

$$(3a) \quad A_{it} = \alpha_0 + \sum_k \alpha_k A_{i,t-k} + \sum_k [\beta_{1k} I_{i,t-k}(S^u B^u) + \beta_{2k} I_{i,t-k}(S^u B^d)$$

$$+ \beta_{3k} I_{i,t-k}(S^u B^u) + \beta_{4k} I_{i,t-k}(S^d B^d)] \, |R_{i,t-k}^{stk}|$$

$$+ \sum_k [\beta_{5k} I_{i,t-k}(S^u B^u) + \beta_{6k} I_{i,t-k}(S^u B^d) + \beta_{7k} I_{i,t-k}(S^d B^u)$$

$$+ \beta_{8k} I_{i,t-k}(S^d B^d)] \, |R_{i,t-k}^{bnd}| + \Gamma \mathbf{X}_{t-1} + \Delta \mathbf{D}_{t-1} + \varepsilon_{it},$$

where A_{it} is one of the action variables available to BHC i's managers during quarter t; $k(\leq 3)$ is the lag length, in quarters, between market signal (return) and managerial action; $I_{i,t}(S^u B^u)$ is a dummy variable equal to one for a quarter for which BHC is stock return (S) was up and its bond return (B) was up, and the variables $I_{i,t}(S^m B^n)$ are defined analogously, where $m, n = u$ indicates that the security's value went up, and $m, n = d$ indicates that the security's value fell down; $|R_{i,t-k}^{stk}|$ is the absolute value of the ith BHC's stock return over period $t - k$; $|R_{i,t-k}^{bnd}|$ is the absolute value of the ith BHC's bond return over period $t - k$; $\mathbf{X}_{t-1}$ is a vector of exogenous shock variables; and $\mathbf{D}_{t-1}$ is a vector of dummy (control) variables indicating the years.

The specification in equation (3a) captures the interaction of the BHC's stock and bond returns, as well as the magnitude of each return. The coefficients on lagged values of $I_{i,t}(S^d B^d)|R_{i,t-k}^{stk}|$ (for example) measure the impact of a negative stock return accompanied by a decline in bond value. (As noted in section 4.4, this combination of stock-bond movements is consistent with a decrease in the firm's asset value.) The coefficients on $I_{i,t}(S^d B^d)|R_{i,t-k}^{bnd}|$ indicate the effect of a negative *bond* return under the same circumstances. Finding that the R^{stk}-related coefficient is significant and of the appropriate sign while the R^{bnd}-related coefficient is not significant would suggest that managers are more responsive to the welfare of shareholders than to that of bondholders. Of the eight potential combinations of absolute excess returns with direction of movement indicators, only some make good economic sense. Suppose the coefficients on $I_{i,t}(S^d B^d)$ $|R_{t-k}^{bnd}|$ and $I_{i,t}(S^d B^u)|R_{i,t-k}^{bnd}|$ are both significant and signed to suggest influence. This combination of directional dummies suggests that a decrease in stock price is influential, regardless of the direction of bond price movement. However, it is difficult to understand why the influence of a stock decline should be proportional to the magnitude of the *bond* excess return!

The specification in equation (3a) requires that managerial actions be proportional to preceding realized returns. However, we noted above that a security return reflects in part the anticipated managerial response, and this endogeneity may bias the estimated a_1 in equation (1c). Moreover, the absolute returns specification in equation (3a) requires that the scale or probability of managerial action be proportional to the return. To assess whether our results depend on this implied restriction, we repeated the analysis using a three-way classification scheme for returns (as shown in table 4.2, headings A and B).

$$(3b) \quad A_{it} = \alpha_0 + \sum_k \alpha_k A_{i,t-k} + \sum_k [\beta_{1k} J_{i,t-k}(S^u B^u) + \beta_{2k} J_{i,t-k}(S^u B^f)$$

$$+ \beta_{3k} J_{i,t-k}(S^u B^d) + \beta_{4k} J_{i,t-k}(S^f B^u) + \beta_{5k} J_{i,t-k}(S^f B^d)$$

$$+ \beta_{6k} J_{i,t-k}(S^d B^u) + \beta_{7k} J_{i,t-k}(S^d B^f) + \beta_{8k} J_{i,t-k}(S^d B^d)]$$

$$+ \Gamma \mathbf{X}_{t-1} + \Delta \mathbf{D}_{t-1} + \varepsilon_{it},$$

where A_{it} and X_t are defined as in equation (3a) and the dummy variables $J_{i,t}(S^a B^b)$ take the value 1 if the excess stock return (S) is a and the excess bond return (B) is b. The superscripts a and b can take on one of three values: u = an up return, ranking in the upper third of excess returns on like securities in the sample; f = a flat return, ranking in the middle third of excess returns on like securities; and d = a down return, in the lowest third of excess returns for like securities. The regression in equation (3b) permits managers to respond to eight types of market signal, corresponding to the outside cells of headings C and D of table 4.2. These measures of stock and bond returns permit us to incorporate some information about return magnitudes while minimizing the potential bias caused by the reflection of anticipated managerial actions in R_{t-1}. Note that we retain a constant term in equation (3b) while omitting the least interesting case $(S^f B^f)$ from the specification.

The Response Equation

The response equation (2) is estimated separately for stock and bond excess returns. Instead of a single action surprise driving the excess return, we now specify that period t security returns depend on a complete set of n action surprises:

$$(4a) \quad R_t^{stk} = b_0 + \gamma R_{t-1}^{stk} + b_1[A_{1,t} - E_{t-1}(A_{1,t})] + \dots$$

$$+ b_n[A_{n,t} - E_{t-1}(A_{n,t})]\Phi X_t + \Lambda D_t + \eta_t,$$

$$(4b) \quad R_t^{bnd} = b_0^* + \gamma^* R_{t-1}^{bnd} + b_1^*[A_{1,t} - E_{t-1}(A_{1,t})] + \dots$$

$$+ b_n^*[A_{n,t} - E_{t-1}(A_{n,t})] + \Phi^* X_t^* + \Lambda D_t^* + \eta_t^*.$$

The observed managerial actions $(A_{i,t})$ can be combined with the influence regression shown in equation (3a) or (3b) to compute the surprise component of each action. The sign of b_i (b_i^*) immediately implies the stockholders' (bondholders') preferred managerial action. We can thus determine whether, on average over the entire sample, an unexpected dividend cut, for example, is viewed as valuable to bondholders. The vector $\mathbf{X}_t$ contains both lagged and contemporaneous (time t) exogenous shock variables.

The Set of Managerial Actions

We have implicitly assumed that managers can effectively control the actions that investors are trying to affect. Finding measurable variables with this characteristic presents something of a challenge. Suppose, for example, that BHC share prices fall in response to large loan losses. The firm's leverage therefore rises, and bondholders would like managers to reduce leverage back toward its ex ante level. (The shareholders' preference is less clear.) In testing for stockholder and bondholder influence, one might be tempted to designate book leverage as a managerial action variable. In the long run, managers can surely reduce book leverage if they wish. In the short run, however, an effort to lower leverage by tightening credit standards might be ineffective. Because loan demand is not perfectly controllable or predictable, leverage might still increase in the short run despite management's sincere efforts to reduce it.[21] Leverage is thus an ambiguous indicator of managerial action. One response to this situation is to permit (empirically) managerial changes to occur over several quarters, and we do this. Another response is to define managerial action more narrowly, for example, as the sale of new stock or a dividend cut. Managers unambiguously control dividends and stock issues.

It is difficult to establish that a particular set of action measures is complete or appropriate. Some legitimate action measures may be omitted, and managers may only imperfectly control some of the included measures. Our approach is to seek systematic linkages in the data that appear to be consistent with managers taking responsive actions in the wake of security losses or gains. By considering a number of regression specifications and various ways of measuring the key variables, we hope to determine if the preponderance of the evidence supports the market influence hypothesis. Table 4.4 lists our measures of managerial action. We divide these actions into three subgroups: those affecting leverage, those affecting asset portfolio risk, and others. For some action variables we include both a binary classification (e.g., dividends up versus not up) and a continuous measure.[22]

Exogenous Shock Variables

In a dynamic firm, managerial action variables may vary through time for reasons other than the immediate desires of stock or bondholders. In

---

21. One reason why managers cannot perfectly control loan volumes is that many customers have prenegotiated lines of credit, which can be draw down (or not) without advance notice.

22. For binary action measures, we estimate equation (3a) or (3b) as a probit and report the likelihood ratio index (Greene 1993, 651) as a goodness-of-fit statistic.

Table 4.4   **Action Variables Used to Measure Managerial Responses to Market Signals**

Variable Name	Variable Description
	Factors Affecting BHC Leverage (continuous variables)
CMINCR	Increase in value of common stock, as percentage of book value of equity.
PFINCR	Increase in value of preferred stock, as percentage of book value of equity.
EQINCR	Increase in equity, as percentage of book value of equity (sum of CMINCR and CFINCR).
dSHCRSP	Percentage change in number of CRSP common shares outstanding.
dCDIVP	Change in common dividend declared as percentage of book value of equity.
dDIVP	Change in common plus preferred dividends declared, as a percentage of book value of equity.
dQSUBDB	Percentage change in sub debt as percentage of quarter-average total assets.
dBVEQ	Change in book value of equity as a percentage of total assets.
TAGROW	Quarter to quarter change in total assets divided by beginning of quarter total assets.
	Factors Affecting BHC Leverage (dummy variables)
DCDIVUP	1 if dividend payment (measured in dollars) increased from prior quarter, 0 otherwise.
DCOMUP	1 if increase in common outstanding, 0 otherwise.
DPFUP	1 if increase in preferred outstanding, 0 otherwise.
DEQUP	1 if increase in either type of equity, 0 otherwise.
DSND	1 if debentures rose in $ value, 0 otherwise.
	Factors Affecting Asset Risk
dSECPCT	Change in securities portfolio as a proportion of total assets.
	Other Measures of Managerial Action
dFTEMP	Percentage change in number of full-time equivalent employees.
dUINSINS	Change in uninsured liabilities as a percentage of insured liabilities.
dUNINTA	Change in uninsured liabilities as a proportion of total assets.

order to isolate the effect of past security returns on managerial actions, therefore, we must control for these exogenous factors. We use an agnostic statistical approach to absorb predetermined variation in action variables, regressing changes in each action variable against a large set of control variables, intended to capture any path dependence in managers' decisions. Table 4.5 lists the income and balance sheet variables we include to model predetermined changes in the action variables. Importantly, these exogenous shock variables do not include past stock and or bond returns. We also include in the set of exogenous variables

1. year dummy variables, to control for omitted variations in the banking industry's condition, ease of access to stock and bond markets, regulatory pressures, and so forth;

2. recent quarterly changes in the (dependent) decision variable in the influence equation (1); and

3. one quarterly lag of the dependent variable (a stock or bond return) in the response equation (2).

Note that the lagged BHC ratios in equation (3a) or (3b) may be correlated with the lagged security returns. We include both sets of explanatory variables in the regression, thereby permitting the data to apportion explanatory power between the lagged returns and lagged control variables. As one indicator of the importance of market influence, we will report the marginal contribution to $\bar{R}^2$ for the accounting and security return variables.

4.6 Empirical Results

We now present and interpret estimation results for the influence (equations [3a] and [3b]) and response (equations [4a] and [4b]) regressions. We first consider the estimated coefficients' parametric statistical significance, in the context of table 4.3 and the discussion in section 4.5.2. This approach yields little evidence of beneficial investor influence. We then apply a sign-based analysis that ignores parametric statistical significance and looks for patterns consistent with the beneficial and perverse influence hypotheses. We find some extreme cases, where the signs of all coefficients are consistent with one hypothesis or the other, for which we can reject the null hypothesis of no influence. However, in most cases the signs are not

Table 4.5	Exogenous Variables
Variable Name	Variable Description
CASHTA	BHC's cash, divided by total assets
CILNTA	BHC's commercial and industrial loans, divided by total assets.
CPTA	BHC's commercial paper outstanding, divided by total assets.
GLOANSTA	BHC's gross loans, divided by total assets.
TRADETA	BHC's assets held in trading portfolio, divided by total assets.
NINCTA	BHC's net income, divided by total assets.
TOTLIATA	BHC's total liabilities, divided by total assets.
LNPDTA	BHC's loans past due 90 days or more, divided by total assets.
LNSNATA	BHC's loans on non-accrual status, divided by total assets.
CHRGOTA	BHC's loan chargeoffs, divided by total assets.
RECVRTA	BHC's recoveries on loans previously charged off, divided by total assets.
LNTA	BHC's natural log of total assets.

Notes: All BHC ratios are measured as *changes,* from one end-of-quarter to the next. The total assets divisor is the quarterly average of total assets, not the quarter-end value. Except three quarterly lags ($t - 1$, $t - 2$, $t - 3$) of all control variables are included in influence equations (3). Contemporaneous and three quarterly lags ($t, t - 1, t - 2, t - 3$) of all control variables are included in response equations (4).

all consistent, and we can only note the tendency one way or the other in the data.

4.6.1   Analysis of Influence Regressions

We identify significant influence coefficients (the analogs of a_1 in equation [1]) on the basis of the sum of the three lagged coefficients for each action variable. Table 4.6 presents these sums and their corresponding statistical significance for the influence specification in equation (3a), and table 4.7 presents the results for the specification in equation (3b). The "HO: All return coefficients = 0" rows provide the formal test of the no-influence null hypothesis. In both specifications the null is rejected for twelve of eighteen action variables at the 10 percent level. Applying a 5 percent confidence level, we reject the null for eleven action variables in table 4.6 and nine action variables using the alternative specification of table 4.7.

The two influence specifications in equations (3a) and (3b) exhibit a good deal of similarity in the actions they identify as responding to lagged returns. Both specifications reject the no-influence hypothesis (10 percent level) for nearly half of our continuous action variables (CMINCR, EQINCR, dCDIVP, TAGROW, and dUININS) and four of the five binary action variables (DCOMUP, DPFUP, DEQUP, DSND). Several variables (dSHCRSP, dQSUBDB, dSECPCT) carry jointly insignificant coefficient sums (10 percent level) in both tables. Overall, the frequencies with which we reject the no-influence null hypothesis in tables 4.6 and 4.7 strongly suggest more than simple sampling variation. These results are consistent with investors exerting some influence over BHC managers.

Moreover, many of the individually significant summed return coefficient combinations are economically sensible. We expect influence to be weakest for $S^u B^u$ combinations and strongest for $S^d B^d$ combinations. The coefficient estimates reflect this general pattern, though not overwhelmingly: Table 4.6 exhibits nine significant coefficients (10 percent level) for the $S^d B^d$ combinations, against five for $S^u B^u$. Table 4.7 exhibits eight significant $S^d B^d$ coefficients against five for $S^u B^u$.

We illustrate the degree to which past security returns contribute to subsequent actions by comparing the full influence model's $\bar{R}^2$ statistic against the $\bar{R}^2$ value when subsets of explanatory variables have been omitted. $\bar{R}^2$ statistics indicate that the full model explains a large fraction of the observed variation in most of the action variables. Dropping the lagged return variables from the right-hand side reduces the explanatory power of the model only marginally, and so does dropping the exogenous shocks. A significant fraction of the explanatory power of these regressions comes from the lagged dependent variables. Thus, although the coefficients on the returns in the influence equation are sometimes statistically significant, the lagged returns do not provide a great deal of additional information.

Finding that managerial actions follow past return patterns is consistent

Table 4.6   Summary Results for "Influence" Regressions (equation [3a]) Using 2-way Classification of Returns as "Down" and "Up", Multiplied by Absolute Value of Return

	OLS, Using Continuous Dependent Action Variables								
	CMINCR	PFINCR	EQINCR	dSHCRSP	dCDIVP	dDDIVP	dQSUBDB	dBVEQ	TAGROW
Sum 3 $S^u B^u |R^{stk}|$	0.00062**	0.00021	0.00091**	0.00035	−0.00004	−0.00005	0.00000	0.00005	0.00019**
Sum 3 $S^u B^d |R^{stk}|$	0.00198***	0.00001	0.00215**	0.00304*	0.00013	0.00010	0.00001	0.00001	0.00010
Sum 3 $S^d B^u |R^{stk}|$	0.00073*	−0.00014	0.00054	0.00051	−0.00050**	−0.00046**	0.00000	−0.00007	0.00025**
Sum 3 $S^d B^d |R^{stk}|$	0.00116**	−0.00003	0.00118**	−0.00035	−0.00016	−0.00014	0.00002	−0.00015**	0.00015**
Sum 3 $S^u B^u |R^{bnd}|$	0.00006	0.00051	0.00067	0.00171	−0.00016	−0.00021	−0.00003	−0.00015*	0.00021
Sum 3 $S^u B^d |R^{bnd}|$	0.00239	−0.00012	0.00255	0.00657	−0.00110**	−0.00109*	−0.00021**	−0.00013	0.00013
Sum 3 $S^d B^u |R^{bnd}|$	0.00088	0.00051	0.00170	0.00378	−0.00021	−0.00020	−0.00003	0.00003	−0.00003
Sum 3 $S^d B^d |R^{bnd}|$	0.00135	−0.00024	0.00115	0.00421	−0.00079**	−0.00083**	−0.00005	0.00034***	0.00075**
H0: all return coefficients = 0	0.0001**	0.7225	0.0004**	0.2975	0.0000**	0.0000**	0.2021	0.0181**	0.0006**
Adjusted R^2									
All variables	0.5843	0.3428	0.5370	0.1081	0.7671	0.7886	0.0626	0.3804	0.9826
Without returns	0.5462	0.3377	0.5080	0.1074	0.7617	0.7841	0.0653	0.3702	0.9822
Without shocks	0.5332	0.3206	0.4939	0.0249	0.7374	0.7597	0.0192	0.0694	0.0323
Without shocks or years	0.5252	0.3145	0.4833	0.0036	0.7298	0.7528	0.0074	0.0412	0.0316
No. of observations	2,045	2,032	2,028	2,043	2,053	2,049	2,053	2,053	2,053

(continued)

Table 4.6   (continued)

	OLS Using Continuous Dependent Action Variables				Probit Using Binary Dependent Action Variables				
	dSECPCT	dFTEMP	dUININS	dUNINTA	DCDIVUP	DCOMUP	DPFUP	DEQUP	DSND
Sum 3 S^uB^u $\|R^{stk}\|$	−0.00013	0.00102**	0.00002	−0.00005	0.01001	0.02711**	0.01807	0.01728	0.00286
Sum 3 S^uB^d $\|R^{stk}\|$	−0.00008	0.00036	0.00019	0.00006	−0.00417	0.01924	0.00267	0.01184	−0.02538*
Sum 3 S^dB^u $\|R^{stk}\|$	0.00053	0.00023	−0.00084	−0.00039	−0.13247**	−0.02192	0.00918	−0.00680	0.01424
Sum 3 S^dB^d $\|R^{stk}\|$	−0.00028	0.00016	0.00059	0.00023	−0.05781**	0.03606**	0.04518**	0.03299**	0.01851
Sum 3 S^uB^u $\|R^{bnd}\|$	0.00058	0.00009	0.00028	0.00017	−0.18891**	0.07786*	−0.02001	0.07263*	−0.11977**
Sum 3 S^uB^d $\|R^{bnd}\|$	0.00123	0.00078	0.00459*	0.00202	−0.28775**	0.17336**	−0.25008**	0.06670	−0.07733
Sum 3 S^dB^u $\|R^{bnd}\|$	−0.00020	−0.00098	0.00028	0.00043	−0.05021	0.16597**	−0.08554	0.07705	−0.24919**
Sum 3 S^dB^d $\|R^{bnd}\|$	0.00041	0.00003	−0.00376**	−0.00162**	−0.09991**	0.04178	−0.16078*	0.02792	−0.10480**
H0: All return coefficients = 0	0.7108	0.1891	0.0713*	0.1045	0.0000**	0.0000**	0.0195**	0.0009**	0.0005**
Adjusted R^2									
All variables	0.3034	0.6341	0.1521	0.1852	0.7404	0.5407	0.4969	0.4816	0.3139
Without returns	0.3031	0.6338	0.1516	0.1831	0.6937	0.5151	0.4741	0.4642	0.2951
Without shocks	0.1429	0.0157	0.0368	0.0613	0.2289	0.4972	0.4052	0.4339	0.2738
Without shocks or years	0.1310	0.0112	0.0205	0.0281	0.2073	0.4723	0.3870	0.4123	0.2686
No. of observations	2,053	2,053	1,851	1,856	2,053	2,045	2,032	2,029	2,053

Notes: Reported coefficients are sums of the three lagged coefficients. Influence regressions were run separately for each action variable, using stock/bond directional dummies for past three quarters, three lags of the dependent variable, three lags of the exogenous variables in table 4.5, and a set of year dummy variables. The adjusted R^2 statistic indicating goodness-of-fit for the probit regressions is the likelihood ratio index (Greene 1993, 651). The numbers reported for "H0: All return coefficients = 0" are *p*-values.

**Significant at the 5 percent level.
*Significant at the 10 percent level.

Table 4.7 Summary Results for "Influence" Regressions (equation [3b]) Using 3-way Classification of Returns as Down, Flat, and Up

	OLS, Using Continuous Dependent Action Variables								
	CMINCR	PFINCR	EQINCR	dSHCRSP	dCDIVP	dDDIVP	dQSUBDB	dBVEQ	TAGROW
Sum 3 S^uB^u	0.0019	0.0054	0.0083	-0.0091	-0.0004	0.0000	-0.0002	0.0011*	0.0047**
Sum 3 S^uB^f	-0.0118*	0.0010	-0.0116	0.0103	0.0038	0.0040	-0.0001	0.0004	0.0024
Sum 3 S^uB^d	0.0143**	-0.0013	0.0141*	0.0194	0.0009	0.0011	-0.0007*	0.0003	0.0007
Sum 3 S^fB^u	-0.0013	0.0035	0.0017	-0.0293	0.0013	0.0017	-0.0004	0.0004	-0.0001
Sum 3 S^fB^d	0.0063	0.0051*	0.0102*	-0.0409	0.0004	0.0003	-0.0007	0.0004	-0.0004
Sum 3 S^dB^u	-0.0014	-0.0039	-0.0053	-0.0107	-0.0040**	-0.0033*	-0.0002	0.0004	0.0036
Sum 3 S^dB^f	0.0112*	0.0052	0.0162**	-0.0669**	-0.0011	-0.0006	-0.0001	0.0002	0.0039
Sum 3 S^dB^d	0.0136**	0.0039	0.0180**	-0.0304	-0.0025*	-0.0019	-0.0002	-0.0003	0.0042**
H0: all returns coefficients = 0	0.0037**	0.0593*	0.0003**	0.2695	0.256**	0.1538	0.4367	0.5975	0.0170**
Adjusted R^2									
All variables	0.5523	0.3387	0.5153	0.1071	0.7617	0.7840	0.0630	0.3696	0.9823
Without returns	0.5462	0.3377	0.5080	0.1074	0.7617	0.7841	0.0653	0.3702	0.9822
Without shocks	0.5012	0.3180	0.4703	0.0271	0.7297	0.7526	0.0151	0.0473	0.0190
Without shocks or years	0.4833	0.3106	0.4515	0.0124	0.7180	0.7416	0.0067	0.0247	0.0147
No. of observations	2,045	2,032	2,028	2,043	2,053	2,049	2,053	2,053	2,053

(continued)

Table 4.7 (continued)

	OLS Using Continuous Dependent Action Variables				Probit Using Binary Dependent Action Variables				
	dSECPCT	dFTEMP	dUNININS	dUNINTA	DCDIVUP	DCOMUP	DPFUP	DEQUP	DSND
Sum 3 $S^u B^u$	−0.0059	0.0232**	0.0027	−0.0026	−0.0308	1.2913**	0.2144	0.7876**	−0.4960
Sum 3 $S^u B^f$	−0.0034	0.0190*	0.0150	0.0038	0.4883	0.7684	−0.2497	0.2488	−0.0286
Sum 3 $S^u B^d$	−0.0030	0.0149*	0.0230**	0.0070*	0.0554	0.8836**	−0.6848*	0.2761	−0.7379**
Sum 3 $S^f B^u$	−0.0001	0.0037	0.0130	0.0039	−0.1024	0.9687**	0.0481	0.5929	−0.4904**
Sum 3 $S^f B^d$	0.0009	−0.0004	0.0209*	0.0083*	0.0657	1.4587**	−0.4863	0.5064	−0.2577
Sum 3 $S^d B^u$	0.0093	0.0144	0.0004	−0.0016	−1.1968**	0.2956	−0.7983*	−0.2177	−0.5376**
Sum 3 $S^d B^f$	−0.0045	0.0111	0.0015	0.0000	0.0750	1.3575**	0.4237	0.7848**	−0.0847
Sum 3 $S^d B^d$	−0.0051	0.0088	0.0149*	0.0044	−0.9633**	1.4655**	0.5190	0.8410**	−0.1623
H0: All returns coefficients = 0	0.5559	0.0413**	0.0496**	0.0646*	0.0002	0.0002**	0.0041**	0.0029**	0.0506*
Adjusted R^2									
All variables	0.3061	0.6367	0.1593	0.1905	0.7136	0.5484	0.4972	0.4854	0.3093
Without returns	0.3031	0.6338	0.1516	0.1831	0.6937	0.5151	0.4741	0.4642	0.2951
Without shocks	0.1475	0.0123	0.0469	0.0690	0.1274	0.4947	0.3976	0.4317	0.2677
Without shocks or years	0.1344	0.0066	0.0259	0.0291	0.0914	0.4640	0.3801	0.4070	0.2642
No. of observations	2,053	2,053	1,851	1,856	2,053	2,045	2,032	2,029	2,053

Notes: See table 4.6.

with influence, but we must look at the response equations to determine if this apparent influence is associated with actions that actually enhance security values.

4.6.2   Parametric Evidence about Influence

Tables 4.8 and 4.9 combine new information about estimated response equations (4a) and (4b) with the influence equation coefficient estimates already presented in tables 4.6 and 4.7. The influence hypothesis is not strongly supported by the response regression coefficients. Stock excess returns respond significantly to only three and four action variable surprises in tables 4.8 and 4.9, respectively, but the only significantly valuable actions that appear in both specifications are dUNINTA and DCDIVUP. (Even then, the significant, opposite signs on the similar variables dUININS and dUNINTA in table 4.9 seem puzzling.) One of the three significant response variables in table 4.8 (dSECPCT) is not associated with significant influence. Table 4.9 provides only two additional actions (dCDIVP and dUININS) that are affected by past returns and that, in turn, significantly affect excess stock returns when action is taken.

The bonds' response regressions exhibit even fewer significant effects. The only action surprises with significant return response coefficients are dSECPCT in table 4.8, and dFTEMP in table 4.9; both are significant only at the 10 percent level.

Investor influence requires $a_1 \neq 0$ and $b_1 \neq 0$. The dearth of significant return responses (b_1) therefore provides scant evidence of investor influence. In table 4.8 the significant stock and bond response coefficients for dSECPCT are not associated with any significant influence coefficients. The significant coefficient on stock response to dUNINTA is associated with a significant influence variable (on $S^d B^d$), and the signs are consistent with beneficial influence. Unhappily, this picture is spoiled by the fact that the significant *stock* response is associated with a significant *bond* influence. Table 4.9 is not much more encouraging. The significant stock response coefficient for dCDIVP is associated with two weak influences in turn associated with stock-down states, consistent with influence. However, the coefficient signs imply perverse, rather than beneficial, influence. The weakly significant bond response coefficient on dFTEMP is associated with a weakly significant influence coefficient on the action for $S^u B^d$, consistent with influence, although again perverse rather than beneficial. The significant dUININS stock response coefficient is associated with three significant influence variables. In this case the signs are consistent with beneficial influence, but the three return states that appear to be influencing the dUININS action variable are all bond-down states. This seems inconsistent with stocks' influencing actions. The significant dUNINTA stock response is associated with bond-down-related influence coefficients, and the signs are consistent with perverse influence. Finally,

Table 4.8   "Influence" and "Response" Regression Results and Sign-Based Test of Beneficial/Perverse Influence Using 2-way Classification of Returns as Down and Up, Multiplied by Absolute Value of Stock or Bond Return

Action Variables	"Influence" Equation (1a)								"Response" Equation (1b)		Beneficial/Perverse Influence	
	Absolute Value of Stock Return Multiplies				Absolute Value of Bond Return Multiplies				Stock	Bonds	Stock	Bonds
	S^uB^u	S^uB^d	S^dB^u	S^dB^d	S^uB^u	S^uB^d	S^dB^u	S^dB^d				
					Continuous Action Variables							
CMINCR	0.0006**	0.0020**	0.0007*	0.0012**	0.0001	0.0024	0.0009	0.0014	13.975	−42.191	BB	PP
PFINCR	0.0002	0.0000	−0.0001	0.0000	0.0005	−0.0001	0.0005	−0.0002	−16.964	−44.674	P	?
EQINCR	0.0009**	0.0022**	0.0005	0.0012**	0.0007	0.0026	0.0017	0.0012	14.645	41.517	BB	BB
dSHCRSP	0.0004	0.0030*	0.0005	−0.0004	0.0017	0.0066	0.0038	0.0042	3.582	0.068	B	BB
dCDIVP	0.0000	0.0001	−0.0005**	−0.0002	−0.0002	−0.0011	−0.0002	−0.0008**	207.221	−161.162	?	BB
dDDIVP	−0.0001	0.0001	−0.0005**	−0.0001	−0.0002	−0.0011**	−0.0002	−0.0008**	−116.735	141.188	B	PP
dQSUBDB	0.0000	0.0000	0.0000	0.0000	0.0000	−0.0002*	0.0000	−0.0001	−129.724	−56.052	PP	?
dBVEQ	0.0001	0.0000	−0.0001	−0.0002**	−0.0002*	−0.0001**	0.0000	0.0003**	136.120	45.047	?	?
TAGROW	0.0002**	0.0001	0.0003**	0.0002**	0.0001	0.0001	0.0000	0.0008***	−15.753	−3.711	PP	PP
dSECPCT	−0.0001	−0.0001	0.0005	−0.0003	0.0006	0.0012	−0.0002	0.0004	19.708**	6.775*	P	B
dFTEMP	0.0010**	0.0004	0.0002	0.0002	0.0001	0.0008	−0.0010	0.0000	−6.234	−2.944	PP	P
dUININS	0.0000	0.0002	−0.0008	0.0006	0.0003	0.0046*	0.0003	−0.0038**	18.375	−4.308	B	P
dUINTA	−0.0001	0.0001	−0.0004	0.0002	0.0002	0.0020	0.0004	−0.0016**	−70.996**	−7.397	?	P

				Binary Action Variables (1 if increase, 0 if decrease)							
DCDIVUP	0.0100	-0.0042	-0.1325**	-0.0578**	-0.1889**	-0.2878***	-0.0502	-0.0999**	2.145**	0.111	P	PP
DCOMUP	0.0271**	0.0192	-0.0219	0.0361**	0.0779*	0.1734***	0.1660**	0.0418	1.478	0.182	B	BB
DPFUP	0.0181	0.0027	0.0092	0.0452**	-0.0200	-0.2501**	-0.0855	-0.1608*	0.258	0.204	BB	PP
DEQUP	0.0173	0.0118	-0.0068	0.0330**	0.0726*	0.0667	0.0771	0.0279	-0.920	-0.055	P	PP
DSND	0.0029	-0.0254*	0.0142	0.0185	-0.1198**	-0.0773	-0.2492**	-0.1048**	-0.284	-0.061	P	BB

Notes: Influence regression results are repeated (in transposed form) from tables 4.6 and 4.7. The numbers reported are sums of the three coefficients on lagged stock/bond return measures.

"Response" equations (4a) and (4b) were estimated separately for stock and bond returns. For each security return, we estimated separate regressions for the set of continuous and discrete action variables. (Including both the OLS and the probit residuals in the same response equation yields very similar results.) Explanatory variables were the unexpected components of all action variables (residuals from the Influence regressions), the lagged security return, year dummies, and the contemporaneous and three lags of the exogenous variables from table 4.5.

Beneficial/perverse influence tests were based on coefficient signs, without regard for significance levels. The classifications from table 4.3 were applied to combinations of influence and response equation coefficients. The sign of b_i implies which direction the action variable must move to increase a security's value. If *all* relevant stock/bond a_i coefficient signs were consistent with beneficial influence, the result was classified as "BB." If the majority of influence coefficients were consistent with beneficial influence, the result was classified as "B," if evenly divided, as "?," etc.

**Significant at the 5 percent level.

*Significant at the 10 percent level.

Table 4.9 "Influence" and "Response" Regression Results and Sign-Based Test of Beneficial/Perverse Influence Using 3-way Classification of Returns as Down, Flat, and Up

Action Variables	"Influence" Equation (1a)						"Response" Equation (1b)		Beneficial/Perverse Influence	
	S^uB^u	S^uB^f	S^uB^d	S^fB^u	S^fB^f	S^fB^d	Stock	Bonds	Stock	Bonds
	Continuous Action Variables									
CMINCR	0.0019	−0.118*	0.0143	−0.0013	0.0063	−0.0014	0.0112*	0.0136**	5.462	−3.758	B	P
PFINCR	0.0054	0.0010	−0.0013	0.0035	0.0051*	−0.0039	0.0052	0.0039	−40.373	−9.828	P	P
EQINCR	0.0083	−0.0116	0.0141*	0.0017	0.0102*	−0.0053	0.0162**	0.0180**	35.558	5.519	B	B
dSHCRSP	−0.0091	0.0103	0.0194	−0.0293	−0.0409	−0.0107	−0.0669**	−0.0304	4.529	0.028	P	P
dCDIVP	−0.0004	0.0038	0.0009	0.0013	0.0004	−0.0040**	−0.0011	−0.0025*	124.920**	38.052	P	?
dDDIVP	0.0000	0.0040	0.0011	0.0017	0.0003	−0.0033*	−0.0006	−0.0019	−17.072	−68.724	?	P
dQSUBDB	−0.0002	−0.0001	−0.0007*	−0.0004	−0.0007	−0.0002	−0.0001	−0.0002	−160.207	−89.684	BB	BB
dBVEQ	0.0011*	0.0004	0.0003	0.0004	0.0004	0.0004	0.0002	−0.0003	128.711	78.941	B	B
TAGROW	0.0047**	0.0024	0.0007	−0.0001	−0.0004	0.0036	0.0039	0.0042**	9.102	18.495	BB	B
dSECPCT	−0.0059	−0.0034	−0.0030	−0.0001	0.0009	0.0093	−0.0045	−0.0051	13.075	7.778	P	P
dFTEMP	0.0232	0.0190	0.0149*	0.0037	−0.0004	0.0144	0.0111	0.0088	−5.451	−5.222*	PP	P
dUININS	0.0027	0.0150	0.0230**	0.0130	0.0209**	0.0004	0.0015	0.0149*	23.194*	−8.080	BB	PP
dUININTA	−0.0026	0.0038	0.0070**	0.0039	0.0083**	−0.0016	0.0000	0.0044	−76.657**	−3.221	P	P
	Binary Action Variables (1 if increase, 0 if decrease)									
DCDIVUP	−0.0308	0.4883	0.0554	−0.1024	0.0657	−1.1968**	0.0750	−0.9633**	1.648**	−0.101	?	B
DCOMUP	1.2913**	0.7684**	0.8836**	0.9687**	1.4587**	0.2956	1.3575**	1.4655**	0.933	−0.313	BB	PP
DPFUP	0.2144	−0.2497	−0.6848*	0.0481	−0.4863	−0.7983*	0.4237	0.5190	−0.718	−0.423	?	?
DEQUP	0.7876**	0.2488	0.2761	0.5929*	0.5064	−0.2177	0.7848**	0.8410**	−0.216	0.631	P	B
DSND	−0.4960**	−0.0286	−0.7379**	−0.4904**	−0.2577	−0.5376*	−0.0847	−0.1623	−0.362	−0.131	BB	BB

Notes: See table 4.8.

in both tables 4.6 and 4.7 the significant stock response on the DCDIVUP action variable is associated with several influences; again predominantly of bond-down states and of signs consistent with perverse influence.

In summary, although there appears to be significant association between return variables and subsequent managerial actions, the evidence from combining the influence and response regression results is very weak, and in no case is there clear evidence of beneficial influence. Obviously, failure to reject a null hypothesis of no influence is not conclusive evidence against stock and bondholder influence, but neither is it evidence for influence. The few instances of influence that we can detect parametrically are consistent with perverse, rather than beneficial, influence.

4.6.3   Nonparametric Evidence about Influence

The broadly insignificant results for the response regressions might reflect a general power failure for the parametric tests applied in the usual sort of regression analysis. We therefore evaluate whether a simple, nonparametric signs test can provide consistent interpretations of the results in tables 4.6 and 4.7. To conserve space we discuss only the tertiary specification results in table 4.9. The results in table 4.8 are similar.

The influence equation specification in table 4.9 includes six explanatory variables that can reasonably be associated with stock return influence on managerial actions: $S^u B^u$, $S^u B^f$, $S^u B^d$, $S^d B^u$, $S^d B^f$, and $S^d B^d$ (stock flat combinations are unlikely to be associated with stock influence). The analogous variables are consistent with bond return influence: $S^u B^u$, $S^f B^u$, $S^d B^u$, $S^u B^d$, $S^f B^d$, and $S^d B^d$. The probability that six coefficients will carry the same sign by chance alone is approximately 1.6 percent. Five out of six coefficients bearing the same sign would appear by chance 18.8 percent of the time. A nonparametric sign test of beneficial or perverse influence would reject the no-influence null at the 5 percent level if all six stock influence coefficients are the same sign as the stock response coefficient (beneficial) or the opposite sign (perverse). Where fewer than six relevant influence coefficients have the same sign, the influence coefficient signs may suggest a relation one way or the other (if not half-positive and half-negative), but these results are statistically inconclusive. Taking the top row of table 4.9 (for the managerial action CMINCR) as an example, the stock response coefficient (5.642) is positive, so beneficial influence requires positive coefficients on the three stock-up and three stock-down influence coefficients. Four of the relevant influence coefficients are positive ($S^u B^u$, $S^u B^d$, $S^d B^f$, $S^d B^d$), and two are negative ($S^u B^f$, $S^d B^u$). This is suggestive of beneficial influence, but not significant. A single "B" in the stock column of the "Beneficial/Perverse Influence" results column denotes this. The dUNINTA results provide clear, significant evidence of beneficial stock influence—denoted "BB" in the stock "Beneficial/Perverse Influence" results column—as well as significant perverse bond influence, denoted "PP" in the bond column. Table 4.8 can only provide weak evidence of influence. For stocks there are only four relevant influence coefficients: those associated with the absolute value of the stock return. The chance of all four coefficients having the same sign is 6.3 percent. Even though this is significant at only the 10% level, we also denote this outcome with "BB" or "PP," if appropriate.

These nonparametric sign tests of beneficial and perverse influence produce mixed results. Over both specifications we find eight (of 36) significant cases of beneficial stock influence, and four significant cases of perverse stock influence. The "suggestive" stock results break down seven beneficial to ten perverse. Less rigorously, some indication (significant or otherwise) of beneficial stock influence obtains in fifteen versus fourteen cases for perverse influence, with seven cases being completely neutral. The corresponding bond results are eight cases of significant beneficial bond influence, seven cases of significant perverse bond influence, fifteen cases at least suggestive of beneficial bond influence, sixteen cases at least suggestive of perverse influence, and five cases completely neutral. Once again, the only strong conclusion we can draw from these results is that the data are *not* uniformly consistent with the presence of beneficial investor discipline for sample banking firms.

4.7 Summary and Conclusions

The concept of market discipline has attained great popularity in discussions of regulatory reform, both in the United States and abroad. Market discipline implies two quite distinct notions, which we have tried to separate: private investors' ability to understand (monitor) a financial firm's true condition, and their ability to influence managerial actions in appropriate ways. A large body of evidence suggests that markets monitor financial firms effectively and promptly, but specific tests of investor influence have been much more limited. Previous research provides some information about shareholders' ability to influence firm managers, particularly in extreme situations; but empirical evidence about bondholders' ability to influence firm behavior has been lacking.

We assembled information about large U.S. BHCs' stock and bond returns for the period 1986–97. One view of corporate capital structure emphasizes the potential conflicts between shareholders and debtholders in a levered firm. In examining quarterly excess returns for our sample, we find that stock and bond prices move in the *same* direction more than half the time. Despite the potential importance of stockholder-bondholder conflicts, the two groups frequently share common interests with respect to firm performance.

To assess whether bondholders can effectively influence banking firms, we explicitly modeled the interaction between investors and managers and showed how beneficial influence should be manifested in the data. Although the methodology is not perfect, we had hoped it would identify appropriate managerial responses to observable, exogenous events that affect BHC value. Some types of beneficial influence will be undetectable: for example, if managers *refrain* from taking actions that they know would elicit investor chagrin, or if managers always respond appropriately to exogenous shocks. Accordingly, we note that our methodology probably identifies a lower bound on the extent of beneficial investor influence.

The empirical results fall into two categories. First, the standard parametric tests provided very little evidence for investor influence. Despite many statistically significant associations between returns and subsequent managerial actions, we could not interpret the overall coefficient estimates as supporting beneficial influence. The weakness in the parametric tests derives from the paucity of meaningful return responses to our managerial action variables. The parametric evidence is not inconsistent with influence. It is simply inconclusive.

A less rigorous, nonparametric interpretation of the regression results identifies evidence consistent with both beneficial and perverse influence. For bondholders, the instances of beneficial and perverse influence are equal in number. Stockholders appear to exert significant beneficial influence about twice as often as they exert perverse influence, consistent with the fact that equity has much more extensive control rights in normal circumstances. However one chooses to interpret these nonparametric results, the evidence cannot be said to unambiguously support the presence of beneficial investor influence on BHC firms over the sample period.

If these conclusions withstand further analysis, the implications for regulatory reliance on market forces are important, but simple. Other research indicates that private investors monitor financial firms and may even anticipate changes in their financial condition. Our results do not address this question and so carry no implication for proposals to more formally incorporated market signals into the government supervisory process. However, in the absence of specific evidence that BHC stock- and bondholders can effectively influence managerial actions under normal operating conditions, supervisors would be unwise to rely on investors—including subordinated debenture holders—to constrain BHC risk taking. At least under current institutional arrangements, supervisors must retain the responsibility for influencing managerial actions.

References

Ang, James S., Rebel A. Cole, and James Wuh Lin. 2000. Agency costs and ownership structure. *Journal of Finance* 55 (1): 81–106.

Basel Committee on Banking Supervision. 1999. A new capital adequacy framework. Consultative paper issued by the Basel Committee on Banking Supervision, June.

Berger, Allen N. 1991. Market discipline in banking. Proceedings of a conference on bank structure and competition, 419–39. Federal Reserve Bank of Chicago.

Brickley, James A., and Christopher M. James. 1987. The takeover market, corporate board composition, and ownership structure: The case of banking. *Journal of Law and Economics* 30 (1): 161–80.

Brickley, James A., James S. Linck, and Jeffrey L. Coles. 1999. What happens to CEOs after they retire? New evidence on career concerns, horizon problems, and CEO incentives. *Journal of Financial Economics* 52 (3): 341–77.

Core, John E., Robert W. Holthausen, and David F. Larcker. 1999. Corporate governance, chief executive officer compensation, and firm performance. *Journal of Financial Economics* 51 (3): 371–406.

Cotter, James F., Anil Shivdasani, and Marc Zenner. 1997. Do independent directors enhance target shareholder wealth during tender offers? *Journal of Financial Economics* 43 (2): 195–218.

Denis, David J., and Diane K. Denis. 1995. Performance changes following top management dismissals. *Journal of Finance* 50 (4): 1029–57.

DeYoung, Robert, Mark J. Flannery, William Lang, and Sorin M. Sorescu. 2001. The information content of bank exam ratings and subordinated debt prices. *Journal of Money, Credit and Banking,* forthcoming.

DeYoung, Robert, Kenneth Spong, and Richard J. Sullivan. 2001. Who's minding the store? motivating and monitoring hired managers at small, closely held commercial banks. *Journal of Banking and Finance,* forthcoming.

Diamond, Douglas W. 1984. Financial intermediation and delegated monitoring. *Review of Economic Studies* 51 (3): 393–414.

Ellis, David M., and Mark J. Flannery. 1992. Does the debt market assess large banks' risk? *Journal of Monetary Economics* 30 (3): 481–502.

Flannery, Mark J. 1998. Using market information in prudential bank supervision: A review of the U.S. empirical evidence. *Journal of Money, Credit and Banking* 30 (3): 273–305.

Flannery, Mark J., and Sorin M. Sorescu. 1996. Evidence of bank market discipline in subordinated debenture yields. *Journal of Finance* 51 (4): 1347–77.

Gilbert, R. Alton. 1990. Market discipline of bank risk: Theory and evidence. *Federal Reserve Bank of St. Louis Review* 72 (1): 3–18.

Greene, William H. 1993. *Econometric analysis,* 2nd ed. New York: Macmillan Publishing Company.

Hadlock, Charles J., and Gerald B. Lumer. 1997. Compensation, turnover, and top management incentives: Historical evidence. *Journal of Business* 70 (2): 153–87.

Hirshleifer, David, and Anjan V. Thakor. 1998. Corporate control through board dismissals and takeovers. *Journal of Economics and Management Strategy* 7 (4): 489–520.

Hubbard, R. Glenn, and Darius Palia. 1995. Executive pay and performance: Evidence from the U.S. banking industry. *Journal of Financial Economics* 39 (1): 105–30.

Jensen, Michael C., and William H. Meckling. 1976. Theory of the firm, managerial behavior, agency costs, and ownership structure. *Journal of Financial Economics* 3 (4): 305–60.

Jensen, Michael C., and Kevin J. Murphy. 1990. Performance pay and top-management incentives. *Journal of Political Economy* 98 (2): 225–65.

Kaplan, Steven N. 1994a. Top executive rewards and firm performance: A comparison of Japan and the United States. *Journal of Political Economy* 102 (3): 510–46.

———. 1994b. Top executives turnover and firm performance in Germany. *Journal of Law, Economics and Organization* 10 (1): 142–59.

Kwan, Simon H. 1996. Firm-specific information and the correlation between individual stocks and bonds. *Journal of Financial Economics* 40 (1): 63–80.

Martin, Kenneth J., and John J. McConnell. 1991. Corporate performance, corporate takeovers, and management turnover. *Journal of Finance* 46 (2): 671–87.

Mikkelson, W., and M. Partch. 1997. The decline of takeovers and disciplinary managerial turnover. *Journal of Financial Economics* 44 (2): 205–28.

Morck, Randall, Andrei Shleifer, and Robert W. Vishny. 1988. Management ownership and market valuation: An empirical analysis. *Journal of Financial Economics* 20 (1/2): 293–315.

Myers, Stewart C. 1977. Determinants of corporate borrowing. *Journal of Financial Economics* 5 (2): 147–75.

Prowse, Stephen. 1997. Corporate control in commercial banks. *The Journal of Financial Research* 20 (4): 509–27.

Shleifer, Andrei, and Robert W. Vishny. 1997. A survey of corporate governance. *Journal of Finance* 52 (2): 737–83.

Smith, Clifford W., Jr., and Jerold B. Warner. 1979. On financial contracting: An analysis of bond covenants. *Journal of Financial Economics* 7 (2): 117–62.

Warga, Arthur D. 1995. *A fixed income database.* University of Houston, Fixed Income Research Program.

Williamson, Stephen. 1986. Costly monitoring, financial intermediation and equilibrium credit rationing. *Journal of Monetary Economics* 18 (2): 159–79.

Comment   Raghuram G. Rajan

This paper examines whether bank actions are, in fact, disciplined by markets. It starts by arguing that market discipline has two components. The first is monitoring, which implies the market's ability to reflect what is happening inside the firm and, sometimes, to predict what will happen to it. The second is influence, which refers to the effect of market movements on managerial actions. The authors argue that both components are necessary for market discipline to work. The paper is very timely in that regulatory authorities are increasingly despairing of supervising the complicated processes that go on inside a modern financial institution and would like to rely on the market to take over some of their tasks. Taken at face value, the results of the paper suggest that it may be premature to delegate supervisory functions to the market because although the market seems to recognize when something is going on, managerial actions do not seem to be influenced by market movements.

Raghuram G. Rajan is the Joseph Gidwitz Professor of Finance at the University of Chicago's Graduate School of Business and a research associate of the National Bureau of Economic Research.

The task the authors undertake is to be commended. There are, however, difficulties in the methodology. They must be able both to interpret what the market reaction suggests is wrong and to specify precisely what actions will be taken to remedy it. This is difficult at the level of a case study, let alone in large samples. But there is a more fundamental concern. If, in fact, market discipline works well, then managers should anticipate the reactions of the market and not mess up. The market should react only to factors beyond managers' control. In this case, however, we should indeed see no effect of the market on managerial actions. So does one conclude from the results that market discipline does not work or that it works too well?

Most of us start with the preconception that managers are not angels, so let us assume, as the authors do, that managers do not do everything perfectly. The problem is that the methodology is even now biased against finding that markets exert influence. As the authors recognize, positive market reactions are unlikely to change managerial actions—if it ain't broke, why fix it? But what does a negative market reaction indicate? The authors' preferred interpretation is that the market may be uncertain about whether managers will be shamed into fixing the problem, and hence it reacts adversely to signs of the problem. The most negative reaction, however, will be when the market is convinced that managers will not fix the problem or that they cannot fix it. In other words, the most adverse reactions will be met by no action, whereas moderate reactions will be met by substantial action. These nonlinear possibilities cloud interpretation of the results. The authors do recognize that the magnitude of the market reaction may not be representative, and also present regressions with dummy variables. I would focus on these.

The last difficulty the authors have is in correlating market reaction to specific operational responses. The problem is that a market reaction could come for any reason. Because the authors do not know why the market has reacted, they can only rely on some very coarse reasoning (I do not use this term pejoratively) about what the appropriate managerial action should be.

In short, even modulo all the caveats, predicting operational reactions is hard. In fact, would a regulator be happy if she saw a bank changing its operations with every blip in market prices? Clintonian management may be appropriate in politics, but what would one conclude about a bank manager who let the market determine his every decision?

This suggests that if one were to look for more comfort about the effects of markets, one may have to rely on coarser but more significant responses. For example, as in Steve Kaplan's studies of German and Japanese firms, does a fall in stock (or subordinate bond) price presage more managerial turnover than the average?

The bottom line is that this paper is interesting in large part because the authors ask very good questions about how one could test for the existence of market influence. I also like the model they present, which highlights the precise assumptions they need to find any evidence of market discipline. Whether the reader leans to their view that the tests have some power, or to the skeptical view that they do not, the paper gives the reader a good way of thinking about the issue. Nevertheless, because the questions they raise are only partially answered, the conclusions must be viewed as tentative.

Discussion Summary

Mark Carey began the discussion by suggesting that the authors augment their work by focusing on events. *Robert Eisenbeis* wondered what the authors were trying to capture. He noted that often firms away from the efficient frontier move back to the frontier using different combinations of actions. He suggested that this might be a good framework.

Charles Calomiris had a somewhat different take on the paper's results for policy. He noted that before the implementation of deposit insurance in the United States markets disciplined banks through depositer exit. He observed that as equity fell, banks had to respond or lose deposits. He noted that bond market discipline might be less organized because covenants are hard to enforce and bondholders are unable to run. He observed that this problem is even more difficult with insured deposits; as bondholders exit banks shift from bond funding to insured deposits. Empirical evidence, he further observed, suggests that bank bond debt shrinks as banks get into trouble.

Doug Diamond began by asking what we should see and do. He noted that from a financial perspective, managers maximize the value of the firm across all claimants. Absent regulation, we should not expect to see actions favoring one claimant over another. He pointed out that at banks there are three claimants—debt, equity and regulators—and that this third claimant will have more clout. This, he observed, leads to the question of whether regulatory interventions cause changes. He concluded that if regulatory actions lead to market response, then we might not expect to see a further response.

Alan Berger noted a key link that has not been investigated—an identification problem. He noted that some apparent actions might in fact be the outcome of previous actions. He suggested that the authors look at nonperforming loans; these may not be actions of the bank but may have been previously identified as bad loans by bondholders. Finally, he noted that the authors face a challenge similar to that of Berger, Kyle, and Scalise: After supervisors identify problems, they then show up as nonperforming loans, making it hard to identify the action and the reaction.

Following up on Berger's argument, *Frederic Mishkin* wondered whether we can identify actions and reactions given that bonds are forward looking. He observed that we might never be able to infer causality: With forward-looking variables it is even harder to get a controlled experiment.

Mark Flannery began the response by noting that these issues are linked. He suggested that the focus on the three claimants may be key. In terms of predicting versus influencing, he noted that the authors do regress residuals on market returns in order to address these concerns partially. He agreed that they should think about Modigliani and Miller and stay away from stockholders.

In response to Eisenbeis, *Robert Bliss* noted that movement back to the frontier might be a third step. He agreed with Calomiris that the current regulatory environment will undermine discipline and could continue under a subordinated debt proposal. To Berger he responded that if there is influence, then it is hard to find evidence. This finding suggests that monitoring-based subordinated debt proposals should be evaluated more closely.

Michael Dooley reopened the discussion by asking what the objective of the third claimant (the regulator) is. He noted that if the insurance fund has a different objective function, then this should be explicit. Berger noted that research (by Flannery and others) suggests that bondholders and supervisors seem to have the same objectives and reactions.

James Wilcox suggested looking at the response to merger announcements—if the acquiring banks stock value falls on the announcement, then why aren't mergers called off? Flannery noted that this related to discussant *Raghuram Rajan*'s first point. He observed that managers who expect a big fall in stock value might not bring mergers to market. He argued that in this case we may not see evidence of discipline even though it is in fact strong.

5

Can Emerging Market Bank Regulators Establish Credible Discipline? The Case of Argentina, 1992–99

Charles W. Calomiris and Andrew Powell

5.1 Introduction

Like those of many other emerging-market countries, Argentina's banking sector was liberalized in the 1990s. That liberalization followed decades of severe financial repression. The return to deposits placed in banks previously was substantially negative; according to Central Bank estimates, if $100 of deposits had been placed in an Argentine bank in 1944, it would be worth roughly 3 cents in real terms today (and 1 cent in 1990). As recently as 1990, bank deposits were frozen as part of an emergency fiscal adjustment. As elsewhere, liberalization involved lifting controls on interest rates, deregulating the banking sector, allowing the entry of foreign capital, privatizing, and adopting international regulatory standards.

Nevertheless, the experience of the Argentine banking sector over the past decade has been unique in several respects. Many observers view Argentina's reforms as among the most radical attempts to overhaul a banking system. In Argentina credit was traditionally allocated either to the

Charles W. Calomiris is the Paul M. Montrone Professor of Finance and Economics at Columbia Business School, a professor of international and public affairs at Columbia's School of International and Public Affairs, a senior fellow at the Council on Foreign Relations, a visiting fellow at the American Enterprise Institute, and a research associate of the National Bureau of Economic Research. Andrew Powell is currently chief economist of the Central Bank of Argentina. He has previously held academic posts at the Universities of Oxford, London, and Warwick, all in the United Kingdom.

The views expressed in this paper are those of the authors and do not necessarily represent the views of the Central Bank of Argentina or any other institution. The authors wish to thank Tamara Burdiso and Laura D'Amato for excellent assistance with the econometric analyses presented in this research. The authors also thank discussant Douglas Diamond, other conference participants, and Charles Himmelberg and Alejandra Anastasi for helpful comments and discussions. All mistakes naturally remain the authors' own.

public sector or, through public intervention, to specific sectors or projects in the private sector. Moreover, the banking sector suffered from ineffective regulation and supervision, and repeated, forced government rescues contributed significantly to Argentina's past fiscal and inflationary problems. In contrast, many have argued that today there is a credible, restrictive safety net as well as high regulatory and supervisory standards. For example, as shown in table 5.1, one World Bank study rated Argentina's regulatory regime on par with Hong Kong, second only to Singapore, and higher than the longer-lived and much admired regime in Chile.[1] In particular, the Argentine system is praised for its attempt to introduce elements of private market discipline as a central component of its regulatory regime.

Private market discipline is enhanced by the following policies: (a) A strictly limited safety net (comprised of a privately funded, limited deposit insurance scheme and restrictions on the Central Bank's potential lender-of-last resort powers) exposes bank depositors to the possibility of loss. (b) High and credible minimum risk-based capital requirements further ensure that stockholders (rather than taxpayers) bear the risk of bank default. (c) National government programs encourage the privatization of provincial government-owned banks. (d) A credit rating scheme has been introduced whereby each bank must solicit a credit rating from an internationally active rating agency. (e) A subordinated debt requirement mandates that banks must issue a subordinated liability for some 2 percent of deposits each year. (f) Banks must satisfy a liquidity requirement in addition to the capital requirement. This not only reduces portfolio risk, ensures systemic liquidity, and further reduces the potential for taxpayer loss from failed banks, but also (because of the structure of the requirement) rewards banks with lower regulatory cost when the market perceives that their risk of failure is low. (g) The Central Bank publishes basic information about bank loans to individuals and firms that borrow from banks (which enhances transparency of credit risk). (h) The quality of accounting data is enhanced by mandatory private audits conducted according to Central Bank guidelines, and auditors must post a forfeitable bond. (i) Argentina permits free entry and competition among foreign and domestic banks, which not only encourages the efficient management of banks but also enhances the ability of bank depositors to punish weak banks by moving their funds to stronger institutions.

The Argentine system's high marks from the World Bank also reflect the fact that the regulatory reforms put in place in the early and mid-1990s have been tested by external shocks. The banking authorities' reactions to those shocks have encouraged advocates of market discipline. Rather than retreat from the reform process in the face of the tequila crisis of 1994–95,

---

1. We note, however, that Chile has since revised and strengthened its capital requirements on banks.

Table 5.1   **World Bank Comparison of Bank Regulatory Quality in Developing Economies**

	Total Score	Capital Position	Loan Classification	Foreign Ownership (management)	Liquidity	Operating Environment	Transparency
Singapore	16	1	6	2	5	1	1
Argentina	21	1	4	3	4	7	2
Hong Kong	21	3	9	1	2	2	4
Chile	25	5	1	4	8	5	2
Brazil	30	7	3	4	3	8	5
Peru	35	5	2	6	1	11	10
Malaysia	41	5	9	8	8	3	8
Colombia	44	3	4	11	6	10	10
Korea	45	7	9	10	11	3	5
The Philippines	47	4	6	7	7	11	12
Thailand	52	7	12	12	8	6	7
Indonesia	52	7	8	9	12	8	8

Source: World Bank (1998, p. 54).

Notes: Numbers indicate rankings (lower numbers mean higher ranking). The total score is a simple average of the six categories.

the Argentine authorities redoubled their efforts to ensure that market discipline prevailed in the banking system. Indeed, many of the features of the current regulatory system just listed were enacted or strengthened after the tequila crisis as part of a new plan for bank oversight developed at the central bank, which is known as the BASIC system of bank regulation.

We define the key elements of that system, and explain its evolution, in section 5.2. These include the new liquidity requirement system (replacing a more traditional reserve requirement approach), capital requirements that reflect banks' trading risks and banking book interest rate risks, an expansion of the publicly available database on the condition of bank borrowers, and the minimum mandatory subordinated debt and credit rating requirement. The authorities have also negotiated a contingent liquidity facility with international banks in order to inject emergency liquidity on the basis of Argentine collateral in the case of a sharp, systemic liquidity shock (this facility currently stands at some $6.45 billion, excluding a $1 billion World Bank/Inter-American Development Bank [IDB] enhancement). Also over this period a significant amount of foreign capital entered the banking system such that, at the time of this writing, some 60 percent of private sector deposits are now in banks under foreign control, accounting for some 40 percent of the whole system. Only one large (top-eight) private retail bank that does not have a foreign controlling interest remains.

The only policy reaction to the 1995 crisis that could be construed as a weakening of the commitment to market discipline was the reestablishment of deposit insurance. The significance of this change for market discipline, however, should not be exaggerated. In November 1992 Argentina abolished its deposit insurance system. When the tequila crisis of 1994–95 hit, Argentina reestablished limited insurance for small deposits, but it did not retreat on its commitment to market reform by bailing out insolvent banks. Banks suffered large outflows of deposits during 1995 (see Banco Central de la República Argentina [BCRA] 1995 and D'Amato, Grubisic, and Powell 1997 for an analysis). Although some critics have pointed to government-assisted acquisitions of banks as a partial bailout of some institutions, it is important to emphasize that, as we describe in detail later, several banks were allowed to fail in the wake of the tequila crisis and that there have been subsequent failures too (see Anastasi et al. 1998). In some of these cases, depositors and other creditors suffered significant losses.

During the recent crises in Asia, Russia, and Brazil, Argentina suffered significant macroeconomic fallout, and thus bank deposit growth and credit growth have slowed and interest rates have risen, as shown in figure 5.1 (which plots deposit growth, the sovereign yield, and an index of economic activity). In contrast to some other emerging countries, however, the weakness of the banking sector has not itself been a source of macroeconomic problems, foreign exchange attack, or capital flight. Indeed, it is widely perceived that the banking sector as a whole has weathered these

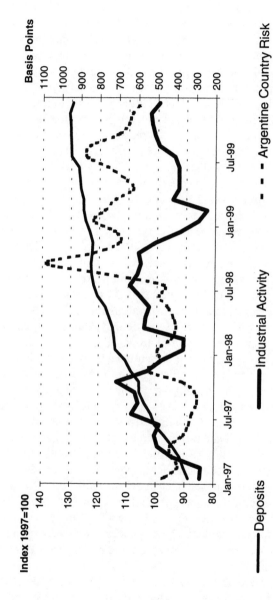

Fig. 5.1   Deposits, economic activity, and country risk

storms extremely well, even though some individual banks have been weakened. That record has added confidence in the credibility of regulation.

In large part, the apparent success of Argentina's banks reflects unique circumstances of history and the current political environment. In particular, Argentina's experience prior to the 1990s with inflation, financial repression, large bank rescues, and low quality in terms of banking services created widespread popular support for the continuation of the currency board as an inflation-fighting tool, a restricted safety net for banks, and tight fiscal discipline. These factors reduced the temptation to bail out financial institutions during the recent crises and also implied that the authorities could allow a significant increase of foreign capital in the sector without fear of any political or popular backlash. Indeed, one puzzle is that although the sector was opened significantly in 1992, and the rest of the economy received large injections of foreign capital between 1992 and 1996, it was only in the years 1997 and 1998 that the banking system saw a very significant increase in foreign capital. One hypothesis is that these international banks waited until the system was tested by its first major external shock before making such significant investment decisions.

Despite this record of apparent success, the reforms and transformation of the banking system have not gone without criticism. Some have suggested that the enactment of limited deposit insurance was unnecessary and counterproductive; that more institutions should have been allowed to fail; and that some assisted mergers, particularly during the tequila period, simply delayed a problem rather than solve it (see World Bank 1998). Other critics have suggested that Argentina's banking regulations are too tight (in particular capital, liquidity, and provisioning) and have diminished banking sector returns and placed the sector at a disadvantage with respect to foreign banks. Other criticisms refer to particular regulations. Some suggest, for example, that a regulatory authority should not establish requirements for the private rating of banks. Others suggest that the effectiveness of the obligation to issue subordinated debt, and therefore market discipline, has been reduced because the penalties for noncompliance have been lowered—a consequence of the perceived difficulties of issuing debt in the wake of the international financial crises of 1997 and 1998. Finally, it has been suggested that the entry of foreign banks may have a drawback; some perceive foreign banks as having more restricted lending practices than national banks and blame those lending policies for exacerbating the current recession.

In this paper we review the record of bank regulation and evaluate that record from the perspective of evidence on the existence of market discipline. We consider evidence on the question of whether and to what extent banks have been disciplined by the market. Section 5.2 provides an overview of the evolution of the regulatory environment from 1992 to the present as well as an evaluation of its consequences for the structure and performance of banks and their exposure to market discipline. Section 5.3 brings econometric evidence to bear on the extent to which market discipline penalizes risk and constrains bank behavior. Thus, in addition to evaluating the record of regulatory enforcement in the narrow legal sense, we also examine the economic evidence that market discipline exists, and that it has in fact achieved its desired goal of limiting bank risk taking.

Specifically, section 5.2 summarizes the experiences with privatization, foreign entry, consolidation, bank failure, and depositor loss. Section 5.3 focuses on differences in bank deposit interest rate risk premiums and in deposit growth, with an emphasis on the degree of diversity within the system with respect to these measures of market discipline. It then develops a framework for identifying links between fundamentals that affect bank default risk and market reactions to that risk (as seen through higher interest rates on deposits and lower deposit growth). Finally, we consider evidence on the effectiveness of market discipline in constraining bank risk taking. Section 5.4 concludes.

5.2   The Development of the Regulatory Framework, 1992–99

5.2.1   The Origins of Banking Reform

The economic turbulence of the late 1980s and the hyperinflations of 1989 and 1990 virtually destroyed the Argentine financial system. M3/GDP, which stood at almost 50 percent in the 1940s, declined over the following decades and then fell very sharply, reaching a mere 5 percent as of 1990. The fiscal reforms of 1989 and 1990 sowed the seeds of the end of inflationary financing in Argentina. However, as part of those reforms, the 1989 Bonex plan (which included replacing bank deposits with Bonex bonds trading at deep discounts) had a significant adverse impact on the financial system. A path to reform based on the seizure of private property housed in the banking system does not encourage rapid faith in the safety of bank deposits.

Nevertheless, since 1990 confidence gradually has returned, and deposits have grown strongly. M3 has risen and is now some 30 percent of GDP. Although this is still a low level for a country of Argentina's GDP per capita and level of development, this financial system growth has been rapid and reflects the transformation of a private banking system that has resumed its role of allocating credit to the private sector.

Macroeconomic stability returned with the imposition of the April 1991 currency board (enshrined in the Convertibility Law) and a very significant opening and further liberalization of the economy, including the banking system. The legal and regulatory environment in the financial system was further defined with a new (September 1992) Central Bank char-

Table 5.2	Main Regulatory Advances in Argentina, 1991–99
April 1991	Currency board adopted (backing of monetary base and ex rate 10,000:1, subsequently 1:1)
September 1992	New charter of the Central Bank
December 1992	Deposit insurance abolished
1992–94	Basel capital requirements adopted, raised to 11.5 percent at December 1994
1994–95	Provisioning requirements tightened
April 1995	Limited, fully funded, deposit insurance, $20,000 (subsequently $30,000)
August 1995	Liquidity requirements system (Raised to 20% of Deposits through 1997)
September 1996	Market risk capital requirements
1997–98	BASIC introduced (B for bonds, C for credit rating, etc.)
March 1999	Capital requirements for interest rate risk

ter. This established Central Bank independence (as in its 1936 creation), and recreated the banking superintendency as a semiautonomous unit within the Central Bank. The Central Bank has ten full-time directors (proposed by the executive and approved by the senate), including the president, vice-president, superintendent, and vice-superintendent of banking supervision. The Central Bank was given a significant degree of autonomy with respect to banking regulation and supervision (e.g., capital and other requirements can be changed by a simple decision of the board), but its role in monetary policy and lender-of-last-resort activities is severely restricted by the 1991 Convertibility Law and 1992 charter.

Table 5.2 lists the main regulatory changes over the period 1992–99. The period 1992–94 was one of strong economic growth and fast development of the financial system, albeit from a very small base. In this context the Central Bank worked to impose international capital, accounting, and provisioning standards, and to improve banking supervision. The financial system had lost virtually all deposits, and hence banks were very highly capitalized—implying that high capital standards were not too difficult to impose at that time. A minimum of 9.5 percent of assets at risk was the standard required as of the end of 1992, rising to 11.5 percent from 1 January 1995 (0.5 percent rises were effected every six months). On top of these requirements, Argentina also introduced a capital requirement for credit risk, which uses the interest rate charged on each loan as a signal of credit risk and requires that capital rise accordingly. Actual minimum capital requirements by the end of 1994 were then some 14 percent of assets at risk—well above the minimum capital requirements set by the Basel standards, or those required in other developing economies. Provisioning requirements were tightened significantly at the end of 1994 and throughout 1995.

Other improvements in banking supervision were underway well before the tequila crisis. In 1992 the Central Bank created a database of the main debtors of the financial system (for loans of more than $200,000). Argentina also maintained a system of high reserve requirements that were viewed explicitly at the time as a liquidity tool (i.e., both as a means of limiting asset risk and as a way of protecting the banking system from the risk of depositor flight). These nonremunerated reserve requirements were also thought of as a tax on banks. The required reserve ratios were set at high levels on sight deposits and at low levels on time deposits. That difference did not reflect underlying liquidity risk differences between time and demand deposits so much as the inelasticity of demand for sight deposits (i.e., the desire to avoid financial disintermediation in reaction to the taxation of banks). As we discuss later, time deposits actually displayed a greater withdrawal propensity during the crisis than did demand deposits.

The 1980s left Argentina with a very large number of small financial institutions, many of which disappeared in the 1990s. In the prereform period, these institutions had become government financing vehicles rather than a proper means of channeling credit to the productive sectors of the economy. With macroeconomic stability, low inflation, and liberalization, many such institutions—which lacked the skills to survive in the new environment—faced the daunting challenge of transforming themselves into bona fide competitive providers of credit. Many survived into the 1990s as they attempted to change their focus. According to one view of that transition period, the strong economic growth and sharp rises in Argentine asset prices in the period 1992–94 (at least until the change in direction of U.S. interest rate policy in February 1994), coupled with high levels of bank capital, gave a breathing space to many institutions as they attempted to adapt to the new circumstances. An alternative interpretation of this period of economic boom is that it allowed many institutions to survive despite underlying weaknesses that only became apparent in subsequent periods of stress.

Table 5.3 gives statistics on the number and type of financial institutions, as well as on the total size of the system, in Argentina over the 1990s. The table shows that there has been substantial restructuring in the Argentine financial system. From 1980 to 1992 over 250 institutions closed. While 210 of these were nonbank financial institutions, 48 were banks. Between 1992 and 1994 there was actually relatively little restructuring activity; and although a set of further nonbanks closed their doors, new banks opened as the system reoriented its focus. Also in this period the privatization process commenced with three entities privatized. There was then a second quite ferocious wave of restructuring activity through 1995 (the so-called tequila period), and to a lesser extent this process continued through 1999. From the end of 1994 to September 1999 over ninety institutions closed, including fifty-four banks and fourteen nonbanks. There were also a significant number of privatizations (eighteen). As these

Table 5.3   Structure of the Financial System

	1980	1992	1994	September 1999
No. of institutions	469	212	205	119
Private	179	131	135	81
Wholesale	n.a.	32	34	31
Retail	n.a.	99	101	50
Foreign-owned	27	31	31	48
Public	35	36	33	15
Nonbank	255	45	37	23
Total deposits[a]	55,020	26,002	42,278	74,693

Note: n.a. = not available.
[a] In millions of 1993 pesos.

privatizations were banks transferred to the private sector, the number of total bank closures (including both private and public banks) was seventy-two (fifty-four plus eighteen).

5.2.2   The Tequila Crisis

Despite the advances in regulation and supervision in 1992–94, the events of late 1994 (particularly after the 20 December Mexican devaluation) and early 1995 exposed weaknesses in many institutions. The tequila period was a very significant event for the financial system, and as such it is worth explaining the main events and regulatory response in some detail. After 20 December a dramatic fall in Argentine asset prices significantly affected the solvency ratios of several wholesale banks with relatively large government bond portfolios or other financial market exposures. At the same time, because these institutions had only a small amount of sight deposits, they had little in the way of liquidity reserves at the central bank. Several such institutions experienced a significant loss of deposits and hence a sharp liquidity crunch. Cooperative and some provincial banks also fared particularly badly, reflecting their low-quality loan portfolios. Nevertheless, although the financial system lost deposits in January and February, this period could not be described as a systemic panic; larger retail banks and large public banks gained deposits, and deposits denominated in dollars also rose overall (see BCRA 1995 and D'Amato, Grubisic, and Powell 1997 for more details). This phase of the shock was largely a flight to quality.

The Central Bank responded to these events in a number of ways. Within the Central Bank was an interesting debate about whether the problem being faced was a run on the currency, which might require a tightening of monetary conditions (i.e., a raising of reserve requirements), or alternatively a liquidity problem, which would require the opposite policy. In the wake of the monetary contraction and a deteriorating macroeconomic environment, it was soon realized that the greater problem was a potential banking sector liquidity crisis, rather than a run on the peso. Hence, reserve requirements were lowered.

The distribution of liquidity within the system was as significant a problem as its aggregate amount. Large retail banks had large reserves in the Central Bank and gained deposits, whereas wholesale banks had low reserves in the Central Bank and were losing deposits. A private liquidity sharing system was negotiated for the banking system. However, the amount of liquidity actually circulated via that mechanism was very restricted. Thus, the authorities also set up an obligatory system through an extra (2 percent) reserve requirement on certain banks, which was then distributed through the publicly owned Banco Nación. Finally the Central Bank extended repos and rediscounts to other affected institutions according to the rules laid down in the Central Bank's 1992 charter.

The end of February 1995 was a critical moment. The Central Bank was finding that the rules on providing rediscounts were very restrictive (being limited to thirty days and to never exceeding the regulatory capital of the borrowing bank), and on 27 February Congress approved a set of changes. These modifications included being able to extend rediscounts for longer periods and, under exceptional circumstances, for an amount exceeding the regulatory capital of the bank. Some interpreted these changes as a weakening of the Convertibility Law itself.

By February Argentina's fiscal position had deteriorated markedly, and there was no agreement yet in place with the International Monetary Fund (IMF). Argentina had missed an IMF fiscal target at the end of 1994, and the authorities had not agreed to a new program. Finally, the May 14th presidential election was looming, and it had been agreed that this election would be fought subject to new electoral rules (a ballotage system) that created new uncertainty. Opinion polls at the time put Carlos Menem in the lead but without enough votes to win comfortably in the first round, prompting speculation of potential second-round coalitions. The opposition parties at the time were not perceived as being strong supporters of the currency board system, nor the very deep liberalization measures that had been pursued.

Rumors abounded in this uncertain economic and political climate. These centered on the state of the banking system and individual banks and the state of the fiscal accounts. A persistent rumor was that the government was considering, as a way out of the crisis, "freezing" bank deposits, as had been done in 1989. The deposit runs that had affected mostly individual banks spread throughout the system, and in the first two weeks of March virtually all banks lost deposits. Indeed, in this two-week period roughly half of the total $8 billion that left the system fled the country.

This more systemic run was halted in the middle of March with the signing of a new agreement with the IMF and an international support package with money from the IMF, the World Bank, and the IDB. A private bond was also launched (known as the Patriotic Bond, with internal and external tranches—an early explicit example of "bailing in"). Part of these funds financed two fiduciary funds for the banking system: one to assist provinces in the privatization of provincial banks, and one to assist in the restructuring of the private banking system. Deposits fell slightly from the day after this agreement was signed until 14 May (the presidential election date). After Carlos Menem's victory in that election, and with much uncertainty thus resolved, deposits started to grow again, and the financial system recovered very quickly.

Despite the fact that the systemic run of March 1995 affected all the banks, depositors fled some banks more than others. Schumacher (1997), Dabós and Sosa-Escudero (2000), and Anastasi and colleagues (1998) all conclude that banks that failed or were forced to merge over this period were much weaker institutions. Each of these papers adopts a logit/probit methodology to explain bank failures as a function of banks' ex ante observable characteristics. Although each study is slightly different in the samples of banks used and the precise specification of the model, the main results are consistent across all the studies. Each study reports that in over 90 percent of the cases the model correctly predicts failure or survival. Thus, although both Type 1 and Type 2 errors are found, they are very small in number.

Anastasi and colleagues (1998) provide more extensive analysis of market discipline of banks using a larger sample of banks, a longer time series, and a more complete set of models than the other papers. In that paper logit estimates are presented as well as results for a survival analysis, where the predicted variable is the number of months a bank is expected to survive (after December 1994). This is estimated using data as of the end of 1994, and predictions are updated on a quarterly basis. A rather small subset of bank fundamentals are found to be significant explanatory variables, and these variables correctly predict over 90 percent of banks' survival experiences even when the set of predictors is constrained to the predicting variables as of December 1994. Little is added to predictive power when explanatory variables are updated quarterly.[2]

D'Amato, Grubisic, and Powell (1997) develop a slightly different approach. Here the authors examine whether the amount of deposits lost during the crisis, on a bank-by-bank basis, could be explained by bank fundamentals, macroeconomic factors, or contagion. Contagion is defined

2. As a caveat it is worth noting that if this model is reestimated over different sample periods, although similar prediction success can be obtained, other bank fundamentals are preferred. This indicates some potential instability in model specification, or an alternative explanation might be a very flat likelihood function with respect to the different model specifications. The superintendency is now employing the results of this analysis in its off-site work.

Table 5.4	The Tequila Crisis	
No. of institutions, December 1994		205
Institutions liquidated		12
No. of mergers		39
New institutions		4
No. of institutions, December 1995		158
Institutions suspended and then merged		2
Total deposits in liquidated institutions[a]		958
Estimated total loss of deposits[a]		477
Estimated total loss of other liabilities[a]		249

[a]In millions of pesos.

here as serially correlated losses across banks that could not be explained either by macroeconomic influences or by changes in individual bank characteristics. This interpretation of significant panel time effects (indicating significant residual correlation) as potential contagion may overstate true contagion, because it could also be accounted for by time-varying coefficients or omitted variables. Nevertheless, what is striking in this study is that even this potentially overstated measure of contagion was not the most important influence on deposit loss. When explicit contagion terms were added (e.g., the loss of deposits of other banks in the previous time period), additional time effects in the panel analysis became insignificant, indicating the importance of serial correlation of risk for the banking sector as a whole. However, fundamental macroeconomic factors remained significant in generating aggregate risk, and the majority of the explained variation in deposits was accounted for by bank fundamentals, indicating the importance of bank soundness in depositors' decisions.

Table 5.4 summarizes the effect of the tequila period on the financial system. Between December and May the system lost $8 billion, or 18 percent, of deposits, and the Central Bank lost some $5 billion, or 30 percent, of international reserves. Over this single year some fifty-one institutions were closed (twelve liquidated and thirty-nine merged), and two institutions were suspended and subsequently merged in 1996. The total deposits in liquidated institutions in 1995 amounted to $958 million, and of this depositors received roughly 50 percent of their investments, losing an estimated $477 million. In addition, other creditors (mainly bondholders) lost an estimated $249 million. This is a record of market discipline (i.e., actual depositor loss) that few countries have matched in recent decades. (Interestingly, Estonia in the early 1990s—a country also constrained by its commitment to a currency board—is the only other example of significant depositor loss of which we are aware.)

5.2.3   Challenges and Reforms after the Tequila Crisis

Argentina had abolished deposit insurance in the early 1990s and managed to weather the tequila storm without it. Nevertheless, there was a perception among some that the complete absence of deposit insurance was too extreme and that its absence may have contributed to the flight from the banking system. A limited deposit insurance scheme was introduced in May 1995 covering deposits of up to $20,000 and funded though premiums on banks calculated using a risk-based pricing formula. This insurance scheme was implemented through a government-sponsored enterprise—Seguro de Depósitos Sociedad Anónima (SEDESA)—that is separate from the Central Bank. The scheme has since been extended to cover deposits up to $30,000.

Originally, SEDESA was seen as a body that would simply pay out to depositors in the case of a bank liquidation. However, over time SEDESA's role and powers have been extended. SEDESA is now formally charged with a minimum cost resolution objective. Additionally, the charter of the Central Bank has been altered to allow the Central Bank to separate the assets and liabilities of a failing bank. In effect, this allows the Central Bank to create a "good" bank that can then be sold and a "residual bank" that can be wound up, thus avoiding the liquidation of the whole bank. The residual bank rests in a "trust" backed by bonds. These bonds are then bought by private investors, and bonds have also been bought with SEDESA's funds—consistent with the minimum cost resolution guidelines. In particular cases, for example when the Central Bank had previously given a rediscount to the bank, the Central Bank has also converted its liabilities into bonds backed by the residual bank trust. Other resources, administered through the government's Bank Capitalization Trust Fund, have also been used essentially to facilitate acquisitions by other banks.

These innovative mechanisms for resolving problem institutions have attracted significant attention. Critics (see World Bank 1998) have suggested that these policies have weakened market discipline. A further related concern highlighted in that report is that acquiring banks were not always of sufficiently high quality to ensure that the merged institution had a sustainable future; the World Bank suggested that acquiring banks should have A credit ratings or even higher. Due to these concerns, the Central Bank formed a committee including three outside experts to review its policies with respect to bank resolution; implementing the findings of that committee became a condition in a World Bank/IDB loan program. Torre (2000) provides a very useful review of these policies and the relevant trade-offs.

Thus far, it seems that little in the way of adverse consequences has resulted from the policies just mentioned, and these policies have produced the tangible benefit of a relatively fast resolution of problem institutions, at least in more recent cases. It is interesting to note that banks rated BB have shown a greater probability of being upgraded than downgraded, and that positive tendency is also reflected in the transition probability matrix of Capital, Assets, Management, Earnings, and Liquidity (CAMEL) ratings (see BCRA 1999). Moreover, although the law in Argentina places depositors in a very senior position and makes it difficult to discriminate between large and small depositors during a liquidation, depositors have lost money in two out of eighteen banks closed since 1995, and losses have been experienced commonly by other liability holders, enhancing market discipline. Finally, although the resolution process has in some cases involved the use of Central Bank funds, the Convertibility Law and the Central Bank charter continue to place strong limits on this activity and ensure that whatever public assistance there is in terms of bank resolution would have to be fiscal and hence transparent in nature. This characteristic of the Argentine financial system continues to provide strong incentives for prudent behavior, reflected in the banking sector's prudence through the recent recession.

Immediately after the tequila shock, beginning in August 1995, there was a very significant reform of the reserve requirement system. During the crisis it was found that sight deposits were more stable than time deposits and that banks with more time deposits had lost a greater fraction of their deposits and (because of the relatively low reserve requirement on time deposits) had less liquidity available to them in the Central Bank. It was decided to replace reserve requirements with a "liquidity requirement" acknowledging explicitly that these reserves were intended for "systemic liquidity protection." These new liquidity requirements were specified on virtually all liabilities (reserve requirements had been placed only on deposits) at rates that declined depending on the residual maturity of each liability and that were required irrespective of the type of liability (sight deposit, time deposit, bond, etc.). Finally, the liquidity requirements introduced were remunerated at rates approximately equal to short-term dollar interest rates, thus alleviating a substantial tax that had been placed on the financial system.

In recent years, the liquidity requirement has been further amended to permit the holding of balances in qualifying foreign banks to count toward as much as 80 percent of the requirement, and to permit the use of standbys from foreign banks as a substitute for deposits held abroad. These rules reflect the intent of the liquidity requirement—a means to insulate the banking system against the flight of deposits—and the recognition that for that purpose hard currency balances held abroad may be as good as or better than deposits held at the Central Bank. Furthermore, the flexibility afforded by the use of standbys provides a market reward to low-risk banks because those banks are able to obtain standbys at low cost from foreign banks.

Another lesson from the tequila crisis had been the importance of market risk as wholesale banks had maintained little regulatory capital against relatively large government bond positions. In 1996, Argentina became one of the first countries to implement an adapted version of the Basel market risk capital requirement amendment to the 1988 Accord. Argentina used the "standardized" approach (with simplified rules for offsetting positions reflecting the more limited Argentine bond market), but with higher risk weights calculated via a value-at-risk formula. The Central Bank publishes the volatilities used to calculate these risk weights on a monthly basis. Capital requirements were further augmented in March 1999 with a requirement to cover interest rate risk on the banking book.

The tequila experience underlined certain structural problems with respect to banking oversight, which encouraged new thinking about the benefits of involving markets in the regulatory process. First, although in large part standard statistics monitored by the superintendency do a fairly good job in predicting bank failure, some failures came as a surprise to the authorities. Among the reasons why banks failed but were not identified in advance as problem institutions is that there is a limit to what reported balance sheet and other statistics tell about a bank. Unsound practices and fraud are an important cause of bank failure, and one that is not likely to show itself in reported financial ratios. For example, off–balance sheet contracts (types of derivative operations) and even undeclared off-shore banks were uncovered in the analysis of some institutions that failed during the tequila crisis. That observation (along with the evidence that market deposit interest rates had been useful in forecasting bank failures during the crisis) led policy makers to consider the potential advantages of relying on market assessments as part of the regulatory process. In an emerging country context, in particular, where supervisory technology and resources are relatively constrained, in some cases the market knows more about the existence of derivatives and offshore transactions than does the superintendency.

Furthermore, there can also be differences between the powers and incentives of regulators and those of markets to discipline banks. The legal powers and the legal protection offered to supervisors who attempt to discipline banks are important issues in some emerging market countries. In Argentina, for example, legal protection of supervisors is weak (a point made in World Bank 1998), and the legal tradition does not give much scope for early Supervisory intervention if an institution is still formally complying with regulations. There is a possibility, therefore, that supervisors cannot close an institution or force remedial action even if they know that an institution is facing serious problems. In that case, the market—if

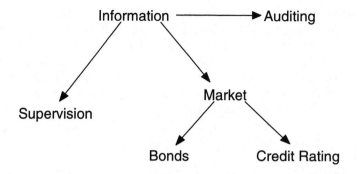

- Information: Disclosure rules on banks, Credit Bureau of the Central Bank.
- Auditing: Auditors supervised by Central Bank, subject to Financial Bonds and Disqualification.
- Supervision: Capital, liquidity and other regulations plus CAMELS system of bank assesment.
- Bonds: Obligation to issue 2% of deposits as subordinated liability each year.
- Credit-Rating: Each bank must obtain a credit-rating from an internationally active authorized rating agency (4 agencies authorized).

Fig. 5.2   BASIC system of bank regulation

it has the correct information—may be more willing and able to discipline weak institutions than are their supervisors (see Powell 1997 on this point).

5.2.4   The BASIC Approach to Bank Regulation

These kinds of considerations led the regulatory authorities in Argentina to develop what has become known in that country as BASIC banking oversight (see Powell 1997 and World Bank 1998 for further details). BASIC is an acronym that stands for Bonds, Auditing, Supervision, Information, and Credit Rating. The main idea behind BASIC is that both market and regulatory discipline are imperfect and that there are complementarities between the two. As we have argued, the superintendency and the market may have different information sets, incentives, and legal powers; hence the quality of monitoring can be improved if both are employed actively to monitor banks. Despite the appeal of the BASIC acronym, the more logical order to discuss the operation of the system is Information, Auditing, Supervision, Bonds, and Credit Rating. Figure 5.2 gives a schematic representation of the main policies under each heading.

Good information is a prerequisite to either market or regulatory discipline. The superintendency in Argentina publishes summarized bank balance sheets, principal regulatory ratios, performance ratios, and details of the nonperforming loans and provisions on a bank-by-bank basis. Moreover, the superintendency's credit bureau has been extended to cover virtually every loan in the financial system (all those above $50). The database includes the name of the borrower and a unique identification number (each person and each company in Argentina has a unique identification number issued by the National Registry and used for many purposes), the name of the bank extending the credit, the amount of the credit, the quality category of the loan (the Central Bank has defined a standard categorization system from 1 = normal to 5 = loss), and the details of any guarantees extended. This information is available free of charge on the Central Bank's website debtor by debtor (www.bcra.gov.ar). In other words, anyone can input the surname of a borrower or a company name and view instantly the total amount of debt that that individual or company has with the financial system and whether that debt is performing or not.

Measures are taken to ensure that the entire database cannot be downloaded. For example, if hundreds of searches are detected from the same source, further access is denied, essentially in an attempt to protect the identity of banks' good creditors from other banks (to ensure that banks can internalize the benefits of their own screening and monitoring investments). However, no measures are taken to protect the identity of individual borrowers. Moreover, the database, except credits of less than $200,000 in categories 1 and 2 (i.e., performing), is sold at very low cost to all interested parties. The main objectives of this policy are not only to promote transparency with respect to the borrowers of the Argentine financial system, but also to enhance the willingness to pay debts, given what is perceived as a weak legal system.[3] The database maintained by the superintendency has recently been expanded to include many more variables (e.g., basic financial ratios of borrowers and other information that would be relevant for determining the quality of the loan), and these data are also available for limited private use, although comprehensive current data are only available for unlimited private use for nonperforming borrowers.

The usefulness of information depends not only on its quantity and availability but also on its quality. The auditing process is vital to ensure the validity of the information published. In previous decades in Argentina auditing firms have been subject to harsh criticism. In response the Central Bank has set up a list of qualified bank auditors who must post a financial bond. In the event of a dispute, this bond may be forfeited, and the auditor may be struck from the authorized list. Additionally, the Central Bank lays down strict guidelines on minimum auditing requirements and supervises the auditing process.

3. The database also has great potential to analyze, for example, whether provisioning and capital requirements are adequate. Falkenheim and Powell (1999) use the database and a simple portfolio model of credit risk in this vein and conclude that in general provisioning and capital requirements are more than adequate in Argentina given loss probabilities (estimated on data for 1998 and 1999).

"Supervision" in BASIC actually refers to both supervision and regulation (and these activities are separated within the internal structure of the Central Bank). The superintendency has now adopted a version of the U.S. CAMELS system of bank rating. The banks' CAMELS ratings are then used in several regulations. In particular the CAMELS score affects capital requirements such that banks with poor CAMELS ratings face a higher requirement.[4]

"Bonds" refers to the requirement that banks in Argentina must issue a subordinated liability for some 2 percent of their deposits each year.[5] The idea behind this kind of regulation (as proposed by Calomiris 1997, 1999) is threefold. First, if banks are forced to attract institutional investors and to go to market to issue debt, that process reveals information about the bank to those debt holders and to supervisors. Supervisors may be able to use that information to discipline the bank. Second, sophisticated investors who hold a subordinated liability then have incentives to monitor the bank and are likely to be a constituency for conservatism within the bank because (like the deposit insurer) their claims are senior to equity. In contrast, equity holders in an insured bank that faces large losses may have incentive to increase risk to take advantage of the put option inherent in deposit insurance. Thus when equity capital is severely depleted, it is not a constituency for conservatism.[6] Third, if debts are traded publicly, then the secondary market prices reveal further information about the default risk of the bank over time. In the case of Argentina, where corporate debt markets are extremely thin, it was thought that the first two objectives would be more important.

The subordinated debt regulation has not performed as well as its advocates had hoped. The regulation was adopted in late 1996, to become effective January 1998. However, over this period the Asian crisis struck global capital markets, and Argentina was also affected (specifically, after the speculative attack on Hong Kong in October 1997). Subsequently, Ar-

---

4. Argentine capital requirements can be expressed as CR = $11.5*w*X*K$ + MR + IR, where CR is the Capital Requirement as a percentage of assets at risk, w is the average-bank Basel risk weight for counterparty risk, X is the average interest rate factor (as described in the text, the interest rate on each loan is used as an indicator of counterparty risk), K is the CAMELS factor, MR is the market risk capital requirement and IR is the interest rate risk (banking book) capital requirement.

5. In this paper we refer to the subordinated debt requirement. In fact, there are several ways to comply, including issuing a bond or holding a deposit/obtaining a loan from certain investors. These investors must be from outside Argentina (and subject to a minimum credit rating) or be local and have already satisfied the requirement. In the case of the bond issue, the bond is not necessarily subordinated to other bonds outstanding, although it is always subordinate to deposits. Meeting the stronger requirement allows subordinated debt to be considered as Tier 2 capital.

6. Bond holders can be depended upon to discipline banks in order to limit their risk taking as long as either (a) equity remains in the bank or, alternatively, (b) an upper limit is placed on the yield on any subordinated debt that counts toward the regulatory requirement (which it is not the case in Argentina, and which Calomiris 1997 argues is a weakness of the current law). For more details, see Shadow Financial Regulatory Committee (2000).

gentina's securities markets suffered further minor shocks as different countries in Asia were affected, then suffered considerably in August 1998 as the result of the Russian debt moratorium, and then was again shaken by the January 1999 Brazil devaluation. To summarize, from roughly October 1997 to mid-1999, the international financial crises made debt or equity issues (foreign or local) from any issuer (sovereign or corporate) difficult. The Central Bank reacted to this by putting back the compliance date for subordinated debt on several occasions, by extending somewhat the range of liabilities that banks could issue in satisfaction of the requirement, and by revising the penalties banks faced for noncompliance.

Currently the regulation remains in force, and banks have a wide range of liabilities that qualify as subordinated debt. Banks that fail to comply face higher capital and liquidity requirements. Banks with foreign parents may comply through their parent.

To investigate how the subordinated debt regulation has been working in practice, we analyze the characteristics of banks according to how they have reacted to this regulation. In particular, in table 5.5 we divide banks into two groups according to whether they have complied with the regulation and how they have complied. In the first group we place banks that either do not have to comply (an exception is made for foreign-owned banks subject to a minimum credit rating) or have complied by issuing a bond or obtaining a two-year deposit from a foreign bank. We call this the high-compliance group. In the second group we place banks that either have complied weakly by obtaining a two-year deposit from a local institution (a category that includes some banks that subsequently failed) or have not complied at all. We designate these low-compliance banks.

The identities of the banks in each of these categories are not a matter of public information. Some critics have argued that the failure to disclose that information weakens the power of subordinated debt to provide signals to the marketplace (i.e., if banks choosing not to comply are weaker, then revealing that information could facilitate market discipline of those banks). The decision not to reveal information about bank compliance reflected supervisors' concerns about creating false impressions of the relative health of banks during the turbulent period of 1998–99. In particular, banks that had issued required subordinated debt early (e.g., before the Asian crisis) did not face the same market challenges as those that had waited to issue debt, and regulators did not think that relative compliance always reflected relative strength. Nevertheless, that lack of confidence in the market's ability to draw proper inferences is somewhat at odds with the motivations for the law in the first place.

Table 5.5 compares various characteristics of these two groups to see if the banks that comply at a high level are the strongest banks (because one would expect that banks with lower default risk would have lower costs of meeting the rigors of market discipline). We report variables that capture

Table 5.5   **Subordinated Debt**

	1993:2–1994	1995	1996–99
Deposit interest rate (US$ deposits)[a]			
High Compliance			
Average	6.16	8.47	6.96
Std. Dev.	2.28	5.33	3.45
Low Compliance			
Average	6.99	9.98	7.93
Std. Dev.	3.18	7.16	2.76
Loan interest rate (US$ loans)[a]			
High Compliance			
Average	15.40	16.69	15.12
Std. Dev.	5.63	6.21	9.29
Low Compliance			
Average	19.02	20.70	17.41
Std. Dev.	10.94	11.80	9.70
Change in deposits[a]			
High Compliance			
Average	2.43	0.44	5.30
Std. Dev.	36.8	31.8	30.8
Low Compliance			
Average	3.58	−1.42	4.49
Std. Dev.	14.6	61.2	27.47
Capital ratio (capital integration)[a]			
High Compliance			
Average	15.97	17.85	15.70
Std. Dev.	10.85	13.98	12.14
Low Compliance			
Average	20.20	17.37	18.31
Std. Dev.	14.55	24.75	16.38
Nonperforming loans[a]			
High Compliance			
Average	13.29	16.24	14.16
Std. Dev.	16.04	16.50	12.91
Low Compliance			
Average	23.10	30.00	25.44
Std. Dev.	19.25	22.37	17.35
Loans/liquid assets			
High Compliance			
Average	6.37	6.92	4.16
Std. Dev.	7.52	6.36	4.06
Low Compliance			
Average	7.14	9.25	5.39
Std. Dev.	7.93	10.14	8.42
No. of observations			
High Compliance	177	237	922
Low Compliance	76	97	412

Note: Low Compliance means either the bank did not comply or the bank complied through a local subordinated insurance.

[a]In percentages.

elements of asset risk and liquidity, as well as market perceptions of the default risk on debt, and the capital ratio.

Default risk on debt is captured alternatively by the average interest cost on debt for the bank (which reflects a market risk premium) and by the growth rate of deposits. When banks' deposits are perceived as riskier, they have a harder time attracting deposits (for theory and empirical evidence on depositors' aversion to risky deposits, see Gorton and Pennacchi 1990, Calomiris and Kahn 1991, Calomiris and Mason 1997, and Calomiris and Wilson 1998).

Asset risk and liquidity differences are captured by (a) the ratio of loans to assets (which, ceteris paribus, indicates higher risk and lower liquidity), (b) the average interest rate on loans (which we view as an indicator of the riskiness of loans), and (c) the ratio of nonperforming loans to total loans (another indicator of the riskiness of loans). This way of defining elements of asset risk isolates three perspectives on asset risk: the proportion of risky assets (loans), the ex ante riskiness of loans, and the riskiness of loans based on actual performance.

Bank default risk reflects a combination of asset risk and leverage. The inverse of leverage (the capital ratio) is measured here using book values (the only available measure because virtually none of the banks have publicly traded stock). For the various measures of asset risk, default risk, and leverage, table 5.5 reports data retrospectively for various dates—that is, compliance is measured in 1998 and 1999, and data are reported for previous periods for the groups defined by their recent compliance.

The simple comparisons presented in table 5.5 indicate that banks that achieved the highest degree of compliance with the rule are relatively strong, as indicated by deposit growth and deposit interest rate differences (the exception is the lack of a difference in deposit growth rates in the prequila period, which predates the subordinated debt regulation by several years). Those differences are also reflected in differences in asset risk, as measured by loan interest rates, nonperforming loans, and loan-to-asset ratios. Capital ratios are higher for the banks that comply least with the law, which reflects a combination of their asset weakness (i.e., that risk-based capital standards are being enforced) as well as the penalty of a higher capital requirement imposed on banks that fail to comply with the rule.

Even though not all banks have complied fully with the subordinated debt rule and there is substantial room for improving the requirement (i.e., disclosing compliance and limiting more what qualifies as subordinated debt), we think the rule can be regarded as a partial success for three reasons: First, compliance patterns with the rule demonstrate the usefulness of market discipline. The fact that weak banks find it difficult to issue subordinated debt, but that strong banks find it easy, is encouraging to advocates of the rule who see it as a way to reward banks for gaining the confidence of the marketplace.

Second, banks that fail to comply outright are penalized in ways that reduce the gains that banks might otherwise obtain from failing to comply, and that protect against the dangerous moral-hazard problem of risk taking (so-called asset substitution) in distress states. By being forced to increase capital and liquidity, noncomplying banks are not encouraged to increase asset risk easily in the face of weakening in their loan quality, which protects the deposit insurer and the taxpayer from the risks of extreme loss attendant to the pursuit of "resurrection" strategies.

Third, the law makes clear to all parties that supervisors are aware of the failure to comply with subordinated debt, and this has the benefit of enhancing discipline over supervisors. When a weak bank with a long record of failure to comply with the subordinated debt rule fails, supervisors cannot claim to have been unaware of the bank's weakness, because the market was providing a clear signal of its lack of confidence in the bank. Although market yields on debt issues are one form of signal, the failure to issue subordinated debt is arguably an even stronger one because it indicates that banks would have a very difficult time attracting uninsured long-term debt. The presence of the subordinated debt rule thus eliminates ex post plausible deniability for supervisors—they cannot claim to have been ignorant about bank weakness if that weakness is known in the marketplace.

Finally, the C in BASIC refers to the credit rating requirement. The idea of this requirement is also to improve information regarding financial institutions. Whereas the subordinated debt requirement looks to institutional investors to provide discipline and information, the idea of a credit rating is to ensure that public information is available to less-sophisticated investors. As in the case of the subordinated debt rule, however, this regulatory requirement has not proved to be free of problems.

The Central Bank first required banks to obtain credit ratings and permitted the ratings to be produced by any of a set of authorized agencies, which included local and internationally active agencies (eight in all). However, the perception was that this regime was expensive and that the ratings were of varying quality. In other words, there was a perception that some agencies were giving higher ratings than others. Arguably this reflected the fact that local capital markets are still not highly developed; Argentina may currently lack a set of institutional investors capable of providing rating agencies incentives to be conservative.

The Central Bank initially responded to the problem of questionable ratings quality by issuing standardized guidelines for rating agencies to follow. This did not appear to solve the problem. Finally, the Central Bank asked banks to have only one rating (reducing the cost of the regime) but also restricted the authorized agencies to only internationally active ones. Currently there are four authorized rating agencies.[7] We show in table 5.6 an estimated transition probability matrix of ratings over the history of this regulation. The table illustrates the distribution of current and past ratings as well as the probability of obtaining a particular current rating given a particular previous rating. Table 5.6 shows that most banks enjoy fairly high private ratings. The vast majority of banks rated (89 out of 103) currently enjoy investment-grade ratings (BBB or higher), and 45 banks are rated AA or AAA. There have been significant changes in ratings for individual banks in both directions during 1998, three of which placed banks that had been rated BB, BBB, and A into the F category. The evidence of such dramatic, negative changes in ratings suggests that the ratings are a meaningful signal of quality.

5.2.5 Banking System Structure and Performance

There have also been extremely important structural changes in the Argentine financial system since the tequila crisis; these have been facilitated by the policies of permitting free entry and encouraging the privatization of public banks. First, the consolidation process begun in the early 1990s, and accelerated by the tequila crisis, has continued, as shown in tables 5.3 and 5.4. As mentioned earlier, some of these mergers were assisted through the use of the fiduciary fund set up during 1995 with funds from multilateral institutions and some through the use of funds from SEDESA (the deposit insurance agency). Moreover, there was also a strong tendency toward privatization in the banking sector, visible in table 5.7. Some seventeen of the twenty-four provincial banks that have been privatized were assisted through a fiduciary fund set up with the assistance of the multilaterals (see appendix).[8] Privatizations have occurred via a mixture of types of sales and have largely been to existing domestic banks or domestic investment groups. Two very large public banks remain in Argentina— Banco Nación, owned by the federal government, and Banco de la Provincia de Buenos Aires (the largest Argentine province in terms of GDP)— and efforts to privatize them have met significant political resistance. As of July 1999, these two banks represent some 27 percent of banking system deposits. Although former President Carlos Menem expressed his desire to privatize Banco Nación in his second term, this was not approved by congress. The ex-governor of the province of Buenos Aires (Eduardo Duhalde) and his successor (Carlos Ruckhauf) have not come out in favor of privatizing its important provincial bank at the time of this writing.

---

7. These agencies are, in alphabetical order, Duff and Phelps, Fitch-IBCA, Standard & Poor's, and Thompson Bankwatch.
8. There have also been a number of privatizations of municipal banks that we do not report here.

Table 5.6 Credit Rating Regulation (transition matrix)

Evaluations[a]	Evaluations in December 1998											
	AAA	AA	A	BBB	BB	B	CCC, CC, C, D	F	Not Available	Orderly Retirement	Revoked, Suspended	Total
AAA	23	1								1		25
AA	2	14										16
A		2	28	2				1	2		1	36
BBB			1	13	2			1	1	1	3	22
BB					5			1	2			8
B						3			1			4
CCC, CC, C, D												0
F								1			1	2
Not Available	2	1							4	8		15
Total	27	18	29	15	7	3	0	4	10	10	5	128

Note: In the cases in which the entity presented two evaluations, the worst one was considered.

[a] Evaluations in December 1997 and March 1998.

Table 5.7   **Bank Privatization in Argentina**

	Number of Institutions	Assets[a]		Deposits[a]	
		Before	After	Before	After
1992–94	3	1,128	321	562	498
1995–96	11	3,093	1,993	1,706	1,316
1997–99	4	1,442	1,078	1,004	793
Total	18	5,663	3,392	3,273	2,606

[a]Assets and deposits after and before privatization, in millions of pesos.

The other very significant structural change in the banking system has been the entry of foreign capital. During 1996–98 several significant transactions took place and resulted in the purchase of domestic banks by Spain's Banco Santander and Banco Bilbao Vizcaya, the United Kingdom's HSBC, and Canada's Bank of Nova Scotia (Scotia International), to name a few. Table 5.8 provides figures on specific transactions. Furthermore, Banco Itau from Brazil entered as a start-up and subsequently purchased a local bank. These entrants added to several existing foreign banks, including Citibank, Bank of Boston, ABM Amro, and Lloyds. Deposits in banks with a foreign controlling share now account for some 60 percent of private sector deposits and some 40 percent of total deposits. Foreign banks have heightened competition, and this is most visible in their strong advertising campaigns and, in some products, in their willingness to wage price wars.[9] Foreign competition has also allowed the introduction of new technology, probably more rapidly than otherwise would have occurred, and has assisted in creating a much more stable deposit base.

To a large extent, this entry of foreign capital in the banking sector is simply a reflection of what has happened in the Argentine economy more generally. In fact, the puzzle is really why this did not happen earlier, given that the sector was liberalized in 1992. As noted before, one hypothesis is that foreign investors were waiting to see that the new policy regime was fully tested before making significant investments. It is worth noting that investors in the financial system were unusually late in entering compared to investors in telephones, electricity, gas, water, railways, mining, and petrochemicals. That difference in timing suggests that potential bank investors had specific policy concerns that did not affect other sectors. In partic-

9. There has also been a tendency among some banks to offer bank accounts combined with lotteries, free computers, and other domestic appliances, and even airline tickets. These marketing campaigns may, of course, reflect an immature market rather than real competition. Still, we note that relative to international standards, banking services in Argentina tend to be expensive; bank administration costs tend to be high; nonperforming loans tend to be high; and bank profitability is low.

Table 5.8   **Entry of Foreign Capital**

	Local Bank	Purchasing Institution	Origin	Percent of Share Purchased
1 September 1996	Tornquist	O'Higgins-Central Hispano	Chile, Spain	100
1 December 1996	Francés del Río de la Plata	Banco Bilbao Vizcaya (BBV)	Spain	30
1 April 1997	Liniers Sudamericano	BT LA Holdings LLC.	U.S.A.	51
1 July 1997	Trasandino	Abinsa	Chile	51
1 July 1997	Crédito de Cuyo	Abinsa	Chile	67
1 July 1997	Banco Río de la Plata	Banco Santander de España	Spain	50
1 August 1997	Banco Roberts	Hong Kong Shangai Banking Corp.	U.K.	100
1 August 1997	Banco de Credito Argentino	Banco Francés del Río de la Plata (BBV)	Spain	28
1 November 1997	Los Tilos	Caja de Ahorros Prov. San Fernando	Spain	40
1 December 1997	Finvercon	Norwest-Finvercon	U.S.A.	100
1 December 1997	Quilmes	Scotia International	Canada	70
1 January 1998	B.I. Creditanstalt	Bank Austria	Austria	49
1 July 1998	Compañía Financiera Argentina	AIG Consumer Finance Group	U.S.A.	91
1 November 1998	Del Buen Ayre	Banco Itaú	Brazil	100
1 January 1999	Bisel	Caisse Nationale de Credit Agricole	France	36
1 May 1999	Entre Ríos	Bisel (Caisse Nationale de Credit Agricole)	France	82

ular, they may have wished to see proof that the government respected the independence of the Central Bank as a regulator and a monetary agency, and that the government would not appropriate resources from the banking sector during a period of stress—e.g., by freezing deposits, as had been done in 1990. According to that interpretation, after the tequila test these investors were more willing to come in.

Despite the dynamism in Argentine banking, bank profitability remains very low by international standards, which partly is a result of regulations that create incentives for banks to limit their risk and partly reflects the high operating costs of banks in Argentina. Table 5.9 gives a breakdown of the profitability of the Argentine banking system in the last three years for public banks, private banks, and the top ten private banks. Even in the top ten private banks, it can be seen that costs remain high (almost 6 percent of assets), and although service income is relatively high, loan-loss charges are also high (at around 2 percent of assets this year), reducing profits to less than 1 percent of assets. Private banks gradually are less profitable (0.5 percent of assets) with higher operating costs (6.4 percent of assets), and public banks show lower interest margin (3.5 percent of assets as opposed to 4.5 percent for the top ten private banks). Public bank profitability also remains low at 0.4 percent of assets.

The combination of low earnings and high recent acquisition prices is interesting. Projecting current levels of profits into the future would appear not to justify the prices paid for recent acquisitions. Thus, in order to explain these prices, one would have to assume a high forecasted growth rate for the financial system. If those growth forecasts do not materialize, it is possible that some foreign entrants may reassess their decisions to enter the Argentine market in the years to come (we note in passing the decision of Deutsche Bank to sell its Argentine retail business to Bank of Boston as an example of foreign exit). On the other hand, if high growth rates resume, the foreign acquisitions of the 1990s could prove quite successful.

What are the prospects for further improvement in the structure and performance of the Argentine banking industry, and what are the risks posed to the system from delaying those improvements? The World Bank (1998) report suggests that the problems of the remaining weak private institutions and the remaining public institutions are quite distinct, and that neither is a systemic threat or a cause for urgent concern. The World Bank (1998) suggests that the weaker private institutions—because of their relatively small size—pose no threat to the stability of the financial system more generally. The remaining public banks, it was argued, also present no threat to the system (because of their separateness from the private sector) but might well present significant fiscal cost if they were to be privatized today (presumably the authors had in mind a significant clean-up of the public banks' balance sheets).

Table 5.9   Breakdown of Banks Profitability (annualized, in percentage of net assets)

	Public Banks			Private Banks			Top Ten Private		
	1997	1998	1999[a]	1997	1998	1999[a]	1997	1998	1999[a]
Interest margin	3.9	3.9	3.5	3.9	4.7	4.6	4.0	4.5	4.5
Service income margin	2.8	2.8	2.5	3.6	3.3	3.1	3.4	3.1	2.9
Gains on securities	0.4	0.6	0.6	1.3	0.8	1.0	1.4	0.6	0.9
Operating costs	−5.5	−5.5	−4.9	−6.8	−6.6	−6.4	−6.3	−6.0	−5.8
Loan-loss charges	−2.8	−1.2	−1.3	−1.9	−1.8	−2.1	−1.8	−1.5	−2.1
Tax charges	−0.3	−0.3	−0.3	−0.5	−0.4	−0.4	−0.5	−0.4	−0.4
Income tax	−0.1	−0.1	−0.1	−0.4	−0.4	−0.4	−0.4	−0.3	−0.5
Other	2.6	0.3	0.4	1.5	1.0	1.2	1.7	1.0	1.2
Total profits	1.1	0.6	0.4	0.8	0.5	0.5	1.5	0.9	0.8

[a] Up to September 1999.

In the eyes of investors, the reforms in the financial system in the late 1990s appear to have produced a very clear positive result. From 1996 to 1998, the financial system grew very strongly, with deposits growing at a roughly 30 percent annualized rate. In the second half of 1998 and through 1999, however, Argentina fell into a recession due to the combination of external factors (high international lending spreads for emerging economies, sharp falls in commodity prices, a high value of the dollar, and a recession in Brazil) and internal factors (political uncertainty leading up to the October 1999 presidential election). That recession has taken its toll on the banking system. Although deposits have kept growing (at just over 10 percent for the year), credit to the private sector has grown very little over the last eighteen months, and interest rates have generally risen, depending on the subperiod analyzed. Nonperforming loans have also risen quite significantly, and thus profitability has suffered.

Although the past year has been a very difficult time in some sectors of the real economy, the banking sector has been very stable. Indeed, the fact that credit supply has tightened in the face of a recession and high loan losses is precisely what one would expect from a banking system subject to market discipline. In that sense, tight credit supply is a sign of the financial system's strength (Calomiris and Wilson 1998).[10] There has been no capital flight from the banking system whatsoever and no capital flight from the country (reserves, in fact, have risen). Thus, the financial system, which had always been an Achilles' heel for Argentina, has recently contributed to the long-run credibility of fiscal, monetary, and regulatory policy, and thus despite the tightness of credit has contributed to macroeconomic stability.

As table 5.10 shows, the reaction by Argentine bank depositors to the recent period of emerging market upheaval (as measured by deposit growth) is strikingly different from the tequila period, even though the recent upheaval (in Brazil) has had larger fundamental consequences for the Argentine economy than did the collapse of the Mexican peso in 1994–95. Not only have deposit growth and international reserves growth remained strong, but interest rates as well have not risen by nearly as much as they did during the tequila period.

---

10. Some observers argue that market discipline is undesirable because it reduces the supply of credit during downturns and thus exacerbates recessions. We see that effect as unavoidable, and attempts to mitigate market discipline with regulatory forbearance as counterproductive. When regulators forbear—in order to permit banks to undertake greater risk than the market would permit—some (especially insolvent) banks will abuse forbearance by undertaking enormous risk as part of a resurrection strategy. These bets (e.g., in foreign exchange markets) often have large negative expected returns and produce enormous losses to taxpayers. Indeed, the credit contraction attendant to a banking collapse, and the fiscal costs of financing those bailouts—both of which are apparent in Mexico recently—can produce a much worse cyclical drag on the economy than can market discipline on banks. For further discussion of these macroeconomic costs, see Caprio and Klingebiel (1996).

Table 5.10   **Comparison of Two Crises**

	Tequila	October 1997 to February 1999
Deposits growth	−18%	19%
Reserves growth	−30%	14%
Maximum rise in interest rates[a]	12.1	7.9

[a]Percentage points increase.

5.3 Is Market Discipline Real? Microeconomic Evidence

In this section we take a more formal look at the evidence that market discipline operates on Argentine banks. We define market discipline as reactions of private debt holders to bank actions such that the bank is penalized for increasing the default risk on its debt, either by a higher risk premium on debt, or by the withdrawal of debt.

There is now a large empirical literature summarizing evidence on the existence of market discipline in banking in a variety of contexts. In the United States, that literature focuses on the usefulness of certificate of deposit yields for predicting bank problems (Baer and Brewer 1986; Berger, Davies, and Flannery 1998; Flannery 1998; Jagtiani, Kaufman, and Lemieux 1999; Morgan and Stiroh 1999), whereas in developing countries the empirical focus is on the predictability of deposit interest rates and the contraction of deposits (Peria and Schmukler 1999). Calomiris and Mason (1997) and Calomiris and Wilson (1998) show that during the interwar period in the United States weak banks (measured either by their probability of failure or by their implied risk of default on debt from an asset-pricing model) were forced to pay higher interest and suffered larger deposit outflows than did other banks.

As we mentioned earlier, several studies of the recent Argentine experience have linked ex ante bank risk with ex ante interest charges and deposit outflows, and ex post bank failure (Schumacher 1997; Dabós and Sosa-Escudero 2000; Anastasi et al. 1998; D'Amato, Grubisic, and Powell 1997). Banks with high deposit interest rates and high observable asset risk were more likely to fail during the tequila crisis and afterward, and lost a greater proportion of deposits than other banks. Thus there is already substantial evidence of the operation of market discipline within the Argentine banking system.

Our approach to measuring market discipline focuses on links between observable characteristics of banks (related to asset risk and leverage) and market reactions to those characteristics as captured in market pricing of deposit risk and contractions in the volume of deposits. A banking system in which market discipline is an important constraining force on bank risk taking should display three characteristics. First, market measures of, and reactions to, deposit default risk should vary across banks. In a banking system in which depositors do not distinguish among banks, market discipline is unlikely to exist. Second, differences in deposit interest rates and deposit growth across banks should reflect differences in bank asset risk and leverage, which, according to economic theory, should be the sources of deposit default risk.

Third, depositor discipline should constrain default risk on deposits. Recent models of banking that emphasize either the liquidity services of bank deposits (as in Gorton and Pennacchi 1990) or delegated monitoring of bank borrowers (as in Calomiris and Kahn 1991) emphasize that depositors do not simply price default risk, but also act to limit it. That is, bank depositors are not only risk-averse, but also risk-intolerant (Calomiris and Wilson 1998). As the level of default risk on deposits increases, deposits become less liquid, and the agency problems inherent in delegated monitoring become magnified. Both of these problems lead to a type of quantity rationing in which depositors withdraw their deposits from risky banks, which acts as a source of discipline over bank risk taking. These arguments imply that increases in default risk caused by adverse shocks to bank asset risk and capital should be mean reverting. Banks that suffer those shocks face a strong incentive to reduce asset risk or increase capital to avoid disciplinary withdrawals of funds by depositors.

Our discussion of microeconomic evidence has three parts. First, we begin by summarizing the evidence on the extent of cross-sectional heterogeneity in the banking system, paying special attention to the heterogeneity in deposit interest rates and flows (our measures of market discipline) during different subperiods. Second, we test a model that relates these two market discipline measures to bank leverage and asset risk measures. That is, according to finance theory (e.g., the Black-Scholes model) default risk should be an increasing function both of asset risk and leverage. In light of that theory, we test to see whether our panel dataset displays observable links that confirm the presence of market discipline in bank debt markets. Third, if depositors are risk-intolerant, then increases in deposit interest rates in response to increased risk should be reversed over time as banks are forced to reduce asset risk and leverage to meet depositors' preferences for low risk. As a first step to testing that theory, we provide some simple tests of mean reversion in deposit interest rates.

5.3.1   Market Discipline and Bank Heterogeneity

Tables 5.11–5.14 provide summary statistics for our measures of asset risk, default risk, leverage, and deposit growth. These are provided for separate subperiods and for different sets of financial institutions. Interest rates on loans and deposits are measured in these tables as premiums over the rates of a benchmark, low-interest rate group of foreign retail banks in order to facilitate a comparison of spreads across subperiods. Our measure

Table 5.11   Pre-Tequila Banking System Heterogeneity, 1994:2–1994:4

Variables	All Institutions			Private Domestic Retail			Private Domestic Wholesale			Foreign Retail			Foreign Wholesale		
	Avg.	Med.	Std.	Avg.	Med.	Std.	Avg.	Med.	Std.	Avg.	Med.	Std.	Avg.	Med.	Std.
Id – avg. Idf	2.21	2.39	2.77	2.42	2.52	1.73	1.51	1.57	2.02	—	—	—	3.02	1.4	4.89
Il – avg. Ilf	5.15	4.38	7.21	4.54	4.6	3.65	2.3	1.21	5.32	—	—	—	0.51	-0.5	6.57
Npl/loans	14.22	9.96	13.74	11.43	9.89	6.71	5.68	4.61	7.95	8.08	8.24	4.0	11.36	5.92	14.05
Loans/assets	69.37	72.74	28.69	70.78	72.78	11.08	43.15	42.56	21.19	70.41	72.51	10.29	46.34	49.58	26.47
Capital/assets	16.98	13.47	12.09	14.06	12.39	6.45	16.65	10.73	21.98	13.43	12.28	4.18	24.97	24.31	13.99
Deposit growth, 1994:2–1994:4	3.69	3.34	17.24	4.18	3.39	9.58	5.29	3.41	20.04	2.46	5.68	16.14	4.15	1.67	40.88
No. of observations	497			124			44			36			36		

Variables	Provincial Public			National Public			Finance Companies			Cooperative		
	Avg.	Med.	Std.	Avg.	Med.	Std.	Avg.	Med.	Std.	Avg.	Med.	Std.
Id – avg. Idf	0.57	0.41	2.76	0.08	-0.16	0.51	3.22	3.74	2.84	3.5	3.3	2.27
Il – avg. Ilf	4.82	3.0	10.41	8.28	6.39	8.42	10.28	9.92	9.36	6.54	6.78	3.77
Npl/loans	34.06	29.21	21.27	17.93	13.94	9.58	10.96	9.34	6.99	12.35	10.49	6.49
Loans/assets	90.33	78.12	54.62	76.33	79.04	12.49	71.63	78.26	20.88	74.31	74.96	7.66
Capital/assets	13.46	12.37	11.69	11.1	10.35	1.64	23.45	19.73	13.57	17.08	15.09	7.93
Deposit growth, 1994:2–1994:4	2.08	0.96	10.36	-0.11	0.53	5.46	3.3	3.06	23.25	4.53	4.37	7.1
No. of observations	75			9			70			103		

Notes: Id is deposit interest rate. Idf is deposit interest rate for foreign retail banks. Il is loan interest rate. Ilf is loan interest rate for foreign retail banks. Interest rates are expressed in dollar units.

Table 5.12   Tequila Crisis Banking System Heterogeneity, 1995:1–1995:4

Variables	All Institutions			Private Domestic Retail			Private Domestic Wholesale			Foreign Retail			Foreign Wholesale		
	Avg.	Med.	Std.	Avg.	Med.	Std.	Avg.	Med.	Std.	Avg.	Med.	Std.	Avg.	Med.	Std.
Id − avg. Idf	2.8	2.0	6.38	3.91	3.01	6.26	2.88	2.4	5.04	—	—	—	2.78	−0.35	12.29
Il − avg. Ilf	3.9	2.6	7.69	3.77	3.14	4.27	4.23	2.5	7.03	—	—	—	1.7	−0.54	9.34
Npl/loans	20.61	16.18	17.75	18.95	16.58	13.58	11.21	7.04	11.33	9.41	8.84	4.57	9.05	2.86	1.34
Loans/assets	69.21	73	30.95	71.7	74.84	15.24	47.48	46.88	24.98	71.15	71.8	8.33	43.84	40.78	27.04
Capital/assets	18.54	14.78	17.12	16.03	13.47	9.61	24.95	19.42	18.54	13.71	12.31	4.8	27.59	22.86	18.0
No. of observations	536			152			61			47			58		
Deposit growth, 1994:4–1995:4	−2.25	0.34	26.65	−1.46	1.07	21.11	−3.8	−2.2	38.71	2.24	4.48	15.66	5.25	4.97	44.39
No. of observations	593			160			70			56			65		

	Provincial Public			National Public			Finance Companies			Cooperative		
	Avg.	Med.	Std.	Avg.	Med.	Std.	Avg.	Med.	Std.	Avg.	Med.	Std.
Id − avg. Idf	0.02	−0.32	3.85	−0.08	−0.05	2.57	5.88	4.78	6.76	4.02	3.64	3.0
Il − avg. Ilf	3.48	0.5	13.7	3.65	2.52	6.39	6.43	6.31	6.3	5.07	5.46	3.89
Npl/loans	43.63	40.37	22.62	23.37	17.96	9.16	22.01	18.17	12.05	19.27	17.87	8.93
Loans/assets	89.86	83.48	54.5	73.18	74.71	9.75	69.16	75.57	24.83	76.75	77.51	8.42
Capital/assets	9.66	10.49	24.51	17.89	9.67	23.27	25.5	22.8	18.69	20.14	18.65	9.6
No. of observations	84			18			53			63		
Deposit growth, 1994:4–1995:4	−4.1	−2.58	13.07	0.1	1.99	8.15	−12.96	−7.4	30.4	−1.52	0.07	18.7
No. of observations	108			17			61			56		

Notes: Id is deposit interest rate. Idf is deposit interest rate for foreign retail banks. Il is loan interest rate. Ilf is loan interest rate for foreign retail banks. Interest rates are expressed in dollar units.

Table 5.13 **Immediate Post-Tequila Banking System Heterogeneity, 1996:1–1997:2**

Variables	All Institutions			Private Domestic Retail			Private Domestic Wholesale			Foreign Retail			Foreign Wholesale		
	Avg.	Med.	Std.	Avg.	Med.	Std.	Avg.	Med.	Std.	Avg.	Med.	Std.	Avg.	Med.	Std.
Id − avg. Idf	1.82	1.65	5.13	1.92	1.98	4.04	2.76	2.58	2.84	—	—	—	0.79	0.86	6.73
Il − avg. Ilf	4.67	3.29	7.09	4.87	3.51	7.25	4.73	3.41	6.78	—	—	—	2.52	0.49	7.76
Npl/loans	20.54	16.57	17.43	22.15	18.53	16.25	16.33	11.38	16.62	10.24	9.71	6.45	11.51	5.28	14.74
Loans/assets	60.10	62.55	20.73	59.74	60.82	18.04	55.61	59.23	18.25	58.22	62.77	16.66	44.10	41.73	26.27
Capital/assets	17.11	12.89	15.41	12.54	11.43	11.64	18.35	15.06	13.57	12.42	11.47	4.56	28.26	18.96	20.71
No. of observations	649			181			52			115			72		
Deposit growth, 1995:4–1997:2	7.05	5.94	22.62	6.75	6.40	16.44	11.95	8.51	24.47	7.51	6.02	9.97	9.73	6.06	36.45
No. of observations	854			286			89			77			100		

Variables	Provincial Public			National Public			Finance Companies			Cooperative		
	Avg.	Med.	Std.	Avg.	Med.	Std.	Avg.	Med.	Std.	Avg.	Med.	Std.
Id − avg. Idf	0.28	0.84	5.17	0.03	0.04	0.54	4.04	4.60	7.92	2.66	2.74	1.56
Il − avg. Ilf	3.21	1.39	8.36	5.95	7.41	3.93	8.60	8.06	7.53	6.34	6.39	3.01
Npl/loans	45.13	44.55	22.58	20.10	20.11	2.31	19.80	15.73	11.25	22.48	21.50	8.86
Loans/assets	69.79	62.83	27.06	63.11	62.69	6.35	68.22	69.00	18.25	62.21	63.18	6.99
Capital/assets	11.87	8.77	20.25	9.22	7.97	2.78	26.47	20.73	16.43	17.91	14.63	9.15
No. of observations	72			16			103			38		
Deposit growth, 1995:4–1997:2	2.48	4.06	28.69	4.68	3.44	10.34	5.74	6.02	23.33	8.57	7.51	8.86
No. of observations	114			23			116			49		

Notes: Id is deposit interest rate. Idf is deposit interest rate for foreign retail banks. Il is loan interest rate. Ilf is loan interest rate for foreign retail banks. Interest rates are expressed in dollar units.

Table 5.14   Post-Asian Crisis Banking System Heterogeneity, 1997:3–1999:1

Variables	All Institutions			Private Domestic Retail			Private Domestic Wholesale			Foreign Retail			Foreign Wholesale		
	Avg.	Med.	Std.	Avg.	Med.	Std.	Avg.	Med.	Std.	Avg.	Med.	Std.	Avg.	Med.	Std.
Id − avg. Idf	1.47	0.97	3.48	1.14	1.08	2.01	2.18	1.98	2.00	—	—	—	1.55	−0.05	6.41
Il − avg. Ilf	4.09	2.26	7.02	4.77	3.44	6.44	2.70	1.90	5.99	—	—	—	1.33	0.01	5.36
Npl/loans	17.5	13.85	15.48	9.00	14.31	10.20	19.39	9.57	10.26	9.69	8.68	6.76	7.99	3.54	12.24
Loans/assets	55.53	58.11	21.17	54.25	57.44	14.80	61.33	60.54	14.73	51.89	54.85	15.42	36.47	29.32	26.77
Capital/assets	16.86	12.10	13.84	12.98	11.23	7.16	18.27	17.64	7.14	11.14	10.16	4.67	25.27	12.74	24.27
No. of observations	811			227			61			161			94		
Deposit growth, 1997:3–1999:1	2.46	1.82	17.73	1.78	1.10	12.45	0.16	−0.71	19.36	4.68	4.15	12.35	4.75	3.90	30.16
No. of observations	722			201			59			159			90		

Variables	Provincial Public			National Public			Finance Companies			Cooperative		
	Avg.	Med.	Std.	Avg.	Med.	Std.	Avg.	Med.	Std.	Avg.	Med.	Std.
Id − avg. Idf	0.77	0.72	2.65	−0.94	−0.39	1.22	3.65	3.35	4.63	1.71	1.81	1.61
Il − avg. Ilf	2.29	1.45	6.56	5.68	0.55	9.64	8.2	7.64	9.19	3.39	3.67	3.45
Npl/loans	41.97	43.38	21.42	21.45	21.18	2.88	20.47	16.96	12.83	23.64	23.04	8.11
Loans/assets	55.24	55.34	17.89	58.87	59.29	10.55	71.15	67.05	17.79	59.11	61.12	5.35
Capital/assets	10.34	9.49	11.38	8.00	7.98	1.51	26.62	23.92	14.40	18.15	14.35	8.4
No. of observations	68			21			140			39		
Deposit growth, 1997:3–1999:1	0.69	1.12	10.50	3.74	3.64	4.48	1.42	0.70	22.44	1.02	2.45	7.75
No. of observations	68			21			146			28		

Notes: Id is deposit interest rate. Idf is deposit interest rate for foreign retail banks. Il is loan interest rate. Ilf is loan interest rate for foreign retail banks. Interest rates are expressed in dollar units.

of deposit interest rates uses interest rates on dollar-denominated deposits to avoid problems from mixing peso-denominated and dollar-denominated debts. Dollar deposits consistently earn lower interest because the peso trades at a forward discount.

The main usefulness of these tables is to (a) indicate the extent of heterogeneity in the reactions of markets to banks (deposit growth and deposit interest rates); (b) describe the average changes over time in measures of asset risk, leverage, deposit growth, and deposit risk premiums; and (c) explore links over time between average bank asset risk and leverage, on the one hand, and average deposit growth and default risk premiums on debt, on the other. A perusal of these tables clearly indicates the pronounced heterogeneity in deposit interest rates and deposit growth, the variation in average performance over time (reflecting the tumult of the 1990s), and the correspondence among measures of asset risk, leverage, deposit interest rates, and deposit growth. We return to those connections among asset risk, leverage, and market discipline in our regression analysis later.

These tables also provide some evidence on how links among asset risk, leverage, and market discipline differ across types of institutions. For example, to the extent that public banks are protected from the risk of insolvency by their sponsoring governments, depositors in those public banks may not penalize asset risk and leverage as much. If that were true, then public bank weakness would not be as evident in deposit interest rate premiums or in lower deposit growth. The tables lend some support for that view. Note, for example, that during the tequila crisis (table 5.12), nonperforming loan ratios for public banks were very high, but deposit interest rates remained very low.

5.3.2   Fundamental Determinants of Market Assessments of Bank Liability Risk

Next, we turn to a regression analysis of market discipline as a reaction to deposit risk, as measured by either the interest rate on deposits or the outflow of deposits. The basic model regresses either of these two dependent variables on our three measures of asset risk (loans/other assets, nonperforming loans/loans, and the loan interest rate), a measure of the liquidity of nonloan assets (cash/government bonds), and the (book) capital ratio. We used lagged capital ratios to avoid correlation by construction between deposit growth and the capital ratio. Other independent variables are taken as exogenous within the quarter in which deposit growth or deposit interest rates are set.

We report a variety of regression specifications, including ordinary least squares (OLS), fixed firm and time effects, and random effects. We ran the regressions for different time periods and for different samples (sometimes including all banks, sometimes confining the sample to private commercial

Table 5.15   Panel Regression Analysis of Bank Deposit Growth Rates, Sample
                  Restricted to Private Commercial Banks (quarterly observations,
                  1993:3–1999:1)

Variables	OLS (1)	Fixed Firm/Time Effects (2)	Random Effects (3)
Constant	0.018	0.018	0.042
	(0.019)	(0.031)	(0.027)
Lagged capital ratio	0.296	0.326	0.277
	(0.064)	(0.087)	(0.074)
Loan interest rate	−0.418	−0.190	−0.254
	(0.106)	(0.153)	(0.121)
Loans/other assets	−0.0047	−0.0028	−0.0032
	(0.0006)	(0.0008)	(0.0007)
Cash/government bonds	0.0000	0.0000	−0.0000
	(0.0002)	(0.0002)	(0.0002)
Nonperforming loans/loans	−0.059	0.025	−0.060
	(0.051)	(0.079)	(0.060)
Adjusted R^2	0.082	0.325	
p-value for Hausman Test			0.309[a]
No. of observations	1,138	1,138	1,138

Note: Numbers in parentheses are standard errors.

[a] The restrictions of the random-effects model are not rejected, implying that the random-effects estimator is preferred.

banks). Our results were generally robust to alternative specifications, although results were stronger when we restricted our sample to private commercial banks. The restrictions imposed by random effects (the orthogonality of regressors with firm and time effects) passed Hausman's test in some cases, and in those cases, random-effects estimation is more efficient. In tables 5.15 and 5.16 we report a subset of our results for the deposit growth and deposit interest rate regressions. Specifically, we report OLS, fixed effects, and random effects specifications for the restricted sample of private commercial banks for the entire period.

Both deposit growth and deposit interest rates reflect fundamental cross-sectional differences in our measures of asset risk. Higher asset risk and leverage are associated with depositor discipline in the form of greater deposit withdrawals, and high asset risk is also reflected in higher interest rates on deposits.

Not all measures of asset risk have the predicted impacts on interest rates and deposit growth in the regressions. The loan interest rate and loan ratio enter significantly and with the right sign in all regressions, whereas nonperforming loans and the ratio of cash to government bonds are either insignificant, or (in the case of the nonperforming loans) switch signs across specifications.

Interestingly, the effect of the capital ratio is of the expected sign for deposit growth (positive); but contrary to our expectation, it is also positive (sometimes insignificantly) for the deposit interest rate. One way to explain the differences in the capital ratio effect between tables 5.15 and 5.16 is to recall that capital ratios are an endogenous variable chosen by the bank. Even though the capital ratio is lagged (to mitigate the endogeneity problem) it is possible that banks anticipate interest rate changes in their deposits one quarter ahead and alter capital ratios to compensate for anticipated increases in default risk.

5.3.3   Does Market Discipline Encourage Prudent Risk Management?

The regressions reported in tables 5.15 and 5.16 do not describe banks' dynamic responses to market discipline. For example, the regressions do not examine whether increases in default risk on debt produce reductions in loan-to-asset ratios, or loan risk, or increases in the ratio of cash to bonds. To accomplish this result, one would have to specify a dynamic system of equations (possibly, a panel vector autoregressive [VAR] model), which requires strong assumptions about the relative endogeneity, and the adjustment frequencies, of our various measures of asset risk, deposit risk, deposit growth, and capital accumulation. We have already argued that

Table 5.16   **Panel Regression Analysis of Bank Deposit Interest Rates, Sample Restricted to Private Commercial Banks (quarterly observations, 1993:3–1999:1)**

Variables	OLS (1)	Fixed Firm/Time Effects (2)	Random Effects (3)
Constant	0.036	0.060	0.058
	(0.002)	(0.003)	(0.004)
Lagged capital ratio	0.035	0.009	0.019
	(0.008)	(0.009)	(0.008)
Loan interest rate	0.142	0.086	0.101
	(0.013)	(0.015)	(0.014)
Loans/other assets	0.00085	0.00034	0.00046
	(0.00007)	(0.00008)	(0.00007)
Cash/government bonds	−0.00002	0.00000	−0.00000
	(0.00003)	(0.00002)	(0.00002)
Nonperforming loans/loans	0.038	−0.0205	−0.007
	(0.006)	(0.0079)	(0.007)
Adjusted R^2	0.269	0.638	
p-value for Hausman Test			0.000[a]
No. of observations	1,138	1,138	1,138

Note: Numbers in parentheses are standard errors.

[a]The restrictions of the random-effects model are rejected, implying that the fixed-effects estimator is preferred.

Table 5.17   **Fixed-Effects Regressions: Deposit Interest Rate Mean Reversion (dependent variable: change in deposit interest rate)**

	1993:3–1994:4 (1)	1995:1–1996:2 (2)	1996:3–1997:4 (3)	1997:4–1999:1 (4)
$r_{i,\,t-1}$	−1.04	−1.06	−1.04	−1.29
	(0.04)	(0.04)	(0.03)	(0.04)
Adjusted R^2	0.475	0.450	0.545	0.577
No. of observations	989	791	762	688

Notes: Data are from quarterly observations of all financial institutions, 1993:3–1991:1. All regressions include fixed firm and time effects, which are not reported here. $r_{i,\,t-1}$ is defined as the lagged deposit interest rate for each bank. Numbers in parentheses are standard errors.

this is treacherous ground; for example, our initial assumption about the exogeneity of capital ratios to interest rate changes is suspect (especially given our findings of a positive partial correlation between deposit interest rates and capital ratios in table 5.16).

Although we think a panel VAR approach to this problem may be promising in future research, here we pursue a simpler approach. We examine whether there is a tendency for individual banks' deposit interest rates to revert to their mean, and whether the speed of mean reversion has changed over time. If depositor discipline forces banks to react to increases in their debt default risk, then high levels of default risk should prompt reductions in interest rates in the future. We test that proposition using a simple model of the time series properties of individual banks' interest rates, and we report our results in table 5.17.

The fixed effects approach to examining mean reversion holds firm and time effects constant and constrains all banks to react similarly to changes in their deposit interest rates. Alternatively, we also estimated the relationship using a random-coefficients approach, which takes advantage of the opportunity to see whether banks differ in the extent to which their deposit interest rates revert to the mean. As the results for these two models were quite similar, we only report the fixed-effects results in table 5.17.

As we discussed at length earlier, regulatory and supervisory monitoring and discipline have improved markedly in Argentina over the period 1992–99. In table 5.17, we investigate whether the speed of mean reversion has increased over time. Specifically, we report results for several subperiods (1993:3 to 1994:4, 1995:1 to 1996:2, 1996:3 to 1997:4, and 1997:4 to 1999:1).

The regression we run for each subperiod is $\Delta r_{it} = c + \alpha r_{it-1} + b_i + f_t + \varepsilon_{it}$, where Δr is the change in the liability interest rate, b and f are fixed firm and time effects, and ε is an error term. The i and t subscripts refer to individual banks and time; α, which we expect to be negative, measures the speed at which the interest rate mean-reverts. If interest rates revert by

100 percent in just one quarter, then we expect the α coefficient to be -1; if there is no reversion at all, then we expect the α coefficient to be 0. We then compare the distribution of the α coefficients (across banks) for the subperiods.[11]

We find that mean reversion is rapid. Within-firm mean reversion occurs within one quarter (α is -1 or smaller) in all subperiods. The most recent period, which has witnessed the implementation of the BASIC plan, shows a significantly higher rate of mean reversion (a coefficient value of -1.29), which is consistent with the view that banks face stronger incentives to resolve problems of high default risk in the more recent period. It is difficult to interpret a coefficient size less than -1 (which seems to imply greater than mean reversion of interest rates). In specifications without fixed time effects, coefficient sizes tended to be smaller (typically in the range of -0.6 to -0.8). Thus we suspect that correlation between average time effects and individual banks' sensitivities to aggregate shocks may explain the apparent overadjustment of rates.

To summarize our empirical results, we find significant cross-sectional differences in market reactions to bank default risk (as measured by deposit interest rates and deposit growth), and our regressions indicate links between those measures and fundamental characteristics of banks related to asset risk and leverage. Furthermore, deposit interest rates revert to the mean very quickly (holding fixed effects and time effects constant), and the rate of mean reversion has increased during the period in which the BASIC framework was implemented. Overall, these results suggest that market discipline is present in measuring bank risk, punishing it, and successfully encouraging banks to pursue risk-management policies that reduce risk after they suffer risk-increasing shocks.

5.4   Conclusion

In this chapter, we reviewed the Argentine experience in the 1990s with bank regulatory reform, which has been one of the most determined efforts, among emerging market countries, to inject credible market discipline into the relationship between banks and depositors, and into the regulatory and supervisory process. We have argued that Argentina successfully implemented a system of bank regulation that achieved credible market discipline over banks. Markets, as well as regulators, punish or reward banks depending on the perceived risk of bank failure, and market

---

11. We also ran regressions excluding fixed firm effects, which constrains all firms to target the same long-run average level of interest rates. Fixed effects have a great deal of explanatory power (raising the adjusted R^2 substantially in all subperiods), and so we only report fixed effects results in table 5.17. In specifications without fixed effects, coefficients on the lagged interest rate were smaller, but the same pattern of increasing coefficient size over time appeared and was even larger in magnitude than the differences reported in table 5.17.

perceptions of risk (as indicated in deposit interest rates and deposit flows) are correlated both with ex ante measures of fundamental asset risk and with ex post incidences of bank failure. Market discipline encourages rapid, risk-reducing adjustments by banks to shocks that raise their risk of failure.

Despite these favorable findings, clearly there is room for improvement in Argentina's bank regulation regime. First, the privatization of public banks remains unfinished—most notably in the cases of the two largest public banks, which account for more than a quarter of banking system deposits. Second, the least-cost resolution mandate that has been given SEDESA thus far has not proved very costly, but it could become a slippery slope—a means to pay for implicit bank bailouts, and thus undermine the hard-won gains of market confidence and market discipline. Limits to the subsidization of acquisitions that prevent least-cost resolution from becoming an implicit bailout mechanism are, therefore, a potentially important area for reform. Finally, the subordinated debt law could also be improved. Disclosing banks' compliance with the law seems a desirable first step. Placing greater limits on what qualifies as compliance (in particular, excluding domestic interbank deposits from the definition of qualifying subordinated debt and ensuring that subordinated debt is held at arm's length) and limiting the yield of qualifying subordinated debt are two additional steps the government should consider.

Does the Argentine regulatory system provide a model that other countries should adopt? We think the capital requirements, liquidity requirements, and BASIC system offer an excellent set of blueprints for any country to consider if it is serious about fostering market discipline in banking. At the same time, experience in developing and developed economies alike has shown that a regulatory system is only as effective as the political will that underlies its enforcement. In many countries—notably Chile in 1982, the United States in 1984, and Venezuela in 1991—de facto deposit insurance was provided despite its de jure absence.

During the tequila crisis of 1995 in Argentina (as during the liberalization of Estonia's banks in 1991) the government chose to force insolvent banks to close and permitted depositors in insolvent banks to lose a significant proportion of their deposits. The political commitment to low inflation and reform of the banking system in Argentina in the wake of the inflation and banking disasters of the earlier era set constraints on government policy toward banks in the 1990s, limiting the possibility of large bailout expenditures or other interventions in the banking system. The ability to apply the Argentine approach successfully to other countries likely depends on the existence of a similar political will backing real reform and limiting bailouts. Thus the challenges for reformers in emerging market countries include not only the technical problem of how to design an effective regulatory system, but also the more difficult problem of how to create the political conditions that make such a system credible.

Appendix

Table 5A.1 The Timing of Privatizations

Bank	Date in Which Law Was Enacted	Date of Loan Agreement	Date of Bid	Date of First Disbursement	Date of Transference	Percentage of Capital Privatized	Total Loan (in millions)
Corrientes[a]	11/1991	—	n.a.	—	5/1993	60	n.a.
La Rioja[a]	n.a.	—	n.a.	—	7/1994	70	n.a.
Chaco[b]	5/1993	8/1995	7/1994	11/1995	11/1994	60	78
Entre Ríos[b]	8/1993	8/1995	8/1994	10/1995	1/1995	60	78
Formosa	2/1995	4/1995	3/1995	7/1995	12/1995	60	80
Misiones	11/1994	4/1995	11/1994	7/1995	1/1996	92.5[c]	78
Río Negro	3/1995	4/1995	8/1995	7/1995	3/1996	85	80
Salta	7/1994	4/1995	8/1995	7/1995	3/1996	70	50
Tucumán	3/1995	6/1995	7/1995	7/1995	7/1996	75	80
San Luis	12/1989	4/1995	4/1996	10/1995	8/1996	100	50
Santiago del Estero	1/1995	4/1995	3/1996	7/1995	9/1996	95	50
San Juan	7/1995	4/1995	11/1995	8/1995	11/1996	75	80
Previsión Social de Mendoza	3/1995	4/1995	11/1995	5/1995	11/1996	90	100
Mendoza	3/1995	4/1995	11/1995	5/1995	11/1996	90	160
Jujuy	6/1995	6/1995	8/1997	12/1995	1/1998	80	50
Santa Fe	7/1996	12/1996	9/1997	5/1997	6/1998	100	160
Santa Cruz	10/1995	3/1998	3/1998	4/1998	10/1998	56	80
Municipal de Tucumán	12/1993	12/1996	2/1997	6/1997	7/1998	100	25
Catamarca	n.a.	—	—	4/1998	—	70	50
Caja Nacional de Ahorro y Seguro[a]	n.a.	—	n.a.	—	5/1996	100	n.a.

Source: Subsecretaría de Programación Regional—Trust Fund for Provincial Development (TFPD).

Notes: The Banco Municipal de Paraná was assisted by the TFPD by an amount of 20 million dollars for closure. n.a. = not applicable.

[a]Privatizations not supported by the TFPD.

[b]The Banco del Chaco and the Banco de Entre Ríos were privatized prior to the TFPD creation.

[c]Corresponds to the privatization of 100 percent of the bank's capital, since the rest was in private hands.

References

Anastasi, Alejandra, Tamara Burdiso, Elena M. Grubisic, and Soledad Lencioni. 1998. Es posible anticipar problemas en una entidad financiera? Argentina 1994–1997. Banco Central de la República Argentina, Working Paper no. 7, October. Available at http://www.bcra.gov.ar.

Baer, Herbert L., Jr., and Elijah Brewer III. 1986. Uninsured deposits as a source of market discipline: Some new evidence. *Federal Reserve Bank of Chicago Economic Perspectives* 10 (September/October): 23–31.

Banco Central de la República Argentina (BCRA). 1995. *Bulletin of Monetary and Financial Affairs,* 1st ed. Available at http://www.bcra.gov.ar, May.

———. 1999. Informe al congreso de la nación [Report to Congress]. Available at http://www.bcra.gov.ar, November.

Berger, Allen N., Sally M. Davies, and Mark J. Flannery. 1998. Comparing market and regulatory assessments of bank performance: Who knows what when? Federal Reserve Board Working Paper no. 32, March.

Calomiris, Charles W. 1997. *The postmodern bank safety net.* Washington, D.C.: American Enterprise Institute.

———. 1999. Building an incentive-compatible safety net. *Journal of Banking and Finance* 23 (October): 1499–519.

Calomiris, Charles W., and Charles M. Kahn. 1991. The role of demandable debt in structuring optimal banking arrangements. *American Economic Review* 81 (June): 497–513.

Calomiris, Charles W., and Joseph R. Mason. 1997. Contagion and bank failures during the Great Depression: The June 1932 Chicago banking panic. *American Economic Review* 87 (December): 863–83.

Calomiris, Charles W., and Berry Wilson. 1998. Bank capital and portfolio management: The 1930s "capital crunch" and scramble to shed risk. NBER Working Paper no. 6649. Cambridge, Mass.: National Bureau of Economic Research, July.

Caprio, Gerard, Jr., and Daniela Klingebiel. 1996. Bank insolvency: Cross-country experience. World Bank Policy Research Paper no. 1620. Washington, D.C.: World Bank.

D'Amato, Laura, Elena Grubisic, and Andrew Powell. 1997. Contagion, bank fundamentals or macroeconomic shock? An empirical analysis of the Argentine 1995 banking problems. Banco Central de la República Argentina, Working Paper no. 2, July. Available at http://www.bcra.gov.ar.

Dabós, Marcelo, and Walter Sosa-Escudero. 2000. Predicción y explicación del momento de caída de bancos en Argentina, usando modelos de duración [Explaining and predicting bank failure in Argentina using duration models]. Universidad de San Andrés, Economic Working Paper no. 26, April.

Falkenheim, Michael, and Andrew Powell. 1999. The use of credit bureau information in the estimation of appropriate capital and provisioning requirements. Banco Central de la República Argentina. Mimeograph.

Flannery, Mark. 1998. Using market information in prudential bank supervision: A review of the U.S. empirical evidence. *Journal of Money, Credit and Banking* 30 (August): 273–305.

Gorton, Gary, and George Pennacchi. 1990. Financial intermediaries and liquidity creation. *Journal of Finance* 45 (March): 49–71.

Jagtiani, Julapa, George G. Kaufman, and Catharine Lemieux. 1999. Do markets discipline banks and bank holding companies? Evidence from debt pricing. Federal Reserve Bank of Chicago, Working Paper, May.

Morgan, Donald P., and Kevin J. Stiroh. 1999. Can bond holders discipline banks? Federal Reserve Bank of New York, Working Paper, August.
Peria, Maria S. M., and Sergio L. Schmukler. 1999. Do depositors punish banks for "bad" behavior? Examining market discipline in Argentina, Chile, and Mexico. World Bank, Working Paper, February.
Powell, Andrew. 1997. Using the market as regulator: Developing BASIC banking oversight in Argentina. Banco Central de la República Argentina. Mimeograph.
Schumacher, Liliana. 1997. Bubble or market discipline? A study of failures and mergers over the Argentine panic. Banco Central de la República Argentina, December. Mimeograph.
Shadow Financial Regulatory Committee. 2000. *Reforming bank capital regulation.* Washington, D.C.: American Enterprise Institute.
Torre, Augusto de la. 2000. Resolving bank failures in Argentina: Recent developments and issues. Policy Research Working Paper no. 2295. World Bank, March.
World Bank. 1998. Argentine Financial Sector Review. Report no. 17864-AR. Washington, D.C.: World Bank, September.

Comment   Douglas W. Diamond

Calomiris and Powell provide a very complete description and analysis of the experience in the market-oriented bank regulatory scheme in Argentina after 1992. They carefully describe the evolution of the system, its great successes, and the surprises along the way. In addition to providing their own analysis of recent data on Argentine banks, they outline the results of important earlier work. Given the importance of Argentina as the most complete experiment with market-oriented bank regulation and supervision, this complete and comprehensive presentation is recommended reading for all concerned with contemporary bank regulation (and not just in emerging markets).

The interpretation given to the experience is evenhanded. It is not self-congratulatory and does not trumpet only one view of how the approach worked or was supposed to work. I will provide my own summary of their evidence and use it to evaluate the potential role for requiring issue of subordinated debt.

The most important fact about the success of the entire approach was that the Argentine banking system managed to survive the tequila shock without initial deposit insurance or a domestic lender of last resort (though with some international help). It appears that the currency board limited the regulator's ability to succumb to the temptation to bail out banks and protect depositors. However, regulators clearly understood the long-run benefits of imposing losses. Some banks were allowed to fail.

Douglas W. Diamond is professor of finance in the Graduate School of Business at the University of Chicago and a research associate of the National Bureau of Economic Research.

After the 1995 tequila crisis ended, the market discipline approach was expanded, but some small safety net was also restored.

Information in Bank Runs during the Tequila Crisis

The cross section of bank runs, deposit losses, and failures during various phases of the tequila crisis is of substantial interest because it provides evidence about the information possessed by depositors. My discussion relies on Schumacher (1996, 2000). Through most of the crisis, it was ex ante low capital banks with poor performance that lost deposits and later failed. The fact that it was not random banks that lost deposits is evidence that some depositors have public information about banks. This, of course, does not show that bank runs do not themselves partly cause banks to increase their losses. Even if runs themselves impose losses on banks, however, this imposition of losses is not indiscriminate. There seems to have been some information that neither regulators nor depositors had: Some of the failures revealed surprise problems, such as fraud.

The crisis deepened and eventually became both a systemic run and a currency run. During this period, runs became indiscriminate (the cross section of severity among domestically owned banks did not depend on a bank's ex ante financial condition). There was little the Argentine government could do to stop it on its own. It needed the help of international agencies. After the new International Monetary Fund, World Bank, and Inter-American Development Bank agreements were reached, the indiscriminate withdrawals stopped, but the runs at poorly performing banks continued.

Regulatory Changes after the Crisis

After the crisis a very limited safety net was established. A limited (and unfunded) deposit insurance for small deposits was introduced, without bailing out losses ex post in failed banks. A new and limited framework to merge banks with some government assistance was set up. In addition, management of liquidity risk was improved. A clearer set of liquidity requirements was imposed, including the use of foreign standby letters of credit as a way to get contingent liquidity.

In addition to the small safety net, an improved regulatory system was put into place: the BASIC system. I want to focus on the most novel part of that system: the subordinated debt requirement.

The intent of the subordinated debt requirement (as well as the credit rating requirement) was to provide verifiable information to avoid deniability by regulators and possibly to provide new information to regulators. At the same time it should increase bank disclosure of information when banks attempt to sell debt or improve their credit rating. In addition, it is possible that the subordinated debt requirement could commit regulators to close banks that are risky and that it would attract outside monitoring of banks. The experience in Argentina suggests that the commitment benefits may be overstated, and that the monitoring benefits depend on the endogenous amount of losses that regulators will impose on subordinated debt holders when choosing the timing of closure.

Investor Commitment, Regulator Commitment, and Creating Liquidity

A regulator's incentive to close banks differs from that of investors and depositors, but there is a common element to these decisions. If banks make unique relationship loans, there is a problem with closing banks or changing management to discipline the bank to take low risks and operate efficiently. When there is relationship lending (or when capital markets do not exist), and borrowers do not have other equally qualified lenders, there are extra losses imposed if a bank is closed. This reduces the incentive for investors or regulators to close poorly performing banks, reducing the discipline that comes from the threat to close or change management. It is possible, of course, that closure imposes trouble on relationship borrowers as well. Diamond and Rajan (2000, 2001) analyze the ability of uninsured demand deposits to provide commitment to run and thus close the bank whenever depositor losses are anticipated. This commitment can be useful to force the imposition of the closure penalty that is painful to those imposing it. Because of the first-come, first-served property rights of demand depositors, they will rush to foreclose even when bank failure is not in the collective interest of depositors. Other claims like capital (in particular, long-term subordinated debt) can be renegotiated and do not provide this extra discipline. Diamond and Rajan view bank capital choice as a trade-off between commitment and stability. Long-term subordinated debt holders will not force inefficient discipline; they may roll over the debt at maturity or buy new issue.

When subordinated debt is closely held, it will provide even less discipline. Closely held debt is even more easily renegotiated and could end up being held by the owners of equity or other banks with business relations with the issuer. It is interesting that the low compliance banks in Argentina included banks that got capital from other Argentine banks. Even a rate ceiling on newly issued subordinated debt, as suggested by Calomiris (1999), may not work as intended if debt is rolled over by an old owner who wishes not to alert regulators of the bank's condition. Given the lack of a bond market in Argentina, its experience may be different from that of more developed countries, but a private placement arrangement might be the only option for smaller banks worldwide.

Did Subordinated Debt Commit Argentine Regulators?

In addition to the discipline imposed at the maturity of debt, there is also a requirement of regular flotation of new debt. Does this impose extra discipline? If regulators close banks or provide other penalties to banks that do not meet this requirement, then it will provide added discipline. However, because regulators will still make closure decisions and can extend the deadline, they may not choose to provide ex post inefficient penalties to banks. This is particularly true when many banks cannot issue new subordinated debt on attractive terms. Because the Argentine requirement became effective after the East Asian crisis, it is not surprising that the regulation was not enforced immediately. More generally, if relationship lending is present and banks are important to lending, regulators will be concerned with the flow of credit in the economy. Even international authorities such as the IMF could be less inclined to force bank closure in a crisis situation, although they should be tougher than most domestic regulators.

This may illustrate a more general point. Commitment to close or punish banks comes from political will and regulatory preferences, when regulators retain discretion not to carry through with the penalty. Commitments to issue subordinated debt may only provide verifiable information that regulators did not enforce their own rules. Although this can provide some commitment, it is not just due to the precise nature of the debt contract, such as its priority. Changing the rules can make more information public, improving transparency, or signal "tough" intent. There is a limit on the amount of market discipline a regulatory system can provide.

The currency board already limits government discretion, which means that some bailouts that require resources would require international help. This by itself provides real commitment to local regulators. However, the timing of closure and implied losses still depend on regulatory action. In this setting, the transparency effect of the BASIC system can be effective. Calomiris and Powell's results suggest that this transparency is very beneficial in helping to make clear to outsiders that there is a given amount of commitment to discipline banks. It is less clear that it adds more commitment than already exists.

References

Calomiris, Charles W. 1999. Building an Incentive-Compatible Safety Net. *Journal of Banking and Finance* 23 (October): 1499–1519.
Diamond, Douglas W., and Raghuram G. Rajan. 2000. A theory of bank capital. *Journal of Finance* 60 (December): 2431–65.
———. 2001. Liquidity risk, liquidity creation and financial fragility: A theory of banking. *Journal of Political Economy* 109 (April): 287–327.
Schumacher, Liliana. 1996. Bubble or depositors' discipline: A study of the Argentine banking panic, December 1994–May 1995. Ph.D. diss., University of Chicago.
———. 2000. Bank runs and currency run in a system without a safety net: Argentina and the "tequila" shock. *Journal of Monetary Economics* 46 (August): 257–77.

Discussion Summary

Ben Bernanke began the general discussion by suggesting that in trying to think about generalizations of the Argentine experience, it is important to consider the role of the currency board. He noted that one needs a substitute for the lender of last resort under a fixed exchange rate regime.

Gerard Caprio cited the Mexican experience, noting that firms as depositors acted as a source of market discipline because of the reliance on trade credit lines. He also wondered about the relationship between credit derivatives and a subordinated debt regime. Finally, he asked if the Argentine model could be exported. He expressed hope that hyperinflation is not a necessary condition.

James Barth pointed out that prompt corrective action was in place in the 1970s for savings and loans and that this highlights the key role of political will. *Martin Feldstein* raised the issue of the importance of foreign banks in Argentina as a safe haven. He wondered why they have not attracted even more deposits. *Michael Dooley* noted that with dollar denominated loans and with two currencies in the system, banks faced spread risk that could be avoided with dollarization.

Eric Rosengren observed that of the three bank failures, two have investment grade ratings, and four of the five banks that were resolved were also investment grade. External debt ratings appear to be poor predictors of banks. He asked if subordinated debt was a better predictor of bank risk. He also asked about the underwriting and associated costs of issuing subordinated debt.

Andrew Powell responded to Bernanke by noting that the Central Bank of Argentina has a systemic liquidity policy. He noted that this mitigates the need for a lender of last resort, and that the run to dollars limits the benefits of a lender of last resort. In response to Caprio, he noted that there was some evidence of even insured depositors leaving banks that subsequently failed. He observed that even though the deposit insurance was ex post credible, the time to resolution may be long and uncertain. He also noted that foreign banks do, in fact, have almost 70 percent of private deposits, but that there are important regional domestic banks in some sectors.

In response to Dooley, Powell noted that dollarization had been considered. He noted that banks were fairly well matched in terms of their peso-dollar books. He noted that there are some short-term peso loans such as overdraft protection and personal loans, but that there were peso deposits as well.

He observed that local rating agencies were competing and that ratings may have had low predictive power, but that now there are only four international-based accredited rating agencies. He conceded that although the Argentine regulatory rating system (CAMELS) outperformed the rating agencies, there were some higher-rated bank failures due to fraud. Lastly, he noted that the cost of issuing subordinated debt varies by type of issuance and that deals with correspondents may be cheaper.

Also in response to Caprio, *Charles Calomiris* noted that in Mexico good and bad banks had different rates for insured deposits as well. He pointed out that banks paying higher rates had little demand deposits. He suggested that it would be good to look at the composition of deposits and debt. He agreed with Feldstein that the presence of foreign banks is a major source of market discipline, but the operating costs for foreign banks can be very high. He agreed that reliance on public ratings is risky. Lastly, he pointed out that Argentina has $80 billion of deposits, so it may be hard to draw lessons for smaller developing economies from the Argentine experience.

6

Dimensions of Credit Risk and Their Relationship to Economic Capital Requirements

Mark Carey

Regulators are now developing a major revision of commercial bank capital adequacy regulations. Regulators are likely to change the treatment of a variety of types of risk, but a primary focus of their effort is improvement of the manner in which the 1988 Basel Accord handles credit risk. Currently, assets making vastly different contributions to portfolio credit risk often receive similar regulatory capital treatment. Because equity is an expensive source of finance, the resulting wedges between regulatory and economic capital allocations have created strong incentives for banks to restructure their activities and balance sheets. For example, many bank-sponsored securitizations are directed at removing from the balance sheet those assets that have relatively high marginal regulatory capital requirements but that contribute relatively little to portfolio credit risk, such as credit card loans and loans to low-risk corporate borrowers (such activity is often called *capital arbitrage*). In contrast, assets for which regulatory capital requirements are too low tend to remain on the balance sheet. By boosting capital ratios, the 1988 Accord reduced bank insolvency risk in the years immediately after its adoption, but if current trends continue to their logical conclusion, an unmodified accord could in the end have the perverse effect of greatly increasing banks' portfolio risk postures and bank failure rates. Moreover, any revision of the Accord that preserves

Mark Carey is senior economist at the Federal Reserve Board.

The views expressed herein are not necessarily those of the Board of Governors, other members of its staff, or the Federal Reserve System. Thanks to Paul Calem, Ed Ettin, Mark Flannery, Michael Gordy, Mark Hrycay, Patricia Jackson, David Jones, John Mingo, Frederic Mishkin, Bill Treacy, and two anonymous referees for useful comments and conversations.

first-order differences between regulatory and economic capital requirements probably will be unsustainable in the long run.[1]

In a recent paper, the Basel Committee on Banking Supervision (1999) briefly outlined three approaches to capital regulation: (a) a revised *standardized* approach architecturally similar to the current accord that would leave in place many distortions; (b) a *full models* approach, similar to that now available for market risk, in which a bank's internal models would compute required regulatory capital for credit risk; and (c) an *internal ratings* approach in which credit risk capital would be computed using formulas involving various relevant portfolio characteristics, such as the fraction of loans assigned each internal rating. Both of the latter two approaches would attempt to make regulatory capital approximate economic capital, but in the internal ratings approach the parameters and architecture of the system would be set by regulators, whereas in the full models approach they would be set by banks and reviewed by regulators.[2]

A principal barrier to adoption of the full models and internal rating approaches is technical uncertainty about the portfolio characteristics that drive credit risk. At least initially, simpler formulas and models are preferred for their lower costs of implementation. However, to avoid a continuation of serious distortions, regulations must take into account all first-order important determinants of portfolio credit risk. The main body of portfolio theory, which was developed largely for equity portfolios and which suggests that correlations of individual loan credit losses with systematic factors are the main determinant of portfolio risk, is of limited use in identifying such determinants. The floating-rate loan portfolios typical of banks have a large credit downside and only modest upside potential, which causes the credit loss distributions for such portfolios to be skewed and to have very long bad tails (fig. 6.1). Though loss correlations are important, factors like individual asset risk, portfolio size, and the behavior of defaulted assets may also be important determinants of debt portfolio bad-tail loss rates.

Empirical uncertainty about the dimensions of credit risk exists among policy makers because relatively few publicly available studies exist and because most such studies have used one of the extant credit risk models to produce evidence. Models like CreditMetrics (Gupton, Finger, and Bhatia 1997) and the Oliver Wyman–like approach described in Ong (1999) esti-

---

1. Economic capital requirements for credit risk means the capital needed for a portfolio so that the chance that credit losses exceed capital is no more than a specified small probability. In many circumstances, economic capital would be the same as that needed to finance an asset or portfolio in a free market transaction with informed counterparties.

2. All three approaches must specify required capital for risks other than credit, such as interest rate risk or operational risk. Although the full models approach has many desirable properties, practical barriers to its implementation are such that the Basel Supervisors Committee is focusing its attention on the standardized and internal rating approaches for possible near-term implementation.

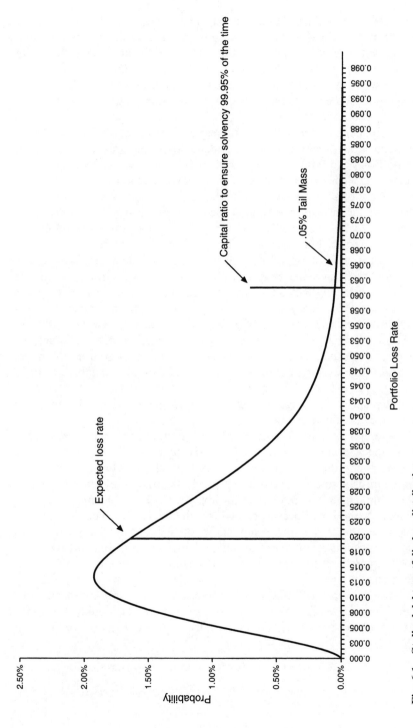

Fig. 6.1 Stylized debt portfolio loss distribution

mate loss rates at different percentiles of the bad tail conditional on portfolio composition. However, model results are quite sensitive to assumptions about values of parameters that are extremely difficult to observe, test, or even develop intuition about (Gordy 2000a). It is difficult to know the reliability of evidence that such models produce about the influence of a given portfolio characteristic on bad-tail loss rates and thus on economic capital requirements.

This paper uses the Monte Carlo resampling method of Carey (1998) to provide nonparametric empirical evidence about the practical importance to portfolio bad-tail loss rates of several different asset and portfolio characteristics. This bootstrap-like method simulates the likely range of loss experience of a portfolio manager who randomly selects assets from those available for investment, while at the same time causing his portfolio to conform to specified targets and limits. For example, the method can be used to compare both average and bad-tail loss rates of portfolios of Baa-rated debt with those of portfolios of Ba-rated debt. The resampling method exchanges the large array of assumptions required by existing parametric models with an assumption that the loss experience in the database from which assets are drawn is representative of the universe of possible experience. That assumption is false, of course, but it is possible to test the sensitivity of results to at least some violations of the assumption. Moreover, the database used in this paper is a principal source of parameter values for existing parametric models (i.e., Moody's database of bond ratings and defaults during 1970–98).[3] To the extent that this database fails to capture the range of likely experience, parametric models may also produce unrealistic estimates.

Although this paper's findings are likely to be useful in parametric credit risk model design and to private sector risk managers as well as regulators, for simplicity the discussion is organized by reference to the internal ratings approach to Basel Accord reform.[4] To the best of my knowledge, current thinking would have such an approach involve (a) an equation or similar method of allocating capital to individual assets according to their characteristics, (b) a simple summation of such allocations to arrive at a portfolio capital requirement, and (c) perhaps some adjustments to the portfolio requirement to account for variations in portfolio size or other portfolio characteristics.

Exercises reported below focus on three questions relevant to such an architecture: (a) Which asset or portfolio characteristics should be included as variables or adjustment factors?; (b) what types of behavior or phenom-

---

3. A similar database available from Standard & Poor's is also a primary source of parameter values.
4. In this paper, the desirability of prudential regulation of bank capital is taken as given.

ena should be considered in estimating the parameters of the system?; and (c) is a linear structure appropriate? That is, does a simple sum of capital allocations appropriate to homogenous pools of assets approximate well the capital required for a mixed pool of assets?

Results imply that borrower default ratings, estimates of the likely loss given default on individual assets (LGD, or one minus the recovery rate), and measures of portfolio size or granularity are important candidate variables for the regulatory formula. Default ratings appear most important, with loss rates at the 99th percentile differing by a factor of about 60 for borrowers rated A or better relative to those rated B. Predictable differences in LGDs (e.g., differences for senior versus subordinated debt) also can have a first-order impact on required capital. Although increases in portfolio size beyond a certain point appear to be associated with relatively modest reductions in risk, small portfolios are significantly riskier than larger portfolios, and thus any regulation might need to be parameterized differently for small and large banks. Moreover, differences in granularity (i.e., the extent to which a large fraction of portfolio is exposed to only a few obligors) can have a material effect on risk.

One natural way of implementing an internal rating–based regulation would be to estimate the capital required for portfolios composed only of assets with each permutation of ratings, expected LGD, and so on. Capital for mixed portfolios would be the sum of the share of the mixed portfolio in each "bucket" times the estimated requirement for that bucket. An exercise in which capital requirements as computed by such a linear approach are compared to direct estimates of required capital for a variety of portfolio risk postures yields mixed results, but on the whole implies that the linear approximation is likely to be adequate.

A potential weakness of the internal ratings approach is that it would ignore differences in certain types of diversification across portfolios. Much of the machinery of CreditMetrics, for example, is designed to estimate differences in credit risk correlations across borrowers as well as the portfolio risk effects of such differences. Correlations are often presumed to be related to the industries and countries in which borrowers operate, but no consensus about values of such correlations exists. Given the lack of consensus, practitioners often use credit risk models to fine-tune formal or informal limits on loans to one industry or loans to one region. Monitoring such limits has long been a part of bank examinations in the United States. However, if bad-tail loss rates are sensitive to modest variations in the limits, it might be necessary to build such variations into the regulatory formula—a difficult task. Fortunately, resampling exercises that vary the loan-to-one-industry limit for a few different sets of industry definitions yield modest differences in bad-tail loss rates. Data limitations complicate resampling analysis of diversification across countries, which intuition suggests might be more important than diversification across industries within a country. See Jackson and Perraudin (1999) and Nickell, Perraudin, and Varotto (1998) for some insights about country effects, and Flannery (1989) for an analysis of incentive effects of capital regulation on portfolio choices.

In estimating the parameters of a formula based on internal ratings, policy makers and technicians should be attentive to implications of the unpredictability of individual LGDs, to the definition of default, and to the fact that capital set to limit bank failure rates in a hypothetical average year may be much less than needed in bad years. For example, many credit risk models appeal to the law of large numbers in assuming that assets that are similarly senior (e.g., having similar collateral) will have similar LGDs if a default occurs. However, LGDs can vary significantly across otherwise similar assets, and the risk that a bank will be unlucky with respect to both the number of defaults and their severity can be material, even if LGD rates and default rates are assumed to be uncorrelated.

On the whole, this paper's results indicate that if the internal ratings approach properly accounts for all the first-order important dimensions of credit risk, it is likely to produce regulatory capital allocations for credit risk that are reasonable approximations to economic capital allocations. However, factors in addition to those considered in this paper are also likely to be important determinants of portfolio risk, so more research is needed before final conclusions are reached. For example, this paper focuses only on losses associated with defaults and distressed restructurings and thus is most consistent with a "default mode" or standard accounting view of credit risk. However, in a mark-to-market view, both variations in borrower credit quality short of default and variations in open market credit spreads are important determinants of changes in portfolio market value. Kiesel, Perraudin, and Taylor (1999) offer evidence that such factors may be comparable in importance to default risk.

The remaining maturity of assets and the proper horizon over which portfolio credit risk should be measured are also probably important, though not analyzed in this paper (see Calem 1999; Jackson and Perraudin 1999; and Kiesel, Perraudin, and Taylor 1999 for some relevant evidence). Although a one-year analysis horizon is conventional in credit risk modeling and is used here, default-mode analyses using such a horizon unrealistically assume that a bank losing almost all its capital in a given year will either be able to recapitalize at the end of the year or will suffer no (or only small) losses in subsequent years.

More generally, the formal modeling of credit and many other risks remains a new and largely untested art. Using existing risk-modeling technologies to engineer regulatory capital requirements to very fine tolerances would amplify model risk—that is, the chance that unforeseen circumstances will produce losses larger than required capital. However, if regulatory requirements are to include substantial margins for model risk, market participants must be persuaded of the need for such margins, or a continuation of capital arbitrage will simply render regulatory requirements ineffective.

This paper's results are not meant to be estimates of the *levels* of capital requirements for credit risk that regulators should require for any given portfolio, but rather to be indicators of likely proportional differences in levels as asset and portfolio characteristics vary. The appropriate level is sensitive to a variety of assumptions, including the degree of systemic and deposit-insurer risk that regulators are willing to tolerate, and is a matter beyond the scope of this paper.[5]

To the extent that a reader does wish to take this paper's estimates as preliminary indicators of levels of economic capital requirements for credit risk alone, it is important to note that the most appropriate point of comparison in the current accord is the 4 percent Tier 1 leverage ratio. Although the bad-tail loss rates reported herein combine expected and unexpected losses, borrowers rated riskier than B3 are omitted from the exercises, and at least in the United States much of the loan loss reserve is allocated to losses associated with such borrowers. Thus, the bad-tail losses reported in the tables conform most closely to those that equity capital would absorb in the United States.

As noted, regulatory applications are emphasized in this paper's discussion, but the results are relevant for credit risk managers at banks and other financial institutions and to sponsors of collateralized debt obligations (CDOs). All such institutions make simultaneous decisions about portfolio risk, capital structure, and remaining risk to be borne by their residual claimants, and knowledge of the determinants of debt portfolio credit risk is helpful to such decision making.

Section 6.1 describes the data, and section 6.2 describes some details of the resampling method. Sections 6.3 through 6.9 report results, and section 6.10 offers concluding comments.

6.1 Data

Information about corporate bonds rated by Moody's, including the ratings of bonds and issuers, the identity and timing of defaults, and some other characteristics, is obtained for the years 1970–98 from the April 1999 release of Moody's Corporate Bond Default Database. The database is a complete history of Moody's long-term rating assignments for both U.S. and non-U.S. financial and nonfinancial firms and sovereigns (no commercial paper ratings, municipal bond ratings, or ratings of asset-backed secu-

5. See Vojta (1973) for an early analysis of the appropriate level and structure of capital requirements.

rities are included). In addition to the ratings of individual bonds, Moody's provides a table of issuer ratings—that is, the actual or likely rating on a senior unsecured bond for each issuer for each date the issuer had any rated bonds outstanding. All analysis is done at the issuer level and is restricted to U.S. issuers (the number of non-U.S. issuers became material only in recent years.)[6]

A loss experience record is constructed for each issuer and year in which the issuer was rated at the start of the year. Those cases in which the issuer defaulted during the year are exposed-and-defaulting records, whereas those in which no default occurred are counted as exposed but not defaulting. Similar to the methods of Moody's annual study of default rates by grade, the rate for any year and grade is the number of defaults divided by the total number of exposures. Cases in which an issuer's rating is withdrawn during the experience year are counted as half a unit of exposure unless the issuer defaults.[7]

In this paper, each exposure-year record is treated as representing all exposures to the borrower. Although a given borrower may have many loans outstanding at a given bank, in the United States a borrower rarely defaults on some but not all obligations. Thus, it is conventional in credit risk analysis to aggregate all loans to a borrower into a single exposure. Loan sizes are simulated according to the rules and purposes of each exercise, as is described later.

Moody's assigns one of about 200 industry codes to each borrower. Some of the codes correspond well to conventional definitions of industries (e.g., "Airlines") but some are quite narrowly focused (e.g., "Hospital supplies" vs. "Hospitals/nursing"). In monitoring their exposure to individual industries and in imposing limits on such exposure, most large banks use internally developed industry classifications involving a few dozen categories. To simulate such procedures, I judgmentally created two separate classification schemes that boil down Moody's 200 categories into 20 and 39 categories, respectively.

Moody's database contains some (but not complete) information on the LGDs of defaulted bonds. Because every study to date has found substantial differences between the LGD experience of loans and bonds (e.g., Society of Actuaries 1998; Asarnow and Edwards 1995; and Hamilton and Carty 1999), the bond LGDs are not used in this paper. Instead, LGDs

---

6. Analysis of the impact of default probabilities versus that of LGDs on portfolio risk would be muddied by use of bond-level rating data. Moody's considers both the quality of the issuer and the terms of the indenture in rating a bond, especially terms like collateral, guarantees, or subordination provisions. In contrast, variations in issuer ratings across borrowers are more likely to be indicative of differences in the probability of issuer default because such ratings are uniformly for a senior unsecured claim.

7. Carty (1996) examined rating withdrawals and found almost all to be associated with maturities and calls of bonds, not with an imminent default. Moreover, the database tracks defaults even if they occur after Moody's withdrew ratings.

for each default are set or simulated according to the rules of each exercise, as is described later.

6.2   Some Details of the Resampling Method and Its Implementation

Events in the bad tail of a financial intermediary's portfolio loss distribution can cause insolvency unless the portfolio is financed entirely with equity. If it is financed partly with debt, the probability of insolvency can be reduced to a given level by choosing a capital structure with enough equity to cover the loss at the percentile of the portfolio loss distribution equal to that level.[8] Estimating how capital ratios must vary to preserve a given insolvency probability as portfolio characteristics change is a matter of estimating how the portfolio loss distribution changes.

The resampling method traces out loss distributions nonparametrically. For each exercise (set of portfolio parameters), 100,000 simulated portfolios are composed by drawing randomly from the loss experience database until the specified portfolio size is reached. Draws for any single simulated portfolio are without replacement. Drawn assets are rejected if they fail to satisfy the parameters for the given exercise. For example, each exercise specifies a target percentage of the portfolio to fall in each rating category. A Baa-rated asset would be rejected for inclusion if sufficient assets with that rating had already been drawn, even if the total simulated portfolio was not yet filled. Looking across simulated portfolios, all will have the same set of specified characteristics, but some will by chance include many defaulting assets and others few. Dollar loss rates are computed for each drawn portfolio, and the frequency distribution of such losses forms an estimate of the loss distribution for portfolios with the specified characteristics. For example, after rank-ordering simulated portfolios by loss rate, the loss rate for the 99,000th portfolio would be the estimated capital ratio sufficient to present insolvency with probability 0.99 for portfolios specified in the exercise.

For any given simulated portfolio (iteration), the draw is in two stages: (a) One of the twenty-nine experience years in the database is drawn, and (b) individual loans exposed during that year are drawn until the simulated portfolio is filled. Using experience from multiple years for a given simulated portfolio would tend to understate tail loss rates because the results of different realizations of systematic economic risk factors would be unrealistically combined.

The resampling method's strength is its lack of assumptions about functional forms of distributions, parameters, and covariances among asset returns. However, when applied to the Moody's database, the method has several weaknesses. Most importantly, the period 1970–98, though long by

---

8. For example, if the loss rate at the 99th percentile is 5 percent, then a 5 percent equity capital ratio will be sufficient to prevent insolvency with probability 0.99.

the standards of credit risk experience databases, does not capture the full range of possible systematic events. For example, the United States did not experience a depression, and many specific industries did not experience severe distress, but both a depression and distress in heretofore untroubled industries are possibilities in the future. Thus, all estimates of tail loss rates are understated in that the effects of very bad systematic events are not modeled.

In principle, parametric credit risk models can avoid this problem by specifying parameters that embody sufficiently pessimistic assumptions about future events. In practice, however, historical data are used to estimate the parameters of such models, and the Moody's and Standard & Poor's (S&P) databases are principal sources of such data. In general, I recommend caution in interpreting the levels of tail loss rates estimated by any available method. In setting levels for capital regulations, policy makers should ask to see bad-tail loss rate estimates for different assumptions about the frequency and severity of future systematic economic events.

A general advantage of the resampling method is that the effects of realistic correlations of losses across individual assets are reflected in estimated bad-tail loss rates because such correlations are embedded in the loss experience database. However, in applications of the method, the realism of embedded correlations is limited by the features of the database being used. Major advantages of the Society of Actuaries database used in Carey (1998) are its focus on private debt instruments and its incorporation of actual LGDs for each credit risk event, so that both cross-default and default LGD correlations typical of loans are captured. However, that database covers a relatively short time period (1986–92) and lacks information about the industries of many borrowers, limiting both the range of correlations reflected in the data and the ability to study the effect of industry diversification on bad-tail loss rates. The Moody's database is in many respects a mirror image. It covers a relatively long time period and has complete information about borrower industries, but it covers only public debt issuers and has LGD information that is not very useful for the purposes of this paper. Fortunately, for exercises that are qualitatively similar here and in Carey (1998), results are usually qualitatively similar.

Because the Moody's data are at the issuer level and bond LGDs differ so much from those for loans, it is necessary to assign both loan sizes and (for defaults) LGDs to each observation rather than using values drawn from the data. To some extent, such generated data are a necessity because studying the effects of variations in portfolio granularity and LGD properties involves perturbing those characteristics. However, to make the base-case data as realistic as possible, both loan sizes and LGDs are assigned randomly such that the distribution of their values closely matches distributions that are realistic for private debt portfolios. Except as otherwise noted, the simulated distribution of individual LGDs matches closely the distribution reported in Society of Actuaries (1998).[9] Except where fixed identical loan sizes are simulated, loan sizes are set as fractions of total simulated portfolio dollar value to match the distribution of fractions for an actual large U.S. bank. In most simulations reported here, about 40 percent of total dollar exposure is associated with the largest 10 percent of individual exposures. Such skewness of sizes is not atypical: I have inspected loan size distributions for a variety of large financial institutions, and they typically involve a significant concentration of assets.

The resampling method is data intensive in that it requires that the database have considerably more loss experience records with a given set of characteristics than are required to populate any given drawn portfolio. For example, if a portfolio of 500 Ba-rated loans is to be simulated and there are only 500 Ba-rated loans in the database for each year, the estimated loss distribution will collapse to the overall average loss rate because all the loans will be drawn for each iteration. Experiments indicate that numbers of observations in database cells must be at least five or six times larger than numbers in simulated portfolio cells. The Moody's database does not satisfy this requirement for virtually all of the exercises reported in this paper.

I address the problem by replicating the base data for each grade a sufficient number of times. For example, to ensure that there are enough Baa loans in every year, for most exercises I create a single replica of each Baa loss experience record in each year. Replicas are identical to base records except that a different borrower ID number is assigned, a different loan dollar size is assigned (as was described previously), and—if it is a default—a different LGD is assigned (as was described previously). For any given exercise, the replication factors are held constant across the different permutations of the exercise.

Such replication represents an intermediate case between sampling from the data with replacement and without replacement. It may seem problematic in that with replication the same defaulting borrower can be drawn twice into the same portfolio, but such a view is not quite correct. In the exercises of this paper, borrower identity is unimportant: Each observation is an exposure to a different simulated borrower, and each borrower is simply a bundle of rating, industry, and default/nondefault characteristics. Replication preserves exactly the proportions of defaulting and nondefaulting borrowers in each grade and industry in each year, as well as the fraction of exposures in each industry.

Different degrees of replication may, however, affect the levels of esti-

9. LGDs are assumed uncorrelated with default rates (e.g., simulated LGDs are not systematically different for defaults in recession and nonrecession years). This assumption of independence is common in the credit risk modeling literature, and is not inconsistent with the limited available empirical evidence, but studies identifying the degree of any correlation are needed.

mated bad-tail loss rates; and thus in some views of credit risk, replication can be thought of as affecting the cross-default correlations embedded in the data. To see the effect, imagine that in Moody's database only two borrowers defaulted in a given grade and year. When simulating a portfolio of 100 loans by drawing without replacement, the maximum estimated default rate for that grade and year is 2 percent—the bad tail is truncated beyond that point because if both borrowers happen to be drawn in building a given simulated portfolio, it is certain that remaining loans drawn into the portfolio will be nondefaulters. This seems unrealistic—there are always more bad loans to be made—and thus drawing without replacement from any actual database seems likely to understate true bad-tail loss rates. That is, as was noted previously, the correlations embedded in any actual finite database, because they represent only a portion of the possible range of experience, seem likely to understate the true correlations. Going to the other extreme, if draws are with replacement, it is always possible to draw another simulated default into a simulated portfolio, and indeed the likelihood of doing so is unaffected by the outcome of any previous draws. This also seems a bit unrealistic. The method most likely to deliver accurate estimates of the levels of bad-tail loss rates—with or without replacement, or with some intermediate method implemented by some degree of replication—is a question for future research. For the purposes of this paper, however, results of interest are qualitatively insensitive to the degree of replication that is applied.

6.3   Results for a Base Case

Table 6.1 presents the parameters of the base case. Subsequent exercises vary one of the parameters while holding the others constant at base-case values unless otherwise noted. The base portfolio has $5 billion of commercial loans with sizes that vary in a manner similar to that of an actual large bank, as was described previously. The number of loans in the portfolio is not fixed, but the parameterization of the loan size distribution keeps the number close to 500. In a few exercises I fix the number of loans and let the portfolio dollar total float, but that requires enforcement of loan-to-one-borrower and loan-to-one-industry limits in terms of fractions of the number of loans rather than fractions of the dollar total, which is unintuitive. Results are qualitatively similar regardless of whether numbers or dollars are fixed.

The loan-to-one-borrower limit is set at 3 percent of portfolio dollar size, whereas the loan-to-one-industry limit is 5 percent of portfolio size and is implemented using the judgmentally developed thirty-nine-industry classification scheme described previously. All loans are presumed to be senior; only actual defaults appearing in the database are treated as credit risk events; and the LGDs for those defaults are generated such that their

Table 6.1   **Parameters of Base Case**

Parameter	Value	Comment
Experience years included	1970–98	Equally weighted
Portfolio size criterion	Dollar limit of $5 billion	
Loan sizes	Mimic actual bank distribution	Mean is near $10 million
Number of portfolio loans	Floats	But close to 500
Loan to one borrower limit	3 percent of portfolio size	
Industry classification type	Carey 39 industries	
Loan to one industry limit	5 percent of portfolio size	
Fraction loans senior	100%	
Included credit events	Only actual defaults	
LGD specification	Mimic Society of Actuaries (1998) distribution for senior loans	Mean is 37 percent
Fraction		Fractions are representative of
rated A or better	20%	the average of large U.S.
rated Baa	30%	banks (close to mean
rated Ba	35%	shares of dollar
rated B	15%	outstandings reported in
		Treacy and Carey 1998).
Replications of each grade	A = 2, Baa = 3, Ba = 5, B = 15	
No. of iterations	100,000	

Note: Simulated portfolios and resampling exercises have the characteristics described in this table for the base case, and for all other cases unless otherwise noted.

distribution matches the distribution for senior loan default LGDs in Society of Actuaries (1998). The distribution of portfolio dollars across ratings conforms to the average distribution for large U.S. banks reported in Treacy and Carey (1998).

The first row of table 6.2 reports results for the base case. The mean or expected loss rate is 0.63 percent, whereas loss rates at the 95th, 99th, 99.5th, and 99.9th percentiles of the distribution are 1.87, 2.71, 3.04, and 3.87 percent, respectively.[10] Clearly, loss rates rise significantly with the percentile, implying, for example, that considerably more capital is required to prevent insolvency in 999 of 1,000 portfolio-years than in 950 of 1,000 experience-years. The mean loss rate of 0.63 percent is less than the 1 percent of the long-run average commercial and industrial (C&I) loan charge-off rate for U.S. banks. However, as noted, issuers rated riskier than B3 are omitted from the exercises, and the set of credit events includes defaults but no negotiated restructurings. Loans to issuers riskier than B3 would generally be considered classified assets on U.S. bank balance sheets. A significant share of real-world average or expected losses is asso-

10. For readers accustomed to unexpected loss rates, those would simply be the loss rates at the far percentiles minus the mean loss rate.

Table 6.2   **Average and Bad-Tail Loss Rates for Base Case**

| | Simulated Loss Rates (percent) | | | | |
| | Mean | At Loss Distribution Percentiles | | | |
Variant	Mean	95	99	99.5	99.9
Base case	0.63	1.87	2.71	3.04	3.87
Base case, replication factor doubled	0.63	1.89	2.77	3.13	3.94
Base case, replication factor = 30 for all grades	0.63	1.85	2.71	3.09	3.85
Base case, replication factor = 80 for all grades	0.63	1.88	2.74	3.11	3.88

Notes: The first row reports loss rates for the base case, the parameters of which are given in table 6.1. Results in remaining rows are for the same parameters except that the number of replications of loans in each year and grade is increased. Loss rates at high percentiles are total loss rates; unexpected loss rates at such percentiles are the total rate less the mean or expected rate as reported.

ciated with such loans and with negotiated restructurings, so their inclusion in simulations would move the mean estimated loss rate much closer to 1 percent.[11]

The second, third, and fourth rows of table 6.2 show that results are little affected when the replication factor for each grade is doubled, set to thirty for all grades, or set to eighty for all grades, respectively. Estimated loss rates at the different percentiles differ from base values by two to nine basis points, representing at most a 0.03 percent proportional change in the base-case loss rate. As was noted previously, although in principle the appropriate degree of replication is uncertain, in practice results appear insensitive to variations in the replication factors.

6.4   Results When All Loans Are in One Grade

Table 6.3 presents results for portfolios composed entirely of assets rated A or better, Baa, Ba, and B, and for comparison results for base-case parameters when the larger replication factors used in this exercise are applied. Focusing on the mean and 99th percentile loss rates, both the mean and bad-tail rates are near zero for assets rated A or better, reflecting the fact that very few issuers with such ratings defaulted over a one-year horizon during the years since 1970. Looking down the grades, the expected loss rate rises by a factor of about 700 between the A and B categories, whereas the 99th percentile loss rate rises by a factor of about 60. Tail rates for the investment grades (Baa and above) are far below that for the

11. No significance should be attached to the fact that the level of the loss rate at the 99.9th percentile is close to the 4 percent Tier 1 capital ratio of the current Basel Accord.

Table 6.3   **Loss Rates for Portfolios with All Loans in a Single Grade**

	Simulated Loss Rates (percent)				
		At Loss Distribution Percentiles			
Variant	Mean	95	99	99.5	99.9
Base case	0.63	1.88	2.74	3.11	3.88
All loans rated A or better	0.00	0.00	0.13	0.26	0.67
All loans rated Baa	0.06	0.42	0.98	1.20	1.81
All loans rated Ba	0.53	1.95	2.96	3.36	4.19
All loans rated B	2.85	6.29	8.12	8.76	9.88

Notes: For comparison with remaining rows, the first row reports results for base-case parameters except that a replication factor of 80 is applied to loans in all grades and years. Remaining rows report results when simulated portfolios are constrained to contain loans only to borrowers with the specified start-of-year rating, with other parameters identified to those of the base case apart from the replication factor of 80.

base case. Straying for a moment into interpretation of levels of results, investment-grade tail rates are also far below current regulatory capital requirements, which is evidence of banks' large incentives to move such loans off the balance sheet. B-rated bad-tail loss rates are well above those of the base case and well above current Tier 1 regulatory requirements, implying that current regulations do not require enough capital for relatively risky loans. In the absence of regulatory reform, the share of risky loans in bank portfolios is thus likely to increase.

Overall, it seems clear from the results in table 6.3 that ratings are an important indicator of a loan's contribution to bad-tail risk and thus of marginal economic capital requirements. Readers accustomed to the findings of standard portfolio theory may find this an uncomfortable result (that indicators of stand-alone asset risk or volatility are highly correlated with portfolio returns). As was noted previously, models that account for the differences between debt and equity imply such a relationship (see Zhou 1997 for an example). Moreover, ratings may also be indicators of the degree of correlation of default risk with systematic economic factors such as the business cycle. In descriptions of their methodologies, the rating agencies state that firms in cyclically volatile industries are more likely to be assigned riskier ratings, other things being equal.

6.5 Seniority Is Important

Although LGDs vary widely across individual defaults and restructurings, with senior secured credit events sometimes imposing a total loss and junior subordinated credit events sometimes imposing no loss, on average the values of LGDs differ with the priority of the debt and the nature of the credit event. For bank loans, which are generally senior or secured,

Table 6.4   Loss Rates as the Fraction of Subordinated Loans Varies,
                   Variable LGDs

| | Simulated Loss Rates (percent) | | | | |
| | Mean | At Loss Distribution Percentiles | | | |
Variant	Mean	95	99	99.5	99.9
Restructurings included, 0% subordinated	0.80	2.25	3.18	3.54	4.32
Restructurings included, 20% subordinated	0.85	2.34	3.28	3.68	4.47
Restructurings included, 40% subordinated	0.91	2.55	3.59	3.99	4.82
Restructurings included, 60% subordinated	0.96	2.70	3.80	4.23	5.20
Restructurings included, 80% subordinated	1.01	2.85	4.03	4.46	5.39

Notes: In the exercises reported in this table, LGDs are permitted to vary randomly across individual credit events in a manner mimicking event-type and seniority-specific distributions from Society of Actuaries (1998). Mean LGDs for senior and subordinated defaults are 44 and 63 percent, respectively, and for senior and subordinated restructurings are 22 and 24 percent, respectively. Other parameters for the exercise are those of the base case.

Carty and colleagues (1998) find that the mean LGD for senior unsecured bank loans to bankrupt firms is 21 percent, whereas it is 13 percent for secured loans. Carty and Lieberman (1996) also report statistics implying that collateral on average is associated with a 10 percentage point difference in LGDs. Asarnow and Edwards (1995) find a 35 percent LGD for C&I loans without distinguishing priority. For bonds, Altman, Waldman, and Kane (1996) find mean LGDs of about 50 percent for senior-secured, about 60 percent for senior-unsecured, and roughly 80 percent for subordinated debt. For private placements, Society of Actuaries (1998) reports mean LGDs of 20 and 44 percent for restructurings and defaults, respectively, and an approximately 15 percentage point difference between the mean LGDs of senior and subordinated defaults. The broad range of values found by the different studies reflects not only different types of debt and different samples but also different methods of measurement.

Priority differs across instruments in bank portfolios, raising the possibility of predictable differences in both average and bad-tail loss rates across portfolios. To obtain evidence about the importance of seniority-related asset characteristics to capital allocations, I vary the proportion of simulated portfolio assets that are subordinated, using two sets of LGD assumptions. Table 6.4 reports results when the percentage of subordinated loans in simulated portfolios varies between 0 and 80 percent and when LGDs for individual credit events have simulated values that mimic the event-type and seniority-specific distributions in Society of Actuaries (1998; means are 44 and 63 percent for senior and subordinated defaults, and 22 and 24 percent for senior and subordinated restructurings). Simulated restructurings are added in proportion to the defaults already in the data, as is described in more detail in section 6.9.1. Here the only role of the restructurings is to provide a platform to allow differences between LGDs on defaults and restructurings to be material to results. In table 6.4, both mean and bad-tail loss rates increase by about 20 to 25 percent from the 0 to 80 percent subordinated case, amounting to about a full percentage point difference in loss rates at the highest reported percentiles.

Table 6.5 shows results for an exercise in which simulated LGDs are set to identical values for all credit events of a given type and seniority (10 and 50 percent for senior and subordinated defaults, respectively, and 5 and 20 percent for senior and subordinated restructurings). The values were chosen to demonstrate the effects of larger differences in asset-type-related LGDs than are embedded in table 6.4's exercises. Unsurprisingly, the effect of varying the subordinated fraction is larger, with loss rates at the 99th percentile increasing by a factor of four.

If the evidence from Carty and colleagues (1998) that collateral yields only about a 10 percentage point improvement in average LGDs reflects reality, and if a secured/unsecured distinction is the only one relevant for bank loan portfolios, then the differences in loss rates shown in tables 6.4 and 6.5 overstate somewhat the possible distortions of ignoring seniority in capital regulations. However, many bankers believe that the type of collateral is as important as the presence of collateral, positing large differences in expected LGDs across types. Moreover, banking organizations increasingly are investing in the full range of capital market instruments, including unsecured junior subordinated debt, for which LGDs are on average far worse than those of secured loans. Thus, results in tables 6.4 and 6.5 probably understate the importance to capital of variations in the seniority of portfolio investments. Overall, it appears that a failure to include in regulatory capital requirements a sensitivity to LGD-related asset characteristics might be quite distortionary.

Table 6.5   Loss Rates as the Fraction of Subordinated Loans Varies, Fixed LGDs

| | Simulated Loss Rates (percent) | | | | |
| | | At Loss Distribution Percentiles | | | |
Variant	Mean	95	99	99.5	99.9
Restructurings included, 0% subordinated	0.18	0.48	0.64	0.71	0.84
Restructurings included, 20% subordinated	0.31	0.88	1.31	1.50	1.87
Restructurings included, 40% subordinated	0.45	1.26	1.83	2.04	2.50
Restructurings included, 60% subordinated	0.58	1.64	2.28	2.52	3.09
Restructurings included, 80% subordinated	0.72	1.97	2.68	2.97	3.54

Notes: In the exercises reported in this table, LGDs are held fixed for each type of credit event and priority. LGD values for senior and subordinated defaults are 10 and 50 percent, respectively, and for senior and subordinated restructurings are 5 and 20 percent, respectively. Other parameters for the exercise are those of the base case.

6.6   Portfolio Granularity Is Important

Standard portfolio theory, as applied to equity portfolios, implies that portfolio risk becomes almost insensitive to portfolio size beyond a rather modest number of assets. However, as was noted previously, debt portfolios are much harder to diversify than are equity portfolios. Moreover, actual banks' loan portfolios tend to contain some loans that are rather large in dollar amount relative to the portfolio dollar size. Intuition suggests that for such portfolios the performance of a relative handful of loans can have a material effect on loss rates.

Full-scale credit risk models, such as CreditMetrics, handle variations in portfolio granularity naturally because individual exposure sizes enter the calculations, but differences in granularity are a bit more problematic for the internal-ratings approach to capital regulation. That approach would place assets with similar ratings, expected LGDs, and so on into groups or buckets, with an implicit presumption that each bucket contains a large number of relatively small loans. However, it seems likely that an internal ratings approach could approximate the effects of differences in portfolio granularity across banks by applying a granularity adjustment factor to each bucket (see Gordy 2000b for an example).

Table 6.6 displays effects of varying both the number of loans in simulated portfolios and the distribution of loan sizes. For these exercises, the size of each simulated portfolio is controlled such that the number of loans is the same for each while the dollar totals vary somewhat around target amounts. Loan-to-one-industry and loan-to-one-borrower limits are enforced in terms of the number of assets and also are roughly enforced in terms of fractions of portfolio dollar amounts.

Table 6.6   **Loss Rates for Different Degrees of Portfolio Granularity**

| | Simulated Loss Rates (percent) | | | | |
| | | At Loss Distribution Percentiles | | | |
Variant	Mean	95	99	99.5	99.9
Base case, but 500 loans, random sizes	0.67	2.01	2.98	3.39	4.34
Base case, but 500 loans, equal sizes	0.65	1.73	2.37	2.58	2.98
Base case, but 100 loans, random sizes	0.66	2.78	4.48	5.14	6.55
Base case, but 1,000 loans, random sizes	0.66	1.84	2.72	3.09	4.11
Base case, but 2,000 loans, random sizes	0.66	1.80	2.67	3.10	3.93

Notes: The first and third through fifth rows report results for base-case parameters, but unlike in other tables, simulated portfolios are considered to be complete when they contain the number of exposures specified in the Variant column, not when they reach the usual specified portfolio dollar size of $5 billion. Portfolio size for the first row is similar to that of the usual base case. Portfolio size is varied in the third through fifth rows. In the second row, portfolio size is fixed at 500 loans, but individual loan dollar sizes are fixed at $10 million each, whereas in other rows the distribution of loan dollar size relative to the approximately $5 billion portfolio size mimics that of an actual large U.S. bank.

Table 6.7   Loss Rates for Different Loan-to-One-Borrower Limits

| | Simulated Loss Rates (percent) | | | | |
| | | At Loss Distribution Percentiles | | | |
Variant	Mean	95	99	99.5	99.9
Base case, no one-borrower limit	0.66	2.09	3.38	4.16	7.81
Base case, 5 percent one-borrower limit	0.66	2.11	3.14	3.55	4.43
Base case, 3 percent one-borrower limit	0.66	2.11	3.14	3.53	4.44
Base case, 2 percent one-borrower limit	0.66	2.03	2.97	3.34	4.10
Base case, 1 percent one-borrower limit	0.66	1.97	2.81	3.13	3.75
Base case, 0.5 percent one-borrower limit	0.65	1.89	2.64	2.89	3.37

Note: Parameters are those of the base case, except that the loan-to-one-borrower limits varies as specified (the limit for the base case is 3 percent).

The first row shows results for parameters similar to those of the usual base case, which features a distribution of loan sizes typical of an actual large bank, whereas the second row shows results when each of the 500 portfolio loans are the same dollar size. Equalizing loan sizes reduces the 99th percentile loss rate by about 20 percent, implying that differences in granularity across banks may have significant implications for the economic capital they require for credit risk.

The third through fifth rows of table 6.6 feature the usual random loan sizes but different numbers of loans. When the number is reduced to 100 loans, bad-tail loss rates increase by 50 percent relative to those in the first row. When the number is increased to 1,000 or 2,000 loans, bad-tail rates are modestly smaller than those in the first row, by as much as 10 percent or so. These results suggest that although differences in numbers of loans across very large banks may not have much impact on portfolio credit risk, differences in size distributions might. Moreover, if an internal ratings approach to regulatory capital is to be applied to small banks as well as large banks, some adjustment of capital requirements for their much smaller portfolios probably is appropriate.[12]

Loan-to-one-borrower size limits are written into formal U.S. bank regulations, and internal limits that are tighter than those of the regulation are part of the policies of every major U.S. bank. Table 6.7 provides some additional insight into the effects of variations in portfolio granularity by varying the tightness of the loan-to-one-borrower limit that is routinely imposed as part of this paper's exercises. The third row has results for the 3 percent limit that is standard in this paper. Looking up the rows, a 5

---

12. In passing, note that granularity differences have essentially no effect on mean or expected losses. They only influence bad-tail loss rates. A practical interpretation of this regularity is that a bank with a concentrated portfolio can experience no problems for many years, but a surprise can more easily be fatal than for a bank with a fine-grained portfolio.

percent limit has essentially no effect. No limit at all also does not change loss rates except at the 99.9th percentile, where the effect is a huge increase of more than 3 percentage points. This pattern is reflective of the fact that the portfolio of the actual bank upon which simulated loan sizes are based has only a few exposures larger than 1 percent of the portfolio, but those are much larger. Thus, in simulations it is rare that the large loan size is assigned and doubly rare that it is assigned to a defaulting asset. With no one-borrower limit at all, huge loans are not screened out of the portfolio; and even though such loans rarely default, their presence is enough to have a major impact on the far tail of the portfolio loss distribution.

Looking farther down the table, tighter loan-to-one-borrower limits have noticeable effects on bad-tail loss rates, especially at the 99.9th percentile. The lesson of these results is that loans that are large relative to portfolio size have a material effect on portfolio risk and economic capital requirements. For banks that use sophisticated credit risk models in making operating decisions, a very tight loan-to-one-borrower limit may not be needed, as such banks are likely to allocate more capital against very large loans than against smaller loans and to adjust loan pricing accordingly. However, other banks might be well served by very tight internal loan-to-one-borrower limits, regardless of the state of regulations.

6.7   Industry of the Borrower Does Not Appear Crucial

Cross-asset default correlations are a central focus of many credit risk models. Though such correlations cannot be measured directly with any confidence with available data, several measurement strategies are employed by practitioners.[13] Some use contingent claim modeling techniques to extract information from equity price correlations, but perhaps more common are methods that base estimated correlations on the industry and country of the borrower plus aggregate information about the performance of the industries and countries.

Traditional credit risk managers have for generations employed a simpler method of appraising and limiting the impact of correlated exposures on portfolio risk: They impose limits on the fraction of portfolio exposure to borrowers in any given industry or country. The limits usually do not vary by industry and are only somewhat specific to different regions of the world, reflecting the fact that a long period of untroubled performance by a given industry or country is no guarantee of an untroubled future.

As a practical matter, a regulatory capital regime cannot include limits or capital charges specific to a given industry (and perhaps not to a given country). In addition to the difficulty of estimating the values of such limits

---

13. McAllister and Mingo (1996) argue that tens of thousands of observations of individual borrower loss experience covering many years are required for confident direct measurement of default correlations.

or charges, their imposition would be seen politically as a form of government-enforced credit rationing. Moreover, inclusion of such limits as part of regulation would be technically challenging because of the lack of a single industry-coding scheme universally recognized as appropriate for all portfolios.

However, limits on exposure to any single industry regardless of identity probably should be a part of supervision, where judgment can be applied in evaluating industry groupings. Such limits have been a part of banking supervision in the United States for many years in that examiners criticize banks for having portfolios that they believe are too concentrated. However, to my knowledge examiners base their reviews on intuition and a sense of standard industry practice. Also, to my knowledge no empirical evidence about the implications for bad-tail loss rates of different industry limits has appeared.

Analysis of industry limits is not entirely mechanical in that it is possible that the details of the industry classification scheme might affect results. Tables 6.8 and 6.9 present evidence for different limits using the 39-industry and 20-industry schemes described previously. Results are qualitatively similar when Moody's 200 industry codes are used directly (not shown in tables). Focusing on table 6.8, the usual base case, which involves a 5 percent loan-to-one-industry limit, is reported in the last row. Raising the limit to 10 percent increases the loss rate at the 99th percentile by about seven percent, from 2.75 to 2.95 percent. Imposing no limit at all raises the rate at the 99th percentile modestly, to 3.11 percent. Table 6.9 displays similar effects of variations in limits when the 20-industry classification scheme is used.

Variations in loan-to-one-industry limits have relatively modest effects because defaults in any given year in the Moody's data tend to be spread across several different industries, with the largest number of defaults in each industry being around ten in any of my classifications. Even where a tight limit screens some exposure out of a relatively high-default industry

Table 6.8   Loss Rates for Different Loan-to-One-Industry Limits,
                   39-Industry Classification

	Simulated Loss Rates (percent)				
		At Loss Distribution Percentiles			
Variant	Mean	95	99	99.5	99.9
Base case, no limit	0.66	2.09	3.11	3.52	4.42
Base case, 20 percent limit	0.66	2.08	3.11	3.52	4.38
Base case, 10 percent limit	0.65	2.02	2.95	3.31	4.15
Base case, 5 percent limit	0.63	1.88	2.75	3.06	3.85

Note: Parameters are those of the base case, but the loan-to-one-industry limit is varied from its usual value of 5 percent.

Table 6.9   Loss Rates for Different Loan-to-One-Industry Limits,
                 20-Industry Classification

| | | Simulated Loss Rates (percent) | | | |
| | | At Loss Distribution Percentiles | | | |
Variant	Mean	95	99	99.5	99.9
Base case, no limit	0.66	2.10	3.13	3.52	4.41
Base case, 30 percent limit	0.66	2.09	3.10	3.52	4.43
Base case, 20 percent limit	0.66	2.09	3.08	3.50	4.38
Base case, 10 percent limit	0.64	1.95	2.84	3.18	4.00
Base case, 7.5 percent limit	0.64	1.92	2.78	3.12	3.86

Note: Parameters are those of the base case, but the loan-to-one-industry limit is varied and the Carey 20-industry classification scheme is used in enforcing the limit rather than the usual Carey 39-industry scheme.

in a given year, there are enough defaults in the same year in other industries to make possible large losses if the lender happens to invest in the wrong borrowers. Moreover, the resampling engine naturally tends to spread exposure across a number of industries (so the results in tables 6.8 and 6.9 do not reflect loss rates if simulated portfolios were *forced* to include only loans to a single industry).

I believe the results imply that for the moment cross-industry correlations can be safely ignored in formal capital regulation for straight loan portfolios. Although supervisors and bank managers should be attentive to concentrations of loans to firms in a single industry, at this time there is little empirical basis for specifying precise loan-to-one-industry limits in regulation. However, for structured products like credit derivatives or subordinated tranches of collateralized loan obligations (CLOs), considerations of cross-industry diversification probably are significant. Moreover, improvements in credit risk measurement may in the future provide an ability to specify loan limits or trade-offs among industries with confidence. Limits on country exposure may be measurable now, but data limitations led me to forego attempting measurement in this paper.[14]

6.8   The Internal Rating Approach's Linear Approximation Might Be Good Enough for Loans

As was noted previously, the internal ratings approach to capital regulation involves an assumption of linearity or perfect correlation across different permutations of key dimensions of credit risk. That is, capital

14. Effects of different country limits are difficult to analyze with the Moody's data because substantial numbers of non-U.S. obligors have appeared in the data only in recent years.

would be computed for each asset or subportfolio according to its characteristics, and such allocations would be summed to obtain a total portfolio
capital requirement. Gordy (2000b) shows that such a setup presumes that
the risk of assets in all buckets is driven by a single systematic risk factor
(e.g., that mixing grades in a portfolio yields no diversification benefits).

Evidence on the accuracy of the linear approximation is provided by
estimating loss rates at the 99th percentile for portfolios with various mix-
tures of loans across grades, both directly and using the linear approximation. Only the mix of grades is varied, with all other parameters fixed at
base-case values. Fractions of portfolio dollars in each of the grades A or
better, Baa, Ba, and B are varied in 20 percent increments, producing fifty-
six different permutations (e.g., 100, 0, 0, 0; 80, 0, 0, 20; 80, 0, 20, 0; etc.).
The 99th percentile loss rate is estimated directly for each permutation.
The linear approximation is computed by multiplying the percentage in
each grade times the 99th percentile loss rate for a portfolio composed of
loans only in that grade.

Differences in direct and approximated capital requirements are expressed as a percentage of the direct estimates in figure 6.2 and in absolute
terms in figure 6.3, one bar per permutation. Permutations are sorted
along the horizontal axis according to the fraction of the portfolio in the

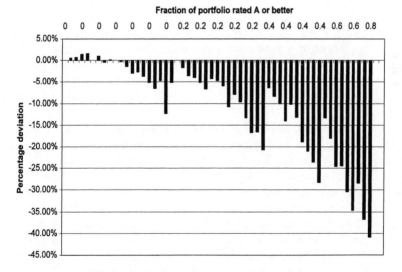

Fig. 6.2   Percentage error from linear capital specification
Notes: Each bar represents the percentage deviation of approximated from directly measured
loss rates at the 99th percentile for a single exercise. Exercises differ in the fraction of loans
in each grade. Results are shown for every possible permutation of grade mixes when fractions in each grade are varied in 20 percent increments. The linear method used to approximate capital is one typical of many internal rating approaches.

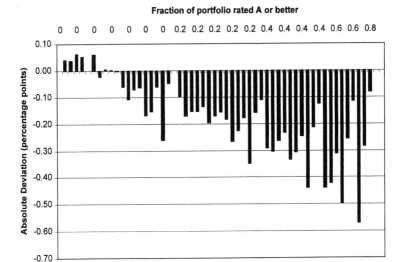

Fig. 6.3   Absolute error from linear capital specification

Notes: Each bar represents the absolute deviation in percentage points of approximated from directly measured loss rates at the 99th percentile for a single exercise. Exercises differ in the fraction of loans in each grade. Results are shown for every possible permutation of grade mixes when fractions in each grade are varied in 20 percent increments. The linear method used to approximate capital is one typical of many internal rating approaches.

A grades, then the fractions Baa and Ba. For example, the permutation with 80 percent of loans rated A or better and 20 percent rated B, the fourth bar from the right, features an absolute error of about 0.6 percentage points of capital, with the approximated requirement of 1.4 percent being about 30 percent below the directly estimated requirement of about 2 percent.

Both percentage and absolute errors generally grow with the fraction in the A grades, and the approximation generally understates the directly estimated requirement. The percentage error can be large, ranging up to 40 percent. However, the absolute errors are modest, almost always less than 0.5 percentage point of capital.

On the whole, I view these results as supportive of the adequacy of the linear approximation. The largest percentage errors arise for high-grade portfolios, and capital requirements are particularly difficult to estimate for such portfolios. At a one-year horizon, defaults by borrowers in the Aaa, Aa, and A grades are extremely rare, and their timing relative to the business cycle is idiosyncratic across databases.[15] Thus, the imprecision of

15. A caveat is that results of a similar exercise using Society of Actuaries (1998) data, though qualitatively similar, produced somewhat larger approximation errors that indicate that the approximation would generally overstate capital requirements. This is symptomatic of the difficulty of measuring diversification effects.

directly estimated tail loss rates for such portfolios may be similar to that of the linear approximation.

6.9   Some Factors to Consider in Parameterizing an Internal-Ratings-Based Regulatory Regime

Several factors that may not be obvious must be taken into account in the parameterization of a credit risk model or regulatory capital regime. Some such factors may appear to be mostly of interest to technicians, but policy decisions that influence their handling can have a large effect on estimated economic capital allocations and thus regulatory requirements.

6.9.1   The Definition of Default Is Important

One such matter is the definition of default to use in estimating and accounting for credit losses. The niceties of the definition are less important in mark-to-market models, but the banking industry's strong past preference for historical cost measures may make the adoption of mark-to-market approaches politically infeasible. If that is the case, the set of credit risk events to be counted as loss-causing events and against which regulatory capital is required is material (and must be reasonably standardized across banks). Most would agree that the payment defaults that are recorded in the Moody's database should be included as loss events. Uncommon in the bond market and thus not in Moody's database are distressed restructurings, in which the payment terms of the original debt contract are altered in negotiations between borrower and lender.[16] Although LGDs for restructurings are smaller on average than those for defaults, restructurings frequently impose losses on banks, which agree to them because the alternative may be bankruptcy and its associated costs. Evidence in Society of Actuaries (1998) shows that restructurings are common in private debt markets and represent a significant share of lenders' total credit losses over time: 127 of 566 credit risk events in that study were restructurings, with a 21 percent mean LGD versus a 45 percent mean LGD for defaults.

I simulate the effect of including restructurings in the definition of default by randomly creating restructuring events in the Moody's data for otherwise nondefaulting experience records. Two exercises are conducted. In the first case, approximately one restructuring is created for every three defaults in each year and grade of the base data. In the second case, the restructuring rate is still proportional to defaults by year and grade, but the rate is twice as high for below-investment-grade borrowers as for investment-grade borrowers, resulting in the creation of approximately one

---

16. Moody's database treats distressed exchanges as defaults. Such exchanges differ from restructurings in that exchanges are usually coercive take-it-or-leave-it offers by the issuer, whereas restructurings are negotiated.

Table 6.10   Loss Rates When Restructurings as Well as Defaults are Included
                    as Losses

| | Simulated Loss Rates (percent) | | | | |
| | | At Loss Distribution Percentiles | | | |
Variant	Mean	95	99	99.5	99.9
Base case	0.63	1.87	2.71	3.04	3.87
One simulated restructuring for every three defaults	0.75	2.10	2.98	3.32	4.16
One simulated restructuring for every two defaults, higher rate for junk loans	0.80	2.24	3.18	3.53	4.37

Notes: Results in the first row are those for the base case, in which only actual defaults as recorded in Moody's database are considered to be credit risk events. In the second and third rows, exposures are randomly designated as restructurings as described in the text. All simulated loans are senior, and simulated LGDs vary across loans such that their distributions mimic those reported in Society of Actuaries (1998) for defaults and restructurings (mean LGDs of 44 and 22 percent, respectively; see section 6.5).

restructuring for every two defaults. Severities for the restructurings are simulated to conform to the distribution of restructuring severities in Society of Actuaries (1998), whereas those for defaults conform to the distribution for defaults in that study.[17]

Results for the two exercises appear in table 6.10. Unsurprisingly, including restructurings raises both mean and tail loss rates, with proportional changes being in the 10 to 25 percent range and larger for the second exercise than for the first. Although the impact of including restructurings in the definition of default is modest relative to the impact of ratings on the bad tail, the effects are economically significant. Thus, regulators and bankers should be attentive to the definition of default in setting up their systems.[18]

6.9.2   That LGDs Vary Across Defaults Is Material

A common assumption in credit risk modeling is that expected LGDs for individual defaults can safely be set to the average value of such LGDs for assets of similar seniority. An appeal is made to the law of large numbers: Although individual-asset LGDs vary widely, annual defaults for any large-bank portfolio are likely to number in the tens or hundreds, and thus for defaults as a whole the LGD will collapse to a value near the population mean. The flaw in this argument is that real portfolios are not com-

17. No controls on the industry of restructured loans are imposed.
18. The effect on loss rates is more modest than if similar numbers of defaults were added to the data because LGDs for restructurings are smaller.

Table 6.11   **Effect of Fixed versus Variable LGDs**

| | Simulated Loss Rates (percent) | | | | |
| | | At Loss Distribution Percentiles | | | |
Variant	Mean	95	99	99.5	99.9
Restructurings included, realistic LGD variation	0.80	2.23	3.15	3.51	4.29
Restructurings included, fixed LGDs (mean values of the realistic distributions)	0.81	2.16	2.91	3.17	3.74

Notes: Results are for an exercise in which simulated restructurings are created, similar to the case reported in the third row of table 6.10. In the first row, LGDs vary across credit risk events by event type in such a manner that the distributions of LGDs mimic those reported in Society of Actuaries (1998). In the second row, LGDs for all credit events are held fixed at the mean values for defaults and restructurings, respectively (all simulated loans are senior).

pletely fine-grained: Even with tens of thousands of assets in the portfolio, the largest 50 or 100 loans usually account for a significant fraction of total dollar exposure. If a few of these large loans default (an event that is usually associated with a portfolio loss rate far out in the bad tail), the idiosyncratic variation in realized LGDs for those few assets can have a material effect on the portfolio loss rate.

Table 6.11 demonstrates the importance of the fixed versus variable LGD assumption. The first row reflects base-case parameters except that simulated restructurings are included, as was described in section 6.9.1. As was noted previously, simulated LGDs vary across defaults in a manner similar to the distributions in Society of Actuaries (1998). In the second row, LGDs are fixed at the sample average rates for each type of credit event (44 percent for defaults and 22 percent for restructurings). Although the fixed-LGD assumption has little effect at the 95th percentile, it materially reduces the estimated loss rate at the 99.9th percentile by about 15 percent. Thus, in parameterizing an internal ratings based capital regulatory regime, if the projected bank failure rate that regulators are willing to tolerate is quite low (corresponding to a percentile very far out in the bad tail), it will be important to take idiosyncratic variation of LGDs into account.

6.9.3   Bad Years Strongly Influence the Tail Loss Rates

It is conventional in credit risk modeling to express the rate of bad tail events in terms of the likelihood of such events implicit in an average year, that is, as though such events might occur at any time. Although bad-tail events are indeed possible at any time, intuition suggests that they are far more likely to occur during times of general economic distress. Estimating portfolio loss distributions by equally weighting events in each database

Table 6.12   **Tail Loss Rates Based on All years, Good Years, and Bad Years**

| | Simulated Loss Rates (percent) | | | | |
| | | At Loss Distribution Percentiles | | | |
Variant	Mean	95	99	99.5	99.9
Base distribution of grades, all years	0.62	1.86	2.72	3.09	3.86
Base distribution of grades, good years only	0.47	1.36	2.04	2.34	3.07
Base distribution of grades, bad years only	1.39	2.74	3.54	3.89	4.64
Investment-grade loans only, good years only	0.02	0.15	0.52	0.74	1.29
Investment-grade loans only, bad years only	0.12	0.64	1.25	1.51	2.27
Junk-grade loans only, good years only	0.93	2.26	3.06	3.39	4.18
Junk-grade loans only, bad years only	2.55	4.50	5.58	5.97	6.82

Notes: This table reports results when the normal equal-weighting of experience years in the Moody's database is varied to put all weight on good or bad years, respectively, with bad-experience years being 1970, 1986, and 1989–91 and good years being all others during the period 1970–98. Results in the first row are for the base case and are for comparison. The second and third rows restrict resampling to good and bad experience years, respectively, while maintaining the usual distribution of loans across grades in simulated portfolios. Remaining rows report results for good versus bad years when all loans are restricted to be in the grades Aaa through Baa3 (investment grade) or Ba1 through B3 (junk), respectively.

year, as is done throughout this paper, tends to understate bad-tail loss rates. In choosing a level of capital requirements, policy makers must decide whether they wish their chosen level of soundness to apply for the average year or for bad years in particular. This section provides a sense of the difference in bad-tail loss rates (and thus capital requirements) associated with such a decision by comparing tail rates when all experience years in the Moody's database are used in simulations with rates when only good years or bad years are used. Bad years include the five years of highest overall average default rates in the data, which are 1970, 1986, 1989, 1990, and 1991, whereas good years are all others during the period 1970–98.

The first three rows of table 6.12 show loss rates for the usual base-case distribution of loans across grades when all years are equally weighted in the simulations and when only good years versus only bad years are used. Both mean and tail loss rates are sharply higher in the bad years than in the good years. The patterns imply that to achieve loss protection at the 99th percentile, capital ratios in the bad years must be about 175 percent of those needed in the good years, and about 130 percent of those estimated to be required when all years are equally weighted. Seen another way, a policymaker choosing to require capital to protect at the 99th percentile estimated with all years equally weighted, and thus requiring about a 2.7 percent equity capital ratio for the typical large bank, would in bad years be likely to experience a large bank failure rate of about 5 in 100, whereas in good years the failure rate would be far less than 1 in 100, more like 1 or 2 in 1000.

The remaining four rows of table 6.12 display good-year versus bad-year loss rates for portfolios composed of purely investment-grade loans versus those composed only of below-investment-grade loans.[19] Tail loss rates are sharply higher in the bad years than in the good for both types of portfolios, but the effect is somewhat more pronounced in the case of the investment-grade portfolio. This is a bit of a surprise, as Carey (1998) found that investment-grade, private-debt portfolio bad-tail loss rates were rather insensitive to good-year versus bad-year distinctions. The difference arises because two of the three defaults of issuers rated A or better appearing in the Moody's data happened to occur in 1989 (a bad year generally), and Baa defaults were unusually high in 1986. In the Society of Actuaries data, investment-grade defaults tend to occur during relatively good years. This difference in results points to the difficulty of reliably parameterizing credit risk models for the investment grades. For investment-grade borrowers, defaults are small in number and their patterns are somewhat idiosyncratic to particular databases.

6.10   Concluding Remarks

The evidence presented in this paper implies that differences across assets in ratings and seniority (expected LGDs) and differences in granularity across portfolios are important influences on differences in portfolio credit risk. Bank capital regulations should take proper account of such differences or risk a continuation of large-scale capital arbitrage. Important but not widely understood considerations in determining the level of regulatory capital requirements are the definition of loss-causing credit risk events, the variability of LGDs across such events, and the extent to which regulators wish to limit failure rates in bad years or in a hypothetical average year.

On the whole, the results imply that for the commercial loan portfolios of large U.S. banks, the internal ratings approach now under consideration by the Basel Committee on Banking Supervision could adequately approximate the capital allocations likely to be produced by a full models approach. However, a number of caveats apply:

---

19. For the former, 40 percent of loans are rated A or better and 60 percent Baa, whereas for the junk exercises 70 percent are rated Ba and 30 percent B.

- More explicit modeling of correlation and other effects than appears in the internal ratings approach may be needed for structured-finance exposures such as credit derivatives.
- The credit risk properties of consumer loans, non-U.S. commercial loans, and other types of exposures may differ from those displayed in this paper.
- The data in this paper represent a mixture of loan and bond loss experience, but there is evidence that loan and bond experiences differ (Society of Actuaries 1998; Altman and Suggitt 2000).
- The results in this paper are most representative of the risks associated with a well-managed bank or portfolio. A poorly managed institution, especially one unable to provide reliable ratings of individual assets or other risk-relevant information, may pose bad-tail risks many times larger than those presented here.
- Regulatory capital must account for risks other than credit, such as operational risks.
- The remaining maturity of an asset may be an important determinant of its contribution to portfolio credit risk. However, maturity effects are intimately related to the time horizon of analysis and the choice between mark-to-market and default-mode analysis. Research on these matters is needed.
- Regulatory choices concerning the definition of capital and the soundness standard to be used will have material effects on the safety and soundness achieved by any new regulation.
- Empirical findings of this and other papers are based on limited panels of data. Allowance should be made for the possibility of economic times that are worse than those reflected in available data.

Many other considerations are also important to the design of an appropriate regulatory capital standard.

I have taken as given in this paper the desirability of prudential regulation and also the necessity of supervision that is adequate to ensure that such regulations are implemented properly. However, even in the absence of capital regulation, the results in this paper are useful to bank examiners, bank investors, risk managers, and asset-backed security designers. All such individuals must evaluate the credit risk embedded in debt portfolios and thus are aided by an understanding of the factors that influence portfolio credit risk.

References

Altman, Edward I., and Anthony Saunders. 1997. Credit risk measurement: Developments over the last 20 years. *Journal of Banking and Finance* 21 (11–12): 1721–42.

Altman, Edward I., and Heather Suggitt. 2000. Default rates in the syndicated bank loan market: A mortality analysis. *Journal of Banking and Finance* 24: 229–53.

Altman, Edward I., Robert A. Waldman, and Christopher P. Kane. 1996. Recoveries on defaulted bonds: By industry and debt seniority. Salomon Brothers High Yield Research, Working Paper. New York, N.Y.

Asarnow, Elliot, and David Edwards. 1995. Measuring loss on defaulted bank loans: A 24-year study. *Journal of Commercial Lending* 77:11–23.

Basel Committee on Banking Supervision. 1999. *A new capital adequacy framework*. Basel, Switzerland: Bank for International Settlements.

Calem, Paul. 1999. The relationship between maturity composition and credit loss exposure for a loan pool. Washington, D.C.: Federal Reserve Board. Internal memorandum.

Carey, Mark. 1998. Credit risk in private debt portfolios. *Journal of Finance* 53 (4): 1363–87.

Carty, Lea V. 1996. An empirical investigation of default risk dynamics. Ph.D. diss. Columbia University, New York.

Carty, Lea V., David T. Hamilton, Sean C. Keenan, Adam Moss, Michael Mulvaney, Tom Marshella, and M. G. Subhas. 1998. Bankrupt bank loan recoveries. New York: Moody's Investors Service. Special comment, June.

Carty, Lea V., and Dana Lieberman. 1996. Defaulted bank loan recoveries. New York: Moody's Investors Service. Special Report, November.

Duffie, Darrel, and David Lando. 1999. Term structures of credit spreads with incomplete accounting information. *Econometrica,* forthcoming.

Flannery, Mark J. 1989. Capital regulation and insured banks' choice of individual loan default risks. *Journal of Monetary Economics* 24:235–58.

Gordy, Michael B. 2000a. A comparative anatomy of credit risk models. *Journal of Banking and Finance* 24:119–49.

———. 2000b. Credit VaR models and risk-bucket capital rules: A reconciliation. Federal Reserve Board, Working Paper, March.

Gupton, Greg M., Christopher C. Finger, and Mickey Bhatia. 1997. *CreditMetrics—Technical document*. [http://www.jpmorgan.com].

Hamilton, David T., and Lea V. Carty. 1999. Debt recoveries for corporate bankruptcies. Moody's Investors Service, Special Comment, June.

Jackson, Patricia, and William Perraudin. 1999. The nature of credit risk: The effect of maturity, type of obligor, and country of domicile. *Financial Stability Review* 7 (November): 128–40.

Kiesel, Rudiger, William Perraudin, and Alex Taylor. 1999. The structure of credit risk. London, Eng.: Birkbeck College, Department of Economics, mimeograph, and forthcoming as Bank of England Working Paper.

McAllister, Patrick H., and John J. Mingo. 1996. Bank capital requirements for securitized loan portfolios. *Journal of Banking and Finance* 20:1381–405.

Mingo, John. 1998. Policy implications of the Federal Reserve study of credit risk models at major U.S. banking institutions. *Journal of Banking and Finance* 24: 15–33.

Nickell, Pamela, William Perraudin, and Simone Varotto. 1998. Stability of rating transitions, Bank of England, Working Paper, December.

———. 1999. Ratings- versus equity-based credit risk modeling: An empirical analysis. Bank of England, Working Paper, July.

Ong, Michael K. 1999. *Internal credit risk models: Capital allocation and performance measurement*. London: Risk Books.

Saunders, Anthony. 1999. *Credit risk measurement*. New York: Wiley.

Society of Actuaries. 1998. *1986–94 credit risk loss experience study: Private placement bonds*. Schaumberg, Ill.: Author.

Treacy, William F., and Mark Carey. 1998. Credit risk rating at large U.S. banks. *Federal Reserve Bulletin* 84 (November): 897–921.
Vojta, George J. 1973. *Bank capital adequacy.* New York: Citicorp.
Zhou, Chunsheng. 1997. Default correlation: An analytical result. Federal Reserve Board, Working Paper no. 1997-27.

Comment   Patricia Jackson

The paper is an extension of Carey's earlier work on the development of nonparametric estimates of the value at risk (VaR) of credit portfolios, using resampling techniques to enable large numbers of portfolios to be generated. For some rating bands, Carey replicates the obligors in his sample to give a pool that is large enough for the resampling. One issue is whether this increases the correlations affecting the VaR estimates. The development of nonparametric methods of estimating credit risk, however, is an interesting way forward given the concerns about the assumptions lying behind some of the parametric models.

Carey looks at the policy implications of the credit risk results, particularly in relation to the development of the new Basel Accord. Under current proposals, one approach for the setting of capital requirements for credit books will be the banks' internal ratings. It is proposed that banks will be able to slot credit exposures into default probability bands for which capital requirements will be set by the Basel Committee at least to cover unexpected loss. These requirements will be calibrated against estimates of unexpected loss at a particular confidence interval.

In this regard, Carey's work raises a number of policy issues. One is whether capital should cover just defaults or economic loss (i.e., a deterioration in credit quality in a bank's book as well as defaults). Carey uses defaults, whereas the research being carried out at the Bank of England looks at economic loss. The difference between the two is significant. Calculations by Bank of England staff indicate that moving from default mode to economic loss increases the VaR estimates by around 70 percent, although less for the lower quality. Economic loss must be important. In any year a bank must be able to withstand the defaults in that year as well as overall weakness in the book that could lead to losses in later years.

This question is also related to the time horizon chosen. Carey calculates losses on the portfolios over one-year periods. That is also the horizon used in the Bank of England work and by many other banks. However, a one-year horizon with default mode, rather than economic loss, implicitly assumes that a bank will be able to raise new capital at the end of the year

Patricia Jackson is head of the Financial Industry and Regulation Division at the Bank of England.

to cover losses in later years. In fact, it would be very difficult for a bank to raise new capital in a severe economic downturn. It also implicitly assumes that a bank will experience only defaults—that is, it will not have any other loans that have deteriorated to such an extent that specific provisions (i.e., reserves) have to be held against them (these are deducted from capital). Default mode is therefore inconsistent with a one-year horizon.

Another issue is whether capital should cover expected as well as unexpected loss. Carey is looking at unexpected plus expected, and the Bank of England research has been looking at unexpected, in line with the way that banks look at their economic capital. This must depend on provisioning and the capital treatment of provisions. Many banks do not provide against expected loss; and where they do, these general provisions are included in Tier 2 capital. Probably it is right, therefore, to set capital requirements against expected as well as unexpected loss or at least require provisions (deducted from capital) against expected loss.

The loss given default assumptions are critical in calculating the VaRs for credit books. These are assumptions about both the level of loss given default and its volatility. The lower-grade credits are particularly sensitive to the recovery rate assumptions. Overall, too little is known about loss given default to be sure which assumptions should be used. In particular, it is not clear which assumptions should be made about mean loss given default and correlations in loss given default when default rates are high. It may well be the case that in extreme recessions, loss given default is generally high. The assumption made in the Bank of England research is that recoveries average 50 percent with a standard deviation of 25 percent, which is in line with the CreditMetrics manual. Carey, in his base-case numbers, assigns loss given default to the exposures in his portfolio by simulating the Society of Actuaries' loss given default distribution produced for private debt. This has a mean of 36 percent, but it is not clear what the standard deviation is.

The different assumptions on default/economic loss and loss given default and its variability have a sizeable effect on the value at risk estimates. Kiesel, Perraudin, and Taylor (1999), using the same approach set out in their paper "The Structure of Credit Risk," calculate the VaR (with a 99.9 percent confidence level) for a portfolio with the same quality distribution as Carey, but they allow for economic loss. Their portfolio consists of 500 equally sized exposures. They also use the loss given default assumptions from the CreditMetrics manual set out previously. They estimate a VaR of 7.5 percent against Carey's 3.3 percent.

Carey suggests that maturity is also an important dimension for VaR for credit books; we have also found this in the Bank of England research (see Jackson and Perraudin 1999). The maturity effect is greater for high-quality portfolios. The policy issue for regulators is whether including this dimension in capital requirements would lead to regulatory arbitrage.

Would banks restructure their books to make longer-term loans appear short-term? Would this matter if they could reprice the credit risk?

Carey mentions some other important issues as well. One is concentration. From the Bank of England work on credit portfolios, highly concentrated portfolios do seem far riskier than less concentrated portfolios. This probably does need to be taken into account in the capital requirements.

References

Jackson, P., and W. Perraudin. 1999. The nature of credit risk: The effect of maturity, type of obligor and country of domicile. *Financial Stability Review* 7 (November): 128–40.
Kiesel, R., W. Perraudin, and A. Taylor. 1999. The structure of credit risk. London, Eng.: Birbeck College, Department of Economics, mimeograph, and forthcoming as Bank of England Working Paper.

Discussion Summary

Doug Diamond began the general discussion with two questions. He noted that given the one-year horizon, banks effectively rebalance their portfolios and are able to recapitalize. He observed that, in practice, banks have some durable relationships and cannot fully rebalance at year-end. He also asked about the risk of bank versus bond portfolios. In good times, he noted, loans may be less risky because of priority, but in bad times loans will be riskier than bonds because they are more illiquid.

Robert Eisenbeis followed, asking how representative the loss given default experience of bonds is for the loss given default of bank loans. He raised a second issue, noting the importance of maturity on default probability. Citing work by Altman, he noted that the default experience of bonds within a given rating class differed by how long the bonds had been outstanding. Bonds tended to have low default incidence in the first couple of years and then to increase significantly.

Mark Flannery noted that Altman compares the recovery of bank loans and bonds. He followed up on Doug Diamond's question and noted that the distinction highlighted by the discussant (*Patricia Jackson*) between mark-to-market losses and losses from default may be semantic. He observed that the key question is whether a bank can raise capital at the end of the year. He noted that the mark-to-market approach advocated by the discussant recognizes the present value of all future losses, whereas the default-mode approach assumes recapitalization.

Taking the discussion in another direction, *James Wilcox* noted the challenge from an approach that leads to procyclical regulatory capital requirements and the difficulty of requiring banks to raise capital in bad years.

Andrew Powell noted that an Argentine database of all loans is available for research. He observed that using parametric approaches, in contrast to the paper's nonparametric approach, shows that estimated transition matrices might be bank specific for this data set.

Martin Feldstein followed with two comments, first noting that within a year, banks will make portfolio adjustments to shed risk so the required capital may be overstated. He also remarked on the importance of credit derivatives. Looking forward, he noted that credit derivatives will be increasingly important as banks originate and sell risk into the market and that this raises the challenge of counterparty credit risk. He wondered how the Basel Committee on Banking Supervision was addressing this issue.

Stephen Cecchetti wondered whether the Basel Accord was becoming overly detailed and urged caution. He asked, if supervisors manage the banking system, do we want all banks responding to shocks in the same way? He noted that this might create systemic risk.

Mark Carey began by responding to Stephen Cecchetti, sharing his worry about the accord's becoming overly detailed, but not for herding reasons. He noted that approximating credit risk and capital needs should not do too much harm if the approximation is reasonably good. If the approximation is bad, however, there will be a problem, particularly if banks that are not well managed base their lending decisions on the regulatory capital rules. In response to Martin Feldstein, he agreed that credit derivatives would need to be addressed, noting that this will be easier for single name protection. He observed that if one does not understand portfolio risk, then addressing credit derivatives would be less useful—the key is to understand the dynamics of the underlying assets. He also agreed that the bank-specific transition matrices brought up by Andrew Powell might be important.

More generally on the question of using a one-year horizon and either a mark-to-market or default-mode approach only, Carey noted that if bad events are serially correlated, then the default-mode assumption that banks can recapitalize will be false and a longer horizon would be appropriate—the question becomes how long a horizon. He asked whether spread risk should be addressed if a mark-to-market approach is employed. He also asked whether this is correct under a hold-to-maturity environment; that is, should a bank cover liquidity risk? He noted that banks are currently wed to historical cost accounting and that a transition to a framework that depends on mark-to-market accounting could be challenging.

In response to James Wilcox, he noted that even without procyclical regulatory capital requirements, banks should be thinking about credit risk in this portfolio framework. He pointed out that banks should raise capital and cut back on lending when the portfolio is riskier (a free-market solution). He also noted that based on Altman's work and other research, there seems to be a significant difference between bonds and bank loans, both for default rates and recovery rates. Finally, he noted that because rebalancing is not allowed within the year, the nonparametric default–only approach employed assumes the portfolio is a one-year portfolio and that the bank is recapitalized at the end of the year.

7

Obstacles to Optimal Policy
The Interplay of Politics and Economics in Shaping Bank Supervision and Regulation Reforms

Randall S. Kroszner and Philip E. Strahan

7.1 Introduction

Economists analyzing depository institution supervision and regulation typically have taken a normative approach and have generated numerous reform proposals. Although agreement exists about the general direction of welfare-enhancing reforms, how to pass and implement such reforms has received much less analysis. This paper provides a positive political-economy analysis of the most important revision of the U.S. supervision and regulation system during the last two decades, the 1991 Federal Deposit Insurance Corporation Improvement Act (FDICIA). We analyze the impact of private interest groups and political-institutional factors on the voting patterns concerning FDICIA to assess the empirical importance of different types of obstacles to welfare-enhancing reforms.

Rather than take regulations as given, the political economy approach we employ here attempts to provide a positive analysis of how and why regulations evolve as they do and what forces can lead to their durability, as well as their potential for change. In section 7.2 we briefly outline a

Randall S. Kroszner is professor of economics at the Graduate School of Business of the University of Chicago, associate director of the George J. Stigler Center for the Study of the Economy and the State, and a faculty research fellow of the National Bureau of Economic Research. Philip E. Strahan is vice president in the Banking Studies Department of the Federal Reserve Bank of New York.

The authors thank Frederic Mishkin, Jeremy Stein, Thomas Stratmann, and conference participants for suggestions on an earlier draft. Kroszner would like to thank both the Lynde and Harry Bradley Foundation for support from a grant to the George J. Stigler Center for the Study of the Economy and the State and the University of Chicago Law School, where he was the John M. Olin Visiting Fellow in Law and Economics when this was written. The views expressed here are strictly those of the authors and do not necessarily reflect the position of the Federal Reserve Bank of New York or the Federal Reserve System.

number of approaches to understanding the political economy of government involvement in the economy. In section 7.3 we apply these theories to describe why, after little change since the end of the Great Depression, legislative reform of bank regulation began in the 1980s. This section also contains a brief review of the major legislative changes during the last twenty years and provides a more detailed description of the legislative history of FDICIA and its amendments.

In section 7.4 we outline hypotheses about the factors that should affect the support for FDICIA and the amendments generated by the positive interest group and political approaches. Concerning private interest groups, we focus on the contrasting interests of large versus small banks (intraindustry rivalry), of banks versus insurance (interindustry rivalry), and of consumers versus the banking industry. Concerning the political-institutional factors, we explore the roles of legislator ideology, partisanship, and congressional committees. We also provide the variable definitions in this section.

Section 7.5 describes our empirical voting model and contains the results. We analyze votes by members of the House of Representatives on three amendments related to FDICIA and its final passage. We find consistent support for the influence of both the intra- and interindustry rivalries on the outcomes but little role for consumer interests. Measures of legislator ideology and partisanship also have an impact. For two of the three amendments, the private interest group factors have greater explanatory power than do the political factors, and we find the opposite for the other amendment. Because both sets of factors do play a role, both should be taken into account in order to implement successful change. A divide-and-conquer strategy with respect to the private interests appears to be effective for bringing about legislative change. The concluding section draws tentative lessons from the political economy approaches concerning ways to make welfare-enhancing regulatory change more likely.

7.2   Alternative Approaches to the Political Economy of Regulation

Both policy reformers trying to effect change as well as researchers trying to develop positive theories of government policy making have tried to understand the patterns of regulation and deregulation. Economists have tended to emphasize the struggle between private interests and the public interest in determining policy outcomes. Political scientists have tended to emphasize the role of ideology and public opinion as well as the structure of the legislative decision-making institutions in shaping outcomes.[1] In this section, we will briefly outline these alternative positive approaches to ana-

---

1. Political scientists, however, have long understood and analyzed the impact of private interest groups on policy outcomes (e.g., Schattscheider 1935), so the distinction between the approaches of economists and political scientists is primarily for expository convenience.

lyzing regulatory change and describe some applications to understanding aspects of banking and financial regulation. Although these approaches are not mutually exclusive, they emphasize different aspects of the interaction between economics and politics. Each captures an important element in the process, and our empirical work will try to gauge their relative importance.

7.2.1 Positive Economic Approaches: Public Interest and Private Interest

Public Interest

The traditional approach that economists once took to explaining the existence of regulation emphasized that regulations exist to correct market failures and protect poorly informed consumers from harm.[2] From this perspective, regulatory intervention occurs primarily to maximize social welfare, so this approach is often called the public interest theory of regulation. Public interest rationales are given for capital regulation and deposit insurance to provide a sound banking system because stability of the financial system can have spillover effects for general macroeconomic performance (e.g., Diamond and Dybvig 1983; King and Levine 1993; Jayaratne and Strahan 1996; Kaufman and Kroszner 1997). Statutory protections of shareholders and creditors from ex post appropriation and supervisory agencies such as the Securities and Exchange Commission (SEC) are rationalized on the grounds of investor and consumer protection.

A key challenge to the public interest theory is that many forms of regulation are hard to understand from a welfare-maximizing point of view. Entry restrictions that protect banks or other financial institutions from competition, portfolio restrictions that hinder diversification, deposit insurance systems that exacerbate moral hazard problems, and geographic restrictions that have prevented expansion within a country or across national borders are generally difficult to rationalize on public interest grounds. Regulation that does not appear to serve a public interest also is common in other sectors (see Stigler 1988).

Virtually all regulation, regardless of whether it may have a public interest rationale, has significant distributional consequences. The parties affected by the regulation thus have an incentive to try to ensure that the government structures the regulation in such a way as to benefit them. A public interest argument is often used to mask the private interests that the intervention serves. Private interests may try to confuse the public debate by providing false or misleading information to make it difficult to discern whether policy would improve social welfare (e.g., Kane 1996; Dewatripont and Tirole 1999).

---

2. Joskow and Noll (1981) call this normative analysis as positive theory.

Private Interest

The private interest theory of regulation, also called the economic theory of regulation, characterizes the regulatory process as one of interest group competition in which compact, well-organized groups are able to use the coercive power of the state to capture rents for those groups at the expense of more dispersed groups (e.g., Olson 1965; Stigler 1971; Peltzman 1976, 1989; Becker 1983). Changes in the size, strength, and organization of interest groups thus provide the key to understanding policy changes. Regulated groups may be sufficiently powerful that they influence the politicians and the regulatory bureaucracy to serve primarily the interests of those subject to the regulation.

The incentives for such regulatory behavior may be direct or indirect. Pressure may be exerted directly on politicians through campaign contributions or votes. The politicians then pass a new statute or pressure the regulators to act sympathetically toward the interest group. Indirect incentives may come through regulators' understanding that cooperative behavior may be rewarded with lucrative employment opportunities in the industry after such supportive regulators leave the government.

The effectiveness of the interest groups depends on a number of factors. First, cohesive groups will find it easier to organize and overcome free-rider problems in lobbying for regulations that may benefit them. Producers of goods and services tend to be more compact and better organized than consumers, so there is a tendency for regulation on net to benefit producers more than consumers (Stigler 1971). As we discuss in more detail later, interests within an industry or section may not be homogeneous, and in such cases competition among well-organized and well-funded corporate interests can offset the tendency for regulation to benefit producers. A group's ability to organize is often inversely related to its size, but many labor unions and trade organizations have been able to develop effective lobbying bodies through carefully crafted incentives that provide a variety of information and support services in return for membership (see Olson 1965).

Second, groups tend to be more effective not only when the benefits are concentrated among group members but also when the costs of the regulation are relatively diffuse. A compact group of potential losers, each of whom would experience high losses associated with the regulation, will be likely to form a lobby that will try to counteract the original interest group's pressure. Interest groups most directly affected by the regulation may attempt to build a large coalition to support or oppose the regulation.[3]

---

3. In addition, groups with completely unconnected interests may form "support trading" or "logrolling" coalitions. Two groups may agree to support each other even if the members of one group are not affected by the regulations that the other wants. Tariffs are a classic

Competition among organized interests is typical, particularly in the financial services area (Kroszner and Stratmann 1998).

Third, in addition to the diffusion of the costs across different groups, the level of the costs relative to the benefits obtained by the interest group plays an important role (Becker 1983). Deadweight loss is defined as precisely the difference between the winner's benefit and the loser's cost from the change in output generated by the regulation. Factors affecting the "efficiency" of the regulatory or transfer mechanism thus may have an important impact on political outcomes. As the deadweight loss grows, for example, the losers are losing more for each dollar of the winner's gain. When this gap widens, losers have a greater incentive to fight each dollar of the winner's gain, and the winners have less incentive to fight for each dollar of the loser's loss. In other words, when deadweight losses are high, an interest group faces greater opposition to its protective regulation on the margin and hence is less likely to be successful.[4]

Similarly, politicians in electoral democracies are concerned about finding an optimal support coalition to promote their reelection chances, so they take into account the marginal costs and benefits to different groups. The rents generated by regulation in an electoral democracy are thus likely to be spread among different groups, even though one group may be the primary beneficiary (Peltzman 1976).[5] Regulation that protects financial institutions from competition and subsidized government deposit insurance[6] generates rents for this sector that may be partially shared through directed credit allocation.[7] Competition among rival interests may then influence the extent and identity of the winners and losers.[8]

---

case of logrolling, in which, say, lumber and glass producers support each other's call for higher protection, thereby providing greater support for higher tariffs than otherwise would be (Schattschneider 1935; Irwin and Kroszner 1996).

4. Becker (1983) argues that competition among lobbying groups thus will lead to the selection of the most efficient (lowest deadweight cost) regulations, so there is a tendency for regulation to be efficient in this sense. Wittman (1995) takes this argument further to conclude that both democratic institutions and outcomes are efficient. On why not all welfare-enhancing reforms may be realized in the political arena, see Rodrik (1996), Rajan and Zingales (forthcoming), and Kroszner (2000b).

5. When the constraint of future elections is less binding on politicians, they may engage in less rent sharing and provide windfalls to targeted groups. McGuire and Olson (1996), however, argue that less democratic regimes may be better able to insulate themselves from rent seeking and might find it in their own interests to pursue economic policies in the public interest.

6. In addition, flat-rate deposit insurance tends to subsidize the smaller and riskier banks at the expense of the larger, better diversified, and safer banks. Lobbying for flat-rate deposit insurance (and for continued protection against geographic diversification through branching) has historically been consistent with this pattern of relative benefits (e.g., White 1983; Calomiris and White 1994; Economides, Hubbard, and Palia 1996; Kroszner 1997).

7. See Kroszner (1999a; 2000a,b), for how this may make the banking and financial system susceptible to political influence.

8. Politicians and the bureaucracy may be considered a distinct interest group concerned about expanding their size and influence over the economy. Niskanen (1971) and Brennan

7.2.2   Positive Political-Institutional Approaches

Ideology

Although the private interest theory has had much success in explaining a wide variety of regulatory interventions that are difficult to rationalize on public interest grounds, it has been less effective in explaining the widespread economic deregulation that has taken place in many countries during the last two decades (Peltzman 1989 and Noll 1989; but see Kroszner and Strahan 1999). Many political scientists and some economists emphasize the importance of beliefs and ideologies of voters and politicians to explain regulation and deregulation (e.g., Kalt and Zupan 1984; Poole and Rosenthal 1997). Differences across countries or among citizens over time in their general beliefs about the appropriate role of the government in economic affairs might affect the extent of intervention. Roe (1994), for example, has argued that populist fear of excessive concentration of power in the hands of financial elites was an important driving force behind many banking and financial regulations in the early part of this century (but see Hellwig 1999 for an alternative interpretation).

Poole and Rosenthal (1997) have undertaken a systematic analysis of voting patterns in the U.S. Congress and argue that ideology is the key to explaining roll-call voting.[9] They have had much success in accounting for a wide variety of economic regulation and deregulation that is not well explained by private interest group variables or party politics.

Poole and Rosenthal (1993), for example, find an important role for ideology in the legislative battles over federal economic regulation in the United States during the nineteenth century. Gilligan, Marshall, and Weingast (1989) had argued that economic interests of constituents were the key to explaining the origins and passage of the Interstate Commerce Act of 1887, which was the first significant piece of federal regulation of private corporations and initiated the "age of economic regulation." When Poole and Rosenthal (1993) included their measures of legislator ideology in the vote prediction regressions, however, the economic interest variables were much diminished in effect and had low incremental explanatory power relative to ideology. In addition, Berglof and Rosenthal (1999) analyze bankruptcy law in the United States and argue that ideology is a key element for under-

---

and Buchanan (1977) suggest that an objective of the government may be to maximize or, on the margin, to increase its size and expenditures, and they discuss institutional structures that can mitigate the tendency toward growth. This view has been characterized as the Leviathan approach.

9. Poole and Rosenthal (1997) create an ideology measure that locates each legislator on a simple left-right scale based on their complete history of roll-call votes. In our empirical work we use the ADA rating, which is based on selected roll-call votes. For our time period, the ADA and the Poole and Rosenthal measures are highly correlated.

standing the voting patterns on bankruptcy legislation during the last two centuries.[10] In the empirical work following, we will examine the incremental explanatory power of private interest and political factors.

Identifying the driving forces behind changes in ideology over time, however, has been difficult. What constitutes the term *ideology* and whether it can be measured independent of private economic interests are the subjects of an extensive and ongoing controversy (see Kalt and Zupan 1984 and Peltzman 1984; and overviews by Bender and Lott 1996 and Poole and Rosenthal 1996).

Institutions

The new institutional economics approach emphasizes transactions costs and institutional arrangements for decision making as key factors influencing the outcome of the policy process (e.g., McCubbins, Noll, and Weingast 1988; North 1990; Williamson 1996; Alston, Eggertsson, and North 1996; Dixit 1996; Irwin and Kroszner 1999). This approach examines how alternative policy-making structures influence the incentives of both special interests and governmental actors to shape policy. These institutional and transactions costs features can in turn affect both the incentives for interest groups to organize and the effectiveness of their lobbying efforts. Interest group size and strength, thus, is not given but may be endogenous, and it is important to take such considerations into account to understand how durable policy change comes about (e.g., Irwin and Kroszner 1999).

The committee structure of Congress creates opportunities for vote trading and issue linkages that may affect coalition formation and policy outcomes (e.g., Shepsle and Weingast 1987; Weingast and Marshall 1988). The selection process for committee membership may lead committees to be composed of "preference outliers" who are not representative of Congress as a whole but, by virtue of their gatekeeping control over legislation in their jurisdiction, may have a disproportionate impact on outcomes (e.g., Shepsle 1978; Shepsle and Weingast 1995). Alternatively, committees may not consist of outliers and may operate as delegated groups to carry out the major party's agenda or as groups of policy experts who gather and process information in order to make well-informed decisions (Hall and Grofman 1990; Krehbeil 1991; Kiewiet and McCubbins 1991; Cox and McCubbins 1993). The standing committees also may function as repeat-dealing devices that permit legislators to develop credible policy positions, and this process then helps the legislators to maximize special interest contributions (Kroszner and Stratmann 1998).

10. On the political economy of bankruptcy, see also Posner (1997), Bolton and Rosenthal (1999), and Kroszner (1999b).

7.3   Legislative Reforms of Bank Supervision and Regulation: Why Do They Occur in the 1980s and 1990s?

Although our main focus will be on the 1991 FDICIA, it is important to investigate whether the positive theories outlined earlier can help explain the general timing of bank regulatory change. From the end of the Depression through the 1970s, there was little reform of the statutes governing the supervision and regulation of the banking sector. As table 7.1 shows, federal legislative change began in 1980. At the same time, states were relaxing restrictions on branching and interstate banking. In the 1990s, regulatory change continued with reform of the financial safety net (FDICIA in 1991), deregulation of restrictions on branching (the Interstate Branching and Banking and Efficiency Act of 1994), and deregulation of the separation of banking and underwriting (the Financial Services Modernization Act of 1999).

Technological, economic, and legal shocks disrupting the long-standing political-economy equilibrium can explain why regulatory change began in

Table 7.1   Legislative Changes to Supervision and Regulation of Banks during the 1980s

	Year Passed	Major Provisions of the Law
Depository Institutions Deregulation and Monetary Control Act (DIDMCA)	1980	Raised deposit insurance from $40,000 to $100,000. Imposed uniform reserve requirements on all depository institutions. Gave access to Federal Reserve services to all depository institutions. Phased out interest rate ceilings. Allowed depositories to offer NOW and ATS accounts nationwide. Eliminated usury ceilings.
Garn St Germain Act	1982	Permitted banks to purchase failing banks and thrifts across state lines. Expanded thrift lending powers. Allowed depositories to offer money market deposit accounts.
Competitive Equality in Banking Act (CEBA)	1987	Allocated $10.8 billion in additional funding to the FSLIC. Authorized forbearance program for farm banks. Reaffirmed that the full faith and credit of the Treasury stood behind deposit insurance.
Financial Institutions Reform, Recovery and Enforcement Act (FIRREA)	1989	Provided $50 billion of taxpayers' funds to resolved failed thrifts. Eliminated the FSLIC and the Federal Home Loan Bank Board (the former regulator of thrifts). Created the Office of Thrift Supervision to regulate and supervise thrifts. Raised deposit insurance premiums. Mandated that the deposit insurance fund reach 1.25 percent of insured deposits. Reimposed restrictions on thrift lending activities. Directed Treasury to study deposit insurance reform.

Source: Mishkin (1997) and FDIC (1997).

the early 1980s. Economic shocks such as rising interest rates and greater competition from the commercial paper and junk bond markets reduced the profitability and capital of banks and thrifts. Because banks and thrifts had less capital at stake, the moral hazard problem associated with deposit insurance worsened in the 1980s, thereby making regulatory changes designed to enhance both regulatory and market discipline in the public interest. At the same time, new technologies such as automatic teller machines (ATMs) and credit scoring models for lending reduced the strength of small banks—the traditional beneficiaries of deposit insurance and restrictions on banks' abilities to expand geographically—relative to large banks. These changes thus set the stage for the regulatory change. We examine these forces later and provide a brief description of the substance of the changes that occurred during the 1980s in section 7.3.1.

Sections 7.3.2 and 7.3.3 then describe FDICIA and its legislative history in detail. We choose this focus for three reasons. First, this act represents the most significant revision to the rules governing federal banking supervision and regulation since the Great Depression. Second, votes on other important pieces of legislation dealing with banking supervision and regulation were either voice votes (hence leaving no record to analyze) or so nearly unanimous that there would not be sufficient variation to do systematic empirical analysis.[11]

The third reason for this focus is that the legislative history of FDICIA allows us to examine roll-call votes on a number of amendments in addition to final passage. Amendments have the advantage of being more narrowly focused than the final bill, thereby making it easier to determine how different interests would be affected. Final bills tend to be the outcome of coalition-building processes that provide an equilibrium balance among interests, so it may be difficult to identify groups that unambiguously lose (see, e.g., Irwin and Kroszner 1996). This may be one reason why so much legislation that ultimately passes does so on a voice vote or with near unanimity (see Krehbeil 1998).

7.3.1   Why Does Bank Regulatory Reform Begin in the 1980s?

A series of technological and economic changes altered the value of the traditional bank regulations and affected the relative strengths of the rival interest groups. The development and spread in the 1970s and 1980s of the checkable money market mutual fund, the Merrill Lynch Cash Management Account, and other opportunities to bank by mail or phone using toll-free numbers, for example, created new competition for bank depositors' funds. In addition, high inflation in the late 1970s and early 1980s led to high interest rates, but depository institutions were not able to offer

---

11. The one exception is the final vote on the Financial Institutions Reform, Recovery, and Enforcement Act (FIRREA), which passed with 77 percent of the House vote.

competitive rates due to Regulation Q interest rate ceilings. What had once been a device supported by the industry to eliminate price competition had become a burden as the new alternatives to bank deposits offered market rates.

The Depository Institutions Deregulation and Monetary Control Act of 1980 (DIDMCA) and the Garn St Germain Act of 1982 both attempted to stem the flow of funds out of financial intermediaries and increase their profitability. DIDMCA raised deposit insurance from $40,000 to $100,000 and phased out the Regulation Q interest rate ceilings.[12] Garn St Germain, in addition to permitting banks to purchase failing thrifts regardless of their location, substantially loosened lending restrictions on thrifts. Together, these two laws laid the groundwork for the rapid growth of the thrift industry in the middle of the 1980s, despite the massive decline in economic capital that led to severe moral hazard problems. High interest rates caused a substantial decline in the capital of thrifts whose portfolios consisted mainly of long-term fixed rate mortgages. The decline in regional real estate values (e.g., in the Southwest after the collapse of the oil industry in the early 1980s) continued to reduce the true net worth of thrifts even after interests rates came down in the mid-1980s. In conjunction with these laws, forbearance by the thrift regulators allowed many economically insolvent thrifts to "gamble for resurrection" (Kane 1989; Kroszner and Strahan 1996).

By the middle of the 1980s, it became increasingly clear that the Federal Savings & Loan Insurance Corporation (FSLIC) had become insolvent. By then, concern about the solvency of the FSLIC had led to increases in interest rates paid on fully insured deposits at weak thrifts (Strahan 1995). After lobbying by the thrift industry that delayed action, the 1987 Competitive Equality in Banking Act took the first step toward bolstering the FSLIC by allocating $10.8 billion to help resolve failed thrifts and by reaffirming that the full faith and credit of the U.S. Treasury stood behind the fund.[13] The insolvency of FSLIC continued to deepen as the industry became weaker (and, consequently, became a less powerful lobbying force) and as the cost of the regulatory regime became clearer to the public (Kane 1996). The 1989 Financial Institutions Reform, Recovery, and Enforcement Act (FIRREA) allocated significantly more funds to resolve failed thrifts. FIRREA also changed and tightened the regulatory authority over thrifts and directed the Treasury to study more significant reforms of the deposit insurance system.

---

12. The elimination of interest rate ceilings on large denomination certificates of deposit during the 1970s appears to have hurt smaller and retail-oriented banks relative to larger, wholesale banks (James 1983).

13. On the political economy of the thrift crisis, see Romer and Weingast (1991).

Table 7.2   **Description of the Federal Deposit Insurance Corporation Improvement Act of 1991 (FDICIA) and Amendment Votes**

	Major Provisions of the Law
FDICIA	Increased the FDIC's authority to borrow from Treasury by $30 billion. Imposed risk-based deposit insurance pricing. Outlined procedure for Prompt Corrective Action of weakly capitalized banks and thrifts. Directed the FDIC to resolve failed banks and thrifts in the least costly way to the deposit insurance fund. Mandated annual on-site examinations and accounting reform. Increased the Fed's role in supervising foreign banks.
Wylie-Neal Amendment	An amendment to permit bank holding companies to purchase banks in any state nationwide, and to permit national banks to open branches across state lines. The amendment also restricted national banks' ability to sell certain insurance products.
Wylie Amendment	An amendment to limit federal deposit insurance coverage for depositors to one account of up to $100,000 per person per institution and an additional $100,000 per person per institution for an IRA account. The amendment would eliminate FDIC coverage for multiple accounts of $100,000 in a single financial institution.
Kennedy Amendment	An amendment to require banks which are authorized to buy or open branches in other states to demonstrate that they are meeting the existing credit needs of the community where they are currently established and to prohibit banks with assets of more than $1 billion from expanding to adjoining states if those banks have exhibited a pattern of closing offices in low- and moderate-income locations, thus effectively levying a "tax" on interstate acquisitions.

Source: Mishkin (1997) and FDIC (1997).

7.3.2   FDICIA: An Important Step toward Improved Supervision and Regulation

FDICIA represents a broad-based attempt to improve the financial safety net by minimizing the moral hazard problems that come with protecting various classes of stakeholders when banks get into trouble (see table 7.2). Flat-rate deposit insurance creates incentives for banks to increase risk in order to raise the value of that insurance (Merton 1977). FDICIA addresses this problem directly by mandating risk-based premiums on deposit insurance. FDICIA also enhanced both regulatory and market discipline over banks' tendencies to take too much risk. The law first enhanced regulatory discipline by prescribing mandatory annual on-site exams of all insured depository institutions and requiring accounting principles applicable to all insured depositories to be uniform and consistent. Both of these changes stemmed from the experience of the thrift industry during the 1980s, when regulatory resources were cut and accounting standards substantially liberalized to conceal large losses (Kane 1989; Kroszner and Strahan 1996).

FDICIA further enhanced regulatory discipline by directing the banking agencies to impose increasingly tighter restrictions on bank activities as capital declined under the Prompt Corrective Action (PCA) section. PCA defines five capital zones: well capitalized, adequately capitalized, undercapitalized, significantly undercapitalized, and critically undercapitalized.[14] As banks fall from the well to adequately capitalized zones, the FDIC must approve their use of brokered deposits. As they fall from adequate to undercapitalized, banks must suspend dividend payments, outline a capital restoration plan, and restrict asset growth, and are prohibited from using brokered deposits. Falling from undercapitalized to significantly undercapitalized, FDICIA restricts interaffiliate transactions and deposit interest rates, and limits payments to bank officers. Finally, when a bank falls into the critically undercapitalized zone, a receiver or conservator must take control of the bank. This provision likely reduces the problem of regulatory forbearance by limiting discretion.[15]

In some prominent cases during the 1980s, all creditors of failing banks were bailed out by the FDIC, and this policy was even made explicit (Kroszner and Strahan 1996). Under such circumstances, bank creditors are not likely to worry about the risks of insolvency, thus worsening the moral hazard problem and encouraging excessive risk taking by large banks. FDICIA addresses this lack of market discipline by directing the FDIC to use the least costly method to resolve troubled or insolvent institutions. Least-cost resolution means that in most cases the FDIC will have to impose losses on uninsured creditors (e.g., subordinated debtholders) and depositors that are less than fully insured. Knowing that the FDIC is directed to resolve failed banks using the least costly approach, these large creditors have an ex ante incentive to impose discipline on a bank's tendency to take too much risk, by both pricing that risk at the outset and withdrawing funds when the bank experiences financial problems.

Although FDICIA's provisions did work to reduce the moral hazard problems associated with deposit insurance, significant issues were not addressed (for critical assessments, see Benston and Kaufman 1994, 1998). Many analysts during the debate over FDICIA, for example, recommended that market value accounting principles replace historical cost accounting to improve the information content in capital ratios as an early warning signal of insolvency. With market value accounting, banks can be

---

14. The capital zones are well-capitalized (total capital-to-risk weighted assets > 10 percent, Tier 1 capital ratio > 6 percent, and leverage ratio > 5 percent); adequately capitalized (total capital-to-risk-weighted assets > 8 percent, Tier 1 ratio > 4 percent, leverage ratio > 4 percent); undercapitalized (total capital-to-risk-weighted assets > 6 percent, Tier 1 ratio > 3 percent, leverage ratio > 3 percent); significantly undercapitalized (total capital-to-risk-weighted assets < 6 percent, Tier 1 ratio < 3 percent, leverage ratio < 3 percent); and critically undercapitalized (leverage ratio < 2 percent).

15. Benston and Kaufman (1994, 1998) argue, however, that the law did not go far enough to reduce regulatory discretion.

closed before significant losses become large, thereby reducing the costs of the deposit insurance. In addition, in response to interest rate risks taken on by many thrifts during the 1980s, FDICIA directed the regulators to account for this risk in capital adequacy requirements but provided little direction about how this would be accomplished. In the end, interest rate risk assessment was left entirely to supervisors on a case-by-case basis.[16]

7.3.3 Legislative Battles over Amendments with Roll-Call Votes

FDICIA emerged out of a debate on safety net reform on House Resolution 6 during 1991. H.R. 6 contained sections that would have allowed interstate branching deregulation and sections on financial services modernization that would have eliminated the Glass-Steagall Act of 1933 by permitting bank holding companies to operate affiliates in banking, securities, and insurance. H.R. 6 also contained sections on safety and soundness reform and deposit insurance coverage. Both the interstate branching and financial modernization sections of H.R. 6 were subsequently dropped prior to passage of FDICIA, but we were able to identify three amendment votes that occurred during the debate over H.R. 6. We analyze each of these amendment votes in addition to analyzing the final vote on FDICIA.

Wylie-Neal Amendment

The first of these votes, on the Wylie-Neal Amendment, would have allowed banks to set up branches in other states, thereby improving diversification of the industry and increasing financial stability. Relaxation of restrictions on branch banking had been occurring at the state level during the 1970s and 1980s as changes in technological and economic conditions altered the political-economy equilibrium that had kept antibranching regulations little changed for at least thirty years (see Kroszner and Strahan 1999). In addition to the development of the checkable money market mutual fund mentioned previously, two other innovations reduced the value

---

16. An important question is why FDICIA occurred when it did rather than years earlier. Its passage following the rapid increase in bank and thrift failure in the 1980s raises the question of whether significant regulatory change can only occur, or perhaps is most likely to occur, following a crisis. Following large losses, public awareness of the costliness of having government-insured but (geographically) undiversified financial institutions likely increased. In the late 1970s the failure rate of banks began to rise, and in the 1980s the thrift crisis and taxpayer bail-out in FIRREA heightened public awareness about the costs of restrictions that make depository institutions more likely to require infusions of taxpayer funds. The failures thus may have heightened public support for branching (Kane 1996). Although this argument seems plausible and can account for the timing of FDICIA, it is difficult to document systematically. For example, banking failures or distress in a state did not affect the speed at which the state deregulated (Kroszner and Strahan 1999). More generally, an economic crisis within a sector is rarely distributionally neutral (Olson 1982). The economic shock could thus have changed the relative importance of different interest groups and thereby led to change in the banking regulatory equilibrium (see Kroszner 1998a; 2000a,b).

to the protected banks of local geographic monopolies. First, ATMs helped erode the geographic ties between customers and banks. Second, technological innovation and deregulation reduced transportation and communication costs, particularly since the 1970s, thereby lowering the costs for customers using distant banks. By increasing the elasticity of deposits supplied to banks, these innovations reduced the value of geographical restrictions to their traditional beneficiaries and thereby reduced their incentives to fight to maintain them (Peltzman 1976).

On the lending side, increasing sophistication of credit-scoring techniques, following innovations in information processing and financial theory as well as the development of large credit databases, began to diminish the value of knowledge that local bankers had about the risks of borrowers in the community. As a result of these innovations, a national market has developed for residential mortgages; credit card receivables have been securitized; and bank lending to small business now relies less on the judgment of loan officers and more on standardized scoring models.

These changes have increased the potential profitability for large banks to enter what had been the core of small bank activities. Large banks' incentives to increase their lobbying pressure to expand into these markets has thus been increasing over time. In fact, small banks' market share began to decline even prior to the branching deregulation (Kroszner and Strahan 1999). As the value of local banking relationships declined, small firms that were the main borrowers from the small banks also probably became more likely to favor the entry of large banks into local markets. With the deadweight costs of preventing the rise of large bank entry, the private interest theory predicts that small local banks would likely become less able to maintain the branching restrictions (Becker 1983). Deregulation that reduces deadweight costs of regulation is consistent also with the public interest theory. The marginal value of lobbying to repeal branching restrictions increased just as the relative value to the small banks of maintaining branching restrictions was declining.

Several details of the Wylie-Neal interstate branching amendment illustrate the influence of interest group politics. For example, the Independent Bankers Association of America, which represents small banks, "strongly opposes the bill, saying it threatens the availability of credit for farmers, ranchers, small businesses, and consumers in rural America" (BNA Banking Reporter, 9/16/91). Perhaps to placate such opposition, the Wylie-Neal interstate branching provision prohibits banks from using interstate offices for deposit production purposes and requires the banking regulatory agencies to set up guidelines to ensure that interstate branches are used to meet the needs of the community in which they operate.

The Wylie-Neal Amendment also included significant concessions to the insurance industry, which had been losing its battle with the banking industry in the courts. In 1986, the Office of the Comptroller of the Currency decided to allow national banks to sell any type of insurance product from small towns. This authority was later upheld by the U.S. Fifth Circuit Court of Appeals in *Independent Insurance Agents of America v. Ludwig* in 1993. In 1995, the U.S. Supreme Court allowed banks to sell annuities nationwide (*Valic v. Clarke*), and then in 1996 the Supreme Court again expanded banks' insurance powers by ruling in the *Barnett Banks v. Nelson* case that states could not bar national banks from selling insurance products from small towns (Seiberg 1996). Wylie-Neal would have scaled back somewhat on bank insurance powers. National banks would be barred from engaging in title insurance, and their ability to sell insurance from small towns of 5,000 or less would have been restricted. In addition, the amendment would limit states' abilities to allow banks to sell insurance products into other states (BNA Banking Reporter, 8/19/91).

Wylie Amendment

We have also identified a roll-call vote on deposit insurance coverage. This provision, also brought by Wylie, would have scaled back deposit insurance to $100,000 per person per institution, rather than $100,000 per account. This measure, along with provisions designed to eliminate deposit insurance coverage for brokered deposits, was supported by the administration; its defeat was considered a "significant setback to . . . efforts to achieve deposit insurance reform" (BNA Banking Reporter, 8/19/91). In the final law, however, regulatory agencies could restrict troubled institutions from issuing brokered deposits and paying interest rates significantly above rates offered on comparable deposits.

The move to scale back deposit insurance marked a sharp change from previous trends and, like the move to unrestricted branching, reflected the declining influence of small banks relative to large. Deposit insurance coverage had been increased in 1950 (from $5,000 to $10,000), in 1966 (to $15,000), in 1969 (to $20,000), in 1974 (to $40,000), and in 1980 (to $100,000). White (1998) argues that small banks supported each of these increases, whereas large banks opposed them. As a result, the real value of deposit insurance rose from $5,000 (1934 dollars) initially to $10,000–15,000 during the 1970s. Since 1980, inflation has eroded the real value of deposit insurance by about 50 percent. Despite this decline, there has been no serious call to raise the limits on insurance over the past two decades because, as we argued earlier, new technologies have increased the ability of large banks to operate in many markets even in the face of regulatory barriers. These changes have weakened the political influence of smaller banks, creating an environment in which they would rather sell out to large banks at a high price than fight to maintain restrictions on branching and a generous deposit insurance system.

Kennedy Amendment

Our last roll-call vote looks at the voting pattern on an amendment brought by Kennedy (which failed) requiring banks authorized to buy or open branches in other states to demonstrate that they are meeting the existing credit needs of the community where they are currently established, and to prohibit large banks (those with assets of more than $1 billion) from expanding to adjoining states if those banks have exhibited a pattern of closing offices in low- and moderate-income locations. The amendment effectively increases the costs of large banks acquiring small banks through increased enforcement of community lending requirements. The Kennedy Amendment goes somewhat further than Wylie-Neal, which would have amended the Community Reinvestment Act of 1977 to require bank supervisors to maintain state-by-state evaluations of bank records of lending to low-income neighborhoods.[17]

7.4 Hypotheses and Variable Definitions

7.4.1 Hypotheses

Intraindustry Rivalry

Small banks have fought to maintain and extend branching restrictions and deposit insurance both historically and in the recent debates.[18] Smaller banks appear to have been the main winners from antibranching laws of the nineteenth century and the 1930s because these restrictions protect them from competition from larger and more efficient banking organizations (see Flannery 1984; Jayaratne and Strahan 1998; and Winston 1993). Branching restrictions thus tend to reduce the efficiency and consumer convenience of the banking system.[19] Small banks also have supported enhanced coverage of federal deposit insurance consistently since its passage in the 1930s.

The interests within the banking industry regarding the Kennedy Amendment depend on whether acquirers (large banks) or targets (small ones) are more likely to bear the "tax" associated with greater scrutiny of

---

17. One of the most important impediments to the recently passed Financial Modernization Act of 1999 (i.e., the Glass-Steagall repeal) were arguments over expansion of the Community Reinvestment Act to a financial holding company's nonbank businesses. See Kroszner (1998b, 2000a).

18. Economides, Hubbard, and Palia (1996) provide evidence that voting in Congress for the McFadden Act of 1927 responded to small state banks' interests in limiting competition from large national banks. See also White (1983) and Abrams and Settle (1993) for historical opposition. On the small bank opposition to the recent branching deregulation, see Kane (1996) and the *Economist* (1994).

19. Flannery (1984) shows that small banks in states with branching restrictions have higher costs than do small banks in states without such restrictions.

their low-income and community development lending. Because prior research suggests that most of the gains associated with takeovers accrue to targets, we expect smaller banks to oppose this amendment.[20] The private interest theory therefore predicts that legislators from states with more small banks will be more likely to oppose each of these three amendments.

Interindustry Rivalry

As broad competitors for household savings, the insurance industry would tend to favor legislative changes that raise their rivals' costs, and vice versa. Thus, the private interest theory predicts that legislators from states with a larger insurance industry would tend to oppose branching deregulation and to favor limits on deposit insurance. Because the Kennedy Amendment effectively raises the cost to banks wanting to open branches across state lines, insurance would tend to favor this provision.

In addition, a number of states permit state-chartered commercial banks to sell insurance. The insurance lobby would thus more intensely oppose the relaxation of branching restrictions on when banks can sell insurance because such deregulation might permit banks to provide a more efficient insurance distribution network. Similarly, their support for limits on deposit insurance and the tax on banks expanding into new states would tend to be much greater in states where banks may sell insurance.

Consumer Interests

Banks are a major source of credit for small firms (Cole and Wolken 1994). Branching deregulation tends to reduce banks' local market power (Jayaratne and Strahan 1998). In addition, Strahan and Weston (1998) find that lending to small businesses increases on average when small banks are purchased by other banking organizations, and Berger and colleagues (1998) find that credit availability to small businesses increases in the years following a large banking organization's takeover of a smaller bank. Because bank borrowers tend to benefit from branching deregulation in particular and from bank consolidation in general, the private interest theory would predict that legislators from states with numerous small, bank-dependent firms would support branching deregulation.[21]

The vote to restrict deposit insurance would likely have its greatest effect on households that use banks and that would potentially be affected by limiting deposit insurance to a single account under $100,000. Because

20. For a survey of the literature on takeovers, see Jensen and Ruback (1983) and Jarrell, Brickley, and Netter (1988).

21. On the other hand, local banking monopolies created by branching restrictions could strengthen relationships between banks and small- and medium-sized firms and increase the availability of credit to these firms (Petersen and Rajan 1994). Also, some have argued that small business lending declines when large banks take over small banks (e.g., Berger, Kashyap, and Scalise 1995).

elderly people typically have more liquid assets than younger people and tend to use bank deposits as a savings vehicle, the private interest theory suggests that legislators from states with more older people will be less likely to vote to scale back on deposit insurance.

The Kennedy Amendment vote would likely increase lending to low-income neighborhoods. Thus, the private interest theory suggests that voting in favor of this amendment is more likely among legislators from states with more low-income people.

Political-Institutional Factors

Republicans are typically perceived as more likely to favor deregulation than Democrats, so the political-institutional theories suggest that Democrats would oppose branching deregulation and limits to deposit insurance. In addition, Democrats are perceived to support the interests of lower- and middle-income households, so they would tend to favor the Kennedy Amendment.[22] We also investigate whether voting behavior depends on ideology and committee structure. Note that these political effects must be interpreted with caution, because the views of the politicians may simply reflect the economic interests of the constituents in the state (see Peltzman 1984).

7.4.2   Variable Definitions and Data Sources

Our main proxy for the strength of the small banks is the fraction of banking assets in the state that is in small banks. We define banks as small if they have assets below the median size in each state. By allowing the definition of small to vary across states, we take into account cross-state heterogeneity in bank sizes. We also include the median capital-asset ratio for all banks operating in a state in our voting models, in part to control for the fact that small banks typically hold more capital than do large ones. In addition, well-capitalized banks may be more likely to support limits to deposit insurance than poorly capitalized banks. Data on bank size and capital are from the 1991 *Reports of Income and Conditions* (call reports) from the Federal Reserve Board.

To measure the effects of the rival insurance industry, we first construct an indicator variable that is 1 if the state permits banks to sell insurance. For each state, we then measure the size of the insurance sector (total value added in the state) relative to the sum of the banking and insurance sectors in 1991. We will examine the effect separately for states that permit banks to sell insurance and those that do not. Data on value added by industry are from U.S. Commerce Department, Bureau of Economic

---

22. For more detail on the importance of legislative structures, party politics, and ideology, see Poole and Rosenthal (1997), Kahn and Matsusaka (1997), and Irwin and Kroszner (1999).

Analysis, *Survey of Current Business* (August 1994; available at http:// www.bea.doc.gov/bea/regional/gsp/).

We also include the share of total contributions to each legislator from banking and insurance that comes from the insurance industry. Previous research on the relationship between contributions and votes has typically included the level of giving by an interested group, but our emphasis here is on the competition between the groups; hence we choose this relative measure.[23] Special interests sponsor political action committees (PACs) that must disclose their contributions to the Federal Election Commission (FEC). Corporations, for example, cannot legally give money directly to a candidate for federal office, but must give through PACs. For each two-year House election cycle, the FEC produces a file that identifies the contributing PAC, the recipient, and the dollar amount, and we use the data from the 1991/92 cycle. We then identify which PACs are sponsored by the banking industry or the insurance industry. The financial services sector is one of the largest contributors of PAC money, accounting for nearly 20 percent of the total (see Kroszner and Stratmann 1998). Because PAC giving is negligible for challengers and for legislators in their last term, we calculate the share of giving variable for only incumbents running for reelection who receive at least some contributions from banking or insurance. We then estimate all of our models with and without PAC contributions.

To measure the relative importance of small, bank-dependent borrowers, we include the proportion of all establishments operating in the state with fewer than twenty employees. These data are compiled by the Bureau of the Census.[24] Our measure of the importance of elderly constituents equals the share of the population in the state over sixty-five, and our measure of the importance of poor people equals the share of the population below the poverty line. Each of these comes from the 1990 Census.

We include three political variables to test for the importance of party politics, ideology, and committee structure. First, we include an indicator equal to 1 if the legislator is a Democrat. Second, we include the Americans for Democratic Action (ADA) scores for each legislator. The ADA scores are based on legislators' past voting records, measured on a scale of 0 to 1, where 1 represents the more liberal position on each vote. Third, we include an indicator equal to 1 if the legislator is a member of the

---

23. Research relating voting to contribution levels has had mixed results when political factors are controlled for (see Stratmann 1991 and 1995 for exceptions). Note that we cannot distinguish whether money is influencing legislators to vote differently than they otherwise would or whether money is being used to reward supporters and induce them to spend more time working on the issue (see Bronars and Lott 1997 and Kroszner and Stratmann 1998, 1999).

24. Data on establishments by state are from 1987. See *State and Metropolitan Data Book* (1991; available at http://fisher.lib.virginia.edu/cbp/).

Table 7.3   **Means and Standard Deviations for Voting Outcomes in the House of Representatives on FDICIA and Amendments to FDICIA and Measures of the Size and Stregth of Interest Groups in Financial Services and Political-Institutional Factors**

	Mean	Std. Dev.
Amendment vote to allow interstate branching	0.502	—
Amendment vote to limit deposit insurance	0.367	—
Amendment vote effective to "tax" interstate bank acquisitions by encouraging low-income lending	0.387	—
Final vote on FDICIA	0.804	—
Private interest variables		
Assets in small banks/total bank assets	0.064	0.041
Value added in insurance/value added in insurance + depositories	0.412	0.069
Indicator for states where banks may sell insurance	0.123	—
Median bank capital/asset ratio	0.081	0.007
Insurance share of PAC dollars from insurance + banking	0.461	0.238
Small firm share of the number of firms in the state	0.878	0.029
Share of population below poverty line	0.141	0.031
Share of population over 65	0.127	0.020
Political/institutional variables		
Indicator equals 1 for Democrat	0.618	—
ADA score (from 0 to 1, least to most liberal)	0.470	0.335
Indicator for member of House Banking Committee	0.120	—

House Banking Committee. The sample statistics for all the variables are reported in table 7.3.

7.5   Methods and Results of the Voting Analysis

In order to determine the influence of the private interest and political-institutional factors described earlier, we develop probit voting models for the three roll-call amendment votes and the final passage for FDICIA in the House of Representatives.[25] The dependent variable equals 1 if the legislator voted in favor of the amendment or bill and 0 otherwise. In the tables containing the results (tables 7.4–7.7), we report the marginal effects (slopes) of a one-unit change of each variable on the probability that a legislator will vote in favor of the amendment or bill. Because we have multiple legislators from each state, we adjust the standard errors to correct for the lack of independence among observations clustered in the same state.

25. We found no roll-call votes on amendments to FDICIA from the Senate. The Senate vote on FDICIA was lopsided: eighty-two to fourteen, with just one Republican voting against the law.

Each table contains four specifications of the voting equation. The first two columns are the same for all four votes. Column 1 contains the private interest and political-institutional factors described earlier, with the exception of the PAC contribution variable. Column 2 then adds this variable, which reduces the sample size by roughly 30 percent. The last two columns repeat the specifications from the first two but include additional variables representing the private interest of nonfinancial services groups specifically affected by each amendment. For the final FDICIA vote, we include all three of these private consumer interest variables.

7.5.1   Amendment to Permit Interstate Branching (Wylie-Neal)

Table 7.4 contains the results for the vote on the amendment to relax restrictions on interstate banking and branching. The negative and statistically significant coefficient on the relative share of small bank assets in the state suggests that legislators from areas with a large share of small banks tended to oppose this amendment. This is consistent with the intraindustry rivalry hypothesis. The share of small banks also has a large effect on the probability that a legislator votes for branching: A 1–standard deviation increase in small bank market share reduces the probability of voting for branching deregulation by roughly 20 to 25 percent, depending on the specification.

We also find support for the interindustry rivalry hypothesis. Where banks can sell insurance, legislators from states with larger insurance sectors relative to banking are less likely to vote for the amendment. In states where banks cannot sell insurance, however, the effect of the relative size of the insurance sector is positive in all four specifications and is statistically significant in columns 1 and 3. In the specifications without PAC money, 1–standard deviation increase in the insurance share decreases the probability of voting for branching by 17 percent in states where banks may sell insurance, but *increases* the probability of voting for branching by about 11 percent in states where banks may not sell insurance. This support may be due to the inclusion of provisions within the amendment to limit national banks' insurance powers partially. As we noted earlier, the insurance industry was losing court battles to keep banks from entering the insurance business and, as a whole, lobbied for specific legislative restrictions on banks' insurance powers.

By combining the branching provisions with limitations on bank powers, the amendment appears to have split the insurance industry. Further evidence of this interpretation is found in columns 2 and 4, which include the share of PAC contributions from the insurance industry. This variable does not have a statistically significant effect on voting patterns on this amendment, but it does in all of the other votes we consider. With the insurance interests split on the amendment, contributions from the insur-

Table 7.4   Marginal Effects from Probit Model Relating Voting Outcomes in the House of Representatives on an Amendment (Wylie-Neal) Related to FDICIA to Relax Restrictions on Interstate Branching to Measures of the Size and Strength of Interest Groups in Financial Services and Political-Institutional Factors

	(1)	(2)	(3)	(4)
Assets in small banks/total	−5.08***	−5.98***	−4.97***	−5.96***
bank assets	(0.92)	(1.08)	(0.92)	(1.09)
Value added in insurance/value	1.57**	1.12	1.45**	1.09
added in insurance +	(0.62)	(0.76)	(0.61)	(0.77)
depositories where banks				
may not sell insurance				
Indicator for states where	0.69***	0.84*	0.70***	0.84*
banks may sell insurance	(0.07)	(0.13)	(0.07)	(0.12)
Value added in insurance/value	−2.42**	−6.76*	−2.55**	−6.87*
added in insurance +	(1.16)	(3.80)	(1.17)	(3.81)
depositories where banks				
may sell insurance				
Median bank capital/asset	−0.50	2.56	−1.24	2.39
ratio	(5.00)	(5.96)	(5.14)	(6.06)
Share of PAC contributions	—	0.11	—	0.11
from insurance		(0.13)		(0.13)
Small firm share of the number	—	—	−1.13	−0.34
of firms in the state			(0.71)	(1.34)
Indicator for Democrat	−0.26**	−0.15	−0.26**	−0.15
	(0.10)	(0.10)	(0.10)	(0.10)
ADA score	−0.23*	−0.34***	−0.24*	−0.34***
	(0.12)	(0.13)	(0.12)	(0.13)
Indicator for member of House	0.06	0.07	0.06	0.07
Banking Committee	(0.08)	(0.10)	(0.08)	(0.10)
No. of observations	409	293	409	293
Pseudo-R^2	0.1971	0.2145	0.1992	0.2148
χ^2 for joint significance	83.60	88.42	92.40	90.93
(*p*-value)	(< 0.001)	(< 0.001)	(< 0.001)	(< 0.001)
Incremental R^2				
Private interest variables	0.1045	0.1448	0.1065	0.1450
Political variables	0.0870	0.0632	0.0860	0.0634

Notes: The table reports the marginal effect of a small change in each variable from its mean on the probability that the House member votes in favor of the proposal. For indicator variables, the coefficient represents the change in the probability for a one unit change in the indicator. Each model contains one observation for each vote. The explanatory variables reflect average measures of interest group strength in the states. Standard errors are adjusted to reflect the fact that votes from House members from the same state may be affected by common factors not included in the model. The marginal effects are reported with their standard errors in parentheses. The pseudo-R^2 is based on Estrella (1998). The incremental R^2 is the change in the pseudo-R^2 that results when we add the private interest (political) variables to the model.

***Significant at the 1 percent level.

**Significant at the 5 percent level.

*Significant at the 10 percent level.

ance industry may be supporting both sides of the issue and, in effect, canceling out or at least mitigating the net influence of this interest group.[26] A divide-and-conquer strategy thus may be effective in neutralizing opposition to a bill, but it also demonstrates the obstacles to optimal policy; that is, compromises to pacify at least some segment of the affected industries may be required to secure passage of regulatory reform.[27]

We do not find a statistically significant effect of the share of small firms in the state. Even though this group of consumers of banking services would be directly affected by the regulatory change, they do not appear to have had an impact on the voting pattern.[28]

Turning to the political-institutional factors, partisanship and our measure of ideology do appear to play a role. The Democrats tended to vote against this deregulatory measure, holding the ADA score constant. The coefficient suggests that Democrats were 15 to 25 percent more likely to oppose branching than were Republicans. In addition, holding party membership constant, the more liberal members of the House also were more likely to vote against this amendment. Based on the ADA score, the most liberal legislator was 23 to 34 percent more likely to oppose branching than was the most conservative one. The effect of membership on the House Banking Committee is small and statistically insignificant. This suggests that there is no particular bias of the Banking Committee members, relative to the House as a whole, on this issue. This result is consistent with the contrasting intra- and interindustry interests being represented by members of the Banking Committee (see Kroszner and Stratmann 1998).

At the bottom of table 7.4, we report a goodness of fit measure that is roughly analogous to the traditional R^2 following Estrella (1998). To determine the marginal contribution of the private interest variables relative to the political-institutional factors, we calculate the incremental R^2, defined as the change in the goodness-of-fit measure when we add one or the other group of variables to the probit equation. In each specification, the incremental contribution of the private interest variables is greater than that of the political-institutional variables, but the contribution of the latter is not negligible, so both sets of factors should be taken into

26. We do not investigate the question of how amendments and bills with different characteristics and combinations of provisions get to a roll-call vote.

27. The significance of splitting industry interests in order to achieve regulatory change is not unique to financial services. Heterogeneity of interests between interstate and intrastate airlines and the breakdown of a unified opposition to deregulation among the major interstate carriers was important to bringing about the Airline Deregulation Act of 1978 (see Bailey, Graham, and Kaplan 1985). Divide-and-conquer strategies also have played an important role in effecting economic reforms in Russia (see Shleifer and Treisman 2000).

28. In earlier work on state-level (not federal interstate) branching deregulation, we do find that states with more small firms relaxed their restrictions on branching earlier than did states with fewer small firms. See Kroszner and Strahan (1999).

Table 7.5   **Marginal Effects from Probit Model Relating Voting Outcomes in the House of Representatives on an Amendment (Wylie) Related to FDICIA to Limit Deposit Insurance to a Single Account to Measures of the Size and Strength of Interest Groups in Financial Services and Political-Institutional Factors**

	(1)	(2)	(3)	(4)
Assets in small banks/total	−4.15***	−5.04***	−4.13***	−5.04***
bank assets	(0.67)	(0.85)	(0.66)	(0.85)
Value added in insurance/value	0.79*	1.18**	0.72*	1.17**
added in insurance +	(0.41)	(0.51)	(0.43)	(0.51)
depositories where banks				
may not sell insurance				
Indicator for states where	−0.62***	−0.85***	−0.62***	−0.85***
banks may sell insurance	(0.06)	(0.05)	(0.06)	(0.05)
Value added in insurance/value	5.84***	11.23***	5.82***	11.23***
added in insurance +	(1.15)	(1.46)	(1.16)	(1.46)
depositories where banks				
may sell insurance				
Median bank capital/asset	1.45	3.82	0.95	3.74
ratio	(4.29)	(4.66)	(4.46)	(4.84)
Share of PAC contributions	—	0.32***	—	0.32***
from insurance		(0.11)		(0.12)
Percent of population over 65	—	—	0.56	0.08
			(1.38)	(1.38)
Indicator for Democrat	0.04	0.01	0.04	0.01
	(0.05)	(0.06)	(0.05)	(0.06)
ADA score	−0.14**	−0.09	−0.14*	−0.09
	(0.06)	(0.09)	(0.07)	(0.10)
Indicator for member of House	0.01	0.06	0.01	0.06
Banking Committee	(0.09)	(0.13)	(0.09)	(0.13)
No. of observations	406	285	406	285
Pseudo-R^2	0.1079	0.1627	0.1082	0.1627
χ^2 for joint significance	63.88	83.10	78.14	90.06
(p-value)	(< 0.001)	(< 0.001)	(< 0.001)	(< 0.001)
Incremental R^2				
Private interest variables	0.1012	0.1619	0.1016	0.1619
Political variables	0.0087	0.0041	0.0084	0.0040

Notes: See table 7.4.

account when trying to understand the political economy of regulatory change.

7.5.2 Amendment to Limit Deposit Insurance (Wylie)

The analysis of the vote on the amendment to limit deposit insurance coverage is reported in table 7.5. Smaller, less diversified banks tend to reap a greater benefit from the deposit insurance system than do larger banks, and this intraindustry rivalry is evident in the voting pattern. Legislators from areas where small banks have a relatively large market share consistently oppose this amendment. Again, the effect of small bank share is economically relevant: A 1–standard deviation increase in this variable is associated with a 20–25 percent decrease in the probability of voting to limit deposit insurance. In addition, although it is not statistically significant, we do find a positive coefficient on the median capital ratio of banks in the state.

The interindustry rivalry also is manifest in the vote on this amendment. The insurance industry generally favors measures that would reduce implicit government subsidy to the banking industry through federal deposit insurance. Regardless of whether banks can sell insurance products in the state, a larger insurance sector relative to banking in the state increases the likelihood that a legislator will support the amendment. The magnitude of the effect is much larger for legislators from states where banks do have insurance powers, but the coefficients are positive and statistically significant for both groups. For instance, a 1–standard deviation increase in the insurance share raises the probability that a legislator votes to limit deposit insurance by 40 percent in states where banks may sell insurance; in states where banks may not sell insurance, a 1–standard deviation increase in the insurance share raises this probability by only about 5 percent. This difference is statistically significant at the 1 percent level. In addition, a legislator who receives a high proportion of PAC contributions from the insurance industry relative to banking is more likely to support the amendment.

As we noted earlier, older people who tend to hold relatively large amounts of wealth in depository institutions preferred to keep the existing deposit insurance structure that permitted multiple accounts to be insured. Our proxy for this consumer interest is the percent of the population over 65 in each state, and we include this variable in columns 3 and 4. As with the other consumer interest variables, this one appears to have little effect on the voting pattern.

Unlike for the other two amendment votes analyzed, the political factors contribute very little beyond the information contained in the private interest variables. The effect of the Democratic Party indicator variable is negligible and not statistically significant. In specifications 2 and 4 the ADA rating does have a small statistically significant effect, but the effect is even smaller and not statistically significant in the other two specifications. Membership on the House Banking Committee again appears to have no impact. The incremental R^2 calculation shows that virtually all of the explanatory power is from the private interest variables.

7.5.3 Amendment to Raise Effective Cost of Acquisition through Low-Income Lending Enforcement (Kennedy)

Table 7.6 reports the results for the amendment that would increase the scrutiny of an acquiring bank's low-income lending. As with voting on the

Table 7.6   Marginal Effects from Probit Model Relating Voting Outcomes in the House of Representatives on an Amendment (Kennedy) Related to FDICIA Effectively to "Tax" Interstate Acquisitions by Encouraging Low Income Lending by Acquiring Banks to Measures of the Size and Strength of Interest Groups in Financial Services and Political-Institutional Factors

	(1)	(2)	(3)	(4)
Assets in small banks/total	−2.56**	−2.88**	−2.41*	−2.68
bank assets	(1.23)	(1.44)	(1.38)	(1.65)
Value added in insurance/value	0.65	1.14*	0.50	0.95
added in insurance +	(0.63)	(0.65)	(0.60)	(0.60)
depositories where banks				
may not sell insurance				
Indicator for states where	−0.58**	−0.70***	−0.57**	−0.67**
banks may sell insurance	(0.11)	(0.11)	(0.11)	(0.14)
Value added in insurance/value	4.13***	6.65***	3.77**	6.02***
added in insurance +	(1.45)	(1.75)	(1.66)	(2.28)
depositories where banks				
may sell insurance				
Median bank capital/asset	−5.02	1.31	−5.62	0.33
ratio	(5.89)	(7.34)	(5.67)	(7.16)
Share of PAC contributions	—	0.29***	—	0.28***
from insurance		(0.10)		(0.10)
Share of population below	—	—	−0.01	−0.01
poverty line			(0.01)	(0.02)
Indicator for Democrat	0.45***	0.43***	0.45***	0.43***
	(0.04)	(0.05)	(0.04)	(0.05)
ADA score	0.06	0.04	0.06	0.04
	(0.08)	(0.10)	(0.08)	(0.10)
Indicator for member of House	0.01	−0.02	0.01	−0.03
Banking Committee	(0.07)	(0.09)	(0.07)	(0.09)
No. of observations	383	270	383	270
Pseudo-R^2	0.2283	0.2226	0.2291	0.2238
χ^2 for joint significance	113.79	95.40	132.85	107.15
(p-value)	(< 0.001)	(< 0.001)	(< 0.001)	(< 0.001)
Incremental R^2				
Private interest variables	0.0658	0.0810	0.0667	0.0823
Political variables	0.1598	0.1383	0.1606	0.1393

Notes: See table 7.4.

branching amendment, legislators from areas with a larger relative market share of small banks tend to oppose this amendment. Brickley and James (1987) found that the premium paid to targets of bank mergers increases with the number of potential bidders for the target banks. Because this amendment would have been likely to reduce the number of bidders from out of state available to take over a bank that was in trouble (and small banks tended to be experiencing greater distress relative to larger, more diversified banks during this time period), small banks might have found it in their interests to lobby against this measure to try to raise the price at which they might sell out to the entering banks.

Where banks could sell insurance, legislators from states with larger insurance sectors relative to banking tended to support the amendment. Again, the magnitude of this effect is large: A 1–standard deviation increase in the insurance share raises the probability that a legislator votes to tax the bank takeover market by about 30 percent. In these states, the insurance industry did not wish to allow new (and presumably stronger) bank competitors to enter the market. Where banks did not have insurance powers, the relative size of the insurance industry does not appear to have had much of an effect. In columns 2 and 4, which include the PAC contribution variable, we find that legislators who receive a high share of their contributions from insurance relative to banking tended to support the amendment. Generally, the insurance industry opposed legislation relaxing constraints on the geographic expansion of banks unless provisions were included to limit banks' insurance powers (and no such provisions were part of this amendment). There was nothing in this amendment to divide the insurance industry into opposing sides, although the part of the industry that was facing a more direct threat from banks appears to have been more active in influencing legislators.

In columns 3 and 4 we include the share of the population below the poverty line as a rough proxy for a consumer interest that would have benefitted from this amendment. Once again, this consumer interest variable has a very small and not statistically significant effect on the voting patterns. The poor may not be a particularly well-organized interest. Also, people who are more affluent are more likely to vote than those who are less affluent. It also could be that poverty is correlated with the partisan and ideological variables we now analyze.

In contrast to the previous amendments, this issue appears to have been highly partisan. Democratic Party members were about 45 percent more likely to vote for this amendment than were Republicans. Our ideology measure, however, does not have any explanatory power beyond what is already implicitly captured in the Democrat indicator. Once again, membership on the House Banking Committee does not appear to have an impact. When we examine the incremental R^2, we find that the political factors have a greater marginal explanatory power than do the private interest variables. The private interest variables, however, still make a non-negligible contribution to the goodness of fit.

7.5.4   Final Vote on FDICIA

Table 7.7 contains the results for the final passage of FDICIA. In contrast to the three amendment votes, none of the specifications pass a chi-square test for joint statistical significance of the regressors. The R^2 is an

Table 7.7   **Marginal Effects from Probit Model Relating Voting Outcomes in the House of Representatives on FDICIA to Measures of the Size and Strength of Interest Groups in Financial Services and Political-Institutional Factors**

	(1)	(2)	(3)	(4)
Assets in small banks/total	−0.96	−1.20*	−1.10	−1.37*
bank assets	(0.62)	(0.68)	(0.66)	(0.82)
Value added in insurance/value	−0.32	0.10	−0.14	0.19
added in insurance +	(0.58)	(0.50)	(0.57)	(0.51)
depositories where banks				
may not sell insurance				
Indicator for states where	0.08	0.17	−0.01	0.04
banks may sell insurance	(0.41)	(0.26)	(0.56)	(0.67)
Value added in insurance/value	−0.37	−0.38	0.03	0.22
added in insurance +	(1.18)	(1.38)	(1.30)	(1.83)
depositories where banks				
may sell insurance				
Median bank capital/asset	−0.79	−0.07	−0.24	0.01
ratio	(5.40)	(4.93)	(5.32)	(5.26)
Share of PAC contributions	—	−0.13**	—	−0.13**
from insurance		(0.06)		(0.06)
Small firm share of the number	—	—	−0.25	−0.15
of firms in the state			(0.87)	(0.83)
Percent of population below	—	—	0.01	0.01
poverty line			(0.01)	(0.01)
Percent of population over 65	—	—	0.31	0.90
			(1.56)	(1.70)
Indicator for Democrat	−0.03	−0.01	−0.04	−0.01
	(0.05)	(0.05)	(0.04)	(0.05)
ADA score	0.02	0.05	0.02	0.05
	(0.05)	(0.05)	(0.05)	(0.06)
Indicator for member of House	0.06	0.04	0.07	0.04
Banking Committee	(0.05)	(0.07)	(0.05)	(0.07)
No. of observations	417	292	417	292
Pseudo-R^2	0.0182	0.0275	0.0219	0.0304
χ^2 for joint significance	4.63	7.85	5.23	8.00
(p-value)	(0.80)	(0.55)	(0.92)	(0.78)
Incremental R^2				
Private interest variables	0.0140	0.0220	0.0177	0.0249
Political variables	0.0047	0.0030	0.0053	0.0032

Notes: See table 7.4.

order of magnitude lower than for the amendment votes and never exceeds 3 percent. The marginal effects for all of the variables that were statistically significant in the amendment voting equations are much smaller in magnitude here. In columns 1 and 3 none of the variables are individually statistically significant. In columns 2 and 4 the relative market share of small banks and the relative share of PAC contributions from the insurance industry do have small statistically significant effects.

The contrast between the ability of the private interest group and political-institutional factors to explain the voting patterns on the amendments but not on the final passage suggests that the final bill was a "Christmas tree" compromise that included some provision to satisfy each constituency. The amendments are much more focused on specific issues, where it is easier to define whose interests would be favored. The final bill is an amalgam of such haggling and logrolling. This could be thought to represent a version of the divide-and-conquer strategy: In order for a bill concerning fundamental change to banking supervision and regulation to be successful, provisions must be included to pacify rival interests. The necessity of satisfying and balancing the competing interests places obstacles in the path to optimal reforms, but an awareness of this requirement can help to shape welfare-improving policy reforms that can build coalitions for final passage.[29]

7.6 Conclusions

Our results suggest that interest group competition and the battle among the interests are key determinants to explaining regulatory outcomes. Partisanship and ideology also appear to play important roles.[30] By the late 1980s, the demise of the thrift industry allowed many economists to argue persuasively that the moral hazard problem associated with deposit insurance could be very costly. Numerous reforms were proposed, but only some could be integrated successfully into the FDICIA. Debate over the legislation illustrated that policy makers were aware of ways to reduce moral hazard without eliminating the potential benefits of the financial safety net. Our positive analysis of roll-call votes shows, however, that reforms such as branching deregulation and limits to deposit insurance were difficult to put into law due to resistance both within banking and from rival segments of the financial industry. Without an interest group to champion a position, an argument may have little effect.

Our results also illustrate how competition among rival interest groups can increase the likelihood of beneficial reform. Rival groups have an incentive to battle each other in addition to battling the consumer. If they dissipate their efforts against each other, they are less likely to be able to support narrow special interest regulation. A divide-and-conquer strategy

---

29. Consistent with this idea, Strahan and Sufi (2000) find that competing interests in banking, securities, and insurance experienced positive stock price reactions following passage of the Financial Services Modernization Act of 1999.

30. Our proxy for the institutional structure of decision making, the Banking Committee membership indicator, did not have an impact. A cross-country comparison would allow for greater variation in the structures and a more thorough analysis of the role of political institutions, but such a study is beyond the scope of this paper. On the international political economy of financial regulation, see Kroszner (1998a, 1999a, and 2000b).

was used to split the insurance industry's interest in attempting to pass branching deregulation. The insurance industry had traditionally opposed branch banking both because it competes with banks for household savings, and because banks' abilities to sell insurance products had been expanding over time. The Wylie-Neal Amendment would have permitted more branching while limiting national banks' insurance powers, thereby gaining the favor of the insurance industry in states where state-chartered banks could not sell insurance. Heterogeneity in the interests of large and small banks also helped to make welfare-improving legislation more feasible.

For economists arguing for welfare-enhancing reforms, it is important to take into account the necessity of satisfying and balancing competing interests and understanding the role of political-institutional factors (Rodrik 1996). These may place obstacles in the path to optimal reforms, but an awareness of addressing the different constituencies can help shape policy reforms that can build coalitions for final passage of welfare-improving legislation.

References

Abrams, Burton A., and Russell F. Settle. 1993. Pressure-group influence and institutional change: Branch-banking legislation during the Great Depression. *Public Choice* 77:687–705.

Alston, Lee, Thrainn Eggertsson, and Douglass North, eds. 1996. *Empirical studies in institutional change*. New York: Cambridge University Press.

Bailey, Elizabeth, David Graham, and Daniel Kaplan. 1985. *Deregulation the airlines*. Cambridge, Mass.: MIT Press.

Becker, Gary S. 1983. A theory of competition among pressure groups for political influence. *Quarterly Journal of Economics* 98 (3): 371–400.

Bender, Bruce, and John R. Lott. 1996. Legislator voting and shirking: A critical review of the literature. *Public Choice* 87:67–100.

Benston, George J., and George G. Kaufman. 1994. The intellectual history of the Federal Deposit Insurance Corporation Improvement Act of 1991. In *Reforming financial institutions and markets in the United States,* ed. George G. Kaufman, 1–17. New York: Kluwer Academic Publishers.

———. 1998. Deposit insurance reform in the FDIC Improvement Act: The experience to date. Federal Reserve Bank of Chicago, *Economic Perspectives* 22 (2): 2–20.

Berger, Allen, Anil Kashyap, and Joseph Scalise. 1995. The transformation of the U.S. banking industry: What a long, strange trip it's been. *Brookings Papers on Economic Activity,* issue no. 2:55–218.

Berger, Allen, Anthony Saunders, Joseph Scalise, and Gregory Udell. 1998. The effects of bank mergers and acquisitions on small business lending. *Journal of Financial Economics* 50 (2): 2–20.

Berglof, Erik, and Howard Rosenthal. 1999. The political economy of American bankruptcy: The evidence from roll call voting, 1800–1978. Princeton University, Working Paper, April.

Bolton, Patrick, and Howard Rosenthal. 1999. Political intervention in debt contracts: Moratoria and bailouts. Princeton University, Working Paper, March.

Brennan, Geoffrey, and James Buchanan. 1977. Towards a tax constitution for leviathan. *Journal of Public Economics* 8:255–73.

Brickley, James A., and Christopher M. James. The takeover market, corporate board composition, and ownership structure: The case of banking. *Journal of Law and Economics* 30 (April): 161–80.

Bronars, Stephen G., and John R. Lott, Jr. 1997. Do campaign donations alter how a politician votes? Or, do donors support candidates who value the same things that they do? *Journal of Law and Economics* 40 (October): 317–50.

Calomiris, Charles, and Eugene White. 1994. The origins of federal deposit insurance. In *The regulated economy,* ed. Claudia Golden and Gary Libecap, 145–88. Chicago: University of Chicago Press.

Cole, Rebel, and John Wolken. 1994. Financial services used by small businesses: Evidence from the 1993 Survey of Small Business Finances. *Federal Reserve Bulletin* 81:629–76.

Cox, Gary W., and Mathew D. McCubbins. 1993. *Legislative leviathan: Party government in the House.* Berkeley: University of California Press.

Dewatripont, Mathias, and Jean Tirole. 1999. Advocates. *Journal of Political Economy* 107 (February): 1–39.

Diamond, Douglas, and Philip Dybvig. 1983. Bank runs, deposit insurance and liquidity. *Journal of Political Economy* 91:401–19.

Dixit, Avinash. 1996. *The making of economic policy: A transactions-cost politics perspective.* Cambridge, Mass.: MIT Press.

Economides, Nicolas, R. Glenn Hubbard, and Darius Palia. 1996. The political economy of branching restrictions and deposit insurance. *Journal of Law and Economics* 29 (October): 667–704.

Economist. 1994. The struggle to reform America's banking system. 6 August, 59.

Estrella, Arturo. 1988. A new measure of fit for equations with dichotomous dependent variables. *Journal of Business and Economic Statistics* 16 (2): 198–205.

Federal Deposit Insurance Corporation (FDIC). 1997. *History of the eighties: Lessons for the future.*

Flannery, Mark. 1984. The social costs of unit banking restrictions. *Journal of Monetary Economics* 13:237–49.

Gilligan, Thomas, William Marshall, and Barry Weingast. 1989. Regulation and the theory of legislative choice: The Interstate Commerce Act of 1887. *Journal of Law and Economics* 22 (April): 35–61.

Hall, Richard, and Bernard Grofman. 1990. The committee assignment process and the conditional nature of committee bias. *American Political Science Review* 84:1149–66.

Hellwig, Martin. 1999. On the economics and politics of corporate finance and corporate control. University of Mannheim, Germany, Working Paper.

Irwin, Douglas, and Randall Kroszner. 1996. Log-rolling and the Smoot-Hawley Tariff, *Carnegie-Rochester Series on Public Policy* 45 (December): 173–200.

———. 1999. Interests, institutions, and ideology in securing policy change: The Republican conversion to trade liberalization after Smoot-Hawley. *Journal of Law and Economics* 42 (2): 643–73.

James, Christopher. 1983. An analysis of intra-industry differences in the effect of regulation: The case of deposit rate ceilings. *Journal of Monetary Economics* 12:417–32.

Jarrell, Gregg A., James A. Brickley, and Jeffry N. Netter. 1988. The market for corporate control: The evidence since 1980. *Journal of Economic Perspectives* 2:12–19.

Jayaratne, Jith, and Philip E. Strahan. 1996. The finance-growth nexus: Evidence from bank branch deregulation. *Quarterly Journal of Economics* 101:639–70.

———. 1998. Industry evolution and dynamic efficiency: Evidence from commercial banking. *Journal of Law and Economics* 41 (1): 239–74.

Jensen, Michael C., and Richard S. Ruback. 1983. The market for corporate control: The scientific evidence. *Journal of Financial Economics* 11:5–50.

Joskow, Paul, and Roger Noll. 1981. Regulation in theory and practice: An overview. In *Studies in Public Regulation,* ed. Gary Fromm, 1–65. Cambridge, Mass.: MIT Press.

Kahn, Matthew E., and John G. Matsusaka. 1997. Demand for environmental goods: Evidence from voting patterns on California initiatives. *Journal of Law and Economics* 40:137–73.

Kalt, Joseph, and Mark Zupan. 1984. Capture and ideology in the economic theory of politics. *American Economic Review* 74:302–22.

Kane, Edward J. 1989. *The S & L insurance mess: How did it happen?* Washington, D.C.: Urban Institute Press.

———. 1996. De jure interstate banking: Why only now? *Journal of Money, Credit, and Banking* 28 (2): 141–61.

Kaufman, George, and Randall Kroszner. 1997. How should financial institutions and markets be structured? In *Safe and sound financial systems: What works for Latin America?* ed. Liliana Rojas-Suarez, 97–122. Washington, D.C.: Inter-American Development Bank.

Kiewiet, Roderick, and Mathew D. McCubbins. 1991. *The logic of delegation: Congressional parties and the appropriations process.* Chicago: University of Chicago Press.

King, Robert, and Ross Levine. 1993. Finance and growth: Schumpeter might be right. *Quarterly Journal of Economics* 108:717–38.

Krehbiel, Keith. 1991. *Information and legislative organization.* Ann Arbor: University of Michigan Press.

———. 1998. *Pivotal politics: A theory of U.S. lawmaking.* Chicago: University of Chicago Press.

Kroszner, Randall S. 1997. The political economy of banking and financial regulation in the U.S. In *The banking and financial structure in the NAFTA countries and Chile,* ed. George M. von Furstenberg, 200–13. Boston: Kluwer Academic Publishers.

———. 1998a. The political economy of banking and financial regulatory reform in emerging markets. *Research in Financial Services* 10:33–51.

———. 1998b. Rethinking banking regulation: A review of the historical evidence. *Journal of Applied Corporate Finance* 11 (2): 48–58.

———. 1999a. Less is more in the new international financial architecture. In *The Asian financial crisis: Origins, implications, solutions,* ed. W. C. Hunter and G. G. Kaufman, 447–52. Boston: Kluwer Academic Publishers.

———. 1999b. Is it better to forgive than to receive? Repudiation of the Gold Indexation Clause in long-term debt contracts during the Great Depression. University of Chicago, Graduate School of Business, Working Paper, November.

———. 2000a. The economics and politics of financial modernization. Federal Reserve Bank of New York, *Economic Policy Review* 6 (October): 25–37.

————. 2000b. Is the financial system politically independent? Perspectives on the political economy of banking and financial regulation. In *Finanssektorn Framtid* (Government inquiry on the international competitiveness of the Swedish financial sector), vol. D. Stockholm: Swedish Finance Ministry.

Kroszner, Randall S., and Philip Strahan. 1996. Regulatory incentives and the thrift crisis: Dividends, mutual-to-stock conversions, and financial distress. *Journal of Finance* 51 (September): 1285–320.

————. 1999. What drives deregulation? Economics and politics of the relaxation of bank branching restrictions. *Quarterly Journal of Economics* 114 (November): 1437–67.

Kroszner, Randall S., and Thomas Stratmann. 1998. Interest group competition and the organization of Congress: Theory and evidence from financial services political action committees. *American Economic Review* 88 (December): 1163–87.

————. 1999. Does political ambiguity pay? Corporate campaign contributions and the rewards to legislator reputation. N.B.E.R. Working Paper no. 7475. National Bureau of Economic Research, November.

McCubbins, Matthew, Roger Noll, and Barry Weingast. 1988. Structure and process, politics and policy: Administrative arrangements and the political control of agencies. *Virginia Law Review* 78:431–82.

McGuire, Martin, and Mancur Olson. 1996. The economics of autocracy and majority rule. *Journal of Economic Literature* 34 (March): 72–96.

Merton, Robert C. 1977. An analytic derivation of the cost of deposit insurance and loan guarantees. *Journal of Banking and Finance* 1 (1): 3–11.

Mishkin, Frederic S. 1997. *The economics of money, banking and financial markets,* 5th ed. New York: Addison-Wesley.

Niskanen, William. 1971. *Bureaucracy and representative government.* Chicago: Aldine-Atherton.

Noll, Roger. 1989. Comment on Peltzman. *Brookings Papers on Economic Activity, Microeconomics:* 48–58.

North, Douglass. 1990. A transactions cost theory of politics. *Journal of Theoretical Politics* 2:355–67.

Olson, Mancur. 1965. *The logic of collective action.* Cambridge, Mass.: Harvard University Press.

————. 1982. *The rise and decline of nations.* New Haven, Conn.: Yale University Press.

Peltzman, Sam. 1976. Toward a more general theory of regulation. *Journal of Law and Economics* 19 (1): 109–48.

————. 1984. Constituent interest and congressional voting. *Journal of Law and Economics* 27:181–210.

————. 1989. The economic theory of regulation after a decade of deregulation. *Brookings Papers on Economic Activity Microeconomics:* 1–41.

Peterson, Mitchell, and Raghuram Rajan. 1994. The benefits of lending relationships: Evidence from small business data. *Journal of Finance* 49:3–38.

Poole, Keith T., and Howard Rosenthal. 1993. The enduring nineteenth-century battle for economic regulation: The Interstate Commerce Act revisited. *Journal of Law and Economics* 36 (October): 837–60.

————. 1996. Are legislators ideologues or the agents of constituents? *European Economic Review* 40:707–17.

————. 1997. *Congress: A political-economic history of roll call voting.* Oxford: Oxford University Press.

Posner, Eric. 1997. The political economy of the Bankruptcy Reform Act of 1978. *Michigan Law Review* 96 (October): 47–126.

Rajan, Raghuram, and Luigi Zingales. Forthcoming. The tyranny of the inefficient: An inquiry into the adverse consequences of power struggles. *Journal of Public Economics.*

Rodrik, Dani. 1996. Understanding economic policy reform. *Journal of Economic Literature* 34 (March): 9–41.

Roe, Mark. 1994. *Strong managers, weak owners.* Princeton, N.J.: Princeton University Press.

Romer, Thomas, and Barry Weingast. 1991. Political foundations of the thrift debacle. *Politics and economics of the eighties,* eds. Alberto Alesina and Geoffrey Carliner, 175–209. Chicago: University of Chicago Press.

Schattscheider, E. E. 1935. *Politics, pressure, and the tariff.* New York: Prentice Hall.

Seiberg, Jaret. 1996. High court: States must let banks sell insurance. *The American banker* 27 March 1996.

Shepsle, Kenneth. 1978. *The giant jigsaw puzzle: Democratic Committee assignments in the modern House.* Chicago: University of Chicago Press.

Shepsle, Kenneth, and Barry Weingast. 1987. Institutional foundations of committee power. *American Political Science Review* 81 (March): 85–104.

Shepsle, Kenneth, and Barry Weingast, eds. 1995. *Positive theories of Congressional institutions.* Ann Arbor: University of Michigan Press.

Shleifer, Andrei, and Daniel Treisman. 2000. Without a map: Political tactics and economic reform in Russia. Cambridge, Mass.: MIT Press.

Stigler, George J. 1971. The theory of economic regulation. *Bell Journal of Economics and Management Science* 2 (1): 3–21.

———. 1988. *Chicago studies in the political economy.* Chicago: University of Chicago Press.

Strahan, Philip E. 1995. Asset prices and economic disasters: Evidence from the S & L crisis. *Journal of Monetary Economics* 36:189–217.

Strahan, Philip E., and Amir Sufi. 2000. The gains from financial modernization. Federal Reserve Bank of New York. Mimeograph.

Strahan, Philip E., and James P. Weston. 1998. Small business lending and the changing structure of the banking industry. *Journal of Banking and Finance* 22 (2–6): 821–45.

Stratmann, Thomas. 1991. What do campaign contributions buy? Deciphering causal effects of money and votes. *Southern Economic Journal* 57 (January): 606–20.

———. 1995. Campaign contributions and congressional voting: Does the timing of contributions matter? *Review of Economics and Statistics* 72 (February): 127–36.

Weingast, Barry R., and William J. Marshall. 1988. The industrial organization of Congress; or, why legislatures, like firms, are not organized as markets. *Journal of Political Economy* 96 (February): 132–63.

White, Eugene. 1983. *The regulation and reform of the American banking system, 1900–1929.* Princeton, N.J.: Princeton University Press.

———. 1998. The legacy of deposit insurance: The growth, spread, and cost of insuring financial intermediaries. In *The defining moment,* ed. Michael Bordo, Claudia Goldin, and Eugene White. Chicago: University of Chicago Press.

Williamson, Oliver. 1996. The politics and economics of redistribution and efficiency. In *The mechanisms of governance.* Oxford: Oxford University Press.

Winston, Clifford. 1993. Economic deregulation days of reckoning for microeconomists. *Journal of Economic Literature* 31:1263–89.

Wittman, Donald N. 1995. *The myth of democratic failure.* Chicago: University of Chicago Press.

Comment   Jeremy C. Stein

The paper by Kroszner and Strahan is a very interesting and extremely well-done positive analysis of bank regulation. Kroszner and Strahan seek to understand a fundamental question about financial regulation (and regulation more generally), namely: What role do various economic and political forces play in shaping these laws?

Because I find Kroszner and Strahan's empirical work to be clear-cut and convincing, I will not quibble in any way with their specifications or their regression results. Rather, I will try to provide an interpretation of what exactly—in terms of broad lessons—one might take away from these regressions. To begin, it is helpful to note that one can ask different versions of the basic positive question that Kroszner and Strahan pose:

Question 1 (static version): Why do we have the (possibly suboptimal) laws we do? Which types of bad laws are most likely to exist?

Question 2 (dynamic version): Why and when do laws change? Do they respond well to shocks in the external economic environment?

Question 3 (cross-country version): Why do some countries have worse laws than others?

One type of answer—the one favored by Kroszner and Strahan—has to do with special interests. For example, restrictions on interbank competition, as well as excessively generous deposit insurance, can be expected to benefit banks, and especially small banks. In contrast, although restrictions on bank competition may also benefit insurance companies, insurers are likely to be hurt by excessive deposit insurance, particularly if they compete directly with banks. These observations lead to sharp predictions about how congressional voting on various issues will be influenced by the relative strength of the banking and insurance lobbies, among other factors.

Note, however, that at least in principle it is possible that a private interest approach may be more successful in providing answers to the static version of the question, question 1, than to the dynamic or cross-country versions, question 2 or question 3. Suppose that the rents accruing to the banking sector as a result of anticompetitive regulation are large but do not vary much over time and across countries. Then the existence of a strong banking lobby can help explain why such anticompetitive laws are on the books, but it may not give us much insight into why such laws are changed at a particular point in time.

With this observation in mind, let me very briefly review the Kroszner and Strahan's results. In all their regressions, the variables on the left-hand

Jeremy C. Stein is professor of economics at Harvard University and a research associate of the National Bureau of Economic Research.

side are the votes of individual members of the House of Representatives on various amendments to FDICIA. That is, the regressions seek to explain the voting patterns of individual house members. In table 7.4 the amendment being voted on is the Wylie-Neal amendment, which would both relax restrictions on interstate branching as well as limit national banks' insurance powers. Consistent with the private interest approach, Kroszner and Strahan find that house members tend to (a) vote "no" if they are from a state with many small banks; (b) vote "no" if they are from a state that has many insurance companies and that allows banks and insurers to compete directly; and (c) vote "yes" if they are from a state that has many insurance companies, but where banks and insurers do not compete with one another.

In table 7.5 the amendment being considered would limit deposit insurance coverage. Again, the private interest variables loom large. House members tend to (a) vote "no" if they are from a small-bank state, (b) vote "yes" if they are from an insurance industry–heavy state, and (c) vote "yes" if they receive PAC money from the insurance industry. As with table 7.4 one of the really interesting things that comes out in the data is the way in which different industries can be played off against one another, based on their conflicting economic interests.

Finally, in table 7.6 the amendment being voted on is one that would raise the effective cost of making banking acquisitions, by scrutinizing an acquiring bank's low-income lending policies. Here, too, the private interest variables have some explanatory power, with members tending to (a) vote "no" if they are from a small-bank state, (b) vote "yes" if they are from an insurance industry–heavy state, and (c) vote "yes" if they receive PAC money from the insurance industry. However, in this case the most dominant variable is not a private interest one, but a partisan one: Being a Democrat is the single strongest predictor of whether a member votes "yes."

Overall, I would interpret the results in the following way. The regressions do an extremely impressive job of explaining variation in individual members' votes, based on the members' home-state economic interests, the PAC money they receive, and, to a somewhat lesser extent, their party affiliation. This strong explanatory power can be seen in the high pseudo-R^2s of the regressions, which are for the most part in the range of 20 percent.

What do these results tell us about variation in regulatory outcomes, however? And what sort of variation are they best suited to explaining: time series, or cross-sectional? In other words, to what extent do the regression results map directly into question 1, 2, or 3? Kroszner and Strahan argue that there is a very direct mapping: "Our results suggest that interest group competition and the battle among the interests are a key determinant to explaining regulatory outcomes" (261). Although this claim may very well be true, it is worth noting that there is—at least logically—some distance between the authors' results for individual members' voting patterns and any conclusions about regulatory outcomes.

This point is best illustrated with an example. Suppose that every year, a nine-member House committee takes up a proposal to cap damage awards from tobacco litigation. Four of the members of the committee are from tobacco states, and always vote "yes." Four of the members are from states with big law firm lobbies, and always vote "no." The final member is from a neutral state, and the vote is effectively random from year to year.

If we were to run a regression to explain individual member votes based on tobacco and law firm economic influence variables, we would get an R^2 close to 1. Even so, however, we cannot predict at all whether the measure will pass in a given year, nor can we explain any time variation in the outcome of the vote. There is a simple moral here: Competing economic interests may be good at explaining the tails of the voting distribution, and hence may help to generate high R^2s in the sort of regressions that Kroszner and Strahan run. But the voting outcome—unlike, say, market demand—is driven by the person in the middle of the distribution, and it may well be that this median voter's preferences are harder to understand in terms of private economic interests. In the case of the tobacco example, the median voter may be much more influenced by changing social views about smoking, personal experience with a relative who got lung cancer, and so on.

Although the example suggests that, as a matter of logic, one should be a bit cautious in mapping the authors' regressions directly into statements about regulatory outcomes, it is not clear how much weight this caveat deserves in practice. My tentative guess is that the caveat is less relevant for question 1. Said differently, I am more comfortable concluding that the authors' type of analysis allows us to speak pretty directly to question 1. To go back to the tobacco example, if eight of the nine committee members were from tobacco states, a private interest model would do a very good job of explaining why, in steady-state, we observe a cap.

On the other hand, I am less convinced that the authors' type of analysis can speak directly to Q2, because at the time that a law gets changed, it is, almost by definition, one that is on the cusp—that is, one in which, like in the first variant of the tobacco example, the median voter (who is neutral based on private economic interests) is more likely to be pivotal.

This is, of course, not to say that private interest variables cannot ultimately explain at least some aspects of the dynamics of regulation. Indeed, in section 7.3 of their paper, Kroszner and Strahan argue that banking reform occurred in the 1980s and 1990s—as opposed to earlier—in part because the balance of power in the industry changed in such a way as to alter the relative strength of various lobbies. This seems like an eminently plausible hypothesis. My only point is that the evidence that Kroszner and

Strahan present in their paper, while suggestive, does not really provide a decisive test of this sort of private interest hypothesis of regulatory dynamics.

Discussion Summary

Charles Calomiris began the discussion by asking about the use of probits for this type of analysis. He pointed out that political scientists note that in close votes, party discipline may be higher, resulting in a poorer model fit. He pointed out also that the authors find high pseudo-R^2s even in the closer votes. He wondered about differences between the amendments and the final vote. He also suggested the inclusion of additional demographic variables, noting that demographic variables such as industry composition and rural population have mattered in past research and are likely to be correlated with the included explanatory variables.

Raghuram Rajan wondered why agreements could not be reached through rent sharing (and not through the death of small banks).

Mark Flannery advocated naïveté in formulating policy advice. He asked whether economists should necessarily focus on what is feasible. *Frederic Mishkin* noted, however, that the route to achieve optimal policy might be important.

James Wilcox focused on the positive rather than normative findings, noting that it is difficult to identify Pareto or social welfare–improving laws. He also noted the fresh water effect—that is, the concentration of unit banking states away from the two coasts. He suggested that state regulations and preferences may influence the distribution of banking assets within a state and, in turn, the characteristics of a state's representatives.

Mark Carey, picking up on a question raised by the discussant, wondered which countries' political systems and laws are associated with good regulation. He suggested that it will be interesting to observe, as sound policies are advocated by some, how these are implemented across countries.

Finally, *Mark Gertler* suggested a different approach to this problem by focusing on the median voter. He suggested that the authors look at representatives who voted in opposite directions for the different amendments.

Randy Kroszner began his response by noting the difficulties associated with the median voter approach. He pointed out that some of his other work suggests entrenchment and support for clearly stated positions. He noted that only when there are broad technological or economic shocks that change the support among the constituents or the profitability to the different groups do we see changes in outcomes.

He also noted that international comparisons might be difficult, given the important role of foreign banks. He observed that these institutions would typically not be part of the political process, but may be interesting actors. In response to Wilcox, he agreed that there is a risk in designating policies as good or bad for certain interest groups. He noted that in a previous paper with Strahan, they looked at endogenous interest group formation, and found that this did not seem to change other results. He did agree that this was an interesting dynamic that occurs as regulation can create interest groups.

He also supported Flannery's assertion, noting that truth is just another special interest group and one that is not well funded. He observed that academics could affect the productivity of the dollars spent by the different interest groups. He also agreed with Rajan that the dynamics of change will be interesting and that the authors need to consider how to generalize their results.

Finally, in response to Calomiris he noted that political scientists would often include a political party indicator variable that helps explain many votes—in particular, the partisan (and often not close) votes. This might explain the high R^2 in many studies where the votes were not close.

In response to Rajan, *Philip Strahan* noted that there is some evidence of transfers among the various groups that are affected. For example, he noted that state branching requires banks to buy existing branches (or banks), resulting in a payoff to incumbents. One challenge, he observed, is how to share these payoffs among the smaller banks. Finally, he also noted that other variables, including indicators for unit banking and rural versus urban areas, had been examined and were not found to change the results.

8

Synergies between Bank Supervision and Monetary Policy
Implications for the Design of Bank Regulatory Structure

Joe Peek, Eric S. Rosengren, and Geoffrey M. B. Tootell

The current structure of bank supervision in the United States has evolved through regulatory competition whereby banks would choose the regulator that most suited their operations. As a result, bank supervision responsibility has not been closely tied to the institutional function of the supervisor. In this study, we focus on determining which institutions the Federal Reserve should supervise based on one of its institutional functions: The Federal Reserve should regulate those banks that provide the greatest synergies between bank supervision and the conduct of monetary policy.[1] We build on recent research by Peek, Rosengren, and Tootell (1999a,b) that finds that confidential supervisory information can improve the conduct of monetary policy. Although that research has established the potential synergies between bank supervision and monetary policy, the implications of these synergies for regulatory structure have not been examined. If regulatory structure were based on the criterion of which institutions provided the most useful supervisory information for monetary policy, a very

Joe Peek holds the Gatton Endowed Chair in International Banking and Financial Economics at the Gatton College of Business and Economics, University of Kentucky. Eric S. Rosengren is senior vice president in charge of the supervision group at the Federal Reserve Bank of Boston. Geoffrey M. B. Tootell is vice president and economist in the research department at the Federal Reserve Bank of Boston.

The authors thank Peggy Gilligan and Peter Morrow, who provided valuable research assistance. The views expressed are those of the authors and do not necessarily reflect official positions of the Federal Reserve Bank of Boston or the Federal Reserve System.

1. Among the other Federal Reserve functions, other relevant criteria for determining the set of banks to be supervised by the Federal Reserve might be lender of last resort and managing the payments system, in which case the emphasis might be on large institutions that pose the greatest concern for systemic risk. In fact, many of the proposals to restructure bank supervision have given supervisory authority over the largest bank holding companies to the Federal Reserve.

different set of institutions would be selected than if the criterion were based solely on the institutions that posed the greatest systemic risk.

A number of plans to reform the bank supervisory and regulatory structure have been proposed over the past fifty years. Although these proposals differ in varying degrees from the current structure (and from each other), a comparison makes clear that any legislation to alter bank supervisory responsibilities will likely focus on one or more of the following three dimensions: charter type, whether a bank is included in a holding company, and the size of the banking organization. The debate has focused on these three dimensions more for political than for economic reasons. This paper contributes to this debate by focusing on an important economic consideration that has been largely absent from prior discussions about redesigning the bank regulatory structure. We examine recent proposals focusing on the extent to which the proposals are likely to assign to the Federal Reserve regulatory oversight of the set of banks that provides the most useful information for improving macroeconomic forecasts relevant for monetary policy.

As a benchmark, we review the empirical evidence found in Peek, Rosengren, and Tootell (1999a) on the extent to which supervisory information about the set of all banks improves forecasts of inflation and unemployment rates. The percent of bank assets held by those banks that supervisors deem to be the most troubled is the measure of the information acquired through bank supervisory responsibilities that is used in these tests. Next, we investigate the extent to which supervisory information about the set of banks currently regulated by the Federal Reserve provides useful information for the conduct of monetary policy. Because the holding company status of a bank is one of the primary dimensions considered in many regulatory reform proposals, we consider the set of banks for which the Federal Reserve serves as primary federal regulator as well as the broader set of banks included through the Federal Reserve's bank holding company (BHC) supervisory responsibilities.

We then analyze four alternative regulatory structures that have been proposed recently to determine their potential impact on the conduct of monetary policy. The first such reform proposal maintains BHC supervisory responsibilities for the Federal Reserve but eliminates the primary regulator responsibility over state member banks. The second proposal limits Federal Reserve supervisory responsibility to only the twenty largest holding companies (along the lines of the 1994 Treasury proposal) plus state-chartered member banks. The third proposal considered assigns the Federal Reserve regulatory responsibility over all state-chartered banks (along the lines of the 1994 Federal Reserve proposal). This structure ignores the holding company affiliation of the banks. The fourth proposal differs only slightly from the third by taking into account holding company affiliation. Here, the Federal Reserve is assigned regulatory responsibility over all banks in any BHC that has a state-chartered lead bank, plus any state-chartered bank not in a holding company.[2]

Section 8.1 provides some background on bank supervisory structure and potential synergies between supervisory information and the conduct of monetary policy. Section 8.2 provides the methodology. Section 8.3 investigates whether informational synergies vary across sets of banks associated with alternative regulatory structure proposals. Section 8.4 discusses the transferability of supervisory data among regulators. The final section provides some conclusions and policy implications.

8.1 Background

The bank regulatory structure in the United States has evolved into an unusually intricate interlocking web of supervisory responsibilities. Individual banks choose their chartering authority, and in so doing also choose their bank supervisor. If a bank chooses a national charter, it is regulated by the Office of the Comptroller of the Currency (OCC), a part of the U.S. Treasury Department. The OCC regulates many of the largest banks, with responsibility for over one-quarter of all banks, by number, that account for more than half of all bank assets.

The Federal Deposit Insurance Corporation (FDIC) is an independent federal agency. In addition to its responsibility for providing deposit insurance, it has supervisory responsibility for all state-chartered banks that are not members of the Federal Reserve System. The FDIC has responsibility for approximately 60 percent of all banks, but they account for only about one-fifth of all bank assets because of their small average size.

The Federal Reserve has responsibility for supervising all state-chartered banks that are members of the Federal Reserve System. The Federal Reserve is the primary federal regulator for approximately 10 percent of all banks, accounting for less than one-quarter of all bank assets. However, in addition to its responsibility as the primary regulator of all state member banks, the Federal Reserve also has supervisory authority over BHCs. Because most banks are in BHCs, the combination of responsibilities for BHCs and as the primary regulator for state-chartered member banks assigns the Federal Reserve supervisory responsibilities for over three-quarters of banks, representing more than 90 percent of bank assets, including most large entities.

The BHC supervisory responsibility gives the Federal Reserve access to

---

2. In other countries, changes in regulatory structure have been even more extreme, frequently removing the central bank from bank supervisory responsibilities and providing a single financial services regulator for banks, insurance companies, securities firms, and mutual funds. Countries adopting a single regulator model include the United Kingdom, Korea, and Japan. Numerous other countries are considering moving to such a model.

virtually every large bank. Even though they are not the primary regulator of many of the biggest banks, they nonetheless are actively involved in joint examinations of lead banks and the holding companies. In fact, it is required that the examination for the holding company and the lead bank be coordinated under certain conditions related to the size or the health of the BHC. Those conditions include the holding company having over $10 billion in assets and the holding company or lead bank having one of the two lowest supervisory rating categories (four or five), or, if their condition has deteriorated, having a rating of three (BHC Supervision Manual; available at http://www.federalreserve.gov/boarddocs/supmanual/default.htm_bhcsm). In addition, although the exams are expected to be concurrent, they are expected also to include the "performance of certain on-site examination activities by examiners from the agencies on a simultaneous or coordinated basis so as to enhance cooperation" (BHC Supervision Manual). Although in practice the degree of coordination and cooperation will vary by regional reserve bank and the associated OCC or FDIC regional office, the interagency policy statement on 10 June 1993 made clear that the agencies were expected to strengthen coordination and cooperation. Thus, the Federal Reserve is required to have hands-on supervision of any large or troubled bank in a holding company.

An additional layer of regulatory oversight is present for state-chartered banks. Although each state has supervisory powers over the banks it has chartered, the bank must also follow the regulations of its federal regulator. Thus, the state regulatory agency has overlapping supervisory responsibilities with the bank's primary federal regulator, either the Federal Reserve (state member banks) or the FDIC (nonmember banks). In addition, the Federal Reserve has supervisory responsibility for all BHCs. In the extreme, a state-chartered nonmember bank in a holding company would come under the jurisdiction of three different regulators: the state banking supervisor, the FDIC, and the Federal Reserve.

It is debatable whether such a convoluted regulatory structure would be the structure of choice if one were to organize supervisory responsibilities from scratch. A number of proposals to reform bank supervision and regulation have been suggested over the past fifty years, and one motivation underlying these proposals has been to reduce regulatory overlap. Although the proposals vary, and none has resulted in a major restructuring, the assignment of banks to particular regulators in these proposals has been based primarily on three considerations: bank charter, bank size, and whether the bank is in a BHC.

Basing regulatory authority on charter type would be assigning regulators based primarily on historical precedent, because such a split would not allocate banks to regulators by size of institution, potential to cause systemic risk, or importance to monetary policy or the payments system. Prior to 1864, all banks were state chartered, with the exception of the experiment with the First and Second Banks of the United States. Banks were able to issue bank notes partially backed by the banks' gold and silver reserves. However, this haphazard system led to the distribution of a plethora of bank notes and an incentive for banks that got into trouble to issue more notes than they could redeem. With the large outstanding government debt from financing the Civil War, it was decided to establish a national currency secured by government bonds and to charter national banks that could issue bank notes secured by government debt. The OCC was established in 1864 to charter, supervise, and examine all national banks. After the establishment of the Federal Reserve in 1913, the Fed had the authority to supervise member banks, which included all national banks. Thus, supervisory responsibility over national banks was shared initially by the Fed and the OCC, although that was changed in 1917 because of turf battles. The result was the elimination of this regulatory overlap. The OCC examined national banks, but provided information to the Federal Reserve. The Federal Reserve was given primary regulatory responsibility for state-chartered banks that were members of the Federal Reserve System.

The choice between a state or national charter has been left to individual banks, rather than being tied to achieving particular public policy objectives, such as improving information for the conduct of monetary policy or reducing systemic concerns. Thus, a bank's choice is determined by which charter the bank believes most enhances its profitability. Charter preferences have been influenced by numerous factors, including taxes on bank notes, a regulator's willingness to allow extended powers, the direct and indirect costs of bank examinations, and the regulatory authority's regulatory and supervisory stance.

Assigning regulatory responsibilities to the Federal Reserve according to bank size may be related to other central bank responsibilities. Most of the largest financial institutions have substantial interlocking relationships and are often integral to the functioning of the financial markets in which they specialize. Thus, the central bank's responsibilities for the discount window function, for management of the payments system, and for maintaining orderly financial markets and a stable economy would provide an economic rationale for assigning the central bank supervisory responsibilities for the largest banks. However, large bank size and potential systemic risks are not synonymous, insofar as some smaller banks are important niche players in some markets and, as the failure of Penn Square Bank showed, even relatively small banks can have a significant impact on their larger brethren.

Assigning regulatory responsibilities according to BHC status has both economic and historical precedents. Although BHCs were first formed in the early 1900s, it was only in the mid-1900s, as holding companies were formed to avoid interstate and intrastate branching restrictions, that holding companies became more popular. In 1956 the Bank Holding Company Act gave the Federal Reserve supervisory authority over multibank holding companies, and in 1970 this supervisory authority was extended to single-bank holding companies. Thus, although a bank's choice of a holding company structure is driven by self-interest and is determined primarily by legal considerations (e.g., for tax purposes and to circumvent restrictions on forming banking networks and on nontraditional bank activities), choosing a holding company structure that allows Federal Reserve oversight may have some potential economic benefits in a broader public policy context. Because the largest institutions are in holding companies, Federal Reserve supervisory responsibilities over these institutions can provide synergies for the central bank's responsibilities as lender of last resort, managing the payments system, and conducting monetary policy.

Most discussions about restructuring bank supervision have focused on reducing regulatory overlap. However, proposals intended only to reduce regulatory overlap provide no guidance for evaluating the costs or benefits of alternative proposals that have one regulator per institution but that are based on a number of other factors, including charter type, bank size, or holding company affiliation. In part, this absence of a persuasive rationale for restructuring bank supervision, other than satisfying the goal of reducing regulatory overlap, has prevented the adoption of a politically palatable restructuring proposal.

As far back as 1949, President Truman created a task force to examine bank supervision. The task force recommended that all federal bank supervision be combined, preferably in the Federal Reserve. A similar conclusion was drawn by a private study in 1961 by the Commission on Money and Credit, which recommended that the supervisory responsibilities of the OCC and the FDIC be transferred to the Federal Reserve. Two other reports also recommended a single federal regulator, although outside the Federal Reserve System. A study commissioned by the House Banking Committee in 1975 recommended that a single Federal Depository Institutions Commission supervise all banks, thrifts, and credit unions. The Grace Commission reported in 1983 to President Reagan that a single regulator, the Federal Banking Commission, should be given supervisory responsibility for banks currently regulated by the OCC, the FDIC, and the Fed. Although the Hunt Commission in 1971 expanded the proposed number of federal regulators to two (an Administrator of National Banks and an Administrator of State Banks), the Federal Reserve still played no role as a primary supervisor.

In 1984, Vice President Bush provided a blueprint for reform that placed all national banks and BHCs whose lead bank was a national bank under a Federal Banking Administration, while placing all state-chartered banks and BHCs whose lead bank was a state-chartered bank under Federal Reserve supervision. This proposal eliminated the FDIC as a bank supervisor and split supervisory authority according to bank charter. A Treasury study in 1991 recommended replacing the OCC and Office of Thrift Supervision (OTS) with a federal banking agency and placing all state-chartered banks under Federal Reserve supervision.

The most serious recent attempt to alter bank supervisory responsibilities occurred in 1994. The debate again focused on three major criteria for determining supervisory authority: charter type, holding company status, and size of banking organization. The Treasury proposal, which was generally incorporated into S.R. 1633 and H.R. 1214, recommended the creation of a single bank regulator with the supervisory responsibilities then assigned to the OTS, OCC, FDIC, and Federal Reserve. However, the Federal Reserve would still have shared supervisory responsibility over the twenty largest BHCs, including conducting exams and initiating enforcement actions. As an alternative, the Federal Reserve proposed that a Federal Banking Commission be created to supervise all national banks and thrifts, as well as all banks in holding companies with national banks as their lead bank. The Federal Reserve would regulate all state-chartered banks as well as all banks in a holding company with a state-chartered bank as its lead bank. At the BHC level, the Federal Reserve proposed two alternatives: placing them all under Federal Reserve supervision or distributing them according to the charter of the lead bank.

The numerous past proposals highlight that most legislation to alter bank supervisory responsibilities will likely focus on charter type, size of bank, whether a bank is included in a holding company, or some combination of these characteristics. Although numerous economic and political arguments for regulatory restructuring have been proposed, little empirical evidence has been provided on the possible costs or benefits of different regulatory designs. This paper examines recent proposals for redesigning the regulatory structure focusing on the extent to which the proposals are likely to assign to the Federal Reserve regulatory oversight over the set of banks that provides the most useful information for improving macroeconomic forecasts relevant for monetary policy.

Such evidence is particularly relevant given that a number of countries have recently adopted a regulatory structure with a single financial services regulator outside of the central bank. Although the blurring of geographic and product characteristics of financial institutions has encouraged many countries to adopt a single regulator model (United Kingdom, Japan, Korea), the costs to systemic stability, lender of last resort responsibilities, or synergies with monetary policy have not been quantified. Although reducing regulatory overlap and inconsistent regulations may be an important objective, it is important also to understand if possible synergies with other central bank functions might be impaired. In fact, a frequent response to regulatory reform measures has been that the Federal Reserve needs hands-on experience with banks to fulfill its responsibilities properly, including the conduct of monetary policy. If such hands-on experience does affect the quality of information, then one important concern when deciding who the Federal Reserve should regulate would be whether the institutions supervised by the Federal Reserve provide the most useful information synergies with the Fed's monetary policy responsibilities.

8.2   Methodology

Previous work by Peek, Rosengren, and Tootell (1999a,b) has found that confidential supervisory information substantially reduces the forecast errors made by private forecasters who do not have access to this information. However, they did not examine whether the usefulness of supervisory information varied across the three dimensions focused on here: bank charter, size of banking organization, and BHC affiliation. If the value of bank supervisory data for macroeconomic forecasts varies by type of institution regulated, then the choice of regulatory structure may impact the information the Fed has available to conduct monetary policy.

Testing the hypothesis that the information content of bank supervisory data could vary across groups of banks requires examining the effect on private forecast errors of a variable that serves as a proxy for those supervisory data. The basic equation takes the form

$$X_{t+i} = \alpha_0 + \alpha_1 E_{t,j}(X_{t+i}; I_{t,j}) + \alpha_2 Z_t + \varepsilon_t,$$

where X_{t+i} is the realized future value in period $t + i$ of the macroeconomic variable being forecast; $E_{t,j}(X_{t+i}; I_{t,j})$ is the expectation of that variable by forecaster j at time t conditioned on publicly available information at time t when the forecast is made; and Z_t is a proxy variable for the confidential supervisory data available to bank supervisors at time t. Z_t is constructed using alternative subsets of banks corresponding to regulatory reform proposals. One can then use differences in the equation standard errors across equations that differ by including Z_ts calculated for alternative sets of banks to identify the set of banks that provides the Fed with the greatest synergies between bank supervision and the conduct of monetary policy.

This study examines the one-, two-, three-, and four-quarter-ahead forecast errors of inflation and unemployment rates of the Federal Reserve's own internal forecasts (the Greenbook) and three major commercial forecasters: Data Resources, Inc.–McGraw Hill (DRI), Georgia State University (GSU), and the University of Michigan Research Seminar in Quantitative Economics (RSQE). All three private forecasters sell their forecasts commercially and have generally been among those with the best forecast record for the macroeconomic variables examined in this study (McNees 1992).

Both RSQE and GSU provide quarterly forecasts that generally are released in the middle month of each quarter. The Federal Reserve Green-book forecasts are at Federal Open Market Committee meeting frequency, which ensures at least one forecast per quarter. When a quarter contains more than one Greenbook forecast, we use the one closest to the middle of the quarter. DRI provides forecasts monthly, and we use its forecast for the middle month of each quarter so that all forecasters possess roughly the same information set. The sample period begins in 1978:Q1, because the CAMEL data first became available only in late 1977, and ends in 1996:Q2. However, the GSU forecasts begin only in 1980:Q3.

The measure of confidential supervisory information that we use is based on the CAMEL ratings used by bank examiners to rate individual banks. The CAMEL scores given to banks are based on the five categories supervisors analyze when evaluating the health of a bank: Capital, Assets, Management, Earnings, and Liquidity.[3] Each bank is rated from 1, the highest, to 5, the lowest, on each of the component categories and is given a composite rating. Banks with a rating of 1 (sound in every respect) or 2 (fundamentally sound) are not likely to be constrained in any way by supervisory oversight. For banks with a 3 rating (flawed performance), examiners are likely to raise potential problems, but these problems are usually viewed as being correctable. Banks with a CAMEL rating of 4 (potential for failure, impaired viability) have a significant risk of failure. Banks with a CAMEL rating of 5 (high probability of failure, severely deficient performance) represent the set of banks with the most severe problems.

The variable that serves as a proxy for the confidential bank data available to the Federal Reserve is the assets of all commercial and savings banks with a CAMEL rating of 5 measured as a percentage of the total assets of all commercial and savings banks with supervisory ratings. We use the value for the end of the month prior to the forecast. The aggregate CAMEL5 measure was found by Peek, Rosengren, and Tootell (1999a) to improve the private-sector and Federal Reserve forecasts of inflation and unemployment rates substantially. If weakness in the banking sector, as indicated by a high percentage of banks with a CAMEL rating of 5, contains significant information about the economy not included in the available forecasts, the estimated coefficient on CAMEL5 should be positive in the unemployment rate equation and negative in the inflation rate equation. Weaker bank health, measured as a higher CAMEL5, would mean that private forecasters would overestimate the strength of the economy, and thus underpredict the unemployment rate and overpredict the rate of inflation.

We consider six alternatives for allocating supervisory responsibilities

---

3. On 1 January 1997 the CAMEL rating system was expanded to CAMELS. The *S* stands for "sensitivity to market risk" and is intended to measure how well prepared a bank is to handle changes in interest rates, exchange rates, and commodity or equity prices. The sample period for this study ends in 1996:Q2, however.

to the Federal Reserve. Supervisory information for the set of all banks (CAMEL5), as well as for three of the alternatives, serve as the benchmarks. The results for CAMEL5 can be considered as a comparison of two extreme proposals: entirely eliminating the Federal Reserve's role as a bank supervisor and assigning the Federal Reserve supervisory authority over all banks. The other three benchmarks are associated with the set of banks that the Federal Reserve currently supervises. FRS5 refers to the supervisory information about the set of state-chartered member banks for which the Federal Reserve serves as the primary federal regulator. BHC5 corresponds to the set of banks in BHCs for which the Federal Reserve currently has supervisory responsibilities. FED5 corresponds to the broader set of banks for which the Federal Reserve has supervisory responsibilities: banks in BHCs plus state-chartered member banks.

The other three alternatives correspond roughly with recent proposals for restructuring bank supervisory responsibilities. TOP20 + SMB corresponds to the set of banks in the twenty largest BHCs plus all state member banks. This roughly corresponds to a compromise between the 1994 Treasury proposal and the Federal Reserve's response to that proposal. STATE corresponds to the set of state-chartered banks as proposed by the 1991 Treasury study. STATE LEAD corresponds to the set of banks in BHCs that have a state-chartered bank as the lead bank, plus all state-chartered banks not in a holding company. This is consistent with the 1984 blueprint for reform proposed by Vice President Bush and the Federal Reserve response to the 1994 Treasury proposal.

8.3 Empirical Results

Table 8.1 presents the basic results for the aggregate CAMEL5 variable. This measure of confidential supervisory information makes a significant contribution to the reduction in forecast errors for both unemployment and inflation rates. The estimated effect is significant at all four horizons for the unemployment rate forecasts and at the three- and four-quarter-ahead horizons for the inflation rate.[4] The coefficients are both economically and statistically significant; for example, an increase in CAMEL5 of 1 percentage point, roughly 1 standard deviation, would account for an underestimation of the four-quarter-ahead unemployment rate of approximately .25 percentage points.

Table 8.2 contains the results for the unemployment rate when we use alternative subsets of banks for the calculation of the share of banks with a CAMEL rating of 5. Equations similar to those in table 8.1 are reestimated with the alternative supervisory information sets in two ways. First,

---

4. As discussed in detail in Peek, Rosengren, and Tootell (1999a), the standard errors are corrected using a method devised by Keane and Runkle (1990).

Table 8.1 Base CAMEL5 Specification

	Unemployment				Inflation			
Variable	Quarter 1	Quarter 2	Quarter 3	Quarter 4	Quarter 1	Quarter 2	Quarter 3	Quarter 4
Constant	0.022	0.110	0.202	0.333	0.507	0.741	1.112	1.265
	(0.30)	(0.44)	(0.46)	(0.62)	(1.66)	(1.08)	(1.22)	(1.18)
Forecast	0.979***	0.948***	0.923***	0.900***	0.935***	0.929***	0.934***	0.892***
	(87.59)	(25.65)	(14.12)	(11.34)	(26.26)	(10.68)	(7.22)	(5.70)
CAMEL5	0.083***	0.165***	0.233**	0.255**	−0.220	−0.443	−0.882**	−0.959**
	(4.90)	(3.00)	(2.47)	(2.26)	(1.52)	(1.47)	(2.44)	(2.44)
No. of observations	286	286	286	286	286	286	286	286
$\bar{R}^2$	0.988	0.933	0.835	0.739	0.857	0.651	0.530	0.456
Log-likelihood	−157.421	−95.261	−225.352	−292.624	−474.479	−601.870	−639.704	−656.354

Notes: The standard errors in the forecast equation are corrected for the appropriate moving average error terms and for contemporaneous correlation across forecasters. Numbers in parentheses are absolute values of *t*-statistics.

***Significant at the 1 percent level.

**Significant at the 5 percent level.

Table 8.2 Alternative Specifications for Unemployment Rate Forecasts

Specification	Quarter 1	Quarter 2	Quarter 3	Quarter 4
1. FED5	**0.122*** (5.13)**	**0.195** (2.39)**	**0.272 (1.93)**	**−0.054 (0.13)**
	0.090 (1.38)	**−0.155 (0.76)**	**−0.236 (0.69)**	**0.333 (1.96)**
CAMEL5	0.024 (0.54)	0.264 (1.87)	0.381 (1.63)	0.288 (1.05)
2. FRS5	**1.645** (2.22)**	**1.276 (0.55)**	**−0.611 (0.16)**	**−4.374 (0.98)**
	−0.042 (0.05)	**−2.919 (1.22)**	**−7.771 (1.95)**	**−14.090*** (3.06)**
CAMEL5	0.084*** (4.17)	0.206*** (3.24)	0.345*** (3.23)	0.462*** (3.78)
3. BHC5	**0.122*** (5.12)**	**0.196** (2.39)**	**0.274 (1.94)**	**−0.030 (0.08)**
	0.088 (1.37)	**−0.146 (0.73)**	**−0.216 (0.64)**	**0.336** (1.98)**
CAMEL5	0.026 (0.58)	0.258 (1.85)	0.368 (1.60)	0.273 (1.01)
4. Top 20+SMB	**0.070 (1.17)**	**0.199 (1.16)**	**0.316 (1.12)**	**0.457 (1.26)**
	−0.090 (1.50)	**−0.093 (0.51)**	**−0.074 (0.24)**	**0.079 (0.19)**
CAMEL5	0.099*** (5.01)	0.181*** (2.80)	0.245** (2.22)	0.242 (1.85)
5. STATE	**0.128*** (3.52)**	**0.297*** (2.70)**	**0.387** (2.09)**	**0.342 (1.58)**
	−0.076 (1.08)	**0.072 (0.33)**	**0.004 (0.01)**	**−0.310 (0.72)**
CAMEL5	0.116*** (3.29)	0.133 (1.21)	0.231 (1.23)	0.399 (1.71)
6. STATE LEAD	**0.133*** (3.60)**	**0.310*** (2.80)**	**0.401** (2.15)**	**0.357 (1.64)**
	−0.062 (0.88)	**0.112 (0.53)**	**0.047 (0.13)**	**−0.248 (0.58)**
CAMEL5	0.110*** (3.16)	0.115 (1.07)	0.213 (1.15)	0.368 (1.66)

Notes: The standard errors in the forecast equation are corrected for the appropriate moving average error terms and for contemporaneous correlation across forecasters. Numbers in parentheses are absolute values of *t*-statistics.

***Significant at the 1 percent level.

**Significant at the 5 percent level.

we replace the aggregate CAMEL5 measure with the alternative proxy for bank health. For ease of comparison, we show only the coefficients for the relevant variables, and the rows containing the estimated coefficients for the alternative proxies are in bold face. Second, we include the alternative proxy as an additional explanatory variable in the basic equation that includes the aggregate CAMEL5 measure. The first specification can be used to determine if confidential supervisory information for a specific subset of banks can make a significant contribution to reducing forecast errors. The second specification addresses a different issue: whether the confidential supervisory information for the specific subset of banks differs from that contained in the aggregate CAMEL5 measure for the entire set of CAMEL-rated banks. We have calculated all shares using total assets in CAMEL-rated institutions as the denominator to compare the estimated coefficients more easily. However, the results are unaffected (other than the size of the estimated coefficients) when the denominator of the ratio is the sum of assets for the same subset of banks used for the calculation of the numerator.

The first two specifications shown in the table examine whether the confidential information about banks currently supervised by the Federal Reserve provides information that would improve the forecasts of the unemployment rate. The first proxy, FED5, is measured as the assets in institutions with CAMEL ratings of 5 that are supervised by the Federal Reserve, divided by total assets in all CAMEL-rated banks. This includes any bank that is in a holding company plus any other bank that has the Federal Reserve as its primary regulator (i.e., has a state charter and is a member of the Federal Reserve System). When FED5 replaces CAMEL5, the estimated coefficients are positive at each horizon and significant for the one- and two-quarter-ahead forecasts, and they just miss being significant at the 5 percent level for the other two horizons. Thus, the information about banks with a CAMEL rating of 5 that the Federal Reserve currently regulates can improve significantly on forecasts of the unemployment rate. The positive sign on the estimated coefficient indicates that as a larger share of Fed-supervised bank assets is accounted for by banks with a CAMEL rating of 5, the unemployment rate rises relative to forecasts, indicating that forecasters overpredict the strength of the economy. However, when both FED5 and CAMEL5 are included in the equation, neither has a significant estimated effect, likely due to the collinearity between the two measures.

The second specification of table 8.2 contains results for the bank health proxy (FRS5) constructed for the set of banks that have the Federal Reserve as their primary federal regulator. The results are weaker than those for FED5. When FRS5 is included without CAMEL5, the estimated coefficients have the predicted positive sign only for the one- and two-quarter-ahead forecasts, and the effect is significant only for the one-quarter-ahead specification. When CAMEL5 is also included in the equation, its estimated effect remains significant. The estimated coefficient on FRS5 is negative at each horizon and significant at the four-quarter-ahead horizon. Thus, the supervisory information for state member banks appears to be much less useful for unemployment rate forecasts compared to that for the combination of banks in holding companies plus state member banks, indicating that the additional supervisory responsibilities over holding companies contribute information that can strengthen the Federal Reserve's ability to conduct monetary policy.

Although supervisory information for the set of banks the Federal Reserve does supervise (based on the current regulatory structure) provides some improvement over the information available to private forecasters that do not have access to confidential supervisory information, the Federal Reserve may not regulate the set of banks providing the information that can most improve the forecasts. The next four specifications shown in the table investigate the value of confidential supervisory information related to four alternative proposals for the set of banks to be supervised by the Federal Reserve. The third specification analyzes the proposal giving the Fed all banks in BHCs (BHC5). When BHC5 is included without CAMEL5, three of the four estimated coefficients are significant, with the fourth narrowly missing being significant at the 5 percent level. Given the extensive overlap with the set of all banks, it should not be surprising that when CAMEL5 is included, neither BCH5 nor CAMEL5 has an individual effect that is significant at any of the four horizons.

The fourth specification shows the results for the set of banks in the twenty largest holding companies plus all state member banks (TOP20+SMB). Interestingly, when the Federal Reserve retains supervisory responsibility over only the largest holding companies (plus state member banks), the value of supervisory information deteriorates substantially compared to that contained in BHC5. The estimated coefficient on TOP20+SMB is not significant for any horizon when CAMEL5 is omitted from the equation. Furthermore, when CAMEL5 is included in the equation, it has an estimated effect that is significant for the first three horizons. Thus, it appears that supervisory information about banks in holding companies other than the twenty largest contains information that is more useful for improving forecasts compared to that for the largest bank holding companies. This evidence suggests that the set of institutions that pose systemic risks may not substantially overlap with the set of banks for which supervisory information is most valuable for improving unemployment rate forecasts.

The next alternative measure of bank health considered is for the subset of banks consisting of all state-chartered banks (STATE) to determine the extent to which the information synergies between bank supervision and the conduct of monetary policy varies by bank charter type. When estimated without CAMEL5, the coefficients on STATE are significant for the three shorter horizons, indicating that supervisory information about this subset of banks does contribute to the reduction in forecast errors for the unemployment rate. When CAMEL5 is included, its coefficient is significant for the one-quarter-ahead horizon and none of the STATE effects are significant.

The last alternative measure is a minor variation of STATE, with the subset of banks including any bank in a holding company with a state-chartered lead bank plus any state-chartered bank not in a holding company (STATE LEAD). The results are essentially the same as for the STATE specification. When CAMEL5 is excluded from the regression, STATE LEAD has a significant effect for the three shortest horizons. When CAMEL5 is included, STATE LEAD provides no useful information that differs from that contained in CAMEL5.

Table 8.3 contains the results for the inflation rate forecast equations corresponding to those reported in table 8.2 for the unemployment rate. When CAMEL5 is not included in the regression, the estimated coefficient on FED5 has the expected negative sign, but is never significant. When CAMEL5 is included, it has the predicted negative effect with all but that for the one-quarter-ahead horizon being significant. The estimated coefficient on FED5 becomes positive and, for three of the four horizons, is slightly larger than that for CAMEL5 (in absolute value), indicating a net effect for FED5 that is positive. In contrast, the estimated coefficients for FRS5 are not only negative, but are significant for the two- and three-quarter-ahead horizons. When CAMEL5 is included, it has the expected negative effect but is significant only at the four-quarter-ahead horizon. Furthermore, with CAMEL5 included, FRS5 retains its negative effect. Thus, for inflation forecasts, FRS5 appears to be relatively more informative than FED5, even though FED5 dominated FRS5 for unemployment rate forecasts.

Among the other four alternative subsets of banks considered, the BHC5 results are essentially the same as those for FED5, an unsurprising result given the extensive overlap across the two sets of banks. On the other hand, TOP20+SMB has estimated coefficients that are positive for three of the four horizons, although never significant. When CAMEL5 is included, it has estimated coefficients of the predicted negative sign that are significant for the three- and four-quarter-ahead horizons and is close to significance for the two other horizons. Unlike with BHC5 and FED5, however, no estimated effects of TOP20+SMB are significant when CAMEL5 is included in the regression.

The two specifications based on the subset of state-chartered banks appear to be the most informative for reducing the forecast errors for the inflation rate. For both STATE and STATE LEAD, the estimated coefficients always have the predicted negative sign, and they are significant for

Table 8.3   Alternative Specifications for Inflation Rate Forecasts

Specification	Quarter 1		Quarter 2		Quarter 3		Quarter 4	
1. FED5	−0.178	0.380	−0.142	1.536	−0.522	2.252**	−0.550	2.477**
	(0.85)	(0.91)	(0.32)	(1.87)	(0.94)	(2.33)	(0.94)	(2.27)
CAMEL5		−0.448		−1.344**		−2.179***		−2.377***
		(1.56)		(2.38)		(3.33)		(3.20)
2. FRS5	−10.129	−7.632	−25.371**	−22.327	−28.860**	−14.714	−22.111	−3.232
	(1.77)	(1.14)	(2.25)	(1.74)	(2.08)	(0.92)	(1.49)	(0.19)
CAMEL5		−0.124		−0.154		−0.681		−0.916**
		(0.74)		(0.45)		(1.62)		(2.03)
3. BHC5	−0.175	0.382	−0.134	1.534	−0.512	2.235**	−0.545	2.441**
	(0.84)	(0.92)	(0.31)	(1.88)	(0.93)	(2.33)	(0.93)	(2.26)
CAMEL5		−0.448		−1.340**		−2.164***		−2.351***
		(1.57)		(2.39)		(3.33)		(3.19)
4. Top 20+SMB	0.002	0.396	0.476	1.345	0.072	1.590	−0.338	1.201
	(0.00)	(0.82)	(0.58)	(1.45)	(0.07)	(1.46)	(0.34)	(1.08)
CAMEL5		−0.284		−0.652		−1.121***		−1.140**
		(1.73)		(1.96)		(2.82)		(2.59)
5. STATE	−0.487	−0.523	−1.241**	−1.990**	−2.040***	−2.644**	−2.175***	−2.720**
	(1.87)	(1.07)	(2.39)	(2.13)	(3.44)	(2.42)	(3.24)	(2.26)
CAMEL5		0.023		0.504		0.409		0.371
		(0.09)		(0.96)		(0.66)		(0.54)
6. STATE LEAD	−0.490	−0.515	−1.244**	−1.914**	−2.055***	−2.604**	−2.198***	−2.703**
	(1.87)	(1.08)	(2.38)	(2.08)	(3.45)	(2.43)	(3.26)	(2.29)
CAMEL5		0.017		0.455		0.374		0.346
		(0.06)		(0.88)		(0.62)		(0.52)

Notes: The standard errors in the forecast equation are corrected for the appropriate moving average error terms and for contemporaneous correlation across forecasters. Numbers in parentheses are absolute values of *t*-statistics.

***Significant at the 1 percent level.

**Significant at the 5 percent level.

all but the one-quarter-ahead horizon, with or without the inclusion of CAMEL5. In fact, when CAMEL5 is included, its effect is never significant. Thus, it appears that for inflation rate forecasts, the confidential supervisory information about state-chartered banks contains most of the useful information contained in the aggregate CAMEL5 measure.

Table 8.4 provides a comparison of the equation standard errors across the alternative specifications for the set of Federal Reserve Greenbook forecasts. The errors for this forecast alone are used because the loss to monetary policy is being examined. In each instance, the equation standard errors are measured as a percentage of that for the specification that excludes confidential supervisory information (BASE). Each regression contains a constant term, the forecast, and the indicated CAMEL rating measure for a particular set of banks. A value equal to or greater than unity indicates that the confidential information contained in the particular measure of bank health does not improve upon the standard forecasts that do not rely on confidential supervisory information.

The aggregate CAMEL5 measure reduces the equation standard errors for the Greenbook forecasts by 5 to 9 percent in the unemployment rate equations and by 1 to 4 percent in the inflation rate equations. Although the supervisory information about the set of banks the Federal Reserve currently supervises (FED5) improves the unemployment rate forecasts, the contribution is less than that achieved by CAMEL5, except for the one-quarter-ahead horizon. On the other hand, for inflation rate forecasts, the supervisory information contained in FED5 contributes to a reduction in forecast errors only for the one-quarter-ahead horizon. Further limiting the information to that about the set of banks for which the Federal Reserve is the primary federal regulator (FRS5) essentially eliminates any reduction in forecast errors for the unemployment rate. The reduction in the standard error compared to the BASE specification is less than 0.5 percent for the one- and four-quarter-ahead horizons, with no improvement for the other two horizons. For the inflation forecasts, this measure reduces the standard error by less than 3 percent for the two-quarter-ahead forecast and by less than 2 percent for the one- and three-quarter-ahead forecasts, with no improvement for the four-quarter-ahead forecast. Thus, supervisory knowledge about the institutions that have the Fed as their primary regulator provides little useful information that could improve forecasts of the inflation and unemployment rates.

One of the contentious issues in rearranging supervisory responsibility is whether the Federal Reserve should continue to supervise BHCs. When the supervisory information set is limited to that about banks in BHCs, the improvement in the equation standard error for the unemployment rate ranges from 3 to 4 percent, except for the 9 percent improvement for the one-quarter-ahead horizon. Thus, the improvement at the one-quarter-ahead horizon is roughly the same as for the aggregate CAMEL5 measure,

Table 8.4 Standard Errors of Alternative Specifications for Greenbook Forecasts, Measured Relative to Forecast without CAMEL Information

Variable	Unemployment				Inflation			
	Quarter 1	Quarter 2	Quarter 3	Quarter 4	Quarter 1	Quarter 2	Quarter 3	Quarter 4
BASE	1.0000	1.0000	1.0000	1.0000	1.0000	1.0000	1.0000	1.0000
CAMEL5	0.9105	0.9287	0.9227	0.9432	0.9670	0.9888	0.9661	0.9584
FED5	0.9078	0.9671	0.9624	0.9694	0.9906	1.0057	1.0000	1.0007
FRS5	0.9953	1.0063	1.0066	0.9958	0.9833	0.9734	0.9845	1.0009
BHC5	0.9078	0.9674	0.9622	0.9689	0.9910	1.0058	1.0001	1.0009
Top 20+SMB	0.9898	0.9926	0.9909	0.9893	1.0037	1.0033	1.0070	1.0050
STATE	0.9519	0.9224	0.9280	0.9588	0.9563	0.9653	0.9372	0.9234
STATE LEAD	0.9492	0.9186	0.9253	0.9568	0.9561	0.9655	0.9372	0.9230

Note: The calculations are based on standard errors for equations in which the actual value is regressed on a constant, the forecast value, and the variable listed in the "Variable" column.

and substantially less for the other three horizons. For the inflation rate, BHC5 provides a 1 percent reduction in the equation standard error at the one-quarter-ahead horizon and no improvement at the other three horizons.

It is possible that the information content in BHC5 is all coming from the larger institutions. If so, the set of institutions that pose systemic risks would overlap with those institutions that provided confidential supervisory information useful for forecasting inflation and unemployment. However, when supervisory information about only the top twenty holding companies plus state member banks is used, the equation standard errors for the unemployment rate are reduced by only about 1 percent at each horizon, and there is no improvement at any horizon for the inflation rate forecasts.

The two measures based on supervisory information about state-chartered banks tend to dominate all of the other alternatives. Thus, if information synergies were the criteria, splitting supervisory responsibility by charter type rather than by whether the bank is in a holding company would be preferred. For the unemployment rate, they produce the largest reduction in the equation standard error at the two-, three-, and four-quarter-ahead horizons among all the alternatives, and even outperform the aggregate CAMEL5 measure at the two-quarter-ahead horizon. However, at the one-quarter-ahead horizon, both FED5 and BHC5, as well as CAMEL5, produce larger reductions in the equation standard error. On the other hand, for the inflation rate equations, STATE and STATE LEAD produce equation standard errors that are smaller than those for any of the other alternatives, as well as for aggregate CAMEL5.

8.4   Transferability of Supervisory Information

If supervisory information could be comprehensively transferred without loss of information, the Federal Reserve would not need to be directly involved in supervising banks. Any synergies with monetary policy, or for that matter with the discount window or the payments system, could be exploited using regular, timely reports on bank condition provided to the Federal Reserve by the primary bank regulators. However, in practice this is likely to result in some loss of information.

First, highly confidential information is not easily shared across bureaucracies. In fact, even within a bureaucracy, it is often difficult to share confidential information. As Peek, Rosengren, and Tootell (1999a) discuss, economists at the Federal Reserve engaged in economic forecasting generally do not have access to confidential bank supervisory information. Thus, even within an organization, it can be difficult for the right individuals to gain access to useful supervisory information.

Second, supervisory information is useful to the Federal Reserve only if the Fed understands how the rating is formulated and how the rating process may be changing over time. Furthermore, the Fed needs to know whether there are other variables or supervisory practices that may impact the quality or interpretation of the information provided by other bank supervisors. Peek, Rosengren, and Tootell (1999a) show that supervisory ratings may vary across size of institution, and Berger, Kyle, and Scalise (chap. 9, this volume) provide evidence that ratings vary over time. Thus, hands-on experience in bank supervision enables the Federal Reserve to identify nuances in the bank supervisory process, as well as in bank health.

Third, other bank supervisors may have objective functions that differ from those of the central bank. Whereas a bank supervisor may be focused on factors affecting the probability of an individual bank failing, the central bank may be more concerned with systemic risks. Thus, collecting data on concentration of exposures, how these exposures vary across the banking system, and how they may impact other financial institutions may be of greater interest to the central bank. This becomes particularly important when requests for detailed information on bank portfolios are viewed as a regulatory burden to the banks and when evaluating that information may be costly in terms of bank examiner resources. Similarly, the central bank may be more interested in data that improve its ability to forecast the macroeconomy and that may be less directly relevant for pure safety and soundness considerations at the individual bank level. Thus, the availability of supervisory information that has synergies with monetary policy and the discount window function may require some direct involvement in the supervisory process by the central bank.

8.5   Conclusion

Recent research by Peek, Rosengren, and Tootell (1999a,b) has established that confidential supervisory information can be used to improve the conduct of monetary policy. This paper explores the implications of these findings for the structure of bank regulation. We find that supervisory information from Federal Reserve–regulated banks does improve macroeconomic forecasts of inflation and unemployment rates. However, the greatest information synergies with monetary policy are from state-chartered banks. Thus, regulatory proposals that would focus regulatory powers of the Federal Reserve only on BHCs or on large, internationally active banks may sacrifice some information useful for monetary policy.

Loss of regulatory powers would imply a loss of synergies with monetary policy only if the information were no longer easily transmitted to policy makers. Peek, Rosengren, and Tootell (1999a) and Berger, Kyle, and Scalise (chap. 9, this volume) provide some evidence that hands-on experience with institutions may be necessary. Central to the Federal Reserve's proposals for regulatory reform is that the Federal Reserve maintains hands-on experience. As Chairman Alan Greenspan testified, "Without the hands-on experience of regulation and supervision, and the exposure to the operations of banks and markets provided by such experience, the Federal Reserve's essential knowledge base would atrophy" (Greenspan 1994, 88). If synergies to monetary policy were part of this essential knowledge base, any proposal for regulatory structure reform would need to include the smaller banks that have provided the greatest improvement for forecasts of inflation and unemployment rates.

Of course, a variety of other factors should be important for determining optimal bank regulatory structure. Concerns with providing lender-of-last-resort functions, potential concerns with systemic risk, potential cost savings, and concerns with the regulatory burden on financial services firms, as well as many other issues, should also shape the debate on optimal regulatory structure. However, this research indicates that there is potentially a cost to monetary policy if the central bank is excluded from participation in bank regulation in general, or even if central bank oversight is limited only to the largest institutions.

References

Greenspan, Alan. 1994. *Banking industry regulatory consolidation.* Statement of Alan Greenspan, Chairman, Board of Governors, Federal Reserve Board, Washington, D.C. Hearings before the Committee on Banking, Housing, and Urban Affairs, United States Senate, March. Washington, D.C.: GPO.

Keane, Michael P., and David E. Runkle. 1990. Testing the rationality of price forecasts: New evidence from panel data. *American Economic Review* 80:714–35.

McNees, Stephen K. 1992. How large are economic forecast errors? *New England Economic Review* (July/August): 25–42.

Peek, Joe, Eric S. Rosengren, and Geoffrey M. B. Tootell. 1999a. Is bank supervision central to central banking? *The Quarterly Journal of Economics* 114 (2): 629–53.

———. 1999b. Does the Federal Reserve possess an exploitable informational advantage? Working Paper no. 99-8, Federal Reserve Bank of Boston.

Comment   Ben S. Bernanke

This interesting paper is motivated by an important, broader issue: namely, whether central banks should be involved in bank supervision as well as in monetary policy. The issue is of practical relevance, as several countries

Ben S. Bernanke is the Howard Harrison and Gabrielle Snyder Beck Professor of Economics and Public Affairs at Princeton University. He is also a research associate and director of the Monetary Economics Program of the National Bureau of Economic Research.

around the world have recently either eliminated or diluted the authority of their central banks over the bank supervisory process.

In a number of recent papers, Peek, Rosengren, and Tootell have raised a novel argument for a continued role for central banks in bank supervision. Their argument is that confidential supervisory reports provide information that is potentially valuable for forecasting key macroeconomic variables, so that access to this information may help improve the conduct of monetary policy. Specifically, they have provided empirical evidence for the United States that a relatively simple measure of banking system health—the share of banking assets held by poorly rated banks (i.e., those with a CAMEL rating of 5)—improves forecasts of inflation and unemployment at one, two, three, and four quarters, relative to projections made by private forecasting concerns and by the Fed itself. Further—and this is the main contribution of the present paper—the greatest forecasting value appears to lie in information about the condition of state-chartered banks.

These findings are intriguing and worthy of further exploration. In particular, the result that the most useful information comes from supervision of state-chartered banks—which tend to be small and not publicly traded—makes a good deal of sense. Having said that, I am not yet convinced that this line of argument is of first-order importance in the debate about the Fed's appropriate role in bank supervision. In the remainder of this comment I explain why (for now at least) I would prefer not to rely on the authors' argument as an important pillar of the case for Fed involvement in bank supervision. I then take the opportunity to discuss briefly the broader issue of what the Fed's role should be.

My reservations about the authors' argument, at least as it stands at the present juncture, are as follows:

First, I think that regulatory design ought to be based on durable, well-established facts and principles, of which the long and varied history of central banking has provided many. Although the PRT regressions are suggestive, they are of necessity somewhat contingent, being based on limited information and a limited sample. Obviously, future studies might produce different results. To illustrate my concern, suppose for the sake of argument that, based on these findings, we were to give the Fed responsibility for supervising state-chartered banks. Then suppose that a future set of regressions were to show that the most valuable information comes from (say) national banks, or, alternatively, that there is no longer marginal forecasting value in supervisory information. Would we then be prepared to change the regulatory design? This is not really a criticism of Peek, Rosengren, and Tootell, who deserve much credit for opening this line of research. My point is only that, as long as the authors' claims remain better described as intriguing hypotheses rather than robust facts, we should be cautious about using these results for regulatory design.

Second, it has not yet been shown that the use of confidential supervisory information would lead (or has led) to an economically significant improvement in monetary policy outcomes. In particular, it would be useful to know more about the marginal value of supervisory information for forecasting, as the force of the authors' argument depends very much on the conclusion that this information is potentially highly useful for the Fed. It is striking that the Fed currently does not seem to make systematic use of this information in its official Greenbook forecasts—though, as the authors have pointed out in other works, confidential supervisory information does seem to affect the votes of Federal Open Market Committee members in a more informal way. The main evidence on forecast improvement given in the paper is in table 8.4, which shows standard errors for regressions with and without the CAMEL5 measure. However, these have the defect of being in-sample comparisons. Out-of-sample forecasting comparisons would be a useful extension, as would some additional analysis of the forecast errors. For example, is the marginal forecasting power of supervisory information (if it survives in an out-of-sample comparison) concentrated in certain subperiods or certain geographical regions?

Third, the authors acknowledge that their argument depends very much on the assumption that information cannot be effectively transferred between agencies, so that unless the Fed itself is the supervisor of banks it will not have full access to the information relevant to making monetary policy. Unfortunately, this assumption is by its very nature extremely difficult to test. The CAMEL5 variable, which Peek, Rosengren, and Tootell show contains useful information for forecasting, could itself be easily transferred from a supervisory agency to the Fed, as could even more detailed quantitative information about bank condition. Thus the authors' ultimate claim is quite indirect: They must argue that if CAMEL5 contains information, surely less quantifiable information in bank supervision must exist as well. They give a number of anecdotal examples of imperfect transfers of information between bureaucracies, and conference participants added more—all of which seem plausible. Nevertheless, it appears that a leap of faith on this issue is unavoidable. Personally, I think the information transfer argument is much stronger in the context of crisis management, when highly detailed and complex information must be transferred quickly. I return to this point later.

To reiterate, my reservations about using the authors' argument to support a particular policy conclusion do not detract from my admiration for their research on this topic. The information content of bank supervisory reports bears on a variety of issues in macroeconomics and finance and is certainly worth studying. I hope the authors will continue to expand and refine their results in this area.

I turn now, briefly, to the broader issue, of whether the Fed should have a role in bank supervision. The standard argument for involving the central bank in supervision is that monetary policy and banking policy are, inevitably, closely intertwined and complementary. For example, as was emphasized by Bagehot and probably earlier authors, both the economy as a whole and the banking system in particular are strongly affected by the central bank's interest rate settings. Moreover, the sensitivity of the economy to interest rate changes may be affected by the condition of the banking system (recall the "headwinds" of the early 1990s), and vice versa. Good interest rate policies therefore require that the central bank take account of both the state of the economy and the state of the banking system, as well as their interactions. Taking account of the banking system in turn requires intimate knowledge of the condition of banks, which can only be acquired (or so it is claimed) by the central bank's participation in the supervisory process. A similar argument applies to discount-window policy, which affects the money supply (indeed, in the early days of central banking, discount-window lending was the only way to affect the money supply) but is also the principal instrument for fulfilling the lender-of-last-resort function for the banking system.

However, although we are accustomed to seeing the Fed and other central banks play a supervisory role, there are certainly some considerations on the other side. One important issue is supervisory efficiency. The current system, with three supervisors and overlapping jurisdictions, imposes significant costs on both the government and the banks. As the financial system grows larger and more complex, perhaps the most rational solution would be to have a single, specialist regulatory and supervisory agency that is responsible for the system as a whole, or at least for the entire banking system. By avoiding overlap and supervisory fragmentation, by being cognizant of the interconnections among financial institutions and markets, and by developing a high level of supervisory expertise, such an agency (it could be argued) would both improve the quality of supervision and reduce its social costs. Of course, the Fed is a candidate to take on this "superregulatory" role; but one might respond that giving this portfolio to the Fed would both invest too much power in one institution and also distract the Fed from its primary mission of making monetary policy.

Another argument against a bank supervisory role for the Fed is the potential for moral hazard. To the extent that the Fed has institutional objectives other than maximizing social welfare, giving the central bank too broad a range of powers may invite abuse. For example, if the Fed were anxious to conceal the insolvency of some part of the banking system (an impulse that we have seen at times in other supervisory agencies), it might be tempted to distort interest rate policies in a way that increases bank profits or asset values, at the expense of macroeconomic objectives. Conversely, it is also possible that the Fed might use its supervisory authority to pressure banks into making loans that they otherwise would not make, in order to serve some goal such as providing short-term macroeconomic stimulus or helping bail out a country suffering a financial crisis. (Not to say that these are necessarily bad objectives; again, a problem only arises when the Fed's institutional priorities differ from those of the society at large.) At the conference, Charles Calomiris gave a number of possible examples of such behavior. The temptation to distort supervisory policies to serve monetary policy objectives, or vice versa, arises of course from the same complementarities between monetary policy and banking policy stressed earlier. I think the potential for moral hazard is real and should be a concern for those who supervise the supervisors. The risk of moral hazard, by the way, is yet another reason for maximum transparency in central banking.

So what's the bottom line? After thinking about both sides of the issue, and giving due credit to the arguments for regulatory efficiency and moral hazard, my own provisional conclusion is that the Fed should retain its supervisory powers, and that its supervision should focus on the largest and most complex banking firms. The key desideratum, I believe, is the need to have a competent and highly trusted public institution that is empowered to deal effectively and in a timely way with financial crises. The Fed has certainly established its credibility and competence over a period of time. Furthermore, because interest rates and discount-window lending are important instruments for dealing with financial crises, and because crises often have major implications for the economy as a whole, the central bank is the natural agency to serve as command central when the financial system threatens to melt down. To fulfill this role effectively, the Fed needs detailed information about not only the general financial condition of the banking system but also about complex financial linkages and the associated vulnerabilities—and it needs to be able to get this information within hours or even minutes. A role for the Fed in the supervisory process is the most direct way to ensure that the necessary information is available in a crisis.

I would not necessarily rule out future modifications of the regulatory design that preserve Fed access to supervisory information. Indeed, it may be possible to rationalize the system in a way that reduces the regulatory costs imposed on banks without affecting the information flow (a system of jointly conducted examinations under a uniform set of regulations might be worth considering, for example). The Fed should also work as closely as possible with other regulators, including nonbank regulators such as the SEC, to improve its information channels. However, because financial crises are dangerous, unpredictable, and not well understood, we should be extremely cautious about changing a system for dealing with such crises that has served us well for half a century.

Discussion Summary

Frederic Mishkin began by asking which kinds of information a lender of last resort could get if there were no bank examinations. He followed up by asking about what happens to information flows, especially if the central bank is responsible for managing financial crises.

Patricia Jackson noted that there could be real information issues when central banks no longer carry out supervision of banks. She observed that with in-house information one gets information about interlinkages that might be important in identifying systemic problems. She noted that the Bank of England had carried out work to look at the size of exposures between different players in various markets. Central banks needed to consider the likely sources of shocks and the adequacy of capital buffers. Focusing on the recent experience in the United Kingdom, she said that one should not overemphasize the trend toward the separation of supervision and central banking. She noted that England is the only country in the G7 where the monetary authority is not involved at all in prudential supervision or linked to the prudential supervisor. For the United Kingdom it meant that the supervisor and central bank needed to work closely together and share information. Lastly, about the results in the paper, Jackson observed that the lags in economic data are substantial. The Bank of England has regional representatives to gather more immediate information on the economy at a regional level. Maybe it is this type of information that the CAMEL ratings pick up.

Stephen Cecchetti suggested that the authors look out of sample and at other data to see if market information, for example, might be a good predictor. He also noted that the conflict of interest argument might be overstated. He pointed out that a financial system collapse would also be bad for macroeconomic stability. Discount loans are 100 percent collateralized, although there are a few extreme exceptions. Finally, he noted that it might be useful to separate regulation, supervision, and consumer protection.

Mark Carey noted that crisis intervention is a key role of the monetary authority and that this is often done through the banks. He emphasized that the monetary authority needs a credible threat because banks will want others to bear the responsibility. He observed that central bank independence gets supervisors' independence. He concluded by noting that it is also desirable to have multiple supervisors to filter out bad ideas.

Laurence Meyer began by noting that the paper tries to rationalize a Byzantine structure. He noted that it is important for the agencies to cooperate to limit regulatory burden on the banks. He observed that regulatory competition may be good in any areas, but the downside to competition is the potential for a race to the bottom. He agreed with Ben Bernanke, the discussant, that supervisors should be structured to maximize supervision; systematic risk will be key, so it is important for the Federal Reserve to have a good relationship with the OCC. Picking up on other comments, he argued that the recapitalization of the banking system was not a conflict of interest but was complementary. Finally, he asked whether one wants a supervisory authority with no macroeconomic responsibility.

Randy Kroszner observed that if the rationalization for having the monetary authority and bank supervisor under one roof is the role of the Federal Reserve as crisis manager, then we should not stop at banking. He noted that the key is to have coordination.

Andrew Powell observed that the information from the tequila crisis was that information flows were the key, although he noted that Venezuela was a counterexample. He followed up on earlier remarks and pointed out that regulation and supervision could be separate. He observed that this separation might enable policy to break down some resistance from supervisors. He concluded by noting that in the end financial regulation should be independent.

James Wilcox noted that the question of many supervisory agencies is a little different from where supervision is housed, but he wondered whether competition and separation were inefficient. He noted that multiple supervisors might not give consistent answers, as evidenced by the Berger, Kyle, and Scalise paper. He also wondered how well information travels. He noted that the Treasury and the Federal Reserve have been able to coordinate their activities during currency-related crises. Finally, he noted that, given the new rules from the Gramm-Leach-Bliley Act, as insurance and security companies come into the new financial holding companies, the Federal Reserve will need to rely more heavily on insurance regulators and the SEC.

Robert Eisenbeis asked a number of questions about the authors' data and results. First, he asked over what time horizon the forecasts were compared. He suggested that the relevant forecast horizon might be longer than one quarter. Second, he asked about the data vintage: Were the authors using the final or revised data? He also asked how much the addition of the regulatory information improved the precision of the forecasts. Finally, referring back to comments from Ben Bernanke, he noted that the mix of goals is complex. He observed that it is not always true that internalizing the resolution of conflict is good, because goals may have different primacy.

Charles Calomiris noted that the race to the bottom for regulatory competition might be avoided. He argued that regulators might be too risk averse and that they may resist beneficial deregulation in the absence of regulatory competition. He noted that in the United States deregulation was partly a product of such competition. With respect to political pressure, he noted that there are a number of cases from recent history in which supervisors either apparently bow to political pressure or get banks on board. One example he pointed to is the link between bank merger and Community Reinvestment Act policy.

Allen Berger concluded the comments by noting that, as the authors acknowledge, a crucial aspect of the argument is that there must be more information from the exam process than just the CAMEL rating to justify the combination of supervision and central banking. He pointed out that a bank exam goes beyond balance sheet information. He observed that communication from bankers may be key, as was the case in the credit crunch where bankers recognized the difficulties first.

Eric Rosengren began by responding to a number of the technical and data suggestions. He noted that they did look at public information such as call report information and interest rate spreads and that their results did not change significantly. He observed that this is further evidence that private information matters for forecasting. He also noted that they had split the sample. He pointed out that looking at the performance of the model out of sample would be difficult given the recent experience of few poor CAMEL ratings. He noted that the authors were in the process of developing a panel data set of GDP forecasts, but that this can be challenging given the revisions to the data. He also noted that they had looked at forecasts from one to four quarters ahead. Finally, he observed that the authors' *Quarterly Journal of Economics* paper discusses both the statistical and economic significance of the findings.

9

Did U.S. Bank Supervisors Get Tougher during the Credit Crunch? Did They Get Easier during the Banking Boom? Did It Matter to Bank Lending?

Allen N. Berger, Margaret K. Kyle, and Joseph M. Scalise

9.1 Introduction

The main goals of bank supervision are generally to act as a delegated monitor on behalf of insured depositors or other stakeholders, to protect the safety and soundness of the financial system, and to counteract the moral hazard incentives created by the government safety net. However, changes in supervisory policy also may have significant effects on macro-economic or regional economic health if banks respond by altering their lending behavior. These additional effects may be intended or unintended. For example, supervisors may intend for some risky institutions to reduce their lending. However, if too many institutions reduce their supplies of credit simultaneously, this may create an unintended credit crunch or recession. Alternatively, supervisors may try to stimulate lending through supervisory easing. We discuss below some reasons to suspect that supervisory changes over the last decade or so may have had significant effects on the overall lending of the U.S. banking industry.

The purpose of this research is to investigate this possibility by testing

Allen N. Berger is senior economist at the Board of Governors of the Federal Reserve System, Senior Fellow at the Wharton Financial Institutions Center, editor of the *Journal of Money, Credit, and Banking,* and editor of the *Journal of Productivity Analysis.* Margaret K. Kyle is a Ph.D. candidate in economics at the Massachusetts Institute of Technology. Joseph M. Scalise is a consultant with the San Francisco office of Bain & Company.

The opinions expressed do not necessarily reflect those of the Board of Governors or its staff. The authors thank our discussant, Steve Cecchetti, the conference organizer Rick Mishkin, and other conference participants, as well as Bob Avery, Kevin Bertsch, Mark Carey, Sally Davies, Al Gilbert, and Diana Hancock for helpful comments, and Kelly Bryant for outstanding research assistance.

three hypotheses about whether supervisors changed their policies and whether these policy changes affected bank lending behavior:

Hypothesis 1: U.S. bank supervisors got tougher on banks during the credit crunch period of 1989–92, treating banks of a given financial condition more harshly than in previous years.

Hypothesis 2: U.S. bank supervisors got easier on banks during the boom period of 1993–98, treating banks of a given financial condition less harshly than in prior periods.

Hypothesis 3: Changes in supervisory toughness, if they did occur, changed bank lending behavior in the predicted directions.

We test these hypotheses using information on the supervisory process, confidential data on classified assets and CAMEL ratings from bank examinations, bank balance sheet and income data, and other variables for the condition of the bank, its state, and its region over the period 1986–98.

Although we test these hypotheses separately, they are all intertwined in the overall question of the effects of changes in supervision. Under the first two hypotheses, there are significant changes in supervisory policy, and under the third hypothesis, these changes had a significant effect on bank lending. If these hypotheses are true, they may help explain part of the observed wide swings in bank lending to business during the 1990s, and may imply a larger role for financial supervision in the performance of the economy than was previously thought.

To put these issues into context, the period around 1989–92 is often referred to as a credit crunch in the United States, in which commercial banks substantially reduced their lending to business customers, although some researchers choose slightly different dates for the credit crunch period. From 1989 to 1992, domestic commercial and industrial (C&I) loans held by U.S. banks fell by about 23 percent in real terms. This decline may have been particularly difficult for bank-dependent small and medium-sized businesses, which often have few alternatives for external finance. Rough estimates suggest declines in business loans to borrowers with bank credit less than $1 million on the order of 38 percent (Berger, Kashyap, and Scalise 1995). Surveys of small business owners also suggest that it was more difficult for these firms to obtain credit during this time (e.g., Dunkelberg and Dennis 1992; Avery, Bostic, and Samolyk 1998). As discussed in the literature review in section 9.4, a number of hypotheses for this decline in bank credit have been tested, but very few of the tests used supervisory data.

An increase in supervisory toughness could explain a reduction in lending as follows. An unfavorable examination rating may be burdensome to a bank because supervisors may require poorly rated institutions to take costly actions to improve their condition (e.g., raising additional equity capital), or because poorly rated banks may be prohibited from engaging in some profitable activities by prompt corrective action rules or supervisory discretion. Banks may try to reverse the supervisory burdens of an unfavorable rating by reducing their perceived risk, and one way to do so is to reduce lending.

This explanation may be broader than it first appears because it may incorporate some of the changes in capital requirements and other regulatory changes during the credit crunch period. To the extent that these regulatory changes were enforced through the supervisory process by assigning worse CAMEL ratings for the same risk-based capital ratios, leverage capital ratios, and other financial ratios, they may be captured by our tests.

In addition, more classified assets or more serious classifications from an unfavorable examination may force a bank to shift funds from equity to its allocation for loan and lease losses (ALLL). Because equity counts in full as Tier 1 equity under risk-based capital guidelines and ALLL counts only as Tier 2 capital up to 1.25 percent of risk-weighted assets, the shift may directly reduce regulatory capital and require the bank to reduce lending or shrink to comply with capital regulations.

There may also have been a reduction in supervisory toughness during the banking boom period of 1993–1998, consistent with hypothesis 2. In 1993, the main federal supervisors of banks and thrifts (Office of the Comptroller of the Currency [OCC], Federal Deposit Insurance Corporation [FDIC], Federal Reserve Board [FRB], and Office of Thrift Supervision [OTS]) formally recognized a problem of credit availability and began a joint program directed at dealing with this problem. The program focused on five areas in which agencies would take actions to alleviate institutions' apparent reluctance to lend. The program (a) removed impediments to lending to small- and medium-sized businesses, (b) reduced appraisal requirements for real estate lending, (c) eased the appeals of examination decisions, (d) streamlined examination processes and procedures, and (e) reduced paperwork and regulatory burden associated with the supervisory process (Interagency Policy Statement on Credit Availability, 10 March 1993). As a specific example of the implementation of this program, banks that were well or adequately capitalized with satisfactory CAMEL ratings of 1 or 2 (most banks) were allowed to make and carry some loans to small- and medium-sized businesses (loans to borrowers with bank credit less than $900,000) with only minimal documentation, exempt from examiner criticism for doing so up to some limits (e.g., up to 20 percent of the bank's capital). Beyond these limits and for institutions not qualifying because of insufficient capital or CAMEL ratings, deviations from standard documentation could be made without examiner criticism for loans to some customers with past experience with the bank (Interagency Policy Statement on Credit Availability, 1993). This policy may be interpreted as an easing of supervision that may increase lending to relationship-type small and medium-sized business borrowers. In 1993, bank Call Report forms were also amended to begin collecting data each June on small business loans.

From 1993 through the end of our sample in 1998, lending by the U.S. banking industry increased substantially, and the industry enjoyed record profitability. Total domestic C&I loans rose by about 50 percent in real dollars, more than recovering from its 23 percent drop during the credit crunch period. However, small business loans may not have recovered quite as well, with business loans to borrowers with bank credit less than $1 million (as collected on the June Call Reports) rising only about 14 percent in real terms, and falling as a percentage of bank gross total assets from about 4.4 percent to about 3.8 percent.[1]

A number of hypotheses for the improvements in bank profitability during the 1993–98 boom period have been advanced, including favorable macroeconomic conditions, exercise of market power in pricing, a shift toward higher risk–higher expected return investments, and improvements in the quality of banking services (Berger et al. 2000; Berger and Mester 2001). However, little attention has been paid to the possible role of changes in the supervisory process on bank lending behavior. The increase in lending may have occurred in part because of the supervisors' joint program or because supervisors became easier in their assessments in other ways. If banks were assigned more favorable CAMEL examination ratings and lower classified assets for a given financial condition, this may have encouraged banks to increase their lending. To our knowledge, hypotheses 2 (decline in toughness during the boom) and 3 (it mattered to bank lending) have not previously been tested using data from the boom period.

To test for changes in supervisory toughness (hypotheses 1 and 2), we control for bank financial condition and other information that might be used by supervisors. We run weighted least squares regression equations for classified assets and ordered logit equations for CAMEL ratings, and test whether supervisors changed their classified assets or assigned different CAMEL ratings during the credit crunch and boom periods, controlling for the bank's financial condition and economic environment.

Our econometric models mimic as closely as possible the information used in the supervisory process, including the levels, trends, and peer group percentile ranks of all the key balance sheet and income variables specified in the off-site and on-site supervisory procedures. It is important to include these variables, because if any important items used by supervisors in setting the ratings are excluded, the test results may be biased. For

---

1. These numbers may slightly overstate the growth in small business lending. Although we are able to deflate the dollar values of loans to put them in real terms, the cutoff of bank credit less than $1 million remains in nominal terms on the Call Report form.

example, if a key balance sheet variable that worsened during the credit crunch period were excluded from the analysis, this may give a false reading of a toughening of supervisory treatment, since the rating may have changed because of the excluded variable rather than a change in supervisory toughness.

To test whether any changes in supervisory toughness affected bank lending behavior (hypothesis 3), we run ordinary least squares regression equations for changes in the proportions of bank assets invested in different types of loans and test whether these were affected by changes in classified assets and CAMEL ratings. We also include dependent variables for other changes in bank risk to determine whether any changes in supervisory toughness may have affected bank risk taking in other ways.

By way of preview, the data provide some statistically significant support for all three hypotheses, as well as supporting the argument that supervisory assessments affect bank risk-taking behavior. However, our evaluation of economic significance suggests that all of these effects are likely to be quite small. The data suggest that changes in supervisory toughness likely do not explain much of the dramatic changes in overall bank lending over the last decade or so.

Section 9.2 describes the supervisory process, including descriptions of the classified assets and CAMEL ratings, and the off-site and on-site procedures used to arrive at these assessments. Section 9.3 looks at the raw data from bank examinations, illustrating how supervisory ratings have changed over time, and pointing out some sample selection issues. Section 9.4 briefly reviews the literature on the credit crunch and other prior research uses of supervisory data. Section 9.5 presents the data and methodology employed, section 9.6 contains results and their implications, and section 9.7 concludes.

9.2   The Supervisory Process

Current supervisory practice based on the FDIC Improvement Act of 1991 (FDICIA) requires that banks be examined at least once every twelve months for most banks or at least every eighteen months for some small banks in good condition, although prior practice often resulted in significantly lower frequency (Gilbert 1993, 1994). Examination frequency is generally higher for troubled banks—those that are perceived to be in poor condition based on off-site monitoring of their balance sheet ratios, past examination ratings, and so on. Supervisors also speed up the schedules when there are indications of fraud, embezzlement, or other criminal activity. Most examinations are of the full-scope type—an in-depth evaluation of all areas of a bank's operation. A limited-scope exam is less intensive but reviews the same areas, whereas a targeted exam focuses on one or two areas intensively. In most cases, banks receive advance notification so that they can have the necessary documents and information prepared.

After the on-site examination, supervisory assessments in the form of CAMEL ratings and classified assets are determined. However, much of the information used in the evaluation of the bank is gathered in advance off-site. In this section, we first describe the CAMEL ratings and classified assets, and then discuss the off-site tasks and on-site procedures.

9.2.1   CAMEL Ratings and Classified Assets

Based on their assessments of information collected both off-site and on-site, supervisors assign each bank a composite CAMEL rating, which reflects their overall assessment of bank condition. CAMEL ratings are integers ranging from 1 to 5, with 1 being the strongest condition and 5 being the weakest. Most banks have ratings of 1 or 2 and are considered to be in satisfactory condition. Banks with ratings of 3, 4, or 5 are generally encouraged or required to take actions to improve their conditions. Table 9.1 gives more complete descriptions of the composite ratings. The CAMEL ratings are confidential, although some of the research reviewed below suggests that the information in ratings changes becomes incorporated into market prices.

For most of our sample, the composite CAMEL rating was based on five components of supervisory concern—capital adequacy (C), asset quality (A), management (M), earnings (E), and liquidity (L)—each of which also receives a rating on the 1 to 5 scale. Since 1997 supervisors have added a component for sensitivity to market risk (S), and altered the acronym to CAMELS. Although we do use the CAMELS rating for the end of our data set, we continue to refer to the CAMEL acronym throughout for convenience. Table 9.2 gives some of the details about these components.

The other main assessment made by supervisors is the determination of classified assets. In order from highest quality to lowest quality, commercial and industrial (C&I) and commercial real estate (CRE) loans are rated as pass, special mention, substandard, doubtful, or loss. Assets in the three most severe categories are often referred to as classified assets, although this term is sometimes meant to include the special mention category. Table 9.3 gives definitions of the special mention, substandard, doubtful, and loss categories.

Examiners use the following formula to determine the minimum required level of the allocation for loan and lease losses (ALLL), which is based on probability of default for each asset classification:

15% * substandard assets + 50% * doubtful assets + 100% * loss assets
   + (discretionary percentage) * (pass + special mention),

where the discretionary percentage the bank is required to hold against nonclassified assets is usually about 1 to 2 percent. If this minimum level exceeds the bank's actual reserve, the bank must add to its reserve from

Table 9.1   Descriptions of Composite CAMEL Ratings

Rating	Description
1	Institutions in this group are basically sound in every respect; any critical findings or comments are of a minor nature and can be handled in a routine manner. Such institutions are resistant to external economic and financial disturbances and more capable of withstanding the vagaries of business conditions than institutions with lower ratings. As a result, such institutions give no cause for supervisory concern.
2	Institutions in this group are also fundamentally sound, but may reflect modest weaknesses correctable in the normal course of business. The nature and severity of deficiencies, however, are not considered material and, therefore, such institutions are stable and also able to withstand business fluctuations quite well. While areas of weakness could develop into conditions of greater concern, the supervisory response is limited to the extent that minor adjustments are resolved in the normal course of business, and operations continue satisfactorily.
3	Institutions in this category exhibit a combination of financial, operational, or compliance weaknesses ranging from moderately severe to unsatisfactory. When weaknesses relate to financial condition, such institutions may be vulnerable to the onset of adverse business conditions and could easily deteriorate if concerted action is not effective in correcting the areas of weakness. Institutions which are in significant noncompliance with laws and regulations may also be accorded this rating. Generally, these institutions give more cause for supervisory concern and require more than normal supervision to address deficiencies. Overall strength and financial capacity, however, are still such as to make failure only a remote possibility.
4	Institutions in this group have an immoderate volume of serious financial weaknesses or a combination of other conditions that are unsatisfactory. Major and serious problems or unsafe and unsound conditions may exist which are not being satisfactorily addressed or resolved. Unless effective action is taken to correct these conditions, they could reasonably develop into a situation that could impair future viability, constitute a threat to the interests of depositors, and/or pose a potential for disbursement of funds by the insuring agency. A higher potential for failure is present but is not yet imminent or pronounced. Institutions in this category require close supervisory attention and financial surveillance and a definitive plan for corrective action.
5	This category is reserved for institutions with an extremely high immediate or near term probability of failure. The volume and severity of weaknesses or unsafe and unsound conditions are so critical as to require urgent aid from stockholders or other public or private sources of financial assistance. In the absence of urgent and decisive corrective measures, these situations will likely require liquidation and the payoff of depositors, disbursement of insurance funds to insured depositors, or some form of emergency assistance, merger or qcquisition.

Source: Commercial Bank Examination Manual, A.5020.1, pp. 3–4: Uniform Financial Institutions Rating System, effective 3/84.

Table 9.2   **Components of the CAMEL Ratings**

Component	Description
Capital adequacy	A bank's Tier 1, total capital, and leverage ratios in relation to its peer group are the most important factors in assigning a preliminary rating. Peer groups are based on bank asset size, number of offices, and location in a metropolitan or nonmetropolitan area. More capital is required for banks with deficiencies in any other area of the examination, particularly in asset quality. Examiners also pay close attention to how equity and asset growth affect the capital ratios, and look at retained earnings as a ratio of average total equity to determine whether a bank's equity growth is through retained earnings or an unsustainable outside source, and to the size of the dividend payout.
Asset quality	The asset quality rating is an indicator of future losses to the bank and affects the ratings of other areas of examination, which must be considered in light of their adequacy to absorb anticipated losses. The most important factor in the asset quality rating is the bank's weighted classified asset ratio, which is computed as (15% * substandard assets + 50% * doubtful assets + 100% * loss assets)/(Tier 1 capital + allocation for loan and lease losses). Examiners also consider the level, trend and composition of classified assets and nonaccrual and renegotiated loans, loan concentrations, lending policies, and effectiveness in monitoring past-due loans, insider loans, and the types of risks inherent in the banks on- and off-balance sheet portfolios.
Management	Management is evaluated on a number of criteria, including compliance with applicable laws and regulations, whether there is a comprehensive internal or external review audit, internal controls to safeguard bank assets, and systems for timely and accurate information. Examiners also consider the other components of the CAMEL rating, shareholder return, and the extent to which the bank is serving all sectors of its community.
Earnings	Earnings are assessed for ability to absorb future losses, so this rating is affected by asset quality, a bank's level, trend and relation to peer of net interest income, noninterest income, overhead expense and provision for loan and lease losses, extraordinary items, additional required provision for loan and lease losses or other nonrecurring items, and dividend payouts.
Liquidity	The liquidity rating is a determination of a bank's ease in obtaining money cheaply and quickly, and a bank's management of interest rate risk. Considerations include the bank's loan commitments and standby letters of credit, the presence of an "unstable core" of funding, access to capital markets, the ratios of federal funds purchased and brokered deposits to total assets and the ratios of loans to deposits.
Sensitivity to market risk (since 1997 only)	Rating is based on, but not limited to, assessments of the sensitivity of the financial institution's earnings or the economic value of its capital to adverse changes in interest rates, foreign-exchange rates, commodity prices, or equity prices, the ability of management to identify, measure, monitor, and control exposure to market risk given the institution's size, complexity, and risk profile, the nature and complexity of interest-rate risk exposure arising from nontrading positions where appropriate, the nature and complexity of market-risk exposure arising from trading and foreign operations.

Source: Commercial Bank Examination Manual.

Table 9.3   Classified Asset Categories

Component	Description
Special mention	This category includes loans that are potential problems, but that are currently of adequate quality. Loans with inadequate documentation and loans particularly vulnerable to a change in economic conditions may be classified as such. Loans to borrowers with deteriorating but still acceptable financials are another example.
Substandard	Loans in this category are judged to have a well-defined weakness that may result in losses to the bank if left uncorrected. Characteristics include significant deviations from scheduled payments, delinquency, carried-over debt, numerous extensions or renewals without statement of source of repayment, decreased borrower profitability or poor borrower cash flow.
Doubtful	Doubtful loans have problems similar to those of substandard loans, but also have a loss exposure considered severe enough to jeopardize full collection of the loan highly unlikely. However, the loan is not yet considered a loss due to the possibility of mitigating circumstances, such as a proposed merger, capital injection, or refinancing plans. A loan should not be classified as doubtful for two consecutive exams, since it is assumed the status of the loan should be resolved during the time between exams.
Loss	A loan considered uncollectible is classified a loss. Although some probability of partial recovery may exist, it is considered preferable to write off the loan in the current period. Such loans are characterized by severe delinquency.

Source: Commercial Bank Examination Manual.

equity capital. Thus, the greater the fraction of assets classified as substandard, doubtful, or loss, and the more serious the classification, the more the bank may have to shift funds from equity to ALLL. This may require the bank to reduce lending, shrink, or raise capital to comply with capital regulations.

In our empirical analysis, we use both total classified assets (substandard + doubtful + loss) and weighted classified assets (15% * substandard assets + 50% * doubtful + 100% * loss). An increase in supervisory toughness may occur when supervisors shift loans from pass or special mention to substandard, doubtful, or loss, which would raise total classified assets. Alternatively, supervisors might get tougher by shifting already-classified assets into more serious classifications, such as from substandard to doubtful or from doubtful to loss, which would raise weighted classified assets. We include both measures of classified assets in our analysis to allow for these possibilities.

9.2.2   Off-Site Supervisory Tasks

In general, one individual is named Examiner-in-Charge (EIC), and is responsible for coordinating most aspects of an exam and has a number of assistants, depending on the size and complexity of the bank. Prior to an on-site visit, examiners perform several analyses off-site. These include review of past examination reports and the correspondence file for that bank, as well as its Call Report and Uniform Bank Performance Report (UBPR). The UBPR, produced for every U.S. commercial bank by the Federal Financial Institutions Examination Council, summarizes several years of Call Report data for a bank and presents both dollar amounts and financial ratios for most areas of bank operations. The UBPR also includes information on the trends of these variables as well as the peer group average for each variable and the bank's rank within its peer group for that variable. Peer groups are based on bank asset size, number of offices, and location in a metropolitan or nonmetropolitan area. Analysis of the UBPR provides initial evaluations of the individual components of the CAMEL rating (although no preliminary rating is given for the management component), which may be changed during the on-site examination if conditions are not consistent with what was reported or expected (Commercial Bank Examination Manual, 1020.1, p. 1). Generally, the off-site monitoring is helpful in determining potential problems that examiners should scrutinize during the on-site visit, allowing on-site resources to be allocated more efficiently. Off-site monitoring is also useful for identifying troubled banks or those with indications of criminal activity to speed up the examination schedule for these institutions.

Our econometric models control for bank condition by proxying for the information used by supervisors as well as possible. This includes forming the levels, trends, and peer group percentile ranks of the key balance sheet and income variables specified in the UBPR from the appropriate Call Report quarter. Failure to include these variables could bias our tests, because any change in classified assets or CAMEL ratings may reflect changes in the UBPR variables, rather than changes in supervisory harshness.

9.2.3   On-Site Examination Procedures

The most important aspect of the on-site examination is the evaluation of the bank's loan portfolio. This process begins with a review of the institution's loan policies, which should include a description of the bank's market, targeted customers, lending guidelines, documentation, and restrictions or requirements on loans to insiders. Examiners also read the minutes of the bank's loan committee meetings, the credit department's procedures and files regarding the acquisition of borrower financial information, and internal reports on past due or problem loans.

Examiners evaluate a certain proportion of the loan portfolio, depending on the bank's most recent composite and asset quality ratings. This proportion ranges from 40 percent for banks with composite ratings of 1 or 2 and an asset quality rating of 1, to 60 percent or more for banks with worse ratings or other areas of concern.

There are several steps in determining the loan sample. Examiners must review all C&I and CRE loans that are past due, nonaccrual, restructured, renegotiated, made to an insider, internally classified by the bank, or classified at the last exam. Large loans—loans greater than a dollar cutoff determined by the EIC to be appropriate for the bank—must also be reviewed. This set of C&I and CRE loans is considered the core group for review. To achieve the desired coverage of the portfolio (i.e., the 40 to 60 percent or more), additional loans are selected for review in a variety of ways. The dollar cutoff for large loans might be lowered; recent loans or specific loan types might be selected; or random sampling or some other technique may be applied, according to examiner discretion.

Examiners assign ratings of pass, special mention, substandard, doubtful, or loss to each loan sampled. Examiners may assign distinct classifications to different parts of a loan depending on the likelihood of collection of each particular part. Examiners may also assign split classifications, such as substandard/doubtful, in appropriate circumstances. The loan ratings are checked against the bank's own internal ratings as a check of how well bank management is monitoring its own portfolio. Installment loans, residential mortgages, and other consumer credits are classified as pass, substandard, or loss based solely on the number of days past due, not by examiner discretion.

After the examination, the final supervisory assessments are made. The composite CAMEL rating is based on all the components of supervisory concern—capital adequacy, asset quality, management, earnings, liquidity, and (more recently for the CAMELS rating) sensitivity to market risk—and the information incorporated into the rating comes from the data gathered off-site and on-site. The composite CAMEL rating is not an unweighted mean of these components; an examiner may use personal judgment as to the importance of each component for a particular bank. However, quality of the assets in terms of likely future losses and the ability of the bank's capital to absorb these losses are usually the most important components. The composite rating is generally not supposed to be more than one rank better than the capital (C) or asset quality (A) rank.

9.3 A Look at the Raw Data from Bank Examinations

Table 9.4 shows some summary statistics from bank examinations over the entire 1986–98 period. Panel A shows the number of banks with examination data for each year, the mean ratios of total classified assets to loans and weighted classified assets to loans, the mean composite CAMEL rating, and the fractions of banks receiving composite CAMEL ratings of 1, 2, 3, 4, and 5. Panel B of table 9.4 summarizes the information for the precrunch, credit crunch, and boom periods. Figure 9.1 plots the fractions of banks with the different CAMEL ratings over time.

We include exactly one observation for each bank that was examined in each year. Because not every bank is examined in every year, the total number of banks examined in each year is fewer than the number of banks in the nation. In the relatively infrequent cases in which more than one examination was made of the same bank in the same year, we simply include the results of the final examination of the year to avoid double counting. As will be seen, changes over time in the sample of banks that were selected by supervisors to be examined are important in interpreting the data.

In some respects the raw data are consistent with expectations, and in other respects the data are quite surprising. Consistent with expectations, the supervisory assessments are unambiguously the best during the boom period. As shown in Panel A, in each of the boom period years 1993–98, the mean total classified asset ratio, mean weighted classified asset ratio, mean composite CAMEL rating, and fraction of banks receiving CAMEL ratings of 1 (the best rating) were better than the corresponding figures for each of the credit crunch years 1989–92, and better than each of the precrunch years 1986–88 as well. The data in Panel B show that on average during the boom period, the classified asset ratios were on the order of about half—and the fractions of banks assigned CAMEL ratings of 1 were on the order of about double—those in the precrunch and credit crunch periods. The figure shows a steep increase in CAMEL ratings of 1 and steep decreases in CAMEL ratings of 3, 4, and 5 beginning in 1993. These

Table 9.4   Summary Statistics from Bank Examinations over Time

	Number Examined	Total Classified Assets	Weighted Classified Assets	Mean CAMEL	Fraction CAMEL 1	Fraction CAMEL 2	Fraction CAMEL 3	Fraction CAMEL 4	Fraction CAMEL 5
				Panel A					
1986	6,042	0.098	0.028	2.402	0.152	0.480	0.217	0.117	0.034
1987	6,763	0.086	0.024	2.291	0.177	0.515	0.182	0.093	0.034
1988	7,729	0.082	0.022	2.257	0.188	0.521	0.170	0.089	0.033
1989	8,352	0.082	0.022	2.216	0.206	0.525	0.153	0.077	0.039
1990	8,316	0.072	0.018	2.207	0.207	0.519	0.165	0.078	0.031
1991	8,377	0.070	0.017	2.194	0.202	0.523	0.178	0.075	0.023
1992	9,040	0.063	0.015	2.089	0.215	0.566	0.149	0.056	0.014
1993	9,594	0.051	0.012	1.869	0.297	0.580	0.088	0.029	0.007
1994	8,867	0.041	0.010	1.758	0.346	0.575	0.058	0.016	0.005
1995	7,821	0.036	0.008	1.676	0.396	0.547	0.045	0.010	0.002
1996	7,273	0.033	0.008	1.609	0.445	0.509	0.037	0.007	0.001
1997	6,381	0.033	0.008	1.591	0.467	0.488	0.036	0.009	0.001
1998	5,578	0.032	0.008	1.624	0.444	0.500	0.046	0.008	0.002
				Panel B					
Precrunch period	20,534	0.088	0.024	2.311	0.174	0.507	0.187	0.098	0.034
Credit crunch period	34,085	0.072	0.018	2.175	0.208	0.534	0.161	0.071	0.026
Boom period	45,514	0.039	0.009	1.704	0.389	0.539	0.054	0.014	0.003

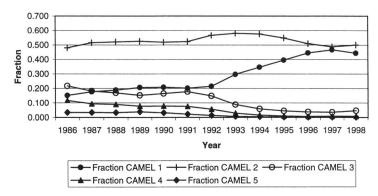

Fig. 9.1   CAMEL Distribution, 1986–98

strong improvements in supervisory assessments during the boom period may reflect the improved condition of banks, any supervisory easing that may have occurred, or a combination of the two. We try to disentangle these effects below in our multivariate empirical analysis.

Contrary to expectations, the supervisory assessments generally did not deteriorate during the credit crunch period. As is shown in Panel A, in each of the credit crunch years 1989–92, the mean total classified asset ratio, mean weighted classified asset ratio, mean composite CAMEL rating, and CAMEL 1 fraction were better than the corresponding figures for each of the precrunch years 1986–88 (although the figures for 1989 are very close to those for 1988 and round to the same three digits for the classified asset ratios). The data in Panel B show that the mean classified asset ratios, mean composite CAMEL, and CAMEL 1 fraction for the credit crunch period are all closer to the precrunch period figures than to the boom period figures, indicating a much smaller improvement in the credit crunch period than in the boom period. This slight improvement in supervisory assessments or failure to deteriorate is surprising given both the recession of the early 1990s and widespread belief that supervisors may have become tougher.[2]

At first blush it might seem unlikely that hypothesis 1 (increase in toughness) could be supported. Banking industry conditions did improve slightly during the credit crunch period in terms of capital ratios and problem loans, but it would not be expected ex ante that controls for bank condition would improve enough to offset a substantial increase in supervisory toughness. As we show next, the improvements in supervisory assessments

---

2. The classified assets figures may have been held down temporarily for some banks during the high bank failure years in the late 1980s and early 1990s in order to allow for orderly bank closures, because high classified assets may have reduced capital to below closure levels for too many banks at the same time.

during the credit crunch period may largely be an artifact of changes in the selection of banks that were examined.

Table 9.5 illustrates the sample selection issue by comparing examined banks with the banking industry as a whole over time. As is shown in Panel A, the fraction of banks with examination data rises each year from 1986 to 1993 and then falls each year thereafter to 1998. The changes are quite dramatic: The percentage of banks with recorded examinations nearly doubles from 42.6 percent to 85.4 percent, and then drops to 62.3 percent. As is shown in Panel B of table 9.5, only 49.4 percent of banks have examination data on average during the precrunch years, versus 69.5 percent during the credit crunch years and 75.4 percent during the boom years. These dramatic changes in the fraction of banks examined may in part reflect changes in supervisory policy, changes in regulation (such as FDICIA, which mandates examinations every twelve or eighteen months), or changes in bank condition.

Importantly, a change in the fraction of banks examined may change the quality pool of the banks examined relative to the industry as a whole. As discussed above, banks that are perceived to be in worse condition based on off-site monitoring of their balance sheet ratios, past examination ratings, and so on are more likely to be examined in a given year. As a consequence, if the fraction of banks examined rises over time, one may expect that the average quality of the pool of banks that are examined will rise relative to the industry as a whole, as better-quality institutions are added to the examination pool. That is, there may be no improvement or even a deterioration in supervisory assessments on average relative to prior examinations, but the addition of better banks to the examination pool makes it appear from the raw data that assessments have improved. This may help explain why the classified asset ratios and CAMEL ratings of examined banks improved during the credit crunch period.

Additional data in table 9.5 are designed to examine this issue further. The table shows the mean total capital ratio and mean nonperforming loan ratio calculated from the Call Report for the year prior to the examinations versus these same ratios for the industry as a whole. For the total capital ratio, the difference between the mean for examined banks and the mean for the industry narrows considerably during the credit crunch period. As is shown in Panel A, the capital ratio for examined banks is 2.4 percentage points lower on average than the industry as of 1986, and this difference narrowed to below 1 percentage point by 1990. As is shown in Panel B, the average difference fell by about one-half from 1.9 percentage points during the precrunch years to 0.9 percentage points during the credit crunch years, consistent with the argument that examinations during the credit crunch period tended to cover a higher-quality cut of the industry than did examinations during the precrunch period, which may explain the slightly improved supervisory assessments. Similar results hold for

Table 9.5   Sample Selection—Examined Banks versus the Industry over Time

	Number of Banks			Total Capital Ratio			Nonperforming Loan Ratio		
	Examined	Industry	Fraction Examined	Examined	Industry	Difference	Examined	Industry	Difference
				Panel A					
1986	6,042	14,197	0.426	0.154	0.178	-0.024	0.061	0.057	0.004
1987	6,763	13,956	0.485	0.157	0.177	-0.019	0.057	0.057	0.001
1988	7,729	13,443	0.575	0.170	0.185	-0.015	0.050	0.049	0.000
1989	8,352	12,863	0.649	0.173	0.185	-0.012	0.044	0.044	0.001
1990	8,316	12,447	0.668	0.178	0.186	-0.008	0.043	0.042	0.000
1991	8,377	12,088	0.693	0.169	0.177	-0.008	0.043	0.043	0.001
1992	9,040	11,677	0.774	0.169	0.178	-0.009	0.042	0.042	0.000
1993	9,594	11,232	0.854	0.179	0.186	-0.007	0.033	0.034	-0.001
1994	8,867	10,778	0.823	0.183	0.191	-0.008	0.029	0.029	0.000
1995	7,821	10,266	0.762	0.184	0.191	-0.007	0.026	0.025	0.000
1996	7,273	9,760	0.745	0.182	0.193	-0.011	0.027	0.027	0.000
1997	6,381	9,346	0.683	0.131	0.137	-0.005	0.028	0.028	0.000
1998	5,578	8,954	0.623	0.173	0.192	-0.018	0.026	0.026	0.001
				Panel B					
Precrunch period	20,534	41,596	0.494	0.161	0.180	-0.019	0.055	0.054	0.001
Credit crunch period	34,085	49,075	0.695	0.172	0.181	-0.009	0.043	0.043	-0.000
Boom period	45,514	60,336	0.754	0.174	0.182	-0.008	0.028	0.028	0.000

other capital ratios (not shown in the table).[3] Perhaps surprisingly, there is much less support for this argument from the nonperforming loan data; examined banks had only slightly higher nonperforming loan ratios than the industry as a whole during the precrunch period, and the difference disappeared during the credit crunch period.[4] Thus, the examination pool seems to have improved substantially relative to the industry in terms of capital, but much less so in terms of nonperforming loans.

Table 9.6 rearranges the raw data in a way that should at least partially offset the changes in sample selection over time. For each examination, we show the changes in composite CAMEL ratings, total classified asset ratio, and weighted classified asset ratio since the previous examination. If a bank did not have an examination in the year or if there are no prior examinations available, the data are excluded from this table (this exclusion is not made in our empirical analysis below). This procedure should partially offset the sample selection problem because each examination is paired with exactly one prior examination of the same bank. As is shown, there are very few observations at the start of the sample because we have data on only a very small number of examinations prior to the start of the precrunch period in 1986. The data are roughly consistent with the expectations that supervisory assessments deteriorated during the credit crunch period and improved during the boom period. As is shown in Panel A, CAMEL downgrades exceed upgrades in the first three years of the credit crunch period from 1989 through 1991, and CAMEL upgrades exceed downgrades in every year from 1992 through 1997 (upgrades, downgrades, and constant CAMEL ratings fractions sum to 1 by construction). Similarly, the percentage of examinations with increases in classified assets is relatively high in 1989 through 1991 and then falls off sharply in the immediately following years (classified asset ratio decreases and increases fractions sum to 1 by construction). The summary data in Panel B confirm this. During the credit crunch period, composite CAMEL downgrades slightly exceed upgrades, whereas upgrades slightly exceed downgrades during the precrunch years and upgrades greatly exceed downgrades during the boom years. Similarly, the fractions of examinations with increases

---

3. The mean Tier 1 and leverage capital ratios for examined banks improved from 0.149 and 0.082, respectively, during the precrunch years to 0.160 and 0.087 during the credit crunch years. For the industry, the corresponding ratios increased from 0.168 and 0.086, respectively, to 0.170 and 0.089. Again, the percentage point difference in capital ratios between examined banks and the industry as a whole dropped by about one-half in the credit crunch period.

4. A potential problem with the nonperforming loan data is that the definition may have changed slightly over time due to changes in supervisory policy in which loans for which no repayments had been missed were recorded as nonperforming. Similarly, there may have been a change in the reported data for C&I and real estate loans, as supervisors became more vigilant in requiring that commercial loans secured by real estate be reported as real estate loans.

Table 9.6   Changes between Examinations in CAMEL Ratings and Classified Asset Ratios

	Number of Banks	CAMEL			Total Classified Asset Ratio		Weighted Classified Asset Ratio	
		Upgrades	Downgrades	Constant	Decreases	Increases	Decreases	Increases
				Panel A				
1986	472	0.131	0.119	0.750	0.523	0.477	0.511	0.489
1987	3,816	0.187	0.155	0.658	0.583	0.417	0.591	0.409
1988	5,426	0.161	0.168	0.672	0.576	0.424	0.586	0.414
1989	7,258	0.157	0.158	0.685	0.554	0.446	0.563	0.437
1990	7,905	0.127	0.175	0.698	0.526	0.474	0.533	0.467
1991	8,072	0.135	0.171	0.694	0.513	0.487	0.522	0.478
1992	8,729	0.182	0.113	0.706	0.557	0.443	0.564	0.436
1993	9,364	0.230	0.060	0.710	0.675	0.325	0.678	0.322
1994	8,777	0.182	0.063	0.755	0.701	0.299	0.691	0.309
1995	7,754	0.164	0.067	0.769	0.645	0.355	0.643	0.357
1996	7,194	0.149	0.066	0.784	0.589	0.411	0.575	0.425
1997	6,277	0.127	0.079	0.794	0.576	0.424	0.568	0.432
1998	5,422	0.095	0.100	0.805	0.557	0.443	0.553	0.447
				Panel B				
Precrunch period	9,714	0.170	0.160	0.670	0.576	0.424	0.584	0.416
Credit crunch period	31,964	0.151	0.153	0.696	0.538	0.462	0.545	0.455
Boom period	44,788	0.165	0.070	0.764	0.633	0.367	0.627	0.373

in the classified asset ratios are greatest during the credit crunch years, whereas the fractions with decreases in these ratios are highest during the boom years. The data in table 9.6 suggest that supervisory assessments began to be somewhat harsher just before the onset of the credit crunch and began to be somewhat less harsh just before the onset of the banking boom. These data are also consistent with our arguments about sample selection. It may be that on average banks of a given quality received worse supervisory assessments in the credit crunch period than in the precrunch period, but that the average assessments improved because the increased examination frequency resulted in a better-quality cut of the industry being examined.

There are several other sample selection issues as well. There may be some missing observations—examinations that took place but were not on the electronic files—particularly at the beginning of our data set. Prior to 1986, the files are very incomplete, making lagged examination data an issue. Some of the data may also be missing for 1986 or other early years. We also may be missing some examinations from 1998 that were not finalized at the time we extracted the data set in the latter part of 1999. In addition, some banks drop out of the sample due to mergers and failures, and others enter the sample through the creation of new charters.

We deal with these sample selection issues in the empirical analysis in several ways. First, we include a large number of controls for bank quality, which may help compensate for changes over time in the quality of the cut of the industry that is examined. Second, we include observations in the regressions even when data for lagged supervisory assessments are missing, and include a dummy variable flagging these observations to account for the average difference of these banks from other banks. This increases representation for new entrants and for banks near the beginning of the data set when examination data are sparse. Third, we try a Heckman correction for sample selection bias, although we acknowledge identification problems with this procedure in our case.

9.4 Literature Review

In this section, we first briefly review the literature on the causes for the decline in bank lending during the credit crunch period. Very little of this research has used supervisory data, despite the widespread belief that an increase in supervisory toughness may be responsible for the reduced lending. We then review prior research that has used the supervisory data to test the timeliness and accuracy of supervisory assessments. To our knowledge there have been no prior tests of whether a decline in supervisory toughness may have contributed to changes in bank lending behavior during the banking boom.

9.4.1 Prior Research on the Causes of the Credit Crunch

A number of hypotheses of the decline in bank credit to business during the credit crunch period have been tested. A few studies have explicitly investigated forms of hypotheses 1 and 3 (i.e., that supervisors got tougher and that this toughness reduced business lending). In the study closest in approach to the current paper, Bizer (1993) ran ordered logit equations for composite CAMEL ratings on a limited number of Call Report items, regional dummies, and primary supervisor dummies. He found that the model predicted tougher CAMEL ratings during the quarters of the credit crunch period than in a single-quarter control period of 1988:4. He also regressed lending on lagged CAMEL ratings and a few control variables and found that worse CAMEL ratings were associated with reduced lending.

Although this was an excellent early attempt, in our opinion a more comprehensive approach is needed. As we discussed earlier, it is important to control for as much of the information used in the supervisory process at the time of the ratings assignment as possible, including the levels, trends, and peer group percentile ranks of the key balance sheet and income variables explicitly used to form the CAMEL ratings. Bizer's CAMEL equations include very few of the specified levels, and none of the trends or peer group percentile ranks. For example, he excluded the risk-based capital ratios, so the effects of enforcing these regulatory requirements through the supervisory process may not be captured. Similar criticisms also apply to the lending regressions, which do not control for problem loan categories. As is indicated later, our strongest results for the lending equations are generated by changes in classified assets, which are excluded from Bizer's analysis. We also include much more information about the condition of banks in the same state and use a three-year precrunch base period in place of a single quarter.

Another study that used supervisory assessments was Peek and Rosengren (1995a). These authors tested a form of hypothesis 3 by evaluating the effects of supervisory enforcement actions in New England during the credit crunch period. They found that banks under enforcement actions reduced lending more than other banks in the same region with the same capital-to-asset ratios, supporting the hypothesis that supervisory actions contributed to the reduction in lending. Again, the conclusions may be somewhat limited because there were very few control variables specified for bank condition, making it difficult to disentangle supervisory actions from the effects of the condition of the banks' portfolios.

A number of studies tested whether implementation of tougher capital standards contributed to the decline in U.S. bank lending to business during the credit crunch period. Some tested the effects of implementation of the Basel Accord risk-based capital standards (e.g., Haubrich and Wachtel 1993; Berger and Udell 1994; Hancock and Wilcox 1994a; Wagster 1999).

Others tested whether supervisors or regulators implemented higher explicit or implicit regulatory capital standards based on leverage ratios (e.g., Berger and Udell 1994; Peek and Rosengren 1994, 1995b; Hancock and Wilcox 1994a; Hancock, Laing, and Wilcox 1995; Shrieves and Dahl 1995). Although there is not full consensus, the empirical results generally do not support risk-based capital as a major contributor to the lending slowdown, but do provide some support for the effects of tougher explicit or implicit leverage capital requirements.

As noted previously, to the extent that capital requirements or other regulatory changes are enforced through the supervisory process by assigning worse CAMEL ratings for the same capital ratio and other balance sheet and income ratios, they may be captured in our tests of supervisory toughness below. That is, if supervisors enforce higher capital ratios, then there should be a worse CAMEL rating assigned for the same capital ratio, all else equal. In our empirical analysis, we include the Tier 1 and total risk-based capital ratios as well as the leverage ratio to capture these effects, although identifying these individual capital effects is quite difficult and is not a goal of this paper.

A notable advantage of our tests is that by including actual supervisory assessments, we can better distinguish between supervisory-induced changes in bank behavior and voluntary changes in bank behavior. It is possible that a reduction in lending during the credit crunch period by banks with capital below the regulatory minimums represents a voluntary retrenchment of risks by banks, rather than the effects of changes in regulation or supervision. Similarly, some studies found that during the credit crunch period, banks facing greater portfolio risks—such as those with more nonperforming loans or those in nations with more banking system risk—also tended to cut back their lending more than other banks (e.g., Berger and Udell 1994; Wagster 1999). Without supervisory information, it is not possible to distinguish whether this represents supervisory or voluntary reactions to risk. Our tests, which control for measures of portfolio risks, may help distinguish among these alternatives.

Other studies tested whether demand or supply factors other than regulatory/supervisory changes contributed significantly to the change in lending during the credit crunch period. Tests have been performed of the effects of the depletion of bank capital from loan loss experiences of the late 1980s (e.g., Peek and Rosengren 1994, 1995b; Hancock and Wilcox 1994a, 1997, 1998), potential choices of lower risk profiles by bank managers (e.g., Hancock and Wilcox 1993, 1994b), reduced loan demand because of macroeconomic or regional recessions (e.g., Bernanke and Lown 1991; Hancock and Wilcox 1993, 1997), or a secular decline in the demand for bank loans because of the growth of alternative sources of credit (e.g., Berger and Udell 1994). All of these hypotheses were supported to at least some degree.

9.4.2 Prior Research on Supervisory Timeliness and Accuracy

Previous research on bank examinations or bank holding company (BHC) inspections has usually focused on either the timeliness or accuracy of supervisory assessments of banking organization condition measured relative to market assessments. Studies of timeliness generally tested whether changes in supervisory assessments (changes in CAMEL; changes in BOPEC, the corresponding rating for bank holding companies; or identification of problem banks) occurred before or after changes in market assessments of banking problems (equity or debt price changes, changes in bond ratings, or changes in share ownership by institutions or insiders).

Most of the early studies of timeliness found that supervisors did not have information in a more timely fashion than market participants. Pettway (1980) performed even studies for six large banks that were placed on the problem bank list during 1972–76 and found significantly negative cumulative abnormal stock returns before the examination that first recognized the banks' problems, suggesting a timeliness advantage for investors over supervisors. Hirschhorn (1987) investigated whether CAMEL rating changes predate stock price changes, using data on examination ratings of the lead banks of the fifteen largest BHCs during 1978–87. He found that CAMEL ratings were approximately contemporaneously correlated with abnormal returns, suggesting that supervisors generally had little if any economically significant informational advantage over equity market participants. Cargill (1989) examined cross-sectional variation in the rates on large certificates of deposit for fifty-eight large banks during 1984–86. He found that CAMEL ratings added no significant explanatory power beyond Call Report financial ratios, again implying that supervisors did not have substantial information prior to market participants.

In contrast, more recent studies generally found that supervisors did have some valuable information on a more timely basis than market participants. Simons and Cross (1991) identified twenty-two BHCs whose lead banks had their composite CAMEL rating lowered to the problem ratings of 4 or 5 during 1981–87. They found that the company's weekly abnormal stock returns for the year preceding the downgrade were equally likely to be positive or negative, and that few news stories chronicled the firms' problems, suggesting that supervisors may have known about problems before market participants. Berger and Davies (1998) used event study methodology to identify abnormal BHC stock returns after 390 lead bank examinations during 1985–89. They separated out the three types of information that may be generated by the examination: private information about bank condition, certification information about the quality of audited financial statements, and supervisory discipline information about whether the bank may have greater or fewer restrictions placed on it. They found that the only type of private information that was transferred to the market was unfavorable private information about bank condition, suggesting that supervisors force the release of unfavorable information. Jordan (1999) found results consistent with these when investigating the effects of examinations of banks in thirty-five BHCs in New England over the period 1988:1–1990:3. He found statistically significant negative abnormal stock returns (below the mean returns of these thirty-five BHCs) in the quarter after CAMEL downgrades involving at least one-third of the BHCs banking assets, but no significant change in market prices for examinations overall. DeYoung et al. (forthcoming) investigated whether national bank examiners' private information significantly predicted changes in the risk premiums on large BHCs subordinated debentures during 1989–95. They found that debenture yield spreads changed after the examination information, suggesting that examiners uncover relevant information before the market. Consistent with Berger and Davies (1998), this predictive effect occurred only for negative supervisory assessments. Flannery and Houston (1999) evaluated the correspondence between market and book valuations for a sample of BHCs in the fourth quarters of 1988 and 1990 and found that investors evaluated financial information differently when the BHC had recently received an on-site inspection, particularly in the relatively normal 1988 period. Inspected BHCs showed a closer correspondence between market and book values, consistent with the hypothesis that investors view examiners as credibly certifying of the financial statements' accuracy. Finally, Berger, Davies, and Flannery (2000) used quarterly data from inspections of 184 large BHCs over the period 1989:4–1992:2 and found that BHC supervisors and bond rating agencies both have some timely prior information that is useful to the other. However, supervisory assessments and equity market indicators were not strongly related to each other, presumably because of differences in incentives regarding risks and expected returns.[5,6]

Studies of supervisory accuracy generally tested whether changes in supervisory assessments added to the predictions of changes in bank condition (e.g., bank failure, book-value insolvency, changes in nonperforming

5. Consistent with this conclusion, Hall, Meyer, and Vaughan (1997) found that supervisors and shareholders responded differently to balance sheet measures of BHC condition.

6. Studies of bank "early warning" systems (e.g., Sinkey 1978; Whalen and Thompson 1988; O'Keefe and Dahl 1997) tested how well supervisory ratings can be predicted from publicly available information, generally Call Report data. These may be viewed as tests of whether supervisors have information not already in the publicly available data, although this was not the main purpose. These studies generally found that the supervisory ratings were far from perfectly predictable from Call Report information, consistent with the supervisors adding timely information. However, these studies are less useful for evaluating timeliness than are studies using stock and bond market data, because market data presumably incorporate much more information than the Call Report.

loans or equity capital) or macroeconomic performance beyond other public or private sources of information (e.g., market assessments, Call Report information, or Federal Reserve staff forecasts). This literature found mixed results. Davies (1993) tested whether CAMEL or BOPEC ratings versus market/book ratios better helped predict future book-value insolvency (bank's capital ratio below either 2 percent or 3 percent of assets) during 1986–91 and found that unsatisfactory bank CAMEL ratings helped predict a higher probability of book-value insolvency, but that unsatisfactory holding company BOPEC ratings had little or no additional predictive power. Cole and Gunther (1998) compared supervisory ratings with Call Report information in predicting future bank failures during 1988:2–1992:1 and found that CAMEL ratings improved forecast accuracy, but only if the examination was in the most recent two quarters. Berger, Davies, and Flannery (2000) similarly found that supervisory assessments are much less accurate overall than both bond and equity market assessments in predicting future changes in performance, but that supervisors may be more accurate when inspections are recent. Finally, Peek, Rosengren, and Tootell (1999a,b) used quarterly data from 1978:1–1996:2 and 1978:1–1994:4, respectively, and found that the proportion of the nation's banking assets in banks with composite CAMEL ratings of 5 (the worst rating) added information in predicting macroeconomic performance beyond what was incorporated in the predictions of private-sector forecasting firms and Federal Reserve staff.

A fundamental problem with tests of supervisory accuracy is that accuracy in predicting future performance may not be the primary goal of supervisors. Supervisors may be more concerned with accurately describing the *current* condition of a BHC in order to exert pressure on institutions to resolve problems, and be less concerned with predicting future condition. Supervisors may be very accurate in assessing current condition while appearing to be very inaccurate at predicting future condition, particularly if supervisors are successful at pressuring institutions to resolve problems. For example, a CAMEL downgrade or an increase in classified assets may encourage an institution to stop making risky loans, eventually reducing its nonperforming loan ratio. The finding in Cole and Gunther (1998) and Berger, Davies, and Flannery (2000) that supervisors may be more accurate than market participants in predicting short-run future performance and less accurate than market participants in predicting long-run future performance is consistent with this argument, because any change in problem loans caused by supervisory pressure is likely to take several quarters to appear in full in the data. Because of these difficulties, we do not try to determine whether any increase or decrease in supervisory toughness in the data represents a change in accuracy.

9.5   Methodology and Data

9.5.1   Tests of Changes in Supervisory Harshness (Hypotheses 1 and 2)

To test for changes in supervisory toughness, we model two types of supervisory assessments—classified assets and composite CAMEL ratings—as functions of measures of bank financial condition and other factors representing the economic environment of the bank. The econometric models mimic as closely as possible the information used in the supervisory process at the time of the supervisory assessments. Of course, it is not possible to include all of the information available to supervisors at the time they set the classified assets and CAMEL ratings, but we address this issue as well as we can by (a) including the key balance sheet and income variables specified in the supervisory procedures in their level, trend, and peer group percentile ranks, as discussed earlier; (b) including a large number of other control variables for bank condition and economic environment; (c) bracketing the information set used by supervisors by running the models with and without information on the future performance of the bank, which is more information than the supervisors could have access to at the time of the supervisory assessments; and (d) running large numbers of robustness checks on the models.

The classified assets model takes the form

$$\ln[\text{class}/(1 - \text{class})] = f[\text{time dummies, lagged supervisory assessments,}$$

$$\text{supervisory agency dummies, bank size, bank}$$
$$\text{balance sheet and income items, state averages}$$
$$\text{of balance sheet and income items, other}$$
$$\text{economic environment indicators,}$$
$$\text{(future performance)}].$$

These variables are shown in table 9.7. There are between 190 and 199 coefficients estimated in each classified assets equations, depending on whether the future performance variables (described later) are included.

The dependent variable is in log-odds form, the natural log of the proportion of loans that are classified divided by one minus this proportion. The equation may be interpreted as a log-odds grouped logit model for the probability that a dollar of loans will be classified. It is estimated by weighted least squares in order to avoid heteroscedasticity problems and the adjusted R^2s are corrected.[7] As is shown in table 9.7, we specify models for both total classified assets and weighted classified assets.

The time dummies are also specified in different ways to ensure robustness of the results. In some equations, we include dummies for each

---

7. Each observation is divided by a number proportional to the estimated standard error of its error term $[\{(1/\text{class}) + [1/(1-\text{class})]\}/\text{total loans}]^{1/2}$.

Table 9.7

Variable Definitions and Sample Statistics for Supervisory Assessment Regressions

Name	Definition	Mean	Std. Dev.
Supervisory Assessments of Bank Condition			
Total classified assets	Proportion of loans classified as substandard, doubtful, or loss.	.060	.065
Weighted classified assets	Weighted proportion of loans classified, weights of .2 on substandard, .5 on doubtful, and 1 on loss.	.015	.020
CAMEL 1	Dummy variable equal to 1 if CAMEL rating is 1.	.275	.447
CAMEL 2	Dummy variable equal to 1 if CAMEL rating is 2.	.521	.500
CAMEL 3	Dummy variable equal to 1 if CAMEL rating is 3.	.128	.334
CAMEL 4 or 5	Dummy variable equal to 1 if CAMEL rating is 4 or 5 (combined because there were so few 5s).	.075	.264
CAMEL satisfactory	Dummy variable equal to 1 if CAMEL rating is 1 or 2.	.797	.403
CAMEL unsatisfactory	Dummy variable equal to 1 if CAMEL rating is 3, 4, or 5.	.203	.143
Time dummies			
1986–88	Precrunch period. This is excluded as the base period in the main regressions.	.216	.412
1989–92	Credit crunch period.	.370	.483
1993–98	Banking boom period.	.414	.493
Individual year dummies	Included in some regressions.		
Lagged Supervisory Assessments			
Lagged total classified assets, weighted classified assets, CAMEL 1, CAMEL 2, CAMEL 3	Lagged values of supervisory assessments for banks with prior examination data, set to zero otherwise (see no lagged examination data variable).		
Time since last recorded examination	Years since last recorded examination, set to zero if no prior data (see no lagged examination data variable).	.994	.701
No lagged examination data	Dummy variable equal to 1 if no lagged examination data are available.	.106	.308
Supervisory Agency			
OCC	Dummy variable equal to 1 if the OCC was the lead agency in the exam.	.248	.432
FDIC	Dummy variable equal to 1 if the FDIC was the lead agency in the exam.	.366	.482
FRB	Dummy variable equal to 1 if the FRB was the lead agency in the exam.	.078	.268

Table 9.7   (continued)

Name	Definition	Mean	Std. Dev.
STATE	Dummy variable equal to 1 if state agency or other federal agency. This is excluded as the base case.	.308	.461
Bank Size variables			
ln(GTA)	Natural log of gross total assets.	11.039	1.221
SIZE1	Dummy variable equal to 1 if GTA ≤ $100 million (excluded from regressions as base case).	.723	.448
SIZE 2	Dummy variable equal to 1 if $100 million < GTA ≤ $1 billion.	.245	.430
SIZE 3	Dummy variable equal to 1 if $1 billion < GTA ≤ $10 billion.	.028	.164
SIZE 4	Dummy variable equal to 1 if $10 billion < GTA.	.004	.065
Bank Balance Sheet and Income Items			
	Total capital ratio, Tier 1 capital ratio, leverage capital ratio, real estate loans/total loans, nonperforming loans/total loans, off-balance sheet items/total loans, other real estate owned/ total loans, return on assets, and volatile liability dependence. All are lagged and all are included as level, trend, and peer group percentile rank.		
State Averages of Balance Sheet and Income Items			
	State averages of the same variables as the bank balance sheet and income items. These variables are also lagged and all are included as level, trend, and peer group percentile rank.		
Other Economic Environment Indicators			
	Regional dummies, state income growth, and state unemployment rate.		
Future Performance			
Future nonperforming loans	Leads of 1, 2, and 3 years included in regressions. Mean for lead 1 shown.	.038	.036
Future charge-offs	Leads of 1, 2, and 3 years included in regressions. Mean for lead 1 shown.	.005	.035
Future total capital ratio	Leads of 1, 2, and 3 years included in regressions. Mean for lead 1 shown.	.169	.078

of our three main time periods: precrunch (1986–88), credit crunch (1989–92), and boom (1993–98). In other equations, we specify dummies for each individual year to allow the data more freedom to "choose for themselves" when changes in supervisory toughness occurred. We use the coefficients of the time dummies to establish the changes in supervisory toughness. That is, after controlling as well as we can for the supervisors' information in the rest of the equation, we test the coefficients of these dummies to see if classified assets tend to be higher in the credit crunch period as predicted by hypothesis 1, and lower during the boom period, as predicted by hypothesis 2.

We also include lagged supervisory assessments to account for stickiness in assessments or additional information inherent in past assessments. We include the lagged total classified assets ratio in the total classified assets regressions and the lagged weighted classified assets ratio in the weighted classified assets equation. In both models we include lagged dummy variables for the last previously recorded composite CAMEL rating (lagged CAMEL 4 or 5 is excluded as the base case). The time since last recorded examination may help predict supervisory outcomes because problem banks are typically examined more frequently, although a shorter lag may also predict less change in condition, because there is less time for changes in condition to occur. Importantly, we also include data for banks without previous examination records to avoid sample selection problems as discussed earlier. For these observations, we set the dummy for "No lagged examination data" to 1 and set the values of the other lagged supervisory assessment variables to zero. In effect, we account for the average difference of these banks from other banks.

We also include supervisory agency dummies to account for the possibility of systematic differences in supervisory standards across government agencies. They may also reflect systematic differences in the quality of banks with different charter types or Federal Reserve membership for which we do not otherwise adequately control.

The bank size variables include a continuous measure of bank assets, as well as dummies for different size classes. These control for many differences between large and small banks that may not be otherwise controlled for in the model, including the degree of industrial and geographic diversification in the loan portfolio, risks from off-balance sheet or international exposures, and any systematic differences in supervisory treatment.

The bank balance sheet and income items are the levels, trends, and peer group percentile ranks of the nine key balance sheet and income variables specified in the UBPR and taken from the appropriate Call Report quarter. These are the total capital ratio, Tier 1 capital ratio, leverage capital ratio, real estate loans/total loans, nonperforming loans/total loans, off-balance sheet items/total loans, other real estate owned/total loans, return on assets, and volatile liability dependence. All of these variables are specified in both first- and second-order terms and interactions, so that each actually appears nine times in the regressor list to allow for a very flexible functional form. That is, for $i = 1, \ldots, 9$, we specify x_{it}, $(x_{it} - x_{it-1})$, $xrank_{it}$, $(x_{it})^2$, $(x_{it} - x_{it-1})^2$, $(xrank_{it})^2$, $x_{it} \times (x_{it} - x_{it-1})$, $x_{it} \times xrank_{it}$, and $(x_{it} - x_{it-1}) \times xrank_{it}$, where x_{it} represents the current value of the variable computed from the Call Report; $(x_{it} - x_{it-1})$ is the trend; and $xrank_{it}$ is the current peer group percentile rank, for a total of eighty-one variables specified (means, standard deviations, and coefficients not shown in tables).

We also include a number of controls for the economic environment of the bank. The state averages of balance sheet and income items are the same eighty-one variables as are specified for the bank itself, except that they are state averages to help control for the economic environment of the bank (data not shown in tables). Other economic environment indicators include regional dummies for the Federal Reserve District (which may capture systematic differences in regional economic conditions or supervisory treatment) as well as state income growth and unemployment rate. Although the local economic environment is not explicitly specified in the examination procedures, it is nonetheless important to control for the environment to account for exogenous changes in bank condition that may be reflected in supervisory assessments. For example, supervisors may be more likely to find problems in the loan portfolio and assign more classified assets and a worse CAMEL rating for a bank in a state with low income growth, a high unemployment rate, and poor state-average bank balance sheet and income items, even after taking into account the bank's own balance sheet and income items. To the extent that there are changes in the macroeconomic or regional environment that affect all banks in the nation or region, these effects may be mostly captured by these state-level variables, because banks were generally legally restricted to have full-service banking offices only in their home state for almost all of our sample.[8] That is, conditions outside the home state are likely to be much less important than those in the state.

Finally, we alternately exclude and include the future performance variables, which are leads of one, two, and three years of nonperforming loans, charge-offs, and the total risk-based capital ratio. As noted earlier, it is not possible to include all of the information available to supervisors at the time of the supervisory assessments, although the variables reviewed thus

---

8. Interstate bank branching was essentially prohibited prior to the implementation of the Riegle-Neal Banking and Branching Efficiency Act in 1997. BHCs were permitted to own banks in different states prior to this time, but our data are on the individual banks, not their holding companies.

far represent our best attempt. One of the ways we attack this problem is to include these future values of nonperforming loans, charge-offs, and capital, which capture more information than the supervisors could have had access to at the time of the assessments and represent fairly well the future condition of the bank that supervisors are interested in predicting or altering. In effect, we try to bracket the information set used by supervisors by running the models alternately with less information and with more information than supervisors have. If the same qualitative result for changes in supervisory toughness holds when we specify both less and more information than supervisors have, then we will feel more confident in drawing conclusions about what occurred with their actual (unobserved) information set. We recognize that the future performance variables are endogenous, that their coefficients are unreliable, and that the model is underidentified with their inclusion; but our purpose is to check the robustness of the main model, which excludes these variables, rather than to rely on equations with the endogenous variables. Fortunately, the results are robust to the inclusion or exclusion of the future performance variables, supporting our interpretation of the time dummies as reflecting changes in supervisory toughness, rather than important excluded variables.

We also run the classified asset model (as well as the CAMEL model below) using a Heckman correction to deal with potential sample selection problems. We first run a probit equation for the probability that a bank has an exam in a given year, and then include the resulting inverse Mills ratio as a regressor in the equations for the classified asset ratios and CAMEL ratings. We specify a separate probit model for each year to take account of the apparent significant changes over time in the probability of an examination. The variables in these models include the same past values of key balance sheet and income variables, past supervisory ratings, and so on, which should affect the decision to examine a bank, just as they affect the supervisory rating on a bank. This creates a problem of identification for the Heckman correction, because we have no variables in the first stage for the probability of an examination that are not also in the second stage for the supervisory assessments at the examinations. Because we do not have any "true" exclusion restrictions, our sample selection correction is identified by (a) the fact that we run separate probit equations for each year, letting all the coefficients vary to take account of changes over time in the probability of an examination, and (b) the nonlinearity inherent in the inverse Mills ratio. The use of the same underlying variables cannot be helped, because all of the variables that supervisors use in off-site monitoring in selecting banks to be examined are also used in their determination of the supervisory assessments at the end of the examination. Fortunately, our main results regarding hypotheses 1 and 2 are robust to including or excluding the Heckman correction.

The model for the composite CAMEL ratings is very similar and takes the form

Probability(CAMEL) = g[time dummies, lagged supervisory
    assessments, supervisory agency dummies,
    bank size, bank balance sheet and income items,
    state averages of balance sheet and income items,
    economic environment indicators,
    (classified assets), (future performance)].

This equation is specified as an ordered logit of the choice among composite CAMEL 1, 2, 3, and (4 or 5). As is indicated in table 9.7, CAMEL 5 is grouped with CAMEL 4 because CAMEL 5 is so rare.[9]

The regressors specified are identical to those in the classified assets model with one exception. We run the CAMEL model three ways: with current total classified assets included as a regressor, with current weighted classified assets included, and with no current classified assets included. The purposes are to allow the data to describe different types of changes in supervisory toughness and to check robustness of the results. One way that changes in supervisory toughness may affect CAMEL ratings is that supervisors may simply assign a higher or lower composite CAMEL grade after an on-site examination for a given evaluation of the loan portfolio, which may be described by the model with current classified assets specified in total or weighted form. That is, supervisors may take as given the set of classifications for the loan portfolio and assign a harsher or laxer rating. Alternatively, supervisors may assign a harsher or laxer CAMEL rating as part of the same process in which loans are classified more or less harshly. In this case, the specification with no current classified assets specified is correct. Fortunately, the results are robust to the inclusion or exclusion of the current classified assets variables as regressors.

9.5.2   Tests of Changes in Supervisory Toughness on Bank Lending Behavior (Hypothesis 3)

To test for the effects of changes in supervisory toughness on bank lending behavior, we model changes in bank lending and other measures of performance as functions of three years of past changes in supervisory assessments and include control variables for three years of other past changes in bank condition and economic environment. Three years of

---

9. As a robustness check, we try running the model with the management (M) component of the CAMEL rating in place of the composite rating, because the supervisors have a significant amount of discretion in assigning a management rating, with results very similar to those for the composite CAMEL. We also rerun the composite CAMEL model as a binomial logit for the probability of a satisfactory rating (1 or 2) versus an unsatisfactory rating (3, 4, or 5).

lagged changes are included because it may take a considerable amount of time for a bank to change the composition of its loan portfolio.

Our model for change in performance takes the form:

Δperformance = h[time dummies, Δsupervisory assessments (3 years of lags), Δbank balance sheet and income items (3 years of lags), Δstate averages of balance sheet and income items (3 years of lags), Δstate averages of supervisory assessments (3 years of lags), Δother economic environment indicators (3 years of lags)].

The Δperformance variables include two types of variables: (a) direct measures of the changes in lending behavior and (b) measures of changes in bank risk. The direct measures of changes in lending behavior are the one-year changes in the ratios of C&I loans, real estate loans, installment loans, and U.S. Treasuries to gross total assets (e.g., $C\&I_t/GTA_t - C\&I_{t-1}/GTA_{t-1}$) as well as the proportional change in gross total assets ($[GTA_t - GTA_{t-1}]/GTA_{t-1}$). We test whether CAMEL downgrades and increases in classified assets predict reductions in lending and assets and increases in Treasuries, and vice versa for CAMEL upgrades and decreases in classified assets.

The measures of changes in bank risk included as Δperformance dependent variables are the ratios of nonperforming loans and charge-offs to gross total assets and the total capital ratio (essentially, changes in the same variables alternately included and excluded in the supervisory assessment regressions above). The predicted signs on supervisory toughness in these regressions could go either way, depending on the extent to which a supervisory downgrade encourages banks to reduce risks versus the extent to which it accurately predicts declining future performance. This tension between supervisory assessments as intended to change behavior versus to predict outcomes is difficult to disentangle, as was indicated in the literature review. The results of these regressions should yield some interesting information on the net effect of these opposing forces, but we do not view the results of the changes in bank risk regressions as clean tests of hypothesis 3, that supervisory changes alter bank lending behavior.

The regressors included in the Δperformance model differ in a number of ways from those in the supervisory assessment equations. For the time dummies, we include the year dummies, rather than the period dummies, to allow maximum flexibility, because these variables are not the main focus of attention here. Data for the year 1986 are dropped, and the dummy for 1987 is the base case, because the data did not go back far enough to cover the lags needed for 1986. The remaining variables are measured as three years of lagged changes to allow time for the bank to adjust its portfolio in reaction to the changes in supervisory assessments and other changes in bank condition and environment. As additional variables, we include state averages of changes in classified assets and CAMEL ratings. We exclude peer group percentile ranks of the balance sheet and income items because these variables should primarily influence supervisors, rather than bank managers.

In the specification of the Δsupervisory assessments variables, we specify three lags of dummies for CAMEL upgrades and downgrades, leaving "no change" as the base case. This allows for an asymmetric response of banks to upgrades and downgrades. We show the results with three lags of changes in total classified assets, but the results were robust to alternately using weighted classified assets. Classified assets are measured here as proportions of assets, rather than as proportions of loans as in the supervisory regressions, in order to form a better indicator of the supervisory pressure on banks to change their behavior.

9.6   Empirical Results

9.6.1   Results of Tests of Changes in Supervisory Harshness (Hypotheses 1 and 2)

Table 9.8 presents the weighted least squares regression equations for classified asset ratios and ordered logit regressions for the composite CAMEL rating. These models include dummies for the main time periods, the credit crunch (1989–92), and boom (1993–98) periods, with the pre-crunch (1986–88) period excluded as the base case. Other models that include dummies for each individual year yield similar results but are not shown in the tables. We also do not show the coefficients for most of the control variables to save space. As indicated previously, there are nearly 200 coefficients estimated in each supervisory equation. The two asterisks indicate statistical significance at the 5 percent level, two-sided.

To test hypothesis 1, that supervisors got tougher on banks during the credit crunch period, we test the coefficients of the time dummies to see if classified assets tend to be higher and composite CAMEL ratings tend to be worse in the credit crunch period than in the precrunch period after controlling as well as we can for the supervisors' information in the equations. The coefficients of the credit crunch dummy (1989–92) in the total classified assets equations in table 9.8 are positive, but small and statistically insignificant. For the weighted classified assets equations, the coefficients of the credit crunch dummy are larger and statistically significant. These findings hold whether or not the future performance variables (leads of one, two, and three years of nonperforming loans, charge-offs, and total capital) are included in the estimation (observations from the final three years of the sample are dropped when the future performance variables are included).

Table 9.8   Regressions of Supervisory Assessments with Period Dummies

	Total Classified Assets				Weighted Classified Assets				CAMEL			
	Estimate	Std. Error	Estimate	Std. Error	Estimate	Std. Error	Estimate	Std. Error	Estimate	Std. Error	Estimate	Std. Error
1989–92	0.005211	0.017926	0.01003	0.018817	0.046267**	0.018059	0.057193**	0.018726	−0.3355**	0.0418	−0.1979**	0.0489
1993–98	−0.16131**	0.030755	−0.13853**	0.033097	−0.15451**	0.030464	−0.11518**	0.032515	−0.1695**	0.0719	−0.1268	0.0863
Lagged classified assets	10.29125**	0.112903	8.977898**	0.12419	25.51462**	0.400763	21.73203**	0.435849	10.9414**	0.3002	10.4541**	0.3654
Lag CAMEL 1	0.47908**	0.028467	0.42174**	0.03119	0.103299**	0.029719	0.084658**	0.032084	6.2138**	0.0674	6.1182**	0.0823
Lag CAMEL 2	0.699025**	0.026069	0.60777**	0.02823	0.405948**	0.027581	0.339049**	0.029372	3.6971**	0.0609	3.6969**	0.0731
Lag CAMEL 3	0.543288**	0.023706	0.464806**	0.025212	0.385124**	0.025478	0.334712**	0.026676	1.9102**	0.052	1.9106**	0.0618
Years since last exam	−0.16398**	0.005336	−0.09785**	0.007547	−0.1304**	0.00555	−0.06696**	0.007341	0.018	0.0143	−0.00672	0.0192
No prior exam	0.744434**	0.031395	0.806143**	0.034212	0.283331**	0.032533	0.359236**	0.034756	4.4846**	0.0766	4.5068**	0.0919
OCC	0.159995**	0.010574	0.168187**	0.013095	0.151008**	0.010116	0.154065**	0.012467	−0.2793**	0.0242	−0.3743**	0.0318
FDIC	0.11576**	0.007679	0.14295**	0.008797	0.115969**	0.007836	0.15533**	0.008961	−0.3258**	0.0208	−0.3874**	0.0259
FRB	−0.00341	0.014849	0.008097	0.016897	0.024116	0.01436	0.024877	0.016248	−0.1479**	0.0347	−0.1559**	0.0431
Total classified assets									−82.938**	0.6564	−85.358**	0.8218
NPF, $t + 1$	2.797067**	0.194073					3.352305**	0.214042			−0.00768	0.9653
NPF, $t + 2$	0.559802**	0.201674					0.965655**	0.217772			−1.4128	0.9934
NPF, $t + 3$	0.549363**	0.173385					−0.27295	0.188366			−4.2268**	0.8816

	(1)	(2)	(3)	(4)	(5)	(6)
Charge-offs, t + 1	1.293406**	0.192597	1.68188**	0.224471	−20.087**	1.9758
Charge-offs, t + 2	2.142689**	0.335742	2.430947**	0.397049	−0.4434	2.0324
Charge-offs, t + 3	0.611406**	0.21981	−0.00928	0.184508	3.9199	2.1816
Total capital, t + 1	0.454978**	0.116291	0.126771	0.148643	2.1243**	0.4814
Total capital, t + 2	0.576912**	0.123038	0.917427**	0.157945	−1.2946**	0.4949
Total capital, t + 3	−0.04714	0.095274	−0.36475	0.118142	−0.2707	0.3772
Adjusted R^2	0.5202	0.5027	0.5312	0.5182		
No. of observations	107,395	107,395	67,425	67,425	107,396	67,426
−2 log-likelihood					101,354.96	64,756.72

Notes: All of these regressions also include the following variables from the bank's Call Report: total capital ratio, Tier 1 capital ratio, leverage capital ratio, real estate loans/total loans, nonperforming loans/total loans, off-balance sheet items/total loans, other real estate owned/total loans, return on assets, and volatile liability dependence. All are lagged and all are included as level, trend, and peer group percentile rank. State averages of all of these items (lagged levels, trends, and peer group percentile ranks). State income growth and the state unemployment rate are also included in all regressions.

**Significant at the 5 percent level, two-sided.

To evaluate whether these results are *economically* significant, we evaluate the contributions of the credit crunch dummy to the probability that a dollar of loans is classified. The dependent variable is in log-odds logistic form [ln(class/(1 − class))], and may be interpreted as a probability model, as discussed earlier. Because the equation is nonlinear, the measured effect will depend on the point of evaluation. We choose the means of total and weighted classified asset proportions during the credit crunch as the most relevant points of evaluation, .072 and .018, respectively (see table 9.4, Panel B). Increasing the dependent variable of the total classified assets equation by .005211 (the coefficient on the credit crunch dummy) increases the predicted proportion of classified loans from 7.2 percent to 7.235 percent, an economically small effect.[10] Similarly, increasing the dependent variable of the weighted classified assets equation by .046267 increases the predicted weighted classified proportion from 1.8 percent to 1.884 percent, which is larger, but would still appear to be a small economic influence. Thus, the data suggest at most a relatively modest effect of examiners getting tougher during the credit crunch period in terms of requiring that banks of a given condition classify more loans or shift loans into more serious classifications. The economic significance results are consistent with on the order of magnitude of about 1 percent or less of the loan portfolio being additionally classified or classified more seriously.

We turn next to the measured effects on the composite CAMEL rating. The negative, statistically significant coefficients on the dummy for the period of 1989–92 indicate that the probability of receiving a favorable CAMEL rating is lower than during the precrunch period, all else held equal. Again, the effects are comparable, whether or not the future performance variables are included. The models shown in table 9.8 control for the current level of total classified assets, but the results are robust with respect to using current weighted classified assets or to excluding current classified assets altogether.

To evaluate the economic significance of the CAMEL results, we compare the predicted values of CAMEL 1, CAMEL 2, CAMEL 3, and CAMEL 4 or 5 with and without the coefficient of the credit crunch dummy variable. That is, we evaluate the predicted CAMEL ratings as if the coefficients reflect the precrunch supervisory regime versus the credit crunch supervisory regime. The point of evaluation is the median of all the variables for the credit crunch period except that the dummy variables are set to one or zero. We assume that the lagged CAMEL rating is a 2 (the modal rating), the region is 1 (New England), the size class is 1 (assets below $100 million), and that the bank was examined by a state supervisory agency. The predicted percentages of CAMEL 1, CAMEL 2,

---

10. Letting P_1 be the new probability of a dollar of loans being classified, the formula for the figure in the text is given by $\ln[P_1/(1 − P_1)] = \ln[.072/(1 − .072)] + .005211$.

CAMEL 3, and CAMEL 4 or 5 are 9.37 percent, 88.91 percent, 1.70 percent, and 0.001 percent, respectively, without the credit crunch dummy coefficient, and 6.89 percent, 90.74 percent, 2.36 percent, and 0.002 percent, respectively, with the credit crunch dummy coefficient. These results suggest that CAMEL ratings are relatively "sticky": Banks rated as CAMEL 2 in the prior examination are about 90 percent likely to receive a 2 during the next examination. These results are consistent with only a modest increase in supervisory harshness during the credit crunch period, worsening the CAMEL ratings for about 3 percent of banks.[11]

To test hypothesis 2, that supervisors got easier on banks during the boom period, we use the same models and test the coefficients of the time dummies to see if classified assets tend to be lower and CAMEL ratings tend to be more favorable in the boom period for a given bank condition and economic environment. The coefficients of the boom period dummy (1993–98) in the classified assets equations in table 9.8 are negative, larger in absolute value than the credit crunch period dummies, and statistically significant in all four cases, consistent with a reduction in supervisory toughness during the boom period. These results are robust to the specification of total or weighted classified assets and to whether or not the future performance variables are included.

To assess the economic significance of the classified asset results for the boom period, we evaluate the contribution to the probability that dollar of loans is classified of the boom period dummy minus the credit crunch dummy, which measures the change between these two periods. We evaluate at the mean proportions of total and weighted classified assets during the boom period, .039 and .009, respectively (see table 9.4). Changing the dependent variable of the total classified assets equation by $(-.16131 - .005211$; the boom period dummy coefficient minus the credit crunch dummy coefficient) reduces the predicted proportion of classified loans from 3.9 percent to 3.322 percent. Similarly, the predicted weighted classified proportion is reduced from 0.9 percent to 0.737 percent. These figures are not economically significant in terms of the reduction in the proportion of loans that are predicted to be classified or receive less serious classifications, on the order of magnitude of 1 percent of loans in both cases. Thus, the data are consistent with very modest reductions in supervisory toughness during the boom period in terms of classified assets.

---

11. We also rerun the CAMEL model as a binomial logit for the probability of a satisfactory rating (1 or 2) versus an unsatisfactory rating (3, 4, or 5; not shown in tables). The results again show a statistically significant effect of the credit crunch dummy variable. The results were also more economically significant than the full model; the data suggest that for a given bank condition at the mean of the data set, the probability of a satisfactory rating decreased about 9 percentage points (from 74.2 to 65.0 percent). The difference from our main result may be due in part to the sparser specification of the satisfactory versus unsatisfactory rating, and in part to the different point of evaluation.

Turning to the potential effects of changes in supervisory toughness on CAMEL ratings during the boom period, we note that the coefficients of the boom period dummy (1993–98) in the CAMEL models are both negative, and the coefficient for the main equation (without the future performance variables) is statistically significant. This suggests that the CAMEL ratings were harsher for a given bank condition in the boom period than in the precrunch period, contrary to the classified assets results. More important for investigating hypothesis 2, however, is that the boom period dummies are less in absolute value than the coefficients of the credit crunch period dummies, so they represent easier ratings for a given condition than during the credit crunch period.

To evaluate economic significance, we again compare the predicted values of the CAMEL probabilities. We evaluate the predicted probabilities with the coefficient of the boom period dummy in place of the credit crunch period dummy, evaluated at the median of the variables for the boom period (as well as lagged CAMEL rating 2, region 1, size class 1, and state agency examination). The predicted percentages of CAMEL 1, CAMEL 2, CAMEL 3, and CAMEL 4 or 5 are 21.98 percent, 77.39 percent, 0.63 percent, and 0.004 percent, respectively, with the credit crunch dummy coefficient specified, and 24.96 percent, 74.50 percent, 0.54 percent, and 0.004 percent, respectively, with the boom period dummy coefficient. These data suggest that bank conditions and economic environments were so strong during the boom period that even banks with lagged CAMEL 2 ratings were predicted to have over a 20 percent probability of rising to a CAMEL 1 rating without any change in supervisory toughness. The effects of any change in supervisory toughness are again rather mild, consistent with supervisory easing resulting in improved CAMEL ratings of about an additional 3 percent of banks receiving better CAMEL ratings. The use of the binomial logit model for the probability of a satisfactory versus unsatisfactory rating also showed very little effect in this case, moving the predicted probability of a satisfactory CAMEL rating during the boom period up by less than 1 percentage point (from 92.1 percent to 93.0 percent).

Overall, the classified assets and CAMEL models are modestly consistent with hypotheses 1 and 2. They generally show statistically significant results in the predicted directions but usually show only fairly small results from an economic viewpoint. In most cases, the findings are consistent with no more than about 1 percent of additional loans becoming classified or put into more serious classifications during the credit crunch period and similarly for the reduction in classifications during the boom period, for a given bank condition and economic environment. Similarly, the data are consistent with movements of CAMEL ratings for about 3 percent of banks in the predicted directions as a result of any changes in supervisory toughness, which is small compared with the effects of stickiness in ratings during the credit crunch period and the trend toward improved ratings from economic conditions during the boom period. These findings are generally confirmed by a number of robustness checks not shown in the tables, including our Heckman correction for sample selection problems.[12]

We briefly discuss the other coefficients shown in table 9.8, but note again that many of the coefficients are not shown. In the classified assets equations, the coefficients of lagged classified assets are positive and statistically significant, consistent with the expectation that a prior problem loan portfolio would predict a current problem loan portfolio, because it takes a considerable amount of time to dispose of problem assets. The coefficients of the lagged CAMEL 1, CAMEL 2, and CAMEL 3 are positive and statistically significant in the classified assets equations. This suggests that a past rating of CAMEL 4 or 5—the base case in the regressions—has a positive effect in encouraging banks to improve their loan portfolios and reduce classified assets relative to their lagged levels. In the CAMEL equations, the positive and statistically significant lagged CAMEL coefficients are consistent with CAMEL stickiness—the higher the past rating, the higher the predicted current rating. As expected, the level of current classified assets has statistically significant negative coefficients in the CAMEL equations, consistent with banks with poor loan portfolios receiving poor CAMEL ratings. However, the lagged classified assets variable has a positive coefficient. Given that the current level of classified assets is in the same equation, this may be interpreted as reward (punishment) for improvement (deterioration) in classified assets since the prior examination. The variable for years since a prior examination has negative coefficients in the classified assets equations, consistent with banks that have problem portfolios being examined more often, although this does not appear to affect the CAMEL rating. The coefficients of the supervisory agency dummies—OCC, FDIC, and FRB—suggest that banks examined by the OCC and FDIC received worse supervisory assessments (higher classified assets, worse CAMEL ratings) than those examined by the Federal Reserve and state agencies (the base case), all else equal. This may reflect differences in supervisory standards or differences in the quality distributions of banks with different supervisors. Finally, the coefficients of the future performance variables generally suggest that banks that are assigned worse supervisory ratings (high classified assets or poor CAMEL ratings) will have higher nonperforming loans and charge-offs in the future, but may also raise their capital ratios. As noted pre-

---

12. We also tried evaluating economic significance by dropping the time dummies and running the model separately for the precrunch, credit crunch, and boom periods, allowing the coefficients of all the regressors to vary. Although this procedure yielded mostly the same qualitative results—consistent with toughening during the credit crunch period and easing during the boom period—the quantitative results were often too large to be believable. For example, at the boom period medians, the CAMEL models predicted a drop from 73.4 to 2.6 percent in the probability of a CAMEL 3 rating from the credit crunch supervisory regime to the boom period regime. Presumably, these models simply did not work very well out of sample.

viously, these variables are endogenous, so we reserve further judgment until we treat them as endogenous variables later.

9.6.2   Results of Tests of Changes in Supervisory Toughness on Bank Lending Behavior (Hypothesis 3)

Table 9.9 presents results from regressions aimed at addressing hypothesis 3, the effect of changes in supervisory toughness on direct measures of bank lending behavior. We regress changes in bank lending on three years of past changes in supervisory assessments and changes in bank condition and economic environment. The main predictions of the hypothesis are that a supervisory downgrade (worsened CAMEL rank, higher classified assets) should result in smaller proportions of assets being devoted to loans, a reduction in asset growth, and a larger proportion of assets being devoted to government securities, and vice versa for supervisory upgrades.

Our regressions appear to explain very little of what drives changes in lending behavior. The adjusted R^2s for the equations in table 9.9 are generally less than 5 percent. Nonetheless, a number of the changes in supervisory assessments are statistically significant. The changes in classified assets all have signs that are consistent with the hypothesis for all lag lengths, and all but one of these coefficients are statistically significant at the 5 percent level. That is, an increase in classified assets is associated with decreases in the future C&I loan ratio, real estate loan ratio, installment loan ratio, and asset growth ratio, and with an increase in the future Treasury holdings ratio. These results are also replicated when changes in weighted classified assets are specified in place of total classified assets (not shown). In addition, we tried rerunning the loan and Treasury ratios with different denominators to ensure that the results were not just driven by changes in asset denominator. We specified $(C\&I_t - C\&I_{t-1})/GTA_{t-1}$ and $(C\&I_t - C\&I_{t-1})/C\&I_{t-1}$ in place of $C\&I_t/GTA_t - C\&I_{t-1}/GTA_{t-1}$, and so forth for the other lending and Treasury ratios, and the results were robust.

To determine if the classified assets results are economically significant, we simply sum the coefficients on the three lags of the change in classified assets. Because the equations are linear, this gives the long-run effect of a change in classified assets (i.e., the sum of the effects of changes one, two, and three years hence). The results suggest that the economic impact of changes in classified assets appears to be rather small. An increase in classified assets of 1 percent of assets is predicted to reduce the C&I loan ratio, real estate loan ratio, installment loan ratio, and asset growth ratio by 0.08 percent, 0.14 percent, 0.11 percent, and 0.72 percent, respectively, and to increase the Treasury ratio by 0.08 percent.

The effects of CAMEL upgrades and downgrades on lending are not very consistent. They sometimes predict changes in lending in the opposite direction of what is expected, and the upgrades and downgrades

Table 9.9 **Regressions of Changes in Lending and Assets on Lagged Changes in Supervisory Assessments and Other Variables**

	ΔC&I Loans		ΔReal Estate Loans		ΔInstallment Loans		ΔU.S. Treasuries		ΔGross Total Assets	
	Estimate	Std. Error	Estimate	Std. Error	Estimate	Std. Error	Estimate	Std. Error	Estimate	Std. Error
1988	−0.0015	0.00114	0.002607	0.001653	0.002231**	0.001008	0.012822**	0.001729	−0.09668**	0.014974
1989	−0.00293**	0.000906	0.003247**	0.001313	0.002629**	0.000801	0.01308**	0.001374	−0.08817**	0.011897
1990	−0.00249**	0.000978	0.001078	0.001418	0.002106**	0.000865	0.021528**	0.001484	−0.07921**	0.012847
1991	−0.00547**	0.000868	0.002569**	0.001257	−0.00152**	0.000767	0.023579**	0.001316	−0.08796**	0.011391
1992	−0.00351**	0.000899	0.00462**	0.001302	−0.0242**	0.000795	0.027741**	0.001363	−0.06352**	0.011802
1993	−0.00224**	0.000932	0.004634**	0.001351	0.000208	0.000824	0.023088**	0.001413	−0.071**	0.012238
1994	−0.00119	0.000897	0.003448**	0.0013	0.00389**	0.000793	0.026555**	0.00136	−0.0726**	0.011779
1995	0.002087**	0.000916	0.002035	0.001327	0.004961**	0.00081	0.011197**	0.001389	−0.06194**	0.012027
1996	0.001892**	0.000878	0.002887**	0.001273	0.003276**	0.000777	0.01199**	0.001332	−0.05113**	0.011532
1997	0.002663**	0.000926	0.011934**	0.001342	0.00199**	0.000819	0.000216	0.001404	0.017994	0.012157
1998	0.002332**	0.000816	0.01318**	0.001182	0.00018	0.000721	−0.00477**	0.001237	0.070603**	0.010709
CAMEL upgrade, $t − 1$	−0.00437**	0.000354	−0.00178**	0.000514	−0.00347**	0.000313	0.002534**	0.000537	−0.00173	0.004653
CAMEL upgrade, $t − 2$	−0.00057	0.000363	−0.00346**	0.000526	−0.00023	0.000321	0.000831	0.00055	−0.01895**	0.004763
CAMEL upgrade, $t − 3$	0.000158	0.000357	−0.00091*	0.000518	0.000357	0.000316	−0.00016	0.000542	−0.00329	0.004692
CAMEL downgrade, $t − 1$	−0.00088**	0.000432	0.010906**	0.000625	0.001593**	0.000382	−0.0027**	0.000654	0.060737**	0.005666
CAMEL downgrade, $t − 2$	−0.00137**	0.000447	−0.00258**	0.000647	0.000706	0.000395	0.003478**	0.000678	−0.03283**	0.005867
CAMEL downgrade, $t − 3$	−0.00137**	0.000444	−0.00147**	0.000644	−0.00046	0.000393	0.002855**	0.000674	−0.0222**	0.005835
Change in total classified assets, $t − 1$	−0.02704**	0.003844	−0.08794**	0.005569	−0.05641**	0.003398	0.037958**	0.005828	−0.39303**	0.00464
Change in total classified assets, $t − 2$	−0.0421**	0.003973	−0.03533**	0.005757	−0.03303**	0.003513	0.028004**	0.006024	−0.14216**	0.052161
Change in total classified assets, $t − 3$	−0.01597**	0.003834	−0.01775**	0.005555	−0.01677**	0.00339	0.009414	0.005813	−0.18002**	0.050334
Adjusted R^2	0.0309		0.0366		0.0202		0.0449		0.0194	0.0309
No. of observations	79,960		79,960		79,960		79,960		79,960	79,960

Notes: All of these regressions also include the following balance sheet variables: total capital ratio, Tier 1 capital ratio, leverage capital ratio, real estate loans/total loans, nonperforming loans/total loans, off-balance sheet items/total loans, other real estate owned/total loans, return on assets, and volatile liability dependence. Three years of lagged changes of the state averages of all of these items as well as three years of lagged changes of state averages of CAMEL and total classified assets, state income growth and the state unemployment rate are also included in all regressions.

**Significant at the 5 percent level, two-sided.

sometimes work in the same direction (i.e., differing in the same way from the excluded case of no change in CAMEL). In most cases, the effects are very small, moving the ratios less than 1 percentage point in the long run for a CAMEL upgrade or downgrade.[13] Thus, the support for hypothesis 3 is mixed and weak. The changes in classified assets are consistent with the hypothesis but are small economically, and the changes in composite CAMEL ratings yield small, inconsistent effects.

Table 9.10 presents the regressions for the effects of changes in supervisory assessments on measures of changes in bank risk—changes in the nonperforming loan, charge-off, and total capital ratios. As discussed earlier, these results combine the effects of supervisory assessments on bank behavior with predictions of how banks choose to adjust their risks. The lagged changes in both classified assets and composite CAMEL ratings generally have statistically significant coefficients that are consistent with each other. A supervisory downgrade of either type is followed by increases in future problem loans, and vice versa for supervisory upgrades. These results suggest a dominance of the predictive ability of the ratings over their effects in persuading banks to change the risk of their loan portfolios. That is, a supervisory downgrade predicts an increase in nonperforming loans and charge-offs that is not fully offset by any changes in bank behavior to reduce their risky lending, likely in part because it takes time to resolve existing problem loans. However, the results are not economically significant; a 1 percent change in classified assets or a CAMEL upgrade or downgrade is predicted to change the nonperforming loan and charge-off ratios by less than 1 percentage point.

The results differ for the change in total capital ratio. The coefficients of the lagged changes in classified assets are statistically significant and predict an increase in future capital, consistent with the possibility that an increase in classified assets encourages banks to increase their capital ratios, more than offsetting the erosion of capital from the change in classification. However, changes in CAMEL ratings appear to have the opposite effect, with downgrades predicting a reduction in capital and upgrades predicting an increase in capital. Once again, all of these changes are economically small.

9.7   Conclusions

We investigate the possibility that overall changes in supervisory toughness may significantly influence bank lending behavior and potentially affect macroeconomic or regional economic health. Specifically, we test three hypotheses about whether U.S. bank supervisors changed their policies

---

13. The one exception of a larger predicted change is that a CAMEL upgrade predicts a decrease of 2.4 percent in the growth rate of assets, which is inconsistent with expectations.

Table 9.10 Regressions of Changes in Performance on Lagged Changes in Supervisory Assessments and Other Variables

	ΔNonperforming Loans		ΔCharge-offs		ΔTotal Capital	
	Estimate	Std. Error	Estimate	Std. Error	Estimate	Std. Error
1988	-0.0008	0.000505	-0.00086**	0.000391	0.011116**	0.001117
1989	-0.00066	0.000401	3.41E-05	0.00031	0.012442**	0.000888
1990	-0.00039	0.000433	-0.00019	0.000335	0.00857**	0.000959
1991	-0.00031	0.000384	0.000207	0.000297	0.013028**	0.00085
1992	-0.0009**	0.000398	0.000461	0.000308	0.016657**	0.000881
1993	-0.00048	0.000412	-4.9E-06	0.000319	0.014444**	0.000913
1994	-0.0004	0.000397	6.26E-05	0.000307	0.010648**	0.000879
1995	4.54E-05	0.000405	0.000406	0.000314	0.009896**	0.000898
1996	-0.00024	0.000389	0.000339	0.000301	0.00954**	0.000861
1997	-0.00027	0.00041	0.000221	0.000317	-0.02143**	0.000907
1998	-0.00072**	0.000361	0.000211	0.000279	0.014723**	0.000799
CAMEL upgrade, $t - 1$	-0.00108**	0.000157	-0.00044**	0.000121	0.006821**	0.000347
CAMEL upgrade, $t - 2$	-0.00062**	0.00016	-0.00036	0.000124	0.001418	0.000355
CAMEL upgrade, $t - 3$	-0.00066**	0.000158	-0.00042	0.000122	4.66E-05	0.00035
CAMEL downgrade, $t - 1$	0.001639**	0.000191	0.001638**	0.000148	-0.00736**	0.000423
CAMEL downgrade, $t - 2$	0.000592**	0.000198	0.000402**	0.000153	-0.00022	0.000438
CAMEL downgrade, $t - 3$	-0.00051**	0.000197	-0.00068**	0.000152	0.001562**	0.000435
Change in total classified assets, $t - 1$	0.083329**	0.0017	0.026872**	0.001317	0.03454**	0.003766
Change in total classified assets, $t - 2$	0.019455**	0.001757	0.011038**	0.001361	0.016247**	0.003892
Change in total classified assets, $t - 3$	-0.00539**	0.001696	-0.00696**	0.001313	0.013343**	0.003756
Adjusted R^2	0.0882		0.0226		0.4184	
No. of observations	79,959		79,960		79,960	

Notes: See table 9.9.

and whether these policy changes affected bank lending behavior during the credit crunch period of 1989–92 and the banking boom period of 1993–98. We test these hypotheses using information on the supervisory process, confidential data on CAMEL ratings and classified assets from bank examinations, and bank balance sheet and income data over the period 1986–98. The data provide some support for all three hypotheses. However, the data also suggest that the economic effects of any policy changes are likely to have been quite small, and likely do not explain a substantial portion of the wide swings in aggregate bank lending to business during the 1990s.

The data provide modest support for hypothesis 1, that there was an increase in toughness during the credit crunch period. During 1989–92, banks of a given measured financial condition and economic environment had statistically significantly worse CAMEL ratings than in the precrunch period of 1986–88, and in some cases also had statistically significantly higher classified assets. Similarly, the data give some support for hypothesis 2, that there was a decline in toughness during the boom period relative to the credit crunch period. During 1993–98, both CAMEL ratings and classified assets are found to be better for a given bank condition than during the credit crunch period.

Despite the statistically significant support for these hypotheses, the data suggest fairly small results in terms of economic significance. The findings are generally consistent with no more than about 1 percent of additional loans becoming classified or put into more serious classifications during the credit crunch period and similarly for the reduction in classifications during the boom period, after controlling for bank condition and economic environment. Similarly, the data are consistent with movements of CAMEL ratings for about 3 percent of banks in the predicted directions as a result of any changes in supervisory toughness. The statistical and economic significance findings are generally confirmed by a number of robustness checks, although some of the checks suggested larger economic significance.

The data provide mixed support for hypothesis 3, that any changes in supervisory toughness affected bank lending in the predicted directions. Increases in classified assets are statistically significantly associated with decreases in the future C&I loan ratio, real estate loan ratio, installment loan ratio, and asset growth ratio, and with an increase in the future Treasury holdings ratio, all consistent with the hypothesis. However, our analysis of economic significance suggests that these effects are rather small, with an increase in classified assets of 1 percent of assets predicted to change these portfolio ratios by less than 1 percentage point each. The changes in CAMEL ratings did not appear to have consistent effects on future lending behavior, although these effects also appeared to be small.

We also tested for the effects of changes in supervisory assessments on other measures of changes in bank risk—changes in the nonperforming loan, charge-off, and total capital ratios. These tests combine the effects of supervisory assessments on bank behavior with predictions of how banks choose to adjust their risks. The findings are statistically significant and suggest that supervisory downgrades in terms of either increases in classified assets or worsened composite CAMEL ranks tend to predict more future nonperforming loans and charge-offs, and vice versa for supervisory upgrades. These findings are consistent with a dominance of the predictive ability of the ratings over their effects in encouraging banks to change the riskiness of their loan portfolios, likely in part because it takes time to resolve existing problem loans. The results differ for the change in total capital ratio: lagged changes in classified assets are statistically significant and predict an increase in future capital, consistent with supervisory discipline that encourages banks to increase their capital ratios, more than offsetting any direct reduction in capital that may occur from classification. However, changes in CAMEL ratings appear to have the opposite effect. As with our tests of the main hypotheses, all of the measured effects of changes in supervisory assessments on bank risk appear to be small, with a 1 percent change in classified assets or a CAMEL upgrade or downgrade predicted to change the risk ratios by less than 1 percentage point.

The findings also suggest that to the extent that regulatory changes like modifications of capital standards are enforced through the supervisory process by assigning worse CAMEL ratings, these regulatory changes may not have much effect on bank lending or portfolio risk, because lending and loan risk do not appear to be influenced substantially through changes in CAMEL ratings. However, these regulatory changes could have strong effects through other channels.

These findings are subject to a number of caveats. First, our results of testing changes in supervisory toughness are subject to bias because we cannot exactly replicate the information set used by supervisors. Part of what we measure as changes in supervisory toughness may be systematic changes in bank conditions or economic environments that supervisors use, but that are not specified in our econometric models. We address this issue in a number of ways, by (a) including the level, trend, and peer percentile rank of the key financial ratios specified in the supervisory procedures, (b) including a large number of other control variables for bank condition and economic environment, (c) bracketing the supervisory information set using data on future performance, and (d) running many other robustness checks. The main findings results are robust to these procedures. We acknowledge that we cannot rule out that omitted-variable bias exists, and we recognize the endogeneity of the measures of future performance to the examination ratings. Ideally, we would include all the information that supervisors have or use a measure of predicted future performance in the absence of the effects of supervisory changes. Nonetheless, we believe that we have gone well beyond prior studies of the credit crunch and other prior studies that used supervisory data in controlling for the information used by supervisors.

Our discussant, Steve Cecchetti, correctly points out that the estimated coefficients of our time dummies—which we interpret as reflecting changes in supervisory toughness in our tests of hypotheses 1 and 2—are highly correlated with macroeconomic series, such as industrial production. This is not surprising, given that the credit crunch period essentially corresponds to a macroeconomic recession and the boom period for bank lending essentially corresponds to a strong macroeconomic expansion. That is, the time dummies virtually *must* be strongly correlated with macroeconomic series if our hypotheses about changes in supervisory toughness are true, because these hypotheses predict a supervisory toughening during the recession and a supervisory easing during the expansion. These hypotheses do not specify reasons behind the changes in supervisory toughness, so if such changes are caused by supervisory reactions to macroeconomic conditions, this is still consistent with the hypotheses. However, a bias may occur if the macroeconomic changes are strongly correlated with significant changes in bank conditions that supervisors consider in making supervisory assessments that are left out of our econometric models. Although such a bias may exist, we do not believe it to be substantial because we control for state income growth, unemployment rate, and state-average bank balance sheet and income items. We expect that these state economic environment variables capture most of the effects of macroeconomic changes on banks, because banks mostly operated within their home states during the sample. That is, we do not expect a strong separate and independent effect from conditions outside the home state, which are represented by the macroeconomic variables, given that we have controlled for state conditions.

Second, part of our measured effects of changes in supervisory toughness on lending and bank risk taking may reflect the reactions of market participants to changes in bank condition or economic environment that are not captured by our control variables, rather than changes in supervisory discipline (hypothesis 3). The fact that these models explain only a small percentage of the variance in the changes in bank lending and the changes in problem loan ratios tends to make this scenario more likely.

Third, our results are subject to sample selection problems. The proportion of banks examined each year changes quite dramatically over time, and the data suggest that a change in the sample selected for examination may alter the quality pool of the banks examined relative to the industry as a whole. Also, some banks drop out of the sample due to mergers and failures, and others enter the sample through the creation of new charters. We deal with these sample selection issues by including a large number of controls for bank quality, by including observations even when data for lagged supervisory assessments are missing, and by using a Heckman correction for sample selection bias.

References

Avery, Robert, Raphael W. Bostic, and Katherine A. Samolyk. 1998. The evolution of small business finance: The role of personal wealth. *Journal of Banking and Finance* 22:1019–61.

Berger, Allen N., Seth D. Bonime, Daniel M. Covitz, and Diana Hancock. 2000. Why are bank profits so persistent? The roles of product market competition, informational opacity, and regional/macroeconomic shocks. *Journal of Banking and Finance* 24:1203–35.

Berger, Allen N., and Sally M. Davies. 1998. The information content of bank examinations. *Journal of Financial Services Research* 14:117–44.

Berger, Allen N., Sally M. Davies, and Mark J. Flannery. 2000. Comparing market and supervisory assessments of bank performance: Who knows what when? *Journal of Money, Credit, and Banking* 32:641–67.

Berger, Allen N., Anil K. Kashyap, and Joseph M. Scalise. 1995. The transformation of the U.S. banking industry: What a long, strange trip it's been. *Brookings Papers on Economic Activity,* issue no. 2:55–201.

Berger, Allen N., and Loretta J. Mester. 2001. Explaining the performance of U.S. banks: Technological change, deregulation, and dynamic changes in competition. Board of Governors of the Federal Reserve System, Working Paper.

Berger, Allen N., and Gregory F. Udell. 1994. Did risk-based capital allocate bank credit and cause a "credit crunch" in the United States? *Journal of Money, Credit, and Banking* 26 (August): 585–628.

Bernanke, Ben S., and Cara S. Lown. 1991. The credit crunch. *Brookings Papers on Economic Activity,* issue no. 2:205–48. Washington, D.C.: Brookings Institution.

Bizer, David S. 1993. Regulatory discretion and the credit crunch. Working Paper. Washington, D.C.: U.S. Securities and Exchange Commission, April.

Cargill, Thomas F. 1989. CAMEL ratings and the CD market. *Journal of Financial Services Research* 3:347–58.

Cole, Rebel A., and Jeffrey W. Gunther. 1998. Predicting bank failures: A comparison of on- and off-site monitoring systems. *Journal of Financial Services Research* 13:103–17.

Commercial Bank Examination Manual, Uniform Financial Institutions Rating System. Available at http://www.federalreserve.gov/boarddocs/supmanual/default.htm#cbem.

Davies, Sally M. 1993. The importance of market information in predicting bank performance. Board of Governors of the Federal Reserve System, Working Paper, April.

DeYoung, Robert, Mark J. Flannery, William Lang, and Sorin Sorescu. Forthcoming. Could publication of bank CAMELS ratings improve market discipline? *Journal of Money, Credit, and Banking.*

Dunkelberg, William C., and W. J. Dennis Jr. 1992. *The small business "credit crunch."* Washington, D.C.: NFIB Foundation.

Flannery, Mark J., and Joel F. Houston. 1999. The value of a government monitor for U.S. banking firms. *Journal of Money, Credit, and Banking* 31:14–34.

Gilbert, R. Alton. 1993. Implications of annual examinations for the bank insurance fund. *Federal Reserve Bank of St. Louis Review* (January/February).

———. 1994. The benefits of annual bank examinations. In *Research in financial services,* vol. 6, ed. George Kaufman, 215–48. Greenwich, Conn.: JAI Press.

Hall, John R., Andrew P. Meyer, and Mark D. Vaughan. 1997. Do equity markets and regulators view bank holding company risk similarly? An comparison of market-based risk measures and regulators' BOPEC scores. Federal Reserve Bank of St. Louis, Supervisory Policy Analysis, Working Paper no. 97-1.

Hancock, Diana, Andrew Laing, and James A. Wilcox. 1995. Bank balance sheet shocks and aggregate shocks: Their dynamic effects on bank capital and lending. *Journal of Banking and Finance* 19:661–77.

Hancock, Diana, and James A. Wilcox. 1993. Has there been a "capital crunch" in banking? The effects on bank lending of real estate market conditions and bank capital shortfalls. *Journal of Housing Economics* 3:31–50.

———. 1994a. Bank capital and the credit crunch: The roles of risk-weighted and unweighted capital regulations. *AREUEA* 22:59–94.

———. 1994b. Bank capital, loan delinquencies, and real estate lending. *Journal of Housing Economics* 4:121–46.

———. 1997. Bank capital, nonbank finance, and real estate activity. *Journal of Housing Research* 8:75–105.

———. 1998. The "credit crunch" and the availability of credit to small business. *Journal of Banking and Finance* 22:983–1014.

Haubrich, Joseph G., and Paul Wachtel. 1993. Capital requirements and shifts in commercial bank portfolios. *Federal Reserve Bank of Cleveland Economic Review* 29:2–15.

Hirschhorn, Eric. 1987. The informational content of bank examination ratings. *Federal Deposit Insurance Corporation Banking and Economic Review* (July/August): 6–11.

Interagency Policy Statement on Credit Availability, 10 March 1993. AD 93-23. Available at http://www.federalreserve.gov/boarddocs/SRLETTERS/1995/sr95 53.htm#pagetop

Jordan, John S. 1999. Pricing bank stocks: The contribution of bank examinations. *New England Economic Review* (May/June): 39–53.

O'Keefe, John, and Drew Dahl. 1997. Scheduling bank examinations. Federal Deposit Insurance Corporation, Working Paper.

Peek, Joe, and Eric S. Rosengren. 1994. Bank real estate lending and the New England capital crunch. *AREUEA* 22:33–58.

———. 1995a. Bank regulation and the credit crunch. *Journal of Banking and Finance* 19:679–92.

———. 1995b. The capital crunch: Neither a borrower nor a lender be. *Journal of Money, Credit, and Banking* 27:625–38.

Peek, Joe, Eric S. Rosengren, and Geoffrey M. B. Tootell. 1999a. Does the Federal Reserve possess an informational advantage? Federal Reserve Bank of Boston. Working Paper.

———. 1999b. Is bank supervision central to central banking? *Quarterly Journal of Economics* 114:629–53.

Pettway, Richard H. 1980. Potential insolvency, market efficiency, and bank regulation of large commercial banks. *Journal of Financial and Quantitative Analysis* 15 (1): 219–36.

Shrieves, Ronald E., and Drew Dahl. 1995. Regulation, recession, and bank lending behavior: The 1990 credit crunch. *Journal of Financial Services Research* 9:5–30.

Simons, Katerina, and Stephen Cross. 1991. Do capital markets predict problems in large commercial banks? *New England Economic Review* (May/June): 51–56.

Sinkey, Joseph F., Jr. 1978. Identifying "problem' banks: How do the banking authorities measure a bank's risk exposure? *Journal of Money, Credit, and Banking* 10:184–93.

Wagster, John D. 1999. The Basle Accord of 1988 and the International Credit Crunch of 1989–1992. *Journal of Financial Services Research* 15:123–43.

Whalen, Gary, and James B. Thomson. 1988. Using financial data to identify changes in bank condition. *Federal Reserve Bank of Cleveland Economic Review* (Second Quarter): 17–26.

Comment   Stephen G. Cecchetti

In their ambitious and thought-provoking paper, Allen N. Berger, Margaret K. Kyle, and Joseph M. Scalise ask the following three questions: (a) Did U.S. bank supervisors get tougher during the credit crunch?; (b) did they get easier during the banking boom?; and (c) did it matter to bank lending? Their answers are yes, yes, and maybe.

These questions are of interest both to students of banking and to researchers interested in macroeconomic phenomena more generally. In the latter case, the hope is that this work will shed additional light on the monetary transmission mechanism. Specifically, proponents of the lending view of the transmission mechanism posit that loan supply shifts are an important channel for the transmission of monetary policy changes to the real economy. Unfortunately, there are virtually no studies that have been able to distinguish loan supply from loan demand shifts in a convincing fashion—all we know for sure is that contractionary monetary policy precedes a reduction in the overall quantity of loans made by banks. The hope is that a change in supervisory toughness that is unrelated to any other macroeconomic variable will provide an instrument, in the econometric sense, that shifts loan supply but not loan demand. In these comments, I will begin with a brief overview of the methods the authors use to reach their conclusions, and then move on to evaluate what I believe can be learned from the paper.

Berger, Kyle, and Scalise examine a panel data set composed of 5,500 to 9,500 banks from 1986 to 1998. Employing the data both from examinations directly and from the call reports, they look for changes in supervisory toughness and bank lending behavior over three periods: 1986–88, their base period; 1989–92, the period generally thought to include a credit crunch; and 1993–98, a boom period for banks and nearly everyone else.

Stephen G. Cecchetti is professor of economics at Ohio State University, and a research associate of the National Bureau of Economic Research.

To address the first two hypotheses, that regulators first became more harsh (hypothesis 1) and then more lax (hypothesis 2), Berger, Kyle, and Scalise study classified assets and CAMEL ratings. As they discuss in detail, the first of these is a supervisory measure of bank asset health, whereas the second is an overall measure of bank soundness. In an attempt to uncover changes in the stance of examiners, the authors estimate two models. The first is a linear regression in which they estimate determinants of (scaled) classified assets, and the second is a probability model in which they try to measure the odds of a shift in a bank's CAMEL rating. Each of their hypotheses is tested by examining dummy variables for the 1989–92 and 1993–98 subperiods. Included in their estimation as controls are numerous bank balance sheet variables as well as measures of regional economic conditions.

The results, reported in table 9.8 of the paper, are encouraging. Berger, Kyle, and Scalise find that total classified assets fell in the 1993–98 period. They also find that the CAMEL rating for a bank with a given balance sheet in a given region of the country was on average worse in the crunch period 1989–92. Unfortunately, there is no real evidence that classified asset levels went up during the crunch period or that CAMEL ratings went down during the period of ease. Nevertheless, things do look pretty good.

But, as the authors point out, when we look further, the results suggest that the change in supervisory stance is statistically, but not economically, significant. That is, the effects can be measured precisely, but are small. To show this, they compute that the change from the precrunch to the crunch period increases the percentage of classified assets by about 0.04 percent. Since the mean in the data set as a whole is about 6 percent, however, this is not a big number. For the CAMEL ratings, again the probability of a shift is also small.

It is worth pausing for a moment and considering two important issues that bear on their results: sample selection problems, and the question of what else was going on during this period. With respect to sample selection, Berger, Kyle, and Scalise provide us with a very thorough description of their data set and make clear a number of things that are going on. They also spend substantial time in section 9.3 addressing sample selection issues and are aware of the difficulties. It is still worth spending a bit of time discussing one of the issues.

As shown in table 9.5, the number of banks examined (and, consequently, in the authors' data set) increased by about 50 percent from 1986 to 1993 and then declined by a similar amount. Furthermore, the fraction of banks examined increased dramatically during the crunch period, from 43 percent in 1986 to 85 percent in 1993. Even more importantly, as is reported in Panel B of table 9.5, the total capital ratio of the banks examined went up during the capital crunch, but the capital ratio for the industry as a whole did not.

What does this all mean for the authors' results? The answer, I think, is that it biases the case against them. It does this for two reasons. First, banks that incurred the most serious wrath of the supervisors—those that were truly bad—will either merge with good banks or cease operation altogether, and so they will drop out of the sample during the crunch period. Second, the change in regulatory strategy meant that more banks were examined, and so more good banks entered the data set. Overall, then, the loss of the bad banks and the addition of the good ones will make it more difficult to find an increase in supervisory toughness because the average bank is getting better and the worst banks are dropping out. The fact that the mean CAMEL rating (table 9.4, Panel A) rises during this period is additional evidence of what was happening.

The second important issue to consider here is what was going on around this time. There were several important events, but they were at the end of the authors' crunch period. First, there was the passage of FIDICIA in 1991, which Krozner and Strahan in this volume refer to as "the most important revision of U.S. supervision and regulations during the past two decades." Associated with this was the implementation of prompt corrective action and the risk-based capital requirements based on the Basel Accord. All of these came essentially in 1992 and would lead one to expect that the most significant regulatory changes should appear in the later part of the sample, not the middle.

Turning to the third hypothesis, Berger, Kyle, and Scalise look at bank balance sheet variables to see if bank behavior was influenced by the changes in supervisory toughness. Here they examine the changes in the proportion of assets attributed to various types of loans and securities and see if changes either in a banks CAMEL rating or in its level of classified assets affect balance sheet composition. I will focus my attention on the changes in commercial and industrial loans (columns 2 and 3 of table 9.9) and the change in U.S. Treasuries (columns 8 and 9 of table 9.9), both measured as a percentage of total bank assets. The results are intriguing. Looking at the CAMEL rating, we find that any change, regardless of whether it is an upgrade or a downgrade, results in a decrease in the percentage of assets held as C&I loans, and increases the percentage of U.S. Treasuries. That is, simply having an examiner change the bank's rating results in a reduction in lending. Although one would expect this for downgrades, surely it is not the expected outcome for upgrades.

As was the case earlier, however, the results indicate that the impact is not quantitatively important. Changes in classified assets of the order we actually see result in bank portfolio movements that are on the order of 0.1 percent of their assets, at most. Again, Berger, Kyle, and Scalise are aware of this and discuss it in the paper.

The overall message of my comment thus far is that the authors' results do not seem to be quantitatively important. But I have left one question

Table 9C.1   **Correlation of Year Dummy Coefficients with Macroeconomic Variables**

Correlation with:	Lag			Lead	
	−2	−1	0	+1	+2
A. Classified Assets					
Risk spread	0.66	0.59	0.03	−0.26	−0.59
Term premium	−0.79	−0.25	−0.07	0.25	0.75
Core inflation	0.54	0.65	0.50	0.25	0.04
M2 growth	0.35	0.34	0.12	−0.16	−0.54
Industrial production growth	−0.16	−0.32	−0.61	−0.68	−0.27
Trade weighted $	−0.20	−0.07	0.09	0.19	−0.42
Unemployment rate	−0.66	−0.37	0.11	0.46	0.67
B. CAMEL					
Risk spread	−0.51	−0.12	0.28	0.55	0.89
Term premium	0.61	0.39	0.06	−0.43	−0.85
Core inflation	−0.32	−0.42	−0.30	0.13	0.32
M2 growth	0.03	−0.02	−0.01	0.26	0.66
Industrial production growth	−0.05	0.31	0.72	0.43	−0.07
Trade weighted $	0.42	0.18	−0.01	0.19	0.48
Unemployment rate	0.66	0.42	−0.13	−0.51	−0.73

Source: Dummy variable coefficients were provided by Berger, Kyle and Scalise.

Notes: Core inflation is measured by the median CPI; the term spread is the difference between the 10 year and the 3 month Treasury (constant maturity); and the risk spread is the difference between the 3 month commercial paper rate and the 3 month treasury bill rate.

unanswered. Is the authors' finding really about supervisory toughness and shifts in loan supply, or could it be about something else? In all of their work, Berger, Kyle, and Scalise do control for economic conditions in a bank's state, but they are unable to remove economy-wide activity. How important might this be? To address this concern, I have taken the annual time dummy variables estimates that come from an extended form of the regressions reported in table 9.8, and I have computed their correlation with a number of macroeconomic variables. That is, I examine the relationship between annual measures of what Berger, Kyle, and Scalise interpret as supervisory stance with measures of the state of the aggregate economy. The results of this exercise for both the total classified assets and the CAMEL regressions are reported in table 9C.1.

Looking at the table, we see that these dummy variables are highly correlated with both growth in industrial production and core inflation. For example, the contemporaneous correlation of the dummy variables with growth in industrial production is −0.61 for classified assets and 0.72 for the CAMEL rating. All of this suggests that what Berger, Kyle, and Scalise are doing is picking up the supervisory reaction to the current general economic environment. As a result, I doubt very much that what they are finding are independent measures of toughness per se.

Discussion Summary

Patricia Jackson began by noting that the CAMEL ratings reflect many things and asked whether these ratings could be disaggregated.

Mark Carey wondered if the findings were possibly a sign of the times. He noted that the press reported dire economic conditions at the time and that these might be the true macroeconomic environment in which the supervisors were operating. He also noted that the Basel Accord went into effect at year-end of 1990 and that FDICIA in 1992 increased the de facto capital requirements. He observed that these changes might have improved bank capitalization over the sample period.

Ed Ettin noted that the backlog of closures at the time might have forced supervisors to delay writing down loans, which would have reduced capital (and forced additional closures). He noted that this might have resulted in the apparent anomaly of seemingly well-capitalized poorly rated (CAMEL 4 or 5) banks. He argued that macroeconomic conditions may not have been fully captured by the included variables.

Eric Rosengren raised the idea of performing nonperforming loans such as collateral impaired loans or loans with no required payments, such as construction loans. He noted that in practice these loans may have been captured as special mention loans, reserved against by the banks, and reflected in bank capital. He observed that these loans would be reflected in the CAMEL ratings, but not captured by the regression analysis that was used in the paper and focused on classified loans.

Joe Peek suggested that the authors should focus on the thresholds for different ratings rather than the level. He argued that the average quality of a given rating might not be of as much interest as the marginal cutoffs between ratings. He suggested that the key question is whether the thresholds between adjacent ratings changed, or possibly changed differently depending on the rating? He raised a second question about the use of loans as a share of assets. Although it will be important to scale the volume and changes of lending, he observed that if the balance sheet is shrinking faster than a bank's loans, the ratio may in fact be increasing. He suggested that the authors might look at the changes in loans scaled by lagged total assets as opposed to the change in the ratio.

Michael Dooley wondered if the forecast of the macroeconomy by supervisors was biased. He also wondered whether supervisors think the economy was in fact worse than the true prediction or the actual economic condition. He noted that past-due loans might not be the best measure of future conditions.

James Barth also suggested looking at the components of the CAMEL ratings, noting that classified loans are most directly linked to the C (capital) rating. He also suggested looking at the examiners' comments because they may reflect more information than the CAMEL ratings. He pointed out that the authors could also look at supervisory actions with respect to specific banks. Finally, he followed up on a comment from the discussant (Stephen Cecchetti) on sample selection bias, noting that bad assets do not drop out of the banking system as a particular institution is resolved.

Randy Kroszner commented on the incentives facing the regulators, suggesting a further analysis of the asymmetric loss and resource constraints faced by the supervisors. James Wilcox noted that the regulatory agencies with more asset downgrades were not the same agencies with the most CAMEL rating downgrades. He noted further that these findings suggest that standards differed across agencies during this time period.

Charles Calomiris raised an issue that is addressed in chapter 8: Is it desirable to combine central banking and bank supervision? He noted that recently most industrialized countries have been removing the bank regulatory authority from the central bank on the theory that there is a conflict of interest between bank regulatory policy and monetary policy.

Doug Diamond asked if the use of the ratings changed over time, and if the outcomes change. He also wondered if there were a change in the persistence of the ratings.

Finally, following on a point made by the discussant about the importance of managing systemic risk, *Marc Saidenberg* suggested looking at CAMEL ratings by the size of the institution. He noted that if supervisors were more concerned about systemic risk, they might have approached larger institutions differently.

In response, *Allen Berger* agreed with many of the suggestions. He noted that he and his colleagues were working on a number of the suggestions already, including the size interactions. In response to Ettin and others, he agreed with the challenge associated with classified assets and the constraints that the supervisors may have faced.

He agreed that the 'performing nonperforming' loans were a potential problem and that the authors will be looking at thresholds between ratings. He also said that the authors would look at lending and asset behavior separately. He noted that they also would be addressing sample-selection bias.

Berger also agreed with comments by Wilcox and Calomiris. He noted that although differences between agencies are controlled for in the paper, it will be difficult to address this issue because banks are not randomly assigned charter types. He noted that he liked Diamond's suggestion to look at these as a function of capital requirements. Berger also noted that generally it is interesting that many of the new capital requirements were in place by 1992, the same time that supervisors appear to be getting easier. He argued that one explanation could be that by 1992 the banks were getting their houses in order so that possibly there is a missing variable, or supervisors felt that they could relax. Berger also responded to the point by Cecchetti and others that the estimated changes in supervisory toughness are highly correlated with macroeconomic changes. He pointed out that this is not inconsistent with the hypotheses. The measured effects virtually have to be strongly correlated with macroeconomic series if the hypotheses are true, because the hypotheses predict a supervisory toughening during the recession and a supervisory easing during the expansion. If the changes in supervisory toughness are caused by reactions to macroeconomic conditions, this is still consistent with the hypotheses. A bias might occur if the macroeconomic changes are strongly correlated with significant changes in bank conditions that supervisors consider in making supervisory assessments that are left out of our econometric models. He argued that although such a bias may exist, it is not believed to be substantial in part because they control for home state economic conditions, and in part because the information on future nonperforming loans and charge-offs are better proxies for the bank conditions that supervisors consider than are general economic conditions outside the home state. Also in response, *Margaret Kyle* noted that they will attempt to disentangle types of regulatory actions, recognizing that the movement from a 1 to a 2 may not be the same as that from a 2 to a 3. She noted that the use of future performance measures is in practice both difficult and endogenous. She also observed that the authors will look further at the components of ratings, but noted that the aggregate CAMEL rating is restricted to be close to the C (capital) and A (asset quality) components. Finally, she agreed that the charter switches would be an interesting topic for future research.

Contributors

James R. Barth
Milken Institute
1250 Fourth Street, 2nd Floor
Santa Monica, CA 90401

Allen N. Berger
Board of Governors of the Federal
   Reserve System
Mail Stop 153
20th & C Streets, NW
Washington, DC 20551

Ben S. Bernanke
Woodrow Wilson School of Public and
   International Affairs
Princeton University
Princeton, NJ 08544

Robert R. Bliss
Research Department
Federal Reserve Bank of Chicago
230 South LaSalle Street
Chicago, IL 60604-1413

Charles W. Calomiris
Graduate School of Business
Columbia University
3022 Broadway Street, Uris Hall
New York, NY 10027

Gerard Caprio Jr.
Financial Strategy and Policy Group
The World Bank
1818 H Street, NW
Washington, DC 20433

Mark Carey
Federal Reserve Board
Mailstop 153
Washington, DC 20551

Stephen G. Cecchetti
Department of Economics
The Ohio State University
1945 N. High Street
Columbus, OH 43210-1172

Douglas W. Diamond
Graduate School of Business
University of Chicago
1101 East 58th Street
Chicago, IL 60637-1511

Mark J. Flannery
Department of Finance, Insurance,
   and Real Estate
Box 117168
University of Florida
Gainesville, FL 32611-7168

Mark Gertler
Department of Economics
New York University
269 Mercer Street, 7th Floor
New York, NY 10003

Patricia Jackson
Bank of England
Threadneedle Street
London EC2R 8AH
England

Randall S. Kroszner
Graduate School of Business
University of Chicago
1101 East 58th Street
Chicago, IL 60637

Margaret K. Kyle
Department of Economics, E52-391
Massachusetts Institute of Technology
50 Memorial Drive
Cambridge, MA 02139

Ross Levine
Finance Department, Room 3-257
Carlson School of Management
University of Minnesota
321 19th Avenue South
Minneapolis, MN 55455

Laurence H. Meyer
Board of Governors of the Federal
    Reserve System
20th & C Streets, NW
Washington, DC 20551

Frederic S. Mishkin
Graduate School of Business
Uris Hall 619
Columbia University
New York, NY 10027

Joe Peek
437C Gatton Business & Economics
    Building
Gatton College of Business &
    Economics
University of Kentucky
Lexington, KY 40506-0034

Andrew Powell
Banco Central de la República
    Argentina
Reconquista 266
1003 Capital Federal
Buenos Aires
Argentina

Raghuram G. Rajan
Graduate School of Business
University of Chicago
1101 East 58th Street
Chicago, IL 60637

Eric S. Rosengren
Research Department, T-8
Federal Reserve Bank of Boston
600 Atlantic Avenue
Boston, MA 02106-2211

Joseph M. Scalise
Bain & Company, Inc.
One Embarcadero Center
San Francisco, CA 94111

Jeremy C. Stein
Department of Economics
Littauer 209
Harvard University
Cambridge, MA 02138

Philip E. Strahan
Banking Studies Department
Federal Reserve Bank of New York
33 Liberty Street
New York, NY 10045-1003

Geoffrey M. B. Tootell
Research Department, T-8
Federal Reserve Bank of Boston
600 Atlantic Avenue
Boston, MA 02106

Author Index

Subject Index